CAN-AM
RACING CARS
1966-1974

Compiled by
R M Clarke

ISBN 9781855205444

BROOKLANDS BOOKS LTD.
P.O. BOX 146, COBHAM,
SURREY, KT11 1LG. UK
sales@brooklands-books.com

www.brooklands-books.com

INTRODUCTION

If ever a motor racing championship series could be said to have captured the spirit of an era, then the Can-Am was a true 'Child of the Sixties'. It was a time of liberation and upheaval throughout society, with an 'anything goes' attitude and an emphasis on enjoying everyday life to the full. The Can-Am embraced all those philosophies and produced a legendary form of pure motorsport that will surely never be repeated, especially in the ever more excessively regulated 21st century - it was a fantastic free-for-all on four wheels.

Even the staid sounding official championship name - the Canadian-American Challenge Cup - was quickly shortened to a much more hip and hard-hitting title, and the Can-Am came to represent a new motor racing ultimate in performance, innovation and excitement. Although classified by the FIA as Group 7 cars, the original Can-Am rule book was remarkably thin and racers faced very few restrictions apart from the basic safety requirements of the day. There was no minimum weight limit, engines could be of any size (with turbochargers unfettered by waste gates to control boost pressure), tyres of any width were acceptable and the materials used in the construction of the car were similarly left to the imagination of the designer.

Big-block Chevrolet V8s mixed it with the largest displacement Ferrari V-12 ever produced and flat-twelve Porsche turbos in a glorious cacophony of raw horsepower. Space age aerodynamic features rubbed shoulders with good, old fashioned, backyard special building techniques, cars sprouted huge sprint car style wings and even motorised fans to enhance down force as what started out as racing sports cars evolved into outrageous machines that went faster than anyone had thought possible.

Of course, the idea of producing a hybrid sports car racer by putting an American V8 into a lightweight home-built or European chassis had been around for many years before the birth of the Can-Am. These days, the most famous exponent of that type of car is probably Carroll Shelby and his Cobra creations. However, in the 1950s it was wealthy enthusiasts like Briggs Cunningham and Lance Reventlow who funded the construction of a number of highly successful sports racers that competed in numerous Sports Car Club of America (SCCA) road racing events.

But if its lineage can be traced back to the late '50s, the Can-Am championship in its prime lasted for only nine short years, between 1966 and 1974. And the cars and drivers that took part were some of the best around and have since become motor racing legends: Denny Hulme (easily the most successful Can-Am driver), Mario Andretti, Dan Gurney, Mark Donohue and many others; plus classic racecars from McLaren, Lola, Shadow, Ferrari, Porsche and Jim Hall's never-to-be-forgotten Chaparrals.

While the racing itself could sometimes be rather processional, the awesome sight and sound of a pack of Can-Am cars hurtling through a corner was enough of a spectacle to thrill the many thousands of spectators who flocked to the tracks across North America. Without the sophisticated technology and on-board cameras we have all come to expect in television coverage of motor racing today, if you couldn't get to the circuit back then the only way to share the experience was to read about it in a magazine. And the writers who reported on the Can-Am were also of championship calibre, producing evocative text that got you right into the heart of the action and the soul of the drivers.

Can-Am was a glorious adventure and one that couldn't last, but as long as cars are raced it will be remembered as an intoxicating period when international championship motorsport was free-spirited and fun.

Tony Beadle

ACKNOWLEDGEMENTS

A few years ago we turned our attention to motor racing and have covered to date all the Mille Miglia and Le Mans events plus the post-war Targa Florio races. It is now the turn of the breath taking Can-Am series. We are covering the subject in three volumes, *Can-Am Racing 1966-1969*, and *Can-Am Racing 1970-1974* which cover the actual races and a third volume Can-Am Racing Cars 1966-1974 which reports on the state-of-the-art cars that made this series so exciting.

Our books are printed in small numbers for enthusiasts and couldn't exist without the generous support of other enthusiasts such as Pete Lyons, whose wonderful book Can-Am was the inspiration for our series. Our thanks also go to motoring writer Tony Beadle for his informative introduction and to Michael Turner, the renowned motoring artist, who has once again come to our aid by allowing us to reproduce four of his meticulous paintings which grace our covers.

Last but not least are the managements of the world's leading motoring journals, who for over forty years have supported our reference works. Our thanks go in this instance to the publishers of *Autosport, Autosport Annual, Car and Driver, Car and Driver Annual, Car Life, Competition Car, Motor, Motorcade, Motor Manual, Motor Racing, Motor Sport, Road & Track, Sports Cars of the World* and *The World Car Catalogue*.

Whereas our other two Can-Am books concentrated solely on race reports, this third volume in the trilogy takes a detailed look at the wide variety of cars that contested the championship.

In chronological order and rising in levels of performance, the machines examined range from the early Lola T70 to the incredible 1100 horsepower, 240mph Porsche 917 that swept all before it in the penultimate year of the Can-Am. McLaren cars dominated the series throughout its nine seasons and are also featured here extensively, but there are many other constructors represented, some less well known than others. Ferrari, Ford and Chaparral will be familiar to most enthusiasts, but how many recall that BRM built a Can-Am contender? Likewise, there was the ill-fated Holman-Moody Hanker II that thwarted even the undoubted ability of the great Mario Andretti to make it competitive and valiant attempts by McKee, Caldwell and the rest to build race-winning cars.

Aerodynamic innovation was also a major part of the typical Can-Am car, whether in the form of the wild-looking Chaparral with its 'flipper' rear wing or the air brakes tried on the Ferrari 612P, and these ideas (and many others) came under the microscope of the magazines of the day.

The freedom of the Can-Am regulations gave rise to some truly unique vehicles that would dramatically influence the shape and style of motor racing around the world, long after the championship itself had passed into history. In these pages you'll find track tests by well-known drivers, comments from ground breaking designers like Bruce McLaren and inside information about the technicalities of the Can-Am which have all been collated to give a comprehensive contemporary overview of what went into producing those awesome Group 7 cars.

R.M. Clarke

Contents

can-am/tech

BY PETE BIRO

During the pause between the
East Coast and West Coast
halves of the Can-Am series,
we take a look at the
technical side of the races.

During the infancy of professional sports car racing in this country, a number of the big-name international drivers had a very cute con game going for them. It involved arriving at the tracks with clapped-out "starting money specials" bolted together for one simple purpose; to separate the rich but gullible colonists from as much cash as possible.

It worked beautifully for awhile. The GP studs would stick around long enough to collect their appearance checks, sign a few autographs for the adoring throngs and put in a few laps before (surprise!) their cars broke. Then they would scuttle back home, but only after they had jettisoned all of their junk machinery on a bunch of rich-yokel American racers. Oh, for *shame*!

Happily, that's all changed. The lucrative Canadian-American Challenge Cup series is upon us, and the old starting money era is over—replaced by a huge, irresistible pot of prize money. A third of a million bucks is being parcelled out to finishers in each race, and another $35,000 or so will be divided up among the best drivers of the whole series, so nobody can afford to run a few laps and pack it in. In a sense, the Can-Am is like a 1200-mile race run in six heats, with prize money for each 200-mile sprint.

The idea of running the fall pro races as a co-operative series originated with Riverside's Les Richter, and is now in full swing. With better than $360,000 in prize and accessory money, both the European and the American drivers are intent on racing for the long green. And unlike the old days, the serious contenders have come loaded with the latest and best of the current crop of Group 7 sports/racing cars. Circuit records aren't just being broken— they're being destroyed. For example, John Surtees lowered his own mark of a year ago at St. Jovite by eight seconds, which is equivalent to lapping Indy at over 175 mph. We

can-am/tech

covered the first half of the series—St. Jovite, Bridgehampton, and Mosport—in the December issue. February will feature the final three events at Laguna Seca, Riverside and Las Vegas. This month we present a look at the technical side of the Can-Am entries.

Representing the Lola factory, Team Surtees' entry for the series is two reworked Type 70 Mk.II Lolas. Surtees' Lolas are highly refined versions of Eric Broadley's original semi-monocoque Type 70. The basic chassis structure is a pair of steel and aluminum fuel-carrying side pontoons with a backboned, sheet steel floor joining them. A steel box structure at the front end locates the suspension and steering components, while two tapered steel box sections, in conjunction with a bridge-type bulkhead at the rear, locate the engine/transmission package and the rear suspension. Chassis rigidity is aided by partially stressing the fiberglass bodywork. The Lola is a big car, with a 95-inch wheelbase and a track of 58 inches, and is at its best on fast, sweeping turns. In tight corners, where oversteer is an advantage, the smaller, shorter McLarens seem to have the edge.

The Type 70 Mk.II, which Surtees used in winning the Player's Quebec

Lola-Chevy features unusual side-draft Webers. Car is the fastest T70 in the series.

At St. Jovite, Surtees debuted huge brakes, with thick, 2-piece disc and machined calipers.

at St. Jovite, has modifications to the rear suspension pick-up points, utilizing a longer-than-stock upper link, with geometry designed to keep the ever-widening tire footprints in better contact with the pavement. To improve braking, Lola machined a set of huge brake calipers, in unit with Girling dual brake cylinders. The calipers wrap around special 2-piece Kelsey-Hayes, 12.5-inch by 0.814-inch ventilated cast iron discs. Surtees explains, "These brakes are similar to those developed for the P3 Ferrari. They don't stop any better, but they greatly increased pad life, so you have just as good braking at the end of a race as when you began." In typical Broadley fashion, they are located well inboard of the hub carriers to provide maximum ventilation and cooling.

At Bridgehampton, Surtees used the newer of his two cars, with the suspension resembling that of the McLarens. Following the layout of the Indy Lola, it had the lower front locating arm angled forward, attaching to pick-up points located by a fabricated tube structure that extends through the radiator air passageway. The Lola was originally fitted with the 475-hp, 364 cu. in. Traco Chevrolet. Later, Surtees had his engines rebuilt in England by Alan Smith. Now he's back with Traco, using the new 359 cu. in., 492-hp version.

The works McLaren team consists of two cars; one for McLaren himself and the other for unassuming but swift Chris Amon, a 22-year-old New Zealander. The Mk.II McLarens feature special ZF transaxles and the well-proven Traco Chevy engines, plus first-rate preparation. The cars utilize nearly the same basic tube-frame chassis as last year, with a stressed undertray riveted and bonded to the lower tubes. New triangulation, added when McLaren switched from the aluminum Oldsmobile engine to the heavier cast iron Chevy, has doubled chassis stiffness—from 1500 lbs. per degree to 3000. Three minutes after the bodywork was lifted off McLaren's car, McLaren's private customers (there were 18 of them in the first three races) looked, measured, and started adding the needed pieces of tubing to stiffen their own store-bought chassis. Most of this year's increased chassis rigidity is in the engine bay—a bolt-in structure developed when McLaren fitted his new fuel injection, and some old tubing had to be removed. "These two are basically production cars," says McLaren, "but we've made them heavier to take the punishment of this six-race series. Dry weight is 1550 lbs., with 330 lbs. of liquids and 160 lbs. of driver, so we're ready to go at 2040 lbs."

McLaren has spent a great deal of development time with suspension, spring and shock settings since switching to the heavier engine. During initial tests with the Olds engine, McLaren added 100 lbs. of lead to the rear of the car to simulate the weight of the heavier Chevy engine, and after a bit of fiddling, went faster than he had before. The Olds developed about 100-hp less than his first Chevys, and now, with a mid-series switch to the 359 Traco Chevy, power will be up from the Olds' 370 to about 490. At Laguna, McLaren ran a new fuel injection unit using a Mickey Thompson manifold, and Hilborn innards. Had he known the competition was going to be so quick, McLaren said, he would have started out with the bigger engines. A great aid to McLaren's and Amon's lap times has been the 5-speed ZF trans-axle. (Production versions are fitted with the more rugged 4-speed Hewland LG500.) To ensure that the ZFs hold up under loads beyond their original design capacity, McLaren's crackerjack crew keeps a log book on each gearbox, and tears down each unit after 500 miles. To take advantage of the increased power output of the new power plants, McLaren has gone from 10- to 12-inch-wide rear rims, which have increased the rear track two inches to 54. Front track remains 51 inches. Brakes are Girling, with BR calipers all around. The discs are unvented cast iron, 12.5-in. front, 11.5-in. rear.

Knowing full well that the Can-Am series would bring out the world's best sports/racing cars, Texan Jim Hall designed and built a pair of the most outlandish ground-effects vehicles ever seen. Even the most jaded journalists were intrigued. When the Chaparral 2Es arrived at Bridgehampton for their first race, the word went around the pits like wildfire, and sponsors, crews and drivers all dashed over to inspect Hall's creations.

It's got this wing. Not a spoiler, a genuine wing, and it towers some 56 inches above ground level. One onlooker walked up to Hill, who had just stepped out of the Chaparral, and asked: "What does that cam do to the car?" "That's not a *cam*, it's a *wing*," tossed back Hill. "Well then, what's the wing there for?" tried the spectator. To which Hill, with a straight face, answered, "It's there to have an effect on the car (pause) in one way or another." Exit Hill. Exit spectator.

Weird Chaparral 2E has vented fenders to prevent air lifting front-end.

Flapper valve in Chaparral's ducted nose works in conjunction with wing.

Water and oil radiators are housed in pods alongside Chaparral engine.

7

can-am/tech

Bare bones of McLaren-Chevy reveal ZF gearbox used by works cars.

A lot of time and trouble went into building and developing the wing, and it seems to have been worth it. Hall, whose competition driving this year prior to the Can-Am Series had been limited to a few laps of Sebring in March, has had the fastest qualifying lap in all three of the three Can-Am events he's run in thus far.

Under the wing of the car Hall drives is a chassis derived from the all-aluminum, semi-monocoque Chaparral 2C, which achieved some success last year. Phil Hill's car is all new, and is designated a 2E. Wholly fabricated in Hall's Midland, Texas, shops, the chassis is composed of a number of aluminum alloy torque boxes, while the bodywork—including the wing—is fiberglass. The choice of aluminum for the chassis, as opposed to plastic, is primarily a weight-saving measure. "The design stiffness in this aluminum chassis is the same as with our plastic cars, but the ultimate stiffness of plastic is about double," said Hall. Smiling, he added, "but aluminum is lighter." Hall will admit to a 1600-lb. Chaparral, ready to race. That figure would include 25 gallons of fuel and 175 lbs. of driver, so the dry weight must be on the or-

Bruce McLaren's McLaren has been consistently strong throughout Can-Am series, but not quite fast enough to catch the winners.

der of 1180 lbs. (We would have guessed slightly less.) With a claimed horsepower rating of 450 from his 327 cu. in., dry-sump, aluminum Chevy engine, Hall isn't pushing as much weight (or frontal area) as his competition. Jim confided, "It's sure nice for once to have a car that can blow somebody off on the straight," which he did at Laguna. Much of the Chaparral's acceleration and speed can be attributed to Hall's aerodynamic studies at Cornell, involving "masses in relation to the control forces about them." Jim Travers, of Traco, feels that Hall is just scratching the surface of aerodynamics with his new wing. "Engine builders," Travers remarked, "have gone about as far as possible in developing horsepower; from now on it's going to be up to the body builders to get these things going faster." Travers and Hall have a lot to talk about.

The wing, or "flapper" as Hall calls it, is attached directly to the hub carriers, thus having its effect directly on the rear wheels without having to operate through the rear suspension. It is pivoted on the hub carriers by two vertical posts just over a yard in length. The wing is mounted high to get it up into un-

Gurney-Weslake heads produce more power than the Ford 289 can handle.

disturbed air. Front-to-rear location is handled by a pair of single trailing arms, one per post, and a single side link attached to the left post, angling downward to the center of the rear chassis bulkhead. The side link is there to keep the post at right angles to the ground. This is the piece that broke during practice at Bridgehampton, causing the posts to sway dramatically.

Up front, in the passageway normally occupied by the water radiator, is another flap—much smaller, and looking something like an oblong throttle butterfly—which operates in unison with the rear airfoil. Because the Chaparral has an automatic transmission, what was once

Dan Gurney's Lola-Ford has had its share of trouble, mainly in the engine department, but took superb victory at Bridgehampton.

the clutch pedal now operates (via hydraulic lines) the airfoil system.

When the driver is on the straight, he holds the pedal down with his left foot, keeping the front flapper valve open and the rear wing near-horizontal. In this position, the wing acts merely as a stabilizer with minimal frontal area, like the feathers on an arrow. As the driver approaches a turn, he takes his foot off the wing pedal, transferring it to the middle pedal for left-footed braking. With the wing pedal released, the front flap and rear wing pivot into a tilted position, giving powerful negative lift (at the expense of added aerodynamic drag) on both ends of the car. This greatly increases traction, making it possible for the Chaparral to brake harder, accelerate with less wheelspin, and scramble around the corners faster. Exiting the corner, the driver again depresses the wing pedal as the car picks up speed. At Laguna Seca, where the turns are close together and top speed is only about 145 mph, winner Hill didn't have much time or necessity to use the wing to its fullest advantage.

What happened to the water radiator? Well, it was split up into two smaller radiators which were moved back to a position in the upper front portion of the rear wheel houses, joined on one side by an oil radiator. All three radiators lean sharply forward for maximum airflow.

Some radiator air is picked up from around the outside of the front fenders (which are vented at the rear to let out lift-producing trapped air) and some from around the pointed windshield. The edges of the car drop straight down to within inches of the ground in an attempt to kill all airflow under the car. Air is picked up under the nose of the car, flows through the ducting inhabited by the front flap, and around the windshield, where it is sucked in through the protruding (to get above the boundary layer of air) radiator ducts. Hot air escapes upward and to the rear via exits on top of the rear fenders, aided at Laguna by small spoilers on the forward lip to induce negative pressure at the outlet.

Complicated, wot?

The long intake ram tubes and short "zoomie" exhaust stacks, long a Chaparral trademark, are gone. A deceptively simple 4-into-2-into-1 (each side) exhaust system with a cross-over balance tube debuted at Daytona in the 2D coupe, and carried over to the 2E. An all-new automatic transmission with greater torque multiplying qualities has enabled Hall to get rid of the long ram tubes and concentrate on top end power. So now you can hear the crisp, clean manual shifts, and watch the 2Es blow off the more conventional iron on the straights. Zap! Maybe we should let Hall take a crack at the Viet Nam thing.

All American Racers' Dan Gurney is running a somewhat out-of-the-box Lola 70 Mk.II, but has a monopoly on the hush-hush Gurney-Weslake heads for his Ford engines. At a mere 305 cu. in., Gurney's Bridgehampton-winning engine was developing 495 horsepower, but recent dyno development at AAR's Santa Ana, California. shop has brought that up to over 525 for the final three Can-Am events. Dan describes the Gurney-Weslake heads as "having wedge combustion chambers, but they breathe like a hemi." Pistons are flat-top, made by Forgedtrue, and utilize Freddy Carrillo's Warren Machine H-beam rods. This set-up also includes a Moldex crank from Dearborn. Valve sizes are Gurney's secret, but we do know that the cam is an Engle roller unit. Maximum power is 525 hp at 7800 rpm, although Gurney took it to 8900 without ill effects on the first lap at Bridgehampton. Maximum torque is 415 lbs./ft. at 6300. An Indy version, running on fuel, has seen 570 hp. The main bearing webs of the Fairlane-based 305 engine can't take the strain of the Gurney-Weslake heads (two blew at Laguna Seca), so by 1967, the Gurney-Weslake heads will be fitted to new 351 cu. in. blocks with a bottom-end design capable of taking over 600 hp.

John Mecom's Fords have been prepared by Bryan Falconer of Sperex Paint's new racing division. The most unusual of these are the 289 and 351 cu. in. Paxton supercharged units fitted to Parnelli Jones' and Jackie Stewart's Lolas. Parnelli's was the fastest Ford-powered car at St. Jovite, but the Ford-Sperex engine suffers from a lack of development, and consequently, reliability. At Laguna Seca, Jones dumped his Ford engine in favor of a Traco Chevy engine bought from Roger Penske. Swaggered wealthy sponsor Mecom: "We're gonna sell all our Ford engines to anyone who needs a boat anchor." This seems to have staggered Ford's corporate imagination, as the Mecom team now possesses a 427 cu. in. Ford engine coupled to Ford's racing automatic transmission. It's amazing what a few well-chosen words can do when delivered at the appropriate time and place. By John Mecom, of course.

Power output for the supercharged 289 is better than 450 at 6500 rpm, which isn't startling, but boost pressure is low, and the power curve is practically flat. The Ford's 400 lbs./ft. of torque come in over a wide range, peaking at 5000 rpm. During the mid-series break (between Mosport and Laguna Seca), Ford was said to be fiddling with an aluminum block 427 cu. in. engine similar to their Le Mans unit, developing something over 500 hp and 500 lbs./ft. of tork (when it gets that high you just can't spell it 'que'). A. J. Foyt had a similar 500-hp engine for Riverside—his only Can-Am appearance—as did Andretti, who drove the automatic transmission Lola supplied to Mecom by Ford.

The tire war has been fought in earnest by Goodyear and Firestone, with the latter currently having the upper hand. Of 27 cars surveyed, Firestones were in use on 16, with Goodyears on 11. The numerical closeness is not borne out in competition, as five of the top six cars in the point standings (after Mosport) were on Firestones. Goodyear scored a win at Bridgehampton with Gurney, but Firestones took the others.

Traco Engineering now has a near-monopoly on the sports/racing engine business. Their ability to get gobs of reliability—from Chevrolet engines—has had them working overtime during the Can-Am season. Right now, their hottest set-up is the 359 cu. in. Chevy, producing 492 hp at 6800 rpm, with 467 lbs./ft. of torque at 4500 rpm. Derived from the 327 block, the 359 cu. in. size was developed by using .040-in. overbore and a quarter-inch stroker crankshaft, bringing stroke to a leather-lunged 3.5. inches. Carburetion on this set-up consists of the gigantic 58mm Weber sidedrafts. Chuck Parsons won the USRRC title with Traco's 333 and 364 engines. The best 333 Traco ever assembled was a honey for Roger Penske that developed 489 hp at 6500 and 435 lbs./ft. of torque at 5500, but the 333s are now considered undersized weaklings in the race for power.

What with Group 7 racing all but chased out of England, the sports/racers have found fertile ground in the Can-Am series. Over a six-race program like the Can-Am, development work is accomplished considerably faster than it ever could be in sporadic, scattered races. If sports/racing cars are rolling laboratories, the Can-Am series is a rolling college. Tune in next month for the graduation exercises.　　**c/D**

FROM THE COCKPIT

By Bruce McLaren

THE bare results of the CanAm sports car series so far don't do anything to convey the excitement, enthusiasm and interest that's being generated for the "big bangers" in America. We haven't won a race yet, but at least we haven't been beaten by the same driver twice!

Four out of the six races have been run. John Surtees won the first with his Lola and our McLaren Elvas were second and third. Dan Gurney's Lola won the next and again we were second and third. In the third race Chris and I were lying first and second when we were both put out by minor accidents while we were lapping slower cars. In the fourth race at Laguna Seca I finished third behind Phil Hill and Jim Hall in the Chaparrals.

Sports car racing is now getting to be the biggest spectator sport in the USA, and the financial support of the motor industry and the accessory companies is on the increase—a very important point for car owners and team managers. You can't run a racing team on just enthusiasm these days!

We started the series reckoning that if our cars were quick and reliable—although

BRUCE McLAREN half in and half out of the McLaren-Chevrolet in the paddock before the Bridgehampton Grand Prix.

not necessarily fastest—we could win. I think we may have been wrong. Our McLaren Elvas are certainly quick and reliable, but it's Phil Hill who leads the series in the automatic Chaparral with a fourth, a second, and a first. Chris and I are right in behind him.

Our mistake was probably in under-rating the Chaparral, because it is undoubtedly the best car. Every year the Chaparrals have been THE competition, but we figured that perhaps with their venture into European long-distance racing this year they may have eased the pace for the CanAm races. We were more worried about the chances of Denny Hulme and John Surtees in their well-developed, proven, race-winning Lolas, and Dan Gurney's Lola with its powerful Weslake modified Ford engine. From the rolling start at Bridgehampton Dan opened up 30 yards in a quarter mile, which was rather off-putting.

But we should have been able to foresee that the Chaparrals would have an immediate weight advantage with their aluminium Chevvy engine which weighs some 200 lbs less than our cast iron engines. I didn't expect them to be as fast as they are on top speed, and I have a sneaking suspicion that their secret automatic transmission is now a 3-speeder.

Fortunately for us we saw the writing on the wall after the opening race at Mosport, and we increased our 5.4-litre Chevvy V8s to just on 6 litres. We were able to make good use of the engine knowledge we have gained on the Formula One engine programme this year, and we fitted stronger con rods and a new fuel injection system that we have been working on.

The Champion Spark Plug people let us use their dynamometer facilities to tune the engines at Long Beach in California, and they helped us considerably with our modifications. We managed to extract 527 horsepower, and in the next race at Laguna Seca the cars were more competitive than they have ever been. At last we had race-winning potential—now all we wanted was some race wins!

In both race heats at Laguna Seca I was right on the tail of the leading Chaparral when trifling problems sent me to the pits, but we're confident that these problems can be sorted out, and we're looking forward to the big-money race at Riverside.

This horsepower boost is quite fantastic when I think back to the neck and neck races we had with the Chaparrals last year when our Oldsmobiles were only giving 370 bhp. We went up to 470 bhp when we changed to Chevvy V8s and now we are looking for 570! The prize money is big in this CanAm series, but so is the horsepower competition. I reckon we've collected more prize money in this series so far than we could have won in three years' racing in England. I'm not saying that no starting money and big prize money is the way to go, but you certainly can't complain if you are finishing regularly.

We know that our cars are handling better than most of the others, and now that we've got some more horses under the bonnet things might start looking up.

At Mosport and Ste Jovite in Canada we were recording quicker times through corners than any of the others, but we were losing ground on the straights. Surtees could leave us four lengths behind when we hit a straight, Gurney would be five or six lengths ahead, and the Chaparrals were making even more ground. It got to the stage where the only cars Chris or I could pass in a straight line were our own! We could lap as quickly as the others, but it meant a lot of ten-tenths stuff in the twisty bits.

However, I reckon we'll be going to the line with a very competitive pair of cars for the 55,000 dollar Riverside race.

Lola 70 Mark III

The latest from Eric Broadley is a car that can be adapted for either Group 7 2-seater racing or the Group 6 prototype class

BY TONY HOGG

ALTHOUGH THE ELDERLY gentlemen of the FIA would be loath to admit it, one of the most competitive, important, and potentially rewarding of the various racing classes is Group 7, the all-out sports-racing 2-seaters. The reason for this state of affairs is the Can Am series. After the 1966 season the cash and the glory went to John Surtees but much of the credit for his victories must go to Lola Cars Ltd, the builders of the Lola 70. It is also significant that Lola man Eric Broadley has already produced a Mk III version of this machine in order to be ahead of the game in 1967.

The Lola 70 has been a very successful sports-racer since its introduction in 1965 and it is now entering its third year of competition. During its life remarkably few changes have been made to the car and even these have been mainly of a minor nature. And so it is with the 1967 Mk III version except that the car is now being offered with an alternative coupe body conforming to the regulations for GT Prototypes in Group 6. By offering this alternative, Broadley has filled the gap left in his business by the decision to drop Group 7 in Europe and he anticipates widening his market considerably by offering a car that can be converted from one Group to another.

With the great popularity of the big sports machines in America, it may seem surprising that they are no longer to be supported in Europe. But the facts of the matter are that European racing is largely dominated by the British oil companies and although these companies have pockets of outstanding depth the bottom is beginning to be reached because of the British government's current squeeze on industry. Therefore it was felt that the available money should go to Formulas 1 and 2, particularly as F1 is now much more exciting and the 1600-cc F2 should attract far greater crowds than its 1000-cc predecessor. Another point is that Group 7 cars employ American engines and the British oil companies much prefer to spend their money helping to develop British engines.

Fiberglass expert Peter Jackson is responsible for Mk III body.

Mk III retains flavor of familiar Lola 70 sports/racing car.

Removable nose and tail shells are held in place by Pip pins.

Prototype rules requiring spare tire result in this rear view.

However, there is still a sizable market for Group 7 cars in America and the idea of the dual-purpose Lola is to cater to Europeans who want to run Group 6 events during the European season and then enter the Can Am series or, alternatively, for Americans who want to run Daytona and Sebring and then enter the big sports car events. As far as the conversion is concerned, Broadley stresses the point that it is not just a snap fastener operation but neither is it a cut-and-weld job. In fact it falls somewhere between the two and would probably take a private owner without experience the best part of a week to carry out, but full instructions will be issued by the factory detailing all the steps.

The basis of the Lola 70 is a central hull composed of the floor, two box side members which house the fuel bags, a box member with an open side in front and two bulkheads in the rear which are situated behind and in front of the engine. A considerable quantity of foam plastic is used at various points to form a sandwich for stiffening purposes. This layout forms an extremely rigid and light structure and Broadley puts them through his shop in dozen lots so that the unit cost is relatively low. Perhaps the biggest change in the car's construction occurred when the Mk II car was introduced. This involved the use of far more aluminum alloy in the hull which decreased the weight considerably but without any loss of rigidity.

The rear suspension uses a lower A-arm of rugged construction attached to the rear bulkhead. The front side of the A is fabricated in hat section and the rear side is tubular. A short upper link passes to the top of the bulkhead and two radius rods go forward to the other bulkhead located in front of the engine compartment. As at the rear, the front suspension is quite conventional with unequal length A-arms and a rack-and-pinion for the steering. For the Mk III version of the car some very minor changes have been made, mainly to alter the roll center and camber changes slightly.

Tests have shown that these modifications have been successful because the car now makes better use of current racing tires when considerable suspension movement is involved and it also handles better in slower turns. Commenting on these changes, Broadley says that in general the car's "dice-ability" has been much improved, by which he means that it can be weaved through traffic more easily and its handling is less critical than previously so that it is more stable for less skilled drivers. Unfortunately it is not possible to incorporate the Mk III suspension modifications in an existing Mk II car.

There are two impressions that one gains immediately from inspection of the Lola 70. The first is that the detail work of even such trivial items as door handles and hinges is first class and that this detail work is carried on throughout the car. Although attention to detail does not necessarily win races it does guard against losing them due to odd but essential pieces starting to come adrift and it is perhaps significant that Lola has lost many more races through engine and transmission failures than through other reasons. The second impression is that, although the overall weight is low, the working parts are remarkably beefy. When the suspension modifications for the Mk III version were carried out, additional strength was one of the objectives and the components certainly look as though they are able to withstand the incredible cornering power of the tires and also the 450 bhp which is passed to them.

The 12.5-in. disc brakes front and rear are very deeply dished to bring them out into the airstream and the GT model, which is 170 lb heavier than the sports car, will be equipped with vented discs to increase pad life during long distance races. The cast magnesium wheels have a 15-in. rim diameter with 8-in. rim widths at the front and 10 in. at the rear to carry the 10.60 x 15 and 12.00 x 15 Firestones.

The body panels are made by Peter Jackson's Specialized Moldings, Ltd. Jackson is relatively unkown outside the close racing circle but he has built up a sizable business employing 25 people which concentrates on building fiberglass

Lola 70 Mark III

bodies for competition cars. His customers include almost everyone in racing, not excepting Enzo Ferrari for whom he has built a number of GP car bodies, and it was largely due to Jackson that the racing world switched from aluminum to fiberglass. The secret of Jackson's success is that he does top quality work and he is equipped to do it in a hurry. He has also always stressed the comparative safety of fiberglass over aluminum in the event of an accident.

In the case of the Lola GT, Broadley gave Jackson an idea of what he wanted, Jackson had his stylist "pretty it up" and then made a quarter-scale model. After the model had been approved by Broadley, it was scaled up and a full size body produced. In this manner a lot of time was saved but only because Jackson knows exactly what he is doing.

The resulting GT body is dramatic and very clean and one hopes that it will not need to be altered by the addition of too many spoilers, fins, slots and louvers as befalls most competition cars these days. The center section of the body is supported by two rollbars, one slightly behind the driver's head and one in front of him, which also serve as mounting points for the gullwing doors. The front and rear body sections are each made in one piece. They are carried on outrigger frame extensions and are quickly detachable by four Pip pins for the front and six for the back after the wiring has been unplugged. The wheelbase of both the open and closed cars is 95 in. but the body of the GT is some 8 in. longer at the rear to accommodate a vertically mounted spare wheel behind the transmission. This is required by the regulations for Group 6 cars and so is the luggage compartment located above the transmission.

The big windshield is very steeply raked and curved and the line of the top flows back horizontally to the sharply chopped-off tail with its molded-in spoiler on top. Obviously great attention has been paid to aerodynamics but as this seems to be an area in which most designers are hopelessly lost, only track testing will tell whether the body is right or not as it stands. Meanwhile, one can say that it certainly looks right and that there is a basic family resemblance to the original Lola GT of 1963 which will be remembered as the origin of the whole Ford GT racing program.

As with most Group 7 cars, the Lola will accept a variety of different engine/transmission combinations. This does not mean that Broadley has left the question of power units entirely to his customers. Unfortunately, the engine requirements for success in Group 6 racing are basically different from those for the Can Am series because of the difference in race duration. For the Group 6 type of event, which includes Daytona and Sebring, Broadley recommends the 333-cu-in. Chevrolet built up by Ryan Falkner of Los Angeles which has been developed in close cooperation with Broadley over the last two years. This is a compromise unit giving 460 bhp at 6200 rpm and it is designed to withstand the pounding of 1000 km round the Nurburgring or similar feats of endurance.

For European customers these engines will be air-freighted across the Atlantic completely prepared and a parts and service organization has been set up to handle them. Commenting on these engines, Broadley stresses that they are produced to his specifications, and not only is the price reasonable for the work involved but also the quality is consistent throughout a batch of units.

The engine is based on the 327-cu-in. Chevy and the bore and stroke are 4.04 x 3.25 in. A fully counterbalanced crank

Rear (left) and front suspension. Front disc is not in place.

First batch of Mark IIIs being built at the Lola works at Slough.

Chassis for one of this year's Indy Lolas under construction.

is used in conjunction with special connecting rods and 4-bolt steel main bearing caps. The camshaft has roller followers and the large valves are operated by light alloy rockers on needle roller bearings. Four Weber 48-mm downdraft carburetors are mounted on a light alloy manifold, and wet sump lubrication is employed using a high capacity oil pump. This engine is by no means in its highest state of tune but should still be going strong at the end of an endurance event provided that the driver sticks to a rev limit determined partly by the duration of the race. In conjunction with this engine, Lola supplies a 4-speed Hewland transmission and it is anticipated that a 5-speed unit will be available shortly.

As we have reported previously, plans have been made for entering two cars at Le Mans powered by Aston Martin's new 5-liter V-8. This marks a welcome return to racing for Aston Martin after a long absence and it provides a much needed

Continued on page 20

14

Left: *TAC's new car with its designers and builders before shipment to the States. Its unconventional lines are clearly shown here, together with the minimal cockpit opening. A Chaparral-type flipper is just one possible modification before this latest Cobra races. Frank Nichols is in the centre of the group, with Len Terry on the right.*

Bottom: *The rear end of the Terry-designed, Nichols-constructed Cobra, showing the transverse coil spring suspension. Idea is to divorce roll stiffness from spring stiffness.*

CAN-AM CONTENDER
New TAC-designed Cobra goes to America

FOR years the backbone of the motor racing industry has been the specialist manufacturer, serving the car builders, the works teams and private entrants alike. If you have an engine problem you probably contact Cosworth or Holbay, if you are in gearbox trouble you get on to Hewland, and if you need a body you probably call up Peter Jackson at Specialised Mouldings.

But until recently if you wanted a complete custom-built racing car, together with the jigs and drawings to make replicas, you had quite a problem. It was this thought as much as any which prompted Frank Nichols to join forces with Len Terry just over six months ago and form Transatlantic Automotive Consultants.

As originally conceived, TAC was to have been a very small organisation, but the pressure of work has been such that already they have twice outgrown their premises, and are now negotiating to expand into land adjacent to their new headquarters at St Leonards-on-Sea, Sussex. TAC offers the motor racing world two main services—the design and manufacture of cars for teams to race, and the design and construction of prototypes for customers' own manufacture. Both services have already been called upon, and there is sufficient follow-up business in the pipeline to keep TAC at full pressure for a long time to come.

Carroll Shelby was the company's first customer, and has recently taken delivery of its first product. Shelby wanted a car to enter for the forthcoming Can-Am Challenge Cup race series and he reckoned that Len Terry's outstanding design ability (his successes have included the World Championship and Indianapolis-winning Lotuses and the Formula 1 and Indy Eagles) made him the obvious choice for the job.

Consequently, TAC were commissioned by Shelby American to design and build one complete car, as well as to supply a second car in component form and a third monocoque chassis-body unit. Initial work was carried out in temporary accommodation close to Frank Nichols' home in Staplecross, Sussex, but in April TAC moved into their new premises on the outskirts of Hastings comprising an administration office, design office, jig room, stores and two assembly bays, amounting in all to 10,000 square feet.

The first Group 7 car has already been completed and shipped to the Shelby American headquarters in Los Angeles, and on completion of the remainder of the contract all the design and assembly drawings will be handed over to Shelby American, who will manufacture further replicas in due course.

It had been intended to enter the Can-Am car as a King Cobra, thereby reviving a name which Carroll Shelby adopted a few years ago for his modified Ford V8-engined Cooper Monacos. But now, apparently, the Terry-designed car will be known simply as a Cobra (probably because the last thing it looks is 'King' size!)

The first car is to be driven in the Can-Am races by 38 year-old Jerry Titus, Editor of the American monthly magazine *Sports Car Graphic*, and currently one of the points leaders in the 1967 Trans-Am Sedan Championship (the US equivalent of the British Saloon Car Championship) in which he is driving a Shelby-prepared Mustang for the Terlingua Racing Team.

The new Cobra had to be shipped out with only a 'dummy' Ford engine installed due to the non-arrival of a new racing version of the Ford V8 351 cubic inch (5.8 litre) engine which Shelby hopes will be available for the car. [Ford have also been developing a 400 cubic inch (6.5 litre) version of this engine.]

As a result, it was not possible to carry out any track-testing in this country and evaluate the performance of Len Terry's ingenious suspension and engine-cooling arrangements. (Shelby American's Phil Remington has been supervising the final assembly work in Los Angeles, and was aiming to have the car ready for Titus to start development tests on August 15.)

Although it was one of Carroll Shelby's design requirements that the car should incorporate Eagle suspension and running gear (Shelby, of course, has an interest in All-American Racers), Terry has broken new ground by replacing the conventional coil springs with a single transverse coil spring at front and rear—a layout he first tried several years ago on one of his early sports cars. One of the design aims of this arrangement is to divorce the car's spring stiffness from its roll stiffness, so that each can be adjusted independently of the other.

Another departure from convention is the car's radiator system, which is so arranged that air is drawn in over the top surface of the almost horizontal matrix and exhausted beneath the car—the reverse of the conventional system. The aim here is to eliminate the need for a low-pressure area above the nose of the car, thereby combating high-speed lift, and also to lower the centre of gravity. In the event of there being insufficient time to fully develop these features before the first Can-Am race on September 3, both the suspension and the radiator system can be quickly converted to a conventional layout.

Len Terry has devised an unusually 'slippery' shape for the Can-Am Cobra, with a minute cockpit opening (by current sports car standards) and a pronounced upsweep at the rear of the underside surface. If time permits, Shelby American may well experiment with a Chaparral-style wing over the tail with compensating modifications at the front.

Although the car was not weighed before it left this country, Terry anticipates an all-up weight in the region of 1,450 pounds, while the car's power expectation is at least 550 bhp. The aluminium monocoque hull (steel is confined to the rear hoop and a few small heavy load-bearing parts) has a centre box carrying all the oil and water lines between engine and radiators, and cooling air is also drawn in through the top of the nose and along the centre tube into the two 'wheelbarrow arms' straddling the engine, and extracted through outlets aimed at the rear brakes and shock absorbers. Fuel is carried in bladders in the side boxes, and there is a total capacity of approximately 56 gallons.

Ford with wings

*New Mark IV-based
group 7 sports-racer
for the Can-Am series*

by Carl Ludvigsen

UNTIL now, Ford have been more interested in sports car racing in Europe than in the United States. Their GT40s and Mk. 2s have raced and won at Sebring and Daytona, to be sure, but Ford never concealed the fact that its main objective was victory at Le Mans. Now, after two straight wins in the French classic, Ford is turning its attention to a new Group 7 car to compete in the Can-Am Championship series, a car that is based closely on this year's Le Mans winner.

Ford's reluctance to go Group 7 has been understandable. Until the Can-Am series was established there was little public interest in the U.S. in this esoteric kind of racing; Ford want to race where their efforts will be noticed and appreciated. Moreover, the design standard of modern Group 7 cars is very high, driven nearer the ultimate in adhesion for sprint-type racing, more at the Grand Prix car level than the endurance-racer level. Until now, Ford themselves have never built a chassis specifically for short-distance events.

Occasional forays into Can-Am competition have given Ford a good feel for the kind of pace required. In late 1965 several starts were made by Chris Amon in the X-1, a lightweight roadster version of that year's prototype GT40 Mk. 2, built for Ford by Bruce McLaren. The X-1 was used to test Ford's two-speed power-shift automatic transmission, which appeared again in 1966 in a Ford-powered Lola for Mario Andretti to try, without special success. In fact Chevrolet engines prepared by Traco and Chaparral dominated the Can-Am racing in 1966, with only occasional interference from Dan Gurney's Lola with a Gurney-Weslake Ford engine. John Mecom was sharply and publicly critical of the engines supplied to him by Ford, supercharged and otherwise, for use in his Lolas. This criticism could only have strengthened Ford's resolve to do the job right in 1967.

Early this year the Dearborn Group 7 battle plan was formulated by the racing stalwarts reporting to Donald N. Frey, Ford's vice president for product development. This was to be an all-FoMoCo project, the cars to be designed and built by

Ford's Kar Kraft subsidiary, a tiny operation composed of talented people headed by Roy Lunn. Newly appointed to oversee the Can-Am cars is Fran Hernandez, who at one time or another has been associated with the racing programmes of every Ford division.

Kar Kraft elected to base its Group 7 car on the frame and suspension of the proven Group 6 J-Car/Mk. 4. This was not the lightest possible way to go but it was likely to be reliable and predictable and safe, especially desirable attributes with the very powerful engines Ford expect to use.

The basic frame is precisely that of the Mk. 4, an angular bathtub made of sheets composed of expanded aluminium honeycomb sandwiched between 0.016-in. aluminium surfaces. At the front, a lateral bulkhead one inch thick transfers the stresses from the leg box to the two side boxes, which are joined by another one-inch bulkhead at the firewall position. All the other frame elements are of half-inch honeycomb, the whole being knitted together by a combination of riveting and epoxy resin bonding. The complete frame, which in a sense *is* the G7 Ford, weighs 123 lb.

The Mk. 4's side boxes carried Goodyear fuel cells containing 42 gallons of fuel, the maximum that the regulations allowed. These ran rearward to the firewall line. On the G7 car the cells run all the way to the rear of the side boxes, expanding the capacity to 64 gallons. A simple but effective system will extract all the fuel from these tanks. At the rear of each tank, kept filled automatically under acceleration, is an integral sump containing a gallon or so of fuel, separated from the main tank by a moulded-in baffle inclined rearward at 45 degrees.

Submerged and drawing from the bottom of each sump is a special electric fuel pump. There is no crossover pipe between the two tanks; instead the left-hand pump has the job of keeping the right-hand tank full. Overflow from the right-hand tank, if any, is bypassed back to the left tank. In this way the right-hand weight bias, for clockwise racing, is positively maintained. When

the left tank is emptied, or at a prearranged mid-race point, its electric pump is simply switched off.

Meanwhile the right-hand pump works *all* the time, sending fuel up to a small "make-up" tank supported on a pylon at the engine's right. This tank supplies a gravity head above the level of the Hilborn fuel injection pump used by Ford, and it also receives the fuel flow that is bypassed by the Hilborn system at low engine speeds. Both these features, often neglected in fuel system design, are very much appreciated by the Hilborn pump.

The steering and suspension, modern conventional race car in concept, are adopted almost unchanged by the G7 version of the Mk. 4. Experience with the latter has allowed Lunn and company to eliminate some alternative wishbone mounting points that are no longer likely to be used. As before, the lower rear suspension radius arms incline upward as they come forward to counter squatting under acceleration, which they do very effectively. The Mk. 4 was exceptional for its flat trim under all conditions, which will also benefit the G7 car, which will be running with less ground clearance, from 3 to 3½ in.

Coil springs are used all round, concentric with aluminium-bodied Koni dampers, and anti-roll bars are provided at both front and rear. With the more rearward tankage and lighter body the weight distribution well to the back, some 65% on the drive wheels. Ford cast their own magnesium wheels for the Mk. 4 and G7, a step taken with reluctance after they found that commercially-available wheels would not consistently clear Kar Kraft's rigorous crack-testing procedures. Even Ford ran into porosity problems with their 16-inch axial-fan wheels for Le Mans; the G7 car runs on 15-inch wheels. The rim widths are 12 in. at the rear and 9 in. in front, adequate to take the widest tyres Goodyear or Firestone will be making for these cars.

The G7 brakes are also of proven Mk. 4 design, using vented 12-in. discs with Kelsey-Hayes calipers, outboard all round. The dual brake master cylinders and the clutch actuation cylinder are all fed with

fluid from a compact common fluid reservoir. Lightness is evident here as in all the detail work on the G7 Ford, showing the effort of Fran Hernandez to keep the weight down as much as possible. The clutch and brake pedals, for example, are on very light fabricated steel arms, lovingly welded into a box section. Other controls include a 12-inch leather-rimmed steering wheel and a gear selection lever on the driver's right.

Ford have a choice of transmissions as well as engines for the G7 cars. They can use the Old Reliable four-speed manual Mk. 2/4 transmission. They can also use the power-shift two-speed automatic box which was developed in late 1965 mainly for the J-Car, and which was race-tested in a GT Mk. 2 at Daytona in 1966. This box uses clutch packs and hydraulic actuation to shift up or down, at the rear of a torque converter, and it can shift with no interruption in acceleration or braking torque to the wheels.

The four-speed and power-shift transmissions weigh about the same. Favoured by Kar Kraft is a unit some 80 lb. lighter, a Chaparral-type automatic, which is fitted in the first G7 Ford. Behind the engine is a simple three-element torque converter of 11 in. diameter. Back of the final drive, with its sprag-type self-locking differential, is a two-speed spur-gear transmission. Gear selection is by Colotti-type dog clutches, each with eight engaging dogs $\frac{3}{16}$ in. in depth. They are simple and very strong, allowing the driver to change gear by backing off on the throttle and punching the short-travel lever, motorcycle style.

A dozen different sets of spur gears are available for the all-indirect gearbox, all fully interchangeable so the driver can have high gear either forward or back, whichever way he wants to push the lever. A complete ratio change inside the one-piece magnesium gear case takes a matter of 25 minutes. The box has its own oil pump and a cooling radiator at the right of the engine.

Use of either of the automatic transmissions will free the clutch pedal for use

The bathtub basic frame of the Group 7 car is built up from expanded aluminium honeycomb sandwiched between aluminium sheets. The engine is the latest Ford light alloy racing unit with three valves per cylinder operated by two camshafts through pushrods and rockers. The gearbox is the new two-speed automatic transmission with a three-element torque converter.

The dual brake master cylinders and the clutch actuation cylinder—when a manual transmission is fitted —are mounted beneath the rack-and-pinion steering gear on the front bulkhead and are fed with fluid from a common reservoir. Front suspension is orthodox, with upper and lower wishbone links and a combined coil spring and Koni damper suspension unit.

The McLaren M6A

by Michael Bowler

Right bank of the McLaren Chevrolet V-8, showing the inlet manifold re-fabricated to accommodate the Lucas fuel injection, the Scintilla magneto and alloy rockers temporarily exposed.

Bare bones of the M6A with designer Robin Herd overlooking. Fuel tanks are housed in side members and another over the knees. Oil cooler is exposed to air through a slot in the upswept tail.

CAN-AM CARS
Ford with wings

as a trim control for the high wing Kar Kraft have designed for the G7 Ford. In height and width the Dearborn airfoil array is like last year's Chaparral 2E, but the Ford approach has been to divide it into two wings, each with a supporting strut at its midpoint for better stress distribution. Like the Chaparral, the strut carries the downthrust direct to the rear wheel hubs through an added pivot in the upper suspension link, and is braced forward by a third trailing arm to both sides of the very solid roll-bar structure.

Unique to Ford's wing system is a third central strut which can be varied in height, experimentally, to position the wings either flat or at an aircraft-type dihedral angle which can increase the car's high-speed stability. A hydraulic cylinder from the central strut is used to vary the incidence angle of the twin wings, angled for corners and flat for the straights. The wings are fabricated in aircraft style, with aluminium skin on punched aerofoil formers along a lateral tubular structure.

Ford's big Hurricane Road wind tunnel was used to pre-test the wing designs, and to develop the body shape also. The outcome is a slippery-looking car with some Chaparral 2E design elements around the radiator air exit and windshield, the currently favoured slab sides, and the general appearance of an Alfa Type 33 gone wild. Made by Ford's styling staff, the glass-fibre body will carry no paint and will have its main colour in the outer coat of epoxy resin, as

another weight-saving measure. One car will be red, to run as a Mercury, and the other will be a blue and white Ford.

What will be under the rear deck of the two G7 Fords when they appear at Elkhart Lake this month, Ford frankly aren't sure. There are several possibilities: one is the famous Indianapolis four-cam Fairlane engine, which would be enlarged to 300 cubic inches (almost 5 litres) and mated to the five-speed ZF gearbox. Another is the 7-litre wedge-chamber V-8, with the latest round ports, which is fully proven in the Mk. 2 and 4 Fords. Either of these could produce in excess of 500 b.h.p. in sprint-race tune.

The third possibility, favoured by Ford at the moment, is an all-new V-8, actually the first engine that Ford themselves (as distinct from Cosworth) have designed and built from scratch for racing. They call it the "calliope", because it has big vertical air inlet stacks, cast integral with the aluminium heads, to feed the two inlet valves per cylinder. A single exhaust valve and a single sparking plug also occupy the semi-spherical combustion chamber. The cylinder block is aluminium, and unlike other large-displacement current Ford V-8s the block is cut off at the crank centre-line to save weight. The bottom end is completed by a deep cast magnesium sump.

Above the "calliope" crankshaft are *two* camshafts, one above the other, both mounted within the block. Through tappets and pushrods the upper one almost certainly operates all the exhaust valves, while the lower one attends to the intake valves. Short rocker arms are used, of similar size for both inlet and exhaust, and each of the 16 inlet valves has its own complete pushrod/rocker system. Somehow, Ford's clever

engine designers get all the pushrods past, or through, the inlet ports.

This all-new engine will probably be raced in 400-cubic-inch form (6.5 litres) in the G7 Fords, which should provide prodigious power without excessive weight. Ford's Engine and Foundry Division went 'way overboard on both weight and bulk when they designed the overhead-camshaft 427 engine. With the "calliope" an obvious attempt was made, successfully, to keep the engine as low and narrow as possible. Overall length was also minimized by using two small water pumps at the front, which can be shallower and need less manifolding than a single large pump.

Sweeping up and away from the engine is a tuned exhaust system, fabricated in mild steel, representing the work of three weeks by two men. At the left of the engine are placed the oil tank for the dry sump system and the oil radiator. Pipes along the left of the cockpit carry water to and from the aluminium radiator. The latter has a four-inch core with finely louvred matrices, made up by Ford's Applied Research Laboratory and fitted with headers by an outside contractor.

The two factory G7 Fords will not be the only Dearborn-powered cars competing for Can-Am points. Alan Mann in England is building two far-out cars for Holman and Moody which will use 351-cubic-inch engines, the same type Skip Scott will use in a new McLaren-Elva. Dan Gurney has a car of his own for a Gurney-Weslake Ford, and Shelby American has built two Eagle-related cars to a Len Terry design and is waiting to see what kind of engines Ford will provide. If Ford engines don't do well in this year's Can-Am competition, it won't be for want of trying.

BRUCE McLaren is one of the few constructors who have made Group 7 cars a commercial success, by combining with the Lambretta Trojan group to produce the McLaren Elvas; the other successful Group 7 producer this side of the Atlantic is obviously Eric Broadley.

The latest McLaren, not yet having earned the Elva suffix, was on show at Goodwood prior to its shipment to Canada where one car will be driven by McLaren himself and the only other M6A by Denny Hulme. Previous Group 7 McLaren cars have used a space frame construction partly because the knowledge available on that theme has been extensive but also because it is cheaper to tool up for this construction with relatively simple jigs. The M6A, however, uses a neatly designed and well made monocoque construction, a mixture of aluminium and magnesium panels held together by "glue" and rivets. Basis of the chassis and responsible for its high torsional rigidity is the centre section with its flat floor braced by twin side box-members housing the rubber fuel tanks and a central small backbone. Fabricated arms reach backwards from the tanks to the rear engine/gearbox bearer, a boxed bulkhead. Forward is a closed box over the pedal area which provides mountings for the transverse suspension links, and forward of that again is the fabricated radiator air intake. This is designed to mate up

Nose down under braking while McLaren establishes which end locks first—tyres by Goodyear. Attractive body by Specialised Mouldings is to showroom finish and shouldn't need fins.

with the beautifully finished glass-fibre bodywork made by Specialised Mouldings.

Aerodynamics for cars is a complicated and only partially understood subject in that practice does not necessarily follow theory. Robin Herd, McLaren's chassis designer, is one of the increasing army of younger engineers in the racing game, their minds untainted by long experience of standard textbooks. This allows the fresh approach, and anyone present at Goodwood some time during the last summer might have seen the McLaren whipping round the circuit with Robin leaning over the back on the straights taking pressure readings at all points both under and on top of the body. This involved racing speeds on the corners so that the car could be held at steady high speeds on the available straights. The result is as pictured, although they admit there is still some way to go even with the state of the art as they

now know it. It is a remarkably clean shape uncluttered by afterthought fins although the tail spoiler has been raised slightly since; something of the Chaparral in the low snow-shovel nose! The nominal wind tunnel drag coefficient is over 0.4. Air flow through the car, both for radiator and brake cooling, is an important factor in body shape, since a high proportion of the disturbed air does pass through these holes creating its own throttling, eddies, etc.

A novel position for the engine oil cooler is in the centre of the upswept tail; for this to be successful, as it is, air must still be flowing along the body and not separate over the cockpit area. The oil cooler for the transmission (a five-speed Hewland LG600), is beneath the tail.

Recent innovations in the suspension field have not yet been proved, apart from the great benefits of ever wider tyres and the minor geometric tailoring to accommodate them and the McLaren car has conventional suspension; at the front it is by simple double wishbones with a speedily removable anti-roll bar—in such a compact and yet beefy layout there is just not room to use the usual adjustable trailing arm alternative. The lower leading link has its rear mounting actually in the cockpit attached to the cross member which holds the seat front mountings. Denny Hulme didn't like the feel of this moving member tickling the back of his thigh so it now has a pad. At the rear, the upper wide angle wishbone has conventional attachment points for its transverse and trailing arms, but the lower one has a triangulated inverted A-arm and the trailing link is attached to a star-bracket on the side of the engine, giving a pivot axis not parallel to that of the upper linkage. Again, the rear anti-roll bar is a quick-change type. At neither end is there any anti-dive or anti-squat angling of the wishbones, since Bruce McLaren prefers to feel the suspension working, and not have the steering feel masked by the kickback and castor changes which are associated with angled axes.

Magnesium wheels are cast to McLaren's own design by Aeroplane and Motor Castings taking 15 in. dia. Goodyear tyres on their large rims. For fast circuits these will be 8½ in. front and 13½ in. rear in width, with 12 in. rims being used on the rear for tighter circuits where some oversteer is necessary. The brakes are again to McLaren specifications, made by Girlings with Ferodo supplying the pads.

Apart from his brief association with the Indy Ford engine and the Serenissima unit, McLaren's cars are usually powered by Traco developed Oldsmobile units. This

Winged Caldwell

This Carl Ludvigsen photograph shows yet another American Group 7 car that has followed the Chaparral lead. Built by Ray Caldwell's Autodynamics Corporation of Marblehead, Massachusetts, for the American driver Sam Posey (extreme right) the new Caldwell has a high two-position wing,

a foam stiffened aluminium monocoque frame and solid axle suspension at front and rear to suit the very wide Goodyear tyres. Wheelbase is only 92 in., the rear track 50 in., and the kerb weight 1,460 lb. Three Caldwells are to be built this year as the start of a two-year development programme.

CAN-AM CARS
The McLaren M6A

time, McLaren has developed his own Chevrolet engine based on the roadgoing 283 cu.in. 4,640 c.c. V-8 (as most are), since this is rather lighter than some of the later GM engines. Speed equipment in the States is big business and McLaren has effectively shopped around picking the best bits from each supplier. Bartz Engine development reground a Camaro crank, Forgetrue supplied pistons, Iskenderian the cam, and Warren Machine Company the rods, which were in fact the sole surviving design from the abortive Formula 1 engine. The crossover inlet manifold is from Mickey Thompson; it is intended for carburetters but has been cut and welded to take Lucas fuel injection. This ensemble gives something over 500 b.h.p. at 7,000 r.p.m. from 5.8 pushrod litres. A cut-out is fitted to prevent anything over 7,500 r.p.m.

The engine is mounted at the front on a magnesium plate and at the rear by a bracket on the rear bulkhead giving fore and aft location as well.

A system of one-way valves between the three fuel tanks can be adjusted according to left or right hand circuits to keep the weight where it is needed and also to prevent the fuel pick-up from being starved.

McLaren was at Goodwood running in one of his Can-Am engines—he is taking six spare and four gearboxes—when I went down there. To the offer of a lift around the circuit, I yielded immediately; although "sports car" suggests two seats, it is a bit difficult to squeeze in with the water pipes running alongside on the left and keep out of the driver's way as well. I almost lay down, half on my left side, and braced my right arm across to the roll bar.

Although still running in, the engine delivered a very useful prod away from rest as we set off around the almost deserted Goodwood. It seemed quite easy at first; I didn't know the circuit and Bruce was just steering; the cornering power seemed fairly high. But in fact he was just being kind, and on the third lap he tried rather harder; it still felt very secure but his hands were tweaking the wheel all the way round the long right-hander that joins Madgwick and Fordwater almost into one, and it felt to me as if the back wanted to come out —he complained of understeer later and changed the roll bars: in fact he was probably giving the front wheels a chance to grip again by straightening the steering slightly. It wasn't until we went into that dipping left hander at St. Mary's that I really appreciated the cornering force when my right arm had to support almost my whole weight as I strove to keep away from the driver. Through Lavant I had time to realize how those large wheel arches really stand out against the road, but not so as to affect visibility unless you aren't going the way you are looking. Down Lavant Straight, the still tight engine was pushed up to around 6,000 r.p.m. or over 150 m.p.h. Into the first of Woodcote's two right-handers we braked all the way, before accelerating hard round the second, a short burst, nose down and hard through the chicane correcting the slight tail wag on the way out. That was probably around 1m. 30s. but Denny Hulme has got down to 1m. 13.4s. (117.7 m.p.h.). Back on the Lavant Straight on the "slower" lap, McLaren took his hands off the wheel, flicked the rim and showed how easily it returned to the straight ahead position —at 120 m.p.h. too! That and the ability to brake really deep into the corners without any tail twitch at all are the outstanding impressions of extraordinary stability. To my own surprise I wasn't frightened; had I been taken round in, say, a saloon car I knew even with a driver of the McLaren calibre I would probably have been terrified, but sitting in a Group 7 sports racer is so far out of one's own world that you can just sit back and enjoy watching a master at his own work, just like seeing the captain on the flight deck of a VC10. It is also a very salutary experience and puts you right back in your place—on the sidelines!

Lola 70 Mark III

Continued from page 14

British entry for the race. The all-alloy 4-cam engine has already been tested in an open Lola Mk III, and the project is going ahead as planned. The Aston engine is reputed to give about 450 bhp, so with a car weight in the region of 1800 lb less fuel and driver, and an efficient body shape, the Lola-Aston Martin should be competitive. When comparing the Aston Martin and the Chevy, it is interesting that one is being introduced in racing form to be used ultimately for passenger cars and the other was introduced for passenger cars and has been brought up to racing specifications. Both were conceived from entirely different points of view but the end result at the flywheel would appear to be almost identical.

Lola sales in America are being handled by John Mecom of Houston who is also one of Broadley's best customers. Asked about the price of the GT, Broadley was unable to quote exactly but estimated the at-the-factory price of $17,000 for a complete car with 333-cu.-in. Chevrolet and Hewland transmission ready to race. To this must be added such items as taxes and freight but of course the cars for American customers will be shipped without engines.

Broadley also mentioned that in his opinion this is a very competitive price for a very competitive car and evidently his customers think so too because he already has firm orders for 16 GTs and another 14 for the sports version.

Predicting the fortunes of the new competition cars is a hazardous occupation but in the case of the Lola 70 Mk III, the hazards are lessened because the car is by no means new and its evolution can be likened to putting old wine into new bottles. The old wine is known to be good and it has undoubtedly matured some more in Broadley's shop during the course of the winter. Assuming the new bottles are as clean as they look, 1967 should be a vintage year for Lola.

THE McLAREN M6A

TWO extremely potent sports-racers have been built by McLaren Motor Racing Ltd for Bruce McLaren and Denny Hulme. After over 2000 miles of testing, the machine—the McLaren M6A— is likely to go into production shortly as the McLaren-Elva Mark 4. Denny Hulme has already lapped Goodwood in 1 m 13.4 s (117.71 mph), which is far quicker than the official lap record and entailed taking Ford-water "flat" at 156 mph!

Most big sports-racers are ugly and many of them are scruffy. When Bruce McLaren demonstrated the big orange car at Goodwood last week it was fit to go straight to a motor show and had no slots, holes, or oddments to spoil the trim lines. Bruce has carried out a great deal of work on aerodynamics and now really knows what stability is all about. He has designed a nose that eliminates the need for front spoilers, and the one at the rear is built in, with a movable blade on variable mountings.

The construction is in the form of a monocoque chassis of bonded and riveted magnesium and aluminium, with quickly detachable glassfibre body panelling. There is a nose section carrying the front of the green plastic screen, two doors also supporting the continuation of the windscreen, and the tail section, through which the neat and compact engine projects, has a built-in spoiler. The power unit is a 5.8-litre Chevrolet V8 with Lucas fuel injection and Mickey Thompson crossover intakes, which have eight separate butterflies, each bank having one full-length throttle spindle. The connecting rods have resulted from Bruce's development of the Indianapolis Ford, and though it was a bad Grand Prix engine it gave a lot of valuable know-how. The camshaft is by Iskenderian and the heads are ported in America, but the valve seats are put in at McLarens. Ignition is by a Scintilla Vertex magneto, which has so far proved to be extremely reliable, and it carries a cutout of McLaren design that operates at 7500 rpm. The engine develops just over 500 bhp at 7000 rpm, and on the five speeds of the Hewland LG600 gearbox a typical set of ratios gives 82, 103, 125, 142, and 178 mph at peak revs. The clutch is a 3-plate Borg and Beck, the half-shafts with roller splines being by BRD Ltd.

The Girling brakes have BR calipers and 12 ins solid cast iron discs. Owing to Mr Hulme's propensity for cutting off later than the Formula 3 boys do, he may be given bigger front discs! The 4-stud 4-spoke 15 ins wheels are 13½ ins wide at the rear, or 12 ins for the slower circuits, the front width being 8½ ins, and the tyres are by Goodyear. The water radiator is at the nose of the car, the engine oil radiator being neatly covered by the rear spoiler, with a

transmission radiator underneath. The fuel tanks are carried along each side and are coupled to a knee tank, the total capacity being 54 gallons. A special system of valves is adopted so that the fuel tends to work towards the inner tank on a given circuit, rather than all being centrifuged to the outer tank, which affects the handling adversely on many cars.

The wheelbase is 7 ft 7 ins, track 4 ft 5 ins, and the weight is 1354 lbs. For the CanAm series the team are taking along six spare engines and four spare gearboxes, plus a thousand and one other parts. These beautifully made cars must be regarded as a very serious challenge and they will certainly be driven to the limit, by which I do *not* mean the Mistress of Transport's pathetic crawl. Indeed, the McLaren could break the law on the M1 without getting out of bottom gear.

JVB.

THE smooth lines of McLaren's latest CanAm contender (top). THE monocoque chassis exposed, showing the bonded and riveted alloy construction (above). THE Lucas fuel injection on the crossover inlet manifold and the Scintilla Vertex magneto (below).

MOTOR RACING
TRACK TEST
('from the cockpit')

NO, Bruce McLaren wasn't crazy enough to hand us his latest £10,000 investment in Can-Am transport, retire to the safety of the pits and grab a pair of stop watches. But he did offer us a ride in the passenger seat of the monocoque M6A sports-racer during a final day of development testing at Goodwood prior to shipping the car to Elkhart Lake, Wisconsin, for the first Can-Am round. As there are probably only a score of drivers in the World competent enough to handle such a car as it really should be handled (and Bruce is very definitely one of them) it seemed sensible to accept, and the resulting trip was so interesting that we make no apology for publishing this first *MOTOR RACING* track test from the somewhat startling viewpoint of a riding mechanic. (It is an experience which no constipated pressman can afford to miss!)

It may be recalled that last year Bruce received less than his share of luck in the Can-Am series, when he was partnered by Chris Amon with a pair of fuel-injected, Chevrolet-engined, spaceframe-chassis McLarens. This year he is making his biggest-ever racing effort, and has brought Denny Hulme into the team—a shrewd move which called for one of the cars to be two inches longer than the other in the wheelbase, but which has already paid off handsomely with Hulme's outright victory in that opening Can-Am race at Elkhart Lake.

No new McLaren has been more highly developed than the M6A. Bruce and his chief designer Robin Herd put a clean sheet of paper on the Colnbrook drawing board at the beginning of April, and the first pieces of metal were being turned a week later. June 19 was the date on which the first running chassis was completed and the initial test runs were made, and between that day and 'our' test laps towards the end of August, McLaren and Hulme between them had been round Goodwood more than 1,000 times. Hulme's fastest lap was in 1m 13.4s, and on the day we were there McLaren put in several laps in 1m 13.9s with Denny's car, despite the fact that he could scarcely see around right-handers because he was so low in the cockpit. For a performance comparison, the previous best by a Group 7 car had been around 1m 16s, and the best-ever time around Goodwood had been Brabham's 1m 15.4s with his Formula 1 car just prior to the Canadian Grand Prix.

The M6A is an amalgamation of ideas seen in several previous McLarens but most of all it can be described as a two-seater version of the Formula 2 and Formula 1 monocoques. A mixture of magnesium and aluminium is used for the 'monocoque chassis, the panels being riveted and bonded with glue, and covered by a glass-fibre body to McLaren's basic design produced by Specialised Mouldings in their new Huntingdon factory. Both the front and rear end sections are quickly removable, being secured in position by pit pins. Both cars are painted in brilliant orange, and it was planned to reverse the colouring of the running numbers and their roundels for easy identification of the two cars.

The front suspension is by outboard-mounted coil springs and Koni shock absorbers between transverse upper and lower links with leading radius arms, and the rear suspension by similar suspension units with double-braced lower wishbones, single top transverse links, and long trailing arms pivoting on the rear cockpit bulkhead. The 15 inch magnesium wheels have

THE CAN-AM McLAR

8½ inch rims at the front carrying Goodyear 10.40 tyres, and there is a choice of 12 inch and 13½ inch rims for the rear for the 12.35 Goodyears. The brakes, like the suspension units, are outboard all round, with 12 inch McLaren-designed discs made by Girling and having BR calipers and either Ferodo DS11 or Raybestos pads.

The M6A looks a small car (the wheelbase is either 89 or 91 inches, and the track 53 inches in each case) but even so it is surprisingly light at 1,354 pounds with oil and water but without fuel. There is tankage in the two side cells and a central knee tank (all rubber bags) for 54 imperial gallons of fuel, and an ingenious system of one-way valves has been built into the layout, one linking one side tank with the central tank, and the other linking the central tank with the other side tank, The idea is to allow fuel to flow one way across the car, towards the inside of the circuit, thereby ensuring that the maximum weight is carried over the inside wheels (the valves are reversed for left and right-handed circuits). Return pipes from the side tanks ensure that these do not balloon up through over-filling.

The Chevrolet engine is based on the familiar 5.3 litre (327 cubic inch) production V8 used in so many General Motors cars, but a 40 thou cylinder over-bore and a stroke increase of 20 thou over the standard long throw used on the Camaro has brought the capacity up to

5.8 litres.

This is believed to be the first American V8 engine to which Lucas fuel injection equipment as used on the Ford Formula 1 engine has been adapted (in this instance with the aid of a Mickey Thompson crossover manifold). The compression ratio is 11.2 to 1, and the output is said to be in excess of 500 bhp at 7,000 rpm (there is an electrical cutout at 7,500 rpm).

The engine conversion is to McLaren's specification throughout, but a good deal of the machine work is done for him in the States. The Bartz Engine Development Company have modified a Camaro crankshaft with small bearing sizes to fit the older and lighter Chevrolet cylinder block, the pistons are Forgedtrue, the Carillo rods are from the Warren Machine Company, and the cams from Iskenderian. Chevrolet's own wet-sump lubrication system is retained with modifications, the oil cooler being mounted in the rear body spoiler, the Champion plugs are sparked by a Scintilla magneto, mounted vertically at the rear of the block, and the whole package including exhausts comes out at 560 pounds, which makes the all-up weight of the car even more commendable.

The Borg and Beck triple-plate diaphragm racing clutch is coupled to one of the new Hewland LG600 five-speed transaxles, the final drive to the rear wheels being through BRD roller-spline shafts. The gear spacing of the LG600 provides road speeds of 82, 103,

No. 65 by John Blunsden

Far left: *The M6A is an impeccably-finished machine, note brake cooling ducts, water pipes, and steering gear here.* **Left:** *Business end, with the 5.8 litre, 500 bhp-plus Chevvy V8 and Hewland LG600 transaxle.* **Left, below:** *Minus its body panels, the M6A is a clean and low-slung car. Teddy Mayer looks on.* **Below:** *The body, looking like a cross between a Lola T70 and a Chaparral 2E, has the customary 'holes to let the air out' in the tail. Note transmission, rear tyre sizes, spoiler, oil cooler and so on.*

EN-CHEVROLET M6A

125, 142 and 178 mph at 7,000 rpm with typical cw and p rating.

Although they are not giving away any secrets, McLaren and Herd admit that their development tests have taught them a lot of new things about aerodynamics, and that a lot of their previously held theories have been thrown to the wind (if you'll excuse the pun!). However, significant features visible on the car are the very steep nose angle, the very low nose line forward of the front wheels, the absence of a rear wing (one was tried but was discarded), the use of a very small tail spoiler with two pre-set positions, one an inch above the other, and the very 'slippery' cockpit area. Also of note is the absence of any anti-lift or anti-dive in the suspension.

The second seat in the McLaren is built strictly to meet regulations, not to carry passengers! The problem is not so much the seat itself as the big wrap-over of the screen, which leaves quite a small 'hole' in the top of the cockpit, through which my borrowed and ill-fitting helmet protruded like a decaying Christmas pudding. But after wedging myself sideways to avoid cooking my left leg on the water pipes, Bruce reckoned there was still room enough for him to work the thing, and so off we set towards Madgwick.

At this stage he was still running-in a new engine, which apparently had an aluminium cylinder block and which, according to Teddy

Mayer, might cause the day's testing to come to an immediate halt at any time. (He needn't have been so pessimistic, because the V8 did nothing worse all day than spew a quantity of oil from a faulty joint.) Bruce was keeping the revs right down at first, therefore, which confirmed the truth of his answer to my earlier question about the revs from which it started to really pull . . . 'around 2,000!'.

There was a slight graunch before first could be selected from rest, and during the early gentle laps Bruce occasionally had to take two or three stabs at selecting a gear, but this was simply due to the comparative lack of torque being put through the box, and later on, when he started to use the revs, he was able to snap through the gears every time.

Though the V8 will pull from 2,000, it becomes 'kick in-the-back' stuff from about 4,000 upwards, After that there is a considerable vibration period around 5,500, where you get the full effect of the solid engine mountings, but gradually this smooths out until at 6,000 it's delivering a lot of power very smoothly. Bruce says it really sings at 6,500 rpm, but I'll take his word for it! A fraction under 6,000 was all we saw in top when I was in the car, and 150 mph felt quite fast enough through Fordwater or down the Lavant Straight!

A trip beside a GP driver is the best ego-crusher I know, and it gave me a completely

new insight into Goodwood. It also taught me that most of us know very little about driving! Bruce was picking out different corners on different laps for really trying, then slacking off (relatively!) while he analysed what had just happened. As a result, our best lap time must have been nearly 1m 30s, whereas had he fitted all the fast bits into one lap it would have been more like 1m 20s. This is what it was all about:

Fifth gear towards the end of the pits straight, brake down into fourth curving right, power on a lot sooner than I expected, a momentary feathering of the throttle as the car gets all light and understeering over the undulation, then foot hard down again for the rest of the turn, coming out on the extreme left side.

Fordwater is taken nearly flat, straightlining it as much as possible, then hard on the brakes and down to fourth for the sharp right-hander at the end, keeping the car in to the right side of the road coming out, then braking again and down to third before swinging left at St Mary's. The extra weight on the left probably helps here, and the revs shoot up quickly coming out on the right side of the track, fourth being taken as soon as the car is straight again.

Accelerate hard, move over to the left of the track, then brake hard and two downshifts into second for the first part of Lavant. This is very rough-surfaced now, so power has to be fed in carefully if a smooth line is to be taken through the two parts of the corner, joining them up into one curve. Unfortunately, third gear is needed right on the second apex, so a very quick shift is called for here. Then up into fourth, through the left-hand kink and into fifth. Woodcote comes up so much quicker than it ever has before as Bruce hits the brakes and drops down twice into third, then puts the power on seemingly 20 yards too soon for a Formula 3 car let alone a Group 7! But he knows what he's doing, we come out on the extreme left of the track, accelerating hard for two seconds, then hard on the brakes again, down into second, a quick right and left through the chicane, a slight correction coming out, up into third, fourth and fifth, and the lap is finished.

Doing my best to 'coolly' analyse what the car was doing, I noticed a comforting overall tendency towards understeer (roll bar sizes are small, ranging from $\frac{5}{8}$ to $\frac{3}{4}$ inch front and rear); the incredible tyre bite and traction, enabling the power to be applied when the 'g' effect on my body told me that the tail was bound to come round; the slightly too firm ride over the rough patches before Bruce went down a size on roll bars; the comparatively low level of wind roar in the cockpit (most of the mechanical and exhaust noise was behind, of course); the fantastic stability of the chassis under braking, despite considerable nose-dive and slight unevenness from the front brakes because of high-spotting; and the clean engine pick-up all the way through the rev range.

With nothing to do but watch, it probably feels even more impressive than it does to the driver, but the new McLaren M6A undoubtedly has outstanding traction, cornering power and high-speed stability. Like all products out of Colnbrook it is also beautifully put together. In fact the whole operation looks utterly professional, and is a credit to one of the hardest-trying outfits in motor racing. They deserve every point they score in the Can-Am Championship and what better start could they have had.

23

THE CANAM CARS

The technical aspects of the Group 7 machines which have contested this year's CanAm Series

By PETER LYONS

DESPITE the smashing success of Bruce McLaren's Kiwis in this year's Can-Am Series, Group Seven is developing into a uniquely North American medium of racing, and properly so. Regarded by some as a White Elephant, the configuration of the two-seater pushed by a big-block V8 is nonetheless the groove in which the American's mind works, be he spectator, builder or driver. The normal race enthusiast here is more orientated towards technology than driving anyway, a phenomenon with complex origins, and the shockingly fast cars making bellowing noises and carrying wings, or at least spoilers, capture his imagination in a way that a delicate single-seater never will. The truth of this is obvious from a glance at the variety of exotic designs for this year's CanAm of purely American origin. Indy cars are monotonous by comparison, and there has only been one native F1 car, the Scarab. From the point of view of even the F1 driver, the fullbodied form is welcome in this particular application because, frankly, of the bad driving they are apt to encounter.

What is developing is a perfectly viable two-seater *formule libre*, practically unhampered by meaningless restrictions and drawing on the full range of local knowhow. This is not to say that Europeans, or Australasians for that matter, will not continue to do well, but increasingly they are going to find themselves aliens if they are not prepared to devote their full energies to North America. The McLaren walkover was a case of a highly competent F1 team being unable to apply themselves to F1, and catching the other G7 people unprepared. The situation will be very different next September. The "visible" CanAm prize money was up 40 per cent this year, and every penny of it was needed. Costs will certainly go up even more sharply next year, not only because of increased competition; the very power and speed of the cars themselves forces development of new materials and fabrication techniques.

In the engine department, the shape of things to come is to be seen in the four-cam Indy Ford unit in the back of Parnelli Jones' Lola. Stroked to just over five litres, it weighs only 400 lb complete and fits easily into the T70 Mk 3, only requiring alterations to the upper radius-rod pickups. Running with alcohol injectors, it developed no more than 525 bhp—and that very much at the top end—and the car was 200 lb overweight and had only a four-speed gearbox, but Jones was able to go right to the front of the three races he started. Everyone expresses a need for more power. To one who remembers when the 4.5-litre Maserati was a monster, Jim Hall's not being satisfied with 570 bhp is dizzying. It's all due to the tyre men, who in the space of 60 days made the rim sizes go from 10½ ins to 13. Hall looks for much more power, and if the tyres reach a plateau he is prepared to go to four-wheel-drive.

Although it's not a point of technology, a word should be said about the organization of the CanAm. A series of such stature requires professional course workers and marshalling. The situation must be rectified whereby a driver (Revson at Las Vegas) is

MIDNIGHT OIL: The preparation of the works McLaren M6As was meticulous. Here the Kiwi team strip the cars between practice and the race (above). THE McLARENS are built with all major parts easily accessible, as can be seen as the gearbox is stripped and the engine checked the night before an event (below).

disqualified for an action which was specifically condoned at an earlier race. And Hulme for one will surely want to see the elimination of the buried-tyre marker, which is far too easily torn out of loose desert soil.

Let's take a look at the new designs of the year, and the lessons they learnt.

McLaren M6A

Its advantage over its competitors—apart from those 2000 laps at Goodwood—was primarily a basic quality that Denny Hulme remarked on delightedly the first time he drove it. "You can toss it about almost like a single-seater." Other drivers, after following either of the cars, expressed it as an ability to take a given corner in a variety of ways, depending on circumstances. "It handles like a sophisticated Go-Kart," said Jerry Titus. Bruce himself points out the high power-weight ratio, and says that the advantage is mostly in the slower corners. In profiling the body he made good use of his experience with the Ford Le Mans project and selected a high down-thrust, high-drag configuration like the original "J-car", which couldn't sustain the speed necessary on the Mulsanne Straight but which is just the thing for all the CanAm circuits, none of which have yet been lapped at 120 mph.

Chaparral 2G

The general layout is well enough known, although it should be made clear that the 2F was a completely different car, made of fibreglass rather than aluminium and two inches longer in the wheelbase.

A talk with Jim Hall is always cordial, but seldom particularly rewarding. You ask a question like, "Why have you removed the little aerofoil-shaped bar at the extreme front of the nose intake?" and he'll reply carefully, "It had an aerodynamic effect . . ." a measured pause ". . . that I'm no longer interested in." He'll acknowledge everything you can see for yourself, like the soft spring rates, but the weight distribution is a secret and you needn't bother asking why he angles the rear suspension travel.

Whenever the car is undressed for work to be done one is reminded irresistibly of spacecraft hardware because of the complex array of braided lines, special tanks and containers, welded brackets and unique little castings. A direct question about what areas had been modified since the first race received a vague answer, but one can see a certain simplification of the aerodynamics at least; the carburetter inlets were fed initially from a tunnel in the engine cover but are now exposed, and the internal ducting in the windscreen to generate a Lotus-like air-curtain has been abandoned. These are minor points, but indicative of the very thorough approach of this CalTech-trained engineer.

Other builders are losing interest in The Wing, but the Riverside race provided a graphic display of its effect on the Chaparral. During the periods when it and the McLaren were lapping nose to tail, Hall was able to press the throttle a split second sooner coming out of a corner and his car seemed to lunge forward and gain two or three yards. As one would expect, the wing is changed between circuits and its working angles altered in the same sense as are anti-roll bars.

Autodynamics D-7

There could hardly be a step greater than that from Formula Vee to Group Seven, and Ray Caldwell's people made an impression far beyond the odds. The under-

A RARE SIGHT: an exposed frontal view of the Chaparral 2G (top). The hoop behind the driver carries pickup points for the rear radius rods. THE REAR SUSPENSION is unusual in that the radius rods are attached to the base of the flipper stanchions, as is the Watts linkage, which has its pickup point in the diaphragm section behind the engine (centre). THE HOOP behind the driver is attached to the monocoque by special fabricated pickup points, making it easily removable (bottom).

RAY CALDWELL's interesting Autodynamics D-7 with its wing, which has now been scrapped; on the straights it caused instability which was not compensated for by the advantage gained in the corners.

current of interest in de Dion suspension continues, but Caldwell is the first in International racing to commit himself to the principle. At the rear of the D-7 proprietary uprights are connected across the car by a lattice of round- and square-section tubing which forms in effect a beam, through which projects the ZF transmission case, located by radius rods and transversely by a Watts' linkage. The front "axle" is similar, though simpler in detail, and the steering is by drag links from a Volkswagen box on the scuttle. Naturally, every nuance of toe-in and camber is adjustable. Sam Posey reports that there is absolutely no "tramp" in the steering, nor is there any particular drama about running up on kerbs and the like, and he is convinced that he gives nothing away in sheer cornering power. The car does seem extremely sensitive to the selection of spring rates, and one of the recurring problems has been a violent porpoising that develops over certain bumps.

Another difficulty has been the use of proprietary parts in ways they weren't stressed for. The first chassis was destroyed in testing after Mosport, going end over end through the trees at Lime Rock when a bolt apparently sheared, and the minor wreck at Las Vegas which kept the replacement car from starting seems to have been a failure of the identical part. This second car, 002, was built up on a magnesium frame, giving a weight saving of 60 lbs. It took a long while and a change of manufacturer to get the brakes right, and the airflow to the carburetters, which are fed from a big bin, has never been perfected; but the big alteration was the scrapping of the wing. Pivoting on chassis-mounted struts, it had seemed effective in the corners, but in feathered position on the straights it caused an unmanageable instability. Posey would have liked to retain it, but points out that he had to operate it with his hand, which gave him just one more job in a busy car.

MASTER MECHANIC John Surtees, with the aid of a mirror, checks a selector fork of the gearbox that caused him trouble at Las Vegas. John was without second and third gears for much of the race, but snatched a sensational last-ditch victory from Donohue nonetheless.

Honker 2

Holman & Moody had more than their fair share of engine failures, and this played havoc with the chassis sorting, which was an involved process entailing in the end a complete repositioning of the suspension pickup points. By Las Vegas the team felt that they had just about got it right, although it seemed to bystanders that Andretti wasn't getting onto the throttle until very late in the corners.

King Cobra

Shelby-American had even less success with their commissioned racer than Holman & Moody, and one thinks inevitably of Pomeroy's dictum about development and design. The Len Terry layout was unquestionably brilliant, but scarcely anything on the finished car worked right. The radiator was moved to the rear and then back up front again, the controversial horizontal springs were replaced, at least temporarily, by conventional arrangements, but the handling still looked erratic to say the least. At Riverside a fuel pump costing £40 failed on the second lap, and at Las Vegas the car crashed after a series of suspension breakages. The quality of the men Shelby employs needs no apology, and there need be no complacency in any other camp. They'll get it right.

Ford G7-A

The Caliope appeared on more magazine covers than it ever did starting grids. There were about three different engines which all produced fabulous power, but the chassis had a weight to match, and the public relations dept at Ford remained more willing to talk about it than show it. One remembers how quiet Bruce McLaren was while testing his own car. . . .

Ferrari

There is nothing wrong with the lightened Group 4 P4 that about another litre wouldn't cure. Jonathan Williams describes a great deal of activity in Maranello as the Commendatore bestirs himself to put down that brash tractor maker, and Mr Harrah wants to sell a lot of cars.

Matich SR-3

Frank Matich made a lot of friends and sold some cars while he was here. His design is workmanlike, and very light by reason of the alloy motor. A big Chevy would probably fit, but one would like to see a larger Repco.

McKee

Bob McKee's proposition is that he can build a competitive car and keep the cost down by using standard production Detroit gears, brakes, etc, wherever possible. Charlie Hayes had a good finishing record with the Oldsmobile-powered version sponsored by TV's Smothers Brothers. To an observer the handling appears a trifle twitchy, with more than a touch of understeer developing under acceleration. Hayes has a good reputation as a serious driver, and things will improve.

Private entrants

The day of the private entrant using bought machinery is as over as it is in F1. The older McLaren or Lola will continue to supply driver-training, but there will come a time when they will have to be cleared off the track. The Penske team will be the exception, for everything they do is first class. Both George Follmer and Mark Donohue turned in lap times out of all proportion to what they had to work with—over-the-counter machinery. Penske is committed to Chevrolet, but it would be the greatest possible fun if he could get General Motors to give him a couple of Chaparral engines!

Tidy, caramel-colored McLaren-Chevrolet M6As were all-new. Unmatched for speed, they easily qualified 1-2 and dominated race. Hulme averaged 104.5 mph, earned $12,550 and 9 points.

GROUP SEVEN, 1967

Charlie Hayes (McKee 7-Olds) leads Jim Hall (Chaparral 2G) and Skip Scott (McLaren-Chevrolet). Hall was 4th, Scott 5th, Hayes 10th.

Chaparral 2G with Chevy 427 resembles 2E but has new spoilers, 2F-type intake "fences," scoop beside headrest.

Holman-Moody Honker with Ford 351 was fast in a straight line, but Mario Andretti had shift problems and car did not run.

USRRC champ Mark Donohue was 2nd after Surtees spun. Lolas of Gurney (36) and Follmer (16) did not go distance.

29

Autodynamics Hudson Wire Chevy for Sam Posey had wing mounted amidships, beam front axle, de Dion rear end. Halfshaft broke on 2nd lap.

Frank Matich brought own SR3-Repco from Australia.

GROUP SEVEN, 1967

Defending Can-Am champion John Surtees ran Lola 3B-Chevrolet with new anti-lift nose, finished 3rd after spinning on oil.

CAN-AM

THE BIGGEST LEAGUE

PHOTOGRAPHY: PETE BIRO

There is real competition in the 1967 Can-Am—
Ford vs. Chevrolet, Goodyear vs. Firestone, the U.S.
vs. the World . . . you need jacks or better to open in this game.

The Canadian-American Challenge was designed with the reasonably ambitious goal of becoming the greatest road racing series in the world. It would bring the top drivers and cars to the North American continent, to run a half dozen or so races under an American formula—big, stock-block engines in fairly sophisticated two-seater sports/racing car chassis—and establish road racing as a major league sport for once and for all.

To do that the Can-Am needed big bucks—and it got them. In its second year, 500,000 of them on the surface and per-

haps several millions where no one could see them, in tire company, accessory company and manufacturer's contracts. It also needed real competition: Ford vs. Chevrolet, Goodyear vs. Firestone, the United States vs. the world—and, as the 1967 series opened in Elkhart Lake, Wisconsin, it looked as though, that, too, was forthcoming.

All this was going to make road racing the spectator sport that it had never been before, because without the oval tracks' yellow flag (which makes a new race of any competition five and six times during

an event—every time there's a spin or an accident), the only substitution was genuine competition; jacks or better to open.

That's what it looked like at Elkhart Lake's Road America circuit on Thursday, August 30, before practice. By the evening of September 3, after the first Can-Am had been run, the series was threatened with disaster.

Denny Hulme in a Goodyear-shod McLaren-Chevy M6A won it wire-to-wire, and the only *real* competition came from a second McLaren M6A, the other team car driven by builder/designer and team

31

leader, Bruce McLaren.

Second man home in the '68 Can-Am opener was USRRC Champion Mark Donohue in a new Lola-Chevy Mk. IIIB; third was another Lola IIIB driven by '66 Can-Am champion, John Surtees.

The Ford effort, which, in fairness, got started very late, did a lot of staying at home. Only John Holman's (half of the Holman-Moody racing shops) imprudence prompted him to bring a 15-seconds-too-slow Honker II—and even Holman (who bills himself as Honker I, a left over from his truck-driving past) had the sense to trailer his car home before the race.

The Honker probably wasn't going to be ready until the third race in the series—Mosport, September 23, and in any case didn't look likely to scare anyone but it's very brave driver, Mario Andretti.

Shelby's cars (only one, probably) stayed home like the rest of the Ford factory and quasi-factory entries because, like them, they suffered from a lack of sorting-out, again, no time. There went the subway series of Ford vs. Chevrolet.

Donohue, whose all American looks and manner challenge Dan Gurney's, kept the isolationist hopes alive, and so, in a way, did Jim Hall, whose 427 cu. in. Chaparral 2G, topped the horsepower race, but who could do no better than fourth. "I guess I better give up team managing and do a little more driving," said an aching Hall after the 200-mile race. Chaparral boosters weren't too worried. Hall, who had spent the season guiding his long distance cars in European endurance races, was rusty as a driver—but sure to regain his driving form. Dan Gurney, on the other hand, was a real contender, and his 378 cu. in. Gurney-Weslake V-8 was the only Ford to work at all well. While he was in there he was as quick as the McLarens, but his throttle stuck, he spun and flat-spotted his tires. He eventually quit with gear shifter problems.

The Ford G7-A didn't even show, the engine wasn't working, and the Ford types thought they would probably go to something less exotic than the three-valve 429 for the West Coast.

Before Elkhart and after Elkhart, the contenders seemed the same: McLaren's two cars, the Penske Lola-Chevy team (Donohue and George Follmer, substituting for Chris Amon, who was tentatively scheduled to drive a Ferrari Group 7 car entered by Bill Harrah), Surtees (Lola) and Hall (Chaparral). All Chevrolet-engined, all extensively tested. Gurney was an outsider from the start, never to be counted out, always the great crowd favorite, but suffering from an inclination to go off in too many different directions instead of down one road very fast and with great determination and preparation.

And that is what's required to win the Can-Am—which still might prove to be what it was originally intended—the greatest road racing series in the world.

Including the 200-mile Elkhart Lake opener, there's 1209 miles of racing in the

McLAREN M6A SLEEK AND SLIPPERY, McLAREN'S MONOCOQUE WONDERS ARE THE '67 CAN-AM FAVORITES.

CHAPARRAL 2G DESPITE A 427 CU. IN. ENGINE, THE MIDLAND ROADRUNNER IS A LONG SHOT.

CALDWELL D-7 A NEW CAR, AN ALMOST NEW DRIVER, AND $500,000 ADD UP TO NEARLY NO CHANCE.

HONKER II THE ONLY NOISE JOHN HOLMAN IS LIKELY TO MAKE THIS YEAR IS A LOUD, SAD SIGH.

LOLA Mk. IIIB DONOHUE, SURTEES, GURNEY; IF McLAREN IS GOING TO BE BEATEN, A LOLA WILL DO IT.

FORD G7-A EXOTIC, STRONG, EXPENSIVE; BUT IT WEIGHS 500 LBS. TOO MUCH, AND IT'S NOT YET READY.

Can-Am: 250 miles of Bridgehampton, September 17; the Player's 200 (actually the Player's 197) at Mosport, September 23; to the West Coast for Monterey—Laguna Seca's 202-miler, October 15; down the coast to Riverside and the 200 mile race there, October 29; and the Stardust for the November 12 finale of 210 miles. Riverside offers the top prize money—$40,000—but they're all close: Elkhart, $39,000; Bridgehampton, $25,000; Mosport, $35,000; Laguna, $35,000; and Stardust, $35,000 plus all you can win at the Las Vegas tables. The point fund is additional, a device to make up for the lack of appearance money (which only one track pays), and this year it's $90,000, with the series winner getting $31,500, the second man $17,000 and paying down to the 10th man with $2,700.

A total of about $500,000 over 1200 miles with about 60 cars competing. If one driver in one car won every race possible and qualified fastest in each, he'd take home $54,200 in prize money, $31,500 in series fund money, and about $15,000 in contingency money—over $100,000. A reasonable budget for a two-car Can-Am team is about $150,000. What makes it all possible if you have to spend more than you can possibly win? The contracts, that's what. And that's what makes it tough on the independents.

Supposedly, one tire distributor, who also races, was dickering for $250,000 from his parent company for a 2-car team, and support for one well-known independent (one car) was pegged at $100,000.

But this is the wildest kind of speculation on the covert money supply in the Can-Am. A closer estimate comes from a team which proposed to field two cars, one with a GP name driver, the other with a name driver without GP experience. The $150,000 figure was taken as projected costs: $75,000 was asked from a tire company sponsor, $25,000 from an auxiliary sponsor, several thousands from smaller sponsors. Given the earlier prize money figures, as well as the appearance money schedule at the one track which pays the name starters (somewhere on the order of $8,000-$6,000-$4,000-$2,500-$1,500 for the top six teams), and the team expected to have about $75,000 in the bank before racing started. Two cars cost $40,000. Engines (Traco Chevys) about $5,000 apiece and travel expenses nearly $1,000 a race. Additionally, the four mechanics were to be paid $200 a week. So the team was into the Can-Am very close to budget if nothing went wrong. In order to break even it would have had to win a couple of races, take some seconds and thirds and at least third overall in the series standings. When the tire sponsor offered only half of its projected contribution, the team pulled out.

Another team, which stayed in the Can-Am, and has a very good chance of winning it, also is fielding two cars, but has an oil company as a primary sponsor. Added to the tire company it represents, the oil company money very probably got the whole effort off the nut before a wheel turned.

Thus, the covert money is what makes the Can-Am go despite the hue and the cry of the $500,000 series. It's more like a $2 million series, if all the figures were known—and publishable.

Will it continue, this underground river of dollars? And is it good for the future of the Can-Am?

If manufacturer entries are classified as "covert money," and if the Ford projects get off the ground—which they still might—the answer is an unqualified "yes." Ford brings A. J. Foyt, Mario Andretti, Jerry Titus and Parnelli Jones to the series with a real chance of winning. Ford money does the same for Dan Gurney, although not to the extent that the company would have you believe. Chevrolet may well be supplying super-secret covert money to Jim Hall and Roger Penske, even if it takes the form of inventory (parts and car) credit for their Chevrolet dealerships. Akron's cross-town war between Goodyear and Firestone has made Indianapolis a brilliant, international race. If it reaches the degree of escalation in the Can-Am it has achieved in USAC's Championship Trail, the prize money in the Can-Am will be almost incidental.

So, if the money continues—and it will, for a while at least—the viability of the Can-Am will depend in a large degree on the continued availability of drivers and, perhaps more importantly, crew chiefs.

Only one of last year's top 10 finishers is out of the Can-Am this year. Phil Hill and Jim Hall have parted company, and, at any rate, Hall is fielding only one car. Amon, who drove for McLaren in '66, may be back with a Ferrari this year but don't break open your piggy bank and bet on it. So the Can-Am drivers are back, and with them are more USAC pilots, including Roger McCluskey in the Pacesetter Homes Lola. Foyt, Andretti and Jones should be mounted in more competitive machinery—always, if Ford gets off the ground—and Frank Matich has come up from Australia to join the chase. On balance about half of the world's top road racing drivers are in the series; but the exceptions are significant, and include Jim Clark, Jack Brabham, Graham Hill (and Phil Hill), Jochen Rindt, Pedro Rodriguez and Lloyd Ruby. Where are the new drivers to come from? A list of qualifiers at Elkhart includes the names of some staggering unknowns—Ronald Courtney, Fred Pipin, Ross Greenville, Gary Wilson and the ever-popular Marshall Doran. Perhaps tomorrow's John Surtees or Jim Hall is among them. If not, they must come from the USRRC lot, or the present Formula Two and Three drivers in Europe.

Nor does the USRRC seem to provide

much in the way of future greats for the Can-Am. Mark Donohue made this year's series look like a cross-country, whistle-stop Clay-Patterson rematch series. He won wherever he went, with one exception, and with the best six races counting for the points crown, came up with a perfect record. But Donohue is an established star—he's a product of a year ago's USRRC and Can-Am. Where is this year's Donohue? It may be a young man from Sharon, Connecticut, Sam Posey. Posey showed great promise in the USRRC this year and has been coming along well. But he has chosen to build a car of his own—in partnership with Ray Caldwell, who designed and built the Autodynamics Formula Vee—and Posey isn't going to win in a league as tough as the Can-Am with a brand-new car. Moreover, he knows it. All he wants to do is get the car running well by the middle of the series. His effort is said to be costing him about half a million dollars. It's not likely he'll win much of that back in '67, but Posey is driver enough, and Caldwell designer enough, that the combination might be very tough a year from now.

Peter Revson is a driver of unquestioned ability, but he's on a second-rate team. Dana Chevrolet tried to win the USRRC with a massive expenditure, and a team of Revson and Bob Bondurant in a pair of McLaren-Chevys. Bondurant crashed and was replaced by Lothar Motschenbacher (who also crashed). The cars didn't work well at all and they were overwhelmed by the Lolas. So Dana has gone out and bought a pair of Lolas. They have Revson and they have Motschenbacher, either of whom might be the next top flight American of the Gurney caliber, but the USRRC effort was beset with changes of mind and reported internal dispute. That sort of thing doesn't win races—let alone the Can-Am.

Brett Lunger, Don Morin and Skip Barber are bright young drivers, all coming along, all capable of putting one good race together—and when they do, of finishing third. But all three are at least two years away. Bill Eve and Mike Goth, who looked very promising last year, were disappointing in the spring pro shakedown.

It is no good looking to USAC or NASCAR for new talent in the Can-Am; they're having a rough enough time providing for their own races. The only possibilities are Al Unser in USAC and maybe, just maybe, Donnie Allison or James Hylton from NASCAR.

Still, they're more drivers looking for cars than the other way around, and the reason for that is the lack of crew chiefs. Crew chiefs and team managers. Once you've said McLaren, Surtees, Penske, Gurney and Hall the list about stops. Caldwell is as good as they come, but the Autodynamics team has car-sorting problems.

Phil Remington and Al Dowd are also major leaguers, but Caldwell's problems look like a taffy-pull compared to what Shelby has on its hands. If you could get a car set up right you could get Brabham, or Ruby in a minute—maybe even Jim Clark. Trouble is, you can't get one set up right—and right now, that's the real bottleneck.

That, and this business with the Ford Motor Company. FoMoCo had a raft of racing types in the pits at the Can-Am opener, cheering Dan Gurney. And all the while in Detroit and Los Angeles and Charlotte, there were the *real* Ford team cars in various states of disarray. The great hope of the series, the thing that was going to put it on the map for once and for all—the gutsy battle between Ford and Chevrolet on the race track—fizzled out by the light of someone's midnight oil. That didn't keep the season's opener from being a beautiful race, and it didn't keep the track owner and promoter, Cliff Tufte, from counting his biggest house ever—53,-100. But if Ford could only, somehow, some way, get going before it was too late, there would be no end in sight to how big the Can-Am could get.

It is already remarkable that the series exists at all—born as it was from the Sports Car Club of America, an-essentially-amateur-organization-gone-partially-professional-but-unable-to-quite-make-up-its-mind-to-go-all-the-way. Ten years ago most of the tracks on which the Can-Am are run were artichoke patches or prairie-dog runs. Ten years ago, the promoters who are making things work were bank clerks or pro football players.

And there is nothing to say that the Can-Am can't get bigger—so that it goes quite beyond North America preaching the gospel of a uniquely American formula. There is talk of expanding it in 1968 to include a race in Germany, a race in England, two in Japan, and perhaps two in Australia.

But it all seems to turn on whether the Can-Am is going to become a success at the box office. And *that* seems to turn on whether Ford Motor Company gets going before the season is over. A sweep of the West Coast races would do it just fine. A very convincing win of two races could even do it. But the West Coast tour in 1967 looks as though it's going to be make-or-break for the Can-Am as a major league enterprise.

The whole thing was said in a curious little interchange in the pits at Elkhart between John Holman and Jim Hall. Holman's new car had just been brought in by Mario Andretti after turning a lap that was 15 seconds or more off the pace. Jim Hall was working on his car, puzzled that he was five seconds quicker than the previous track record . . . and seven seconds slower than the McLarens.

"Say, Jim, what do you think of my new Honker?" asked an oddly proud Holman.

Hall looked up, paused a moment, and answered, "It's perfect." ●

INSIDE THE SPORTS/RACERS

BY PETER L.V. HUTCHINSON

The cars come from all over the world, but the real battle is between Ford and Chevrolet powerplants. It's a thoroughly professional league, and the winners will come from the big teams like Chaparral, Ford, Lola, McLaren, Shelby, and Holman-Moody.

Ford's G7-A underwent extensive wind tunnel development to reduce both lift and drag.

The Ford Motor Company may have a far tougher job dominating the Can-Am sports/racing car series than it had winning Indianapolis and LeMans. At the Brickyard and the Sarthe circuit, Ford brought brand-new technology to bear on relatively archaic rivals.

At Indy, Ford was up against the Establishment's 30-year-old Offenhauser engines and crude roadster chassis. At Le Mans, the Establishment's equipment was comprised mainly of low displacement, high revving motors.

The Can-Am, not yet a full year old, has no Establishment, and the machinery comes from the same blend of American know-how and European design talent that Ford used to blow off the opposition at Indy and Le Mans. So Ford is no longer grenading tried-and-true fish in a barrel; Ford, like everybody else, is starting from scratch. And most significant of all, Ford is locked in a duel with its arch-rival, Chevrolet.

But, don't think that Ford isn't going to be in there fighting. After winning Le Mans for the second time, Ford management began to feel that they had proved their point, and were considering abandoning their annual pilgrimage to road racing's mecca, and concentrating on road racing at home, particularly in the Can-Am, where they had been badly beaten in 1966. Any indecision Ford may have been experiencing was quickly forgotten when the FIA's rules body slapped a 3-liter limit on Group 6 racing, rendering Ford's equipment obsolete.

All the while, however, the Le Mans program had been generating experimental hardware for potential use in 1968, and among this new equipment was one of the wildest engines ever built in Dearborn. Nicknamed the Calliope, it is an all-alloy, dry-sump V-8, with three valves per cylinder set in a shallow, slightly distorted hemispherical combustion chamber. The two intake valves (1.74 in. each) are arranged at a 37° angle (18.5° on either side of the bore centerline) from the single exhaust valve (1.89 in.). The exhaust valve is displaced about 0.5 in. off the bore centerline, allowing the spark plug to be nearly centered in the combustion chamber.

The Calliope's valves are pushrod-operated by two camshafts. But instead of being overhead camshafts, they are arranged one above the other, in the valley between the two cylinder banks. The two cams (exhaust above, intake below) are necessary to provide room for the 24 cam lobes, and to permit reasonable rocker geometry without having to run pushrod tubes through the intake ports (as is done on the latest Ford 427 NASCAR engine, the so-called "tunnel port"). Overhead camshafts were avoided because of the increased bulk they would add to the top of the cylinder heads, and to eliminate the complications of driving overhead cams.

We were told that the displacement of this engine was 427 cu. in., but the bore size (4.33 in.) is not the same as the existing 427 (4.23 in.). The bottom end of the Calliope is based on the "385" series of Ford engines. The only production example of this series, so far, is the new Thunderbird engine, which displaces 429 cu. in., and which has an entirely different crankshaft from the 427. This leads us to believe that, in fact, the Calliope has a 429 crank with a stock 3.59-in. stroke. The resulting bore stroke (4.33 x 3.59 in.) would give the Calliope a 423 cu. in. displacement.

In case any doubts still exist concerning the specialized nature of the Calliope engine, the monster breathes through a fuel injection system, with the manifolds and throttle bodies cast integrally with the cylinder heads—and that spells racing engine.

FORD G7-A

Ford's Can-Am hopes aren't pinned entirely on its Engine and Foundry Division. Dubbed the G7-A (cover), Ford's Group 7 chassis is essentially a Mk. IV roadster with an all new, wind-tunnel-tested body, but has, otherwise, the same brakes and suspension that proved so successful at Sebring and Le Mans. Ford racing car designer, Roy Lunn, has torn a couple of pages from Jim Hall's notebook—not a bad man to copy, if past performance counts—and included a two-speed "automatic" transmission and a wing.

The transmission is a Hewland-like, dog-clutch affair, driven through the same Falcon-based, 3-element torque convertor which has proved so successful in the Ford and Mercury drag-racing "funny" cars. It isn't really an automatic because the driver must shift the gears manually, and while he doesn't have a clutch pedal, he does have to pay attention to his revs. Thus, much of the benefit attributed to fully automatic transmissions is lost.

While the application of the wing concept to modern race car design is generally attributed to Jim Hall (Fritz von Opel used a wing on his 1928 rocket car), Lunn has gone a step further than Hall and put some dihedral (camber) in the G7-A's wings, in an effort to improve lateral stability as well as provide negative lift to the rear end. A fixed control strut supports the inner ends of both wings, while vertical struts to the center of each wing are attached—like the Chaparral's—to the suspension.

Even though the G7-A boasts the above technical credentials—certainly the most impressive of all the Can-Am series entries—some serious problems exist which could negate much of its obvious potential. First, the G7-A isn't light; at 1900 lbs. curb weight, it's the heaviest contender in

Ford's all new "Calliope" engine, while tough on the dyno, isn't yet sorted out.

John Holman (left) looks on as his namesake, the Honker II, takes shape.

Shelby's King Cobra suffered some setbacks during testing; didn't show at Elkhart.

36

John Surtees' Lola is one of three Mk. IIIBs in the 67 Can-Am.

The Matich SR3-Repco is a threat from Down Under.

Bruce McLaren's and Denny Hulme's McLaren M6As had been tested extensively in England. Hulme easily won Elkhart.

1967 CAN-AM CONTENDERS

Car	Drivers	W.B.	Track Front	Track Rear	Tires	Trans.	Engine Size (cu. in.)/Type	Hp	Curb Wt. Lbs.
Caldwell D-7	Sam Posey	92.0	52.0	50.0	Goodyear	ZF 5-speed	365/Traco Chevy	520	1540
Chaparral 2G	Jim Hall	90.0	56.0	53.0	Firestone	auto. (2-speed)	427/aluminum Chevy	560	(1450)
Ford G7-A	Mario Andretti	95.0	55.6	54.8	Firestone	auto. 2-speed	(423)/aluminum 24-valve, V-8	(650)	1900
Holman Honker II	Mario Andretti/ (Parnelli Jones)	92.0	57.0	56.0	Firestone	ZF 5-speed	351/Ford, fuel injected	(500)	1520
King Cobra	Jerry Titus	93.0	56.0	56.0	Goodyear	ZF 5-speed	378/Cobra Ford	(500)	1400
Lola T70 Mk. IIIB	Mark Donohue	95.0	58.0	58.0	Firestone	Hewland 5-speed	365/Traco Chevy	520	1410
Lola T70 Mk. IIIB	John Surtees	95.0	58.0	58.0	Goodyear	Hewland 5-speed	365/Traco Chevy	520	1410
Lola T70 Mk. IIIB	Dan Gurney	95.0	58.0	58.0	Goodyear	Hewland 5-speed	378/Gurney-Weslake Ford	525	1400
Matich SR3 R	Frank Matich	93.5	55.5	55.5	Firestone	ZF 5-speed	268/Repco V-8	400	1360
McLaren M6A	Bruce McLaren/ Denis Hulme	89.0*	51.0	52.5	Goodyear	Hewland 5-speed	358/fuel injected McLaren-Chevy	(550)	1460

Hulme's car has a 91.0-in. wheelbase for driver comfort.
Bracketed information is unconfirmed.

Being ready (or not) will probably be the
story of this year's Can-Am series. After
Elkhart, with the series only one-sixth over,
nobody was saying, like they do at Indy,
"Wait 'til *next* year." There's a lot of
racing left this year.

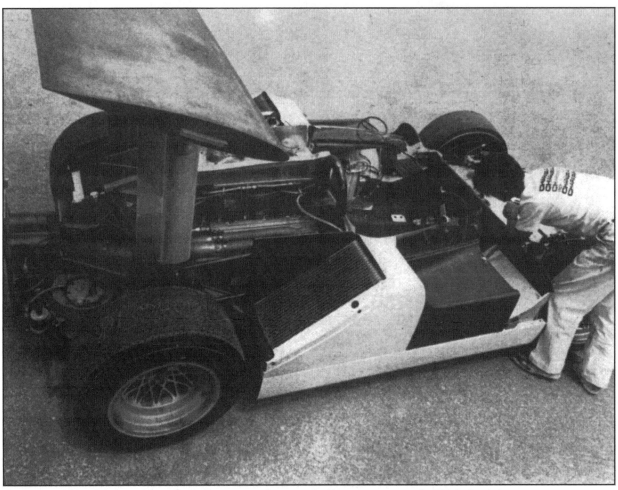

The Chaparral 2G, while derived from the 2E of a year ago, has many detail improvements—and a 427 cu. in. engine.

the series, by some 23%. Unfortunately, all the horsepower in the world (and the Calliope should have at least 650, or 16% more than its next most powerful competition) isn't likely to compensate for the penalty paid in cornering performance by that extra weight. Second, Ford hasn't had sufficient time to shake the car down. Initial testing at Las Vegas in August revealed an abundance of problems. The fuel-injected Calliope engine's throttle response is poor, and the engine transferred water into the oil through suspected casting porosity holes in the block. It isn't as if these very special blocks are readily available. At present, there are two complete engines, with castings around for only three more.

To make matters worse, the wing isn't doing all the magical things for Ford that it did for Jim Hall. In fact, the G7-A went faster *without* the wing than with it. And,

when the first testing session was over, the G7-A was still 14 seconds slower than the lap record at Vegas. It's understandable that Ford didn't bring it to Elkhart Lake for the Can-Am's opener.

In the interests of making an appearance before the 6-race Can-Am season is over, G7-A project manager Homer Perry is seriously considering installing an 875-hp, supercharged version of the 427 NASCAR mill (the Holman-Moody marine racing engine originally brainstormed by Chuck Daigh). If this happens, both the automatic transmission and the wing are likely to fall by the wayside.

HOLMAN & MOODY HONKER II

While Ford's big gun is thus effectively jammed, its secondary armament, comprised of equally unsorted machinery, is faring little better. John Holman, one of

racing's few truly successful businessmen, decided to see if he could come up with a chassis to beat the likes of Lola and McLaren, and, at the same time, develop a Ford-based racing engine that could compete with the Traco-, Bartz-, and Falconer-modified Chevy engines. If successful, these units could be added to Holman & Moody's line of "competition proven" racing gear. Realizing that it would be too expensive to build the chassis in this country, Holman contracted England's Len Bailey (who had designed the Mirage) to lay out a car, and Alan Mann (former team operator for Ford) to build the chassis, and set John Wander (Holman's own right-hand man) to manage the car in the Can-Am.

Named Honker II (Honker I is Holman himself), the car arrived in Charlotte, N.C., looking like an Alfa 33's big brother, both in shape and in workmanship. But the weight (1520 lbs. curb) was in the ball park, the suspension geometry seemed promising during preliminary testing at Goodwood, and Ford's wind tunnel indicated that the body was extremely slippery. A few spoilers were shown to be necessary—nothing extreme, but enough to lose Holman $20 on a bet he had made with a designer/driver that the car could be run as received.

The Honker II has one chassis feature unique to sports/racing cars. Designer Bailey, believing that a tremendous amount of air circulates within the wheel wells, placed the disc brakes inboard of the uprights (like Cooper's Formula One cars). The semi-inboard brakes necessitated moving the front springs and shocks inboard of the suspension pickups, operating through upper control arms acting as rocker arms (again, like the F-I Cooper).

The initial powerplant chosen for the Honker was a fuel-injected (Telcalamit-Jackson), 351 cu. in., cast iron V-8 based on the not-yet-production Ford engine of the same displacement. This engine is not really new, but merely a taller-block version of the old 289. Unfortunately, the 351 retains one of the less desirable features of the 289; the 4-bolt cylinder-head pattern is conducive to head gasket failure in racing applications. The Holman/Wander cure for this is to "dry-deck" the engine (blocking up all the water passages between the head and the block, so that if any lifting of the head occurs, overheating won't be as likely to result).

Several alternate versions of this engine have been built, around such exotica as aluminum cylinder blocks, billet steel crankshafts, and Gurney-Weslake heads— and in displacements ranging from 348 to 398 cu. in. The most popular size may well turn out to be 378 cu. in., which not only seems to run well with a bore and stroke of 4.00 x 3.77, but which also falls very close to being the engine size for a 3500-lb. stock car, the minimum weight under NASCAR's 9.36 lb./cu. in. rule. Could good ol' John Holman be planning to find two markets for his engine?

But even a month in Charlotte wasn't enough to make the Honker II competitive in the company of the field at the Can-Am opener. It had become a sanitary car but virtually untried. Mario Andretti, originally slated to drive the G7-A, tried to turn the Honker on, but could only get within 17 seconds of Bruce McLaren's record-setting time of 2:12.6. The Honker II was loaded on the trailer and taken home to Charlotte before the race started.

SHELBY AMERICAN KING COBRA

The Shelby effort is in even rougher straits. Shelby's King Cobra has been suffering a series of major setbacks and failed to appear at Elkhart. Designed by Len Terry, ex-of Lotus (the Type 38 Indy car) and AAR (the Eagle), and built by Transatlantic Automotive Consultants, a new partnership between Terry, and Frank Nichols (ex-of Elva Cars), the King Cobra has a very unconventional suspension system. Both the front and rear suspension have a single transverse coil spring shared by both the right- and left-hand wheels. Since these springs don't act on the chassis itself, but only on the opposite wheels, the chassis has no built-in roll stiffness. All the roll stiffness is provided by front and rear anti-sway bars, which, by necessity, are considerably larger than they would have to be on a normally sprung car. While this approach has some merit on a car with high-pivot swing axles (in that the "jacking" tendency would be reduced), we don't understand its value on the King Cobra, which already has low roll-centers to prevent jacking. We can even see a disadvantage resulting from the use of the necessarily stiff anti-sway bars—the right-hand wheels are no longer as independent of the left-hand wheels and vice versa.

More important, however, the King Cobra ran into serious trouble during its second shake-down cruise to Riverside. First, there was a problem in the engine lubrication system which delayed testing. Once that problem was fixed, engine overheating made it obvious that the horizontal radiator—designed to exhaust in what turned out to be a positive pressure area under the car—wasn't getting the job done. Work is underway to incorporate rear-mounted radiators, Chaparral-style, to cure this. The final blow came when one of the transverse springs parted company with the suspension while Jerry Titus, who is to pilot the car in the Can-Am, was hurtling through Riverside's first turn. It must have been quite a ride—certainly more exciting than the preceding laps, the best one having been a full seven seconds off the Riverside sports/racing car record. Realizing that the car wasn't anywhere close to being ready, Shelby showed good sense in not bringing the car to Elkhart.

LOLA T70 Mk. IIIB

This leaves Dan Gurney holding the standard for Ford (or at least for modified Ford cylinder blocks), in one of the three Lola T70 Mk. IIIB chassis that were ready for the Can-Am. Running a 351 cu. in. cast iron Ford block with a steel Moldex stroker crankshaft to give 378 cu. in., and his own Gurney-Weslake cylinder heads, Dan managed to qualify his Lola for the inside of the second row. That put him behind the two incredible McLarens, but ahead of the two Chevy-powered Lola Mk. IIIBs of Mark Donohue and John Surtees. A sticking throttle began a train of events which led to Gurney's eventual retirement and the end of the only real Ford threat to the Elkhart Lake "Chevy Show."

The Lola chasis is remarkable. Eric Broadley has made only relatively minor changes to his original T70 design, changes resulting from almost three years of racing development, making the Lola a truly "Competition-Proven" design. The "B" designation refers to slightly altered rear suspension geometry, and some weight savings which are possible only in Group 7 form. (The regular Mk. III is a "convertible," able to run either as a Group 7 car or—in coupe from—as a Group 6 GT prototype.) Otherwise, the "B" is a Lola T70 Mk. III. This continuity of design has contributed to the high level of reliability reflected by Donohue's and Surtees' second and third place finishes at the Can-Am opener—a race which saw less than a third of the starting field take the checkered flag in good running condition.

CHAPARRAL 2G

While the G7-A is Ford's "secret weapon," many of the concepts it embodies were first seen on secretive Jim Hall's Chaparral. Hall has made many detail changes during the year, and designates his 1967 Can-Am Chaparral the 2G. Derived largely from the 2Es that Phil Hill and Hall drove a year ago, the sole 2G (Hall is going it alone this year) retains most of the same features—the wing, the ducted front spoiler, the rear-mounted radiators, the automatic transmission, the 16-inch "spiderweb" wheels, the aluminum monocoque chassis, and the bizarre body. But the engine is new—an all-aluminum 427 (its origin could only be Chevrolet), with a dry sump system developed by Chaparral. The 427, biggest engine so far in the Can-Am, replaces the aluminum 327 used by Hall last year in the 2Es. Fed by four 58mm Weber downdraft carburetors, the new engine is rated at a conservative 560 hp—110 hp more than a year ago.

Jim Hall is probably the most test-minded of all the Can-Am entrants. With his own private test track right behind his shop, he keeps accurate tabs on the worth of each and every innovation, using 13 photo-electric timing pickups planted at strategic points around the course. You can bet that Jim knew his new car was faster than last year's (and how much faster) before he loaded up and headed for Elkhart. It was faster, all right, even much faster, but not fast enough—the other cars were faster still. Such is progress in the Can-Am, although the fact that Hall hasn't driven since the Daytona Continental may have something to do with his qualifying 4.8 seconds off the pace.

GOODYEAR vs. FIRESTONE

Part of Jim's problem may have been that he was running on Firestone tires, which appeared to be inferior to Goodyear's at Elkhart. While Goodyear was ready with a brand-new tire designed specifically for the Can-Am series, Firestone's equivalent is not expected to appear until Bridgehampton, or maybe as late as Mosport.

Continued on next page

INSIDE THE SPORTS/RACERS

Firestone suffered a crippling 91-day strike this summer. Goodyear was also struck, but for only 14 days. John Surtees spent most of practice and qualifying trying out both brands, and even though his car was originally set up for Firestones, he wound up racing on Goodyears. He felt that the Goodyears were good for at least a second a lap. Firestone isn't likely to let this situation persist. Tire design, an extremely competitive and rapidly changing science, lies behind many of the seemingly inexplicable performance differences between cars, and contributes to the spectacular increases in lap speeds each year.

CALDWELL D-7

There are a pair of long shots in the field this year that deserve mention for their novel approaches to sports/racing car design. The Caldwell D-7 was built for Sam Posey, a USRRC contender this year in a McLaren-Ford, by Autodynamics Corp., the Formula Vee builders. Autodynamics president and chief designer, Ray Caldwell, felt that in view of the increasing width of racing tires and the resulting importance of precise camber control in suspension geometry, the simple expedient of live (or rigid) axles was the best plan. This, combined with considerable scale-model wind tunnel testing at MIT—with the assistance of a Dr. Larabee, an aerodynamics consultant retained by Autodynamics—shaped the Caldwell D-7's homely body. While we think that rigid axles are not the best system for the fairly rough Can-Am race tracks, we admire the candid approach that these privateers have taken. Unfortunately, some severe brake and rear axle problems, which were thought to have been overcome during pre-series testing, reappeared at Elkhart and precluded a demonstration of the Caldwell's true potential.

MATICH SR3-REPCO

Another unique approach to Can-Am glory emerged from Down Under. After dominating the Australian racing scene (137 wins in 171 starts over the past three years), Frank Matich has come to the North American continent with two cars (one already sold) of his own design. The Matich SR3-Repco uses a tubular space frame reinforced with stressed aluminum panels. Matich's primary aim is light weight. He furthers this goal by employing a 4.4-liter version of the aluminum Repco V-8 weighing only 363 lbs. complete with accessories. It produces over 400 hp throughout a range of 1700 rpm. With a curb weight of only 1360 lbs., Matich's cars are indeed the lightest in the series. But his SR3-R suffered some teething problems at Elkhart—residue from the fuel bladders clogged the injection pump's fuel filter, and after that was remedied, electrical and oil cooling problems developed.

Frank Matich, like Jock Sturrock, skipper of Australia's America's Cup entry, must be a little dazzled by the competition, right now. But, while we are not too sure about what the future holds in the America's Cup competition, we wouldn't be surprised to see some really impressive Australian challenges in the Can-Am's future. Would you believe Jack Brabham?

McLAREN M6A

Bruce McLaren had enough bad luck in the 1966 Can-Am to cause most men to seek communion with the devil himself. We don't think Bruce sold his soul, but we know that he went back to England with a single-mindedness toward winning in 1967. Almost immediately after Las Vegas in 1966, Bruce signed up Denis Hulme for this year's series, and set about building two brand-new cars. Switching from space frame to monocoque chassis construction, the new cars are designated McLaren M6As. He designed his own bodies, and even built his own 358 cu. in. Chevy engines. Last year, McLaren flirted with fuel injection at the Riverside Can-Am race, and found it promising but unreliable. In the interim, with the help of BRM (wizards with fuel injection) and John Willment (of J. W. Automobiles—Willment and ex-Ford team manager John Wyer—who built the Spa-winning Mirage GT prototype), McLaren developed a Lucas-based fuel injection system that appears to give his Chevys an edge on all the others.

Completing the cars early in the summer, McLaren and Hulme put over 2,000 miles on them at Goodwood, ironing out every detail. Arriving at Elkhart, they proceeded to smash all previous records, and when the smoke had cleared, they were one-two on the grid, a tenth of a second apart and almost two seconds faster than Gurney who, in turn, was 1.3 seconds faster than fourth-fastest qualifier George Follmer (Lola-Chevy 365). In the race, Hulme led flag-to-flag, while McLaren followed on his bumper until a freak oil line fatigue-failure put him out. One thing was obvious to all, however; the McLarens were *ready*.

And being ready (or not) will probably be the story of this year's Can-Am series. All the technically superior equipment in the world won't win this series unless it is fully sorted out—developed to give that kind of continuously reliable service associated only with the aerospace industry in the past.

Ford, on paper, has the hot set-up. Theoretically, Hall's Chaparral 427 should be faster than the McLarens, and so should Roger Penske's forthcoming Lola-Chevy 427 for Mark Donohue. The specifications of Gurney's Lola-Ford make it a potential winner. Technically, the Honker and Shelby's Cobra ought to go like blazes. But the last two didn't even run, and many of the others were ready—but not enough. With the series only one-sixth over, nobody was saying, like they do at Indy, "Wait 'til *next* year." There's a lot of racing left this year. ●

THE fourth round of the CanAm Series at Laguna Seca was a decisive one for us. We knew it had to be. With three wins so far Denny could tie up the title with another win, so the three weeks that we had between Mosport and the Monterey race were just plain hard work.

The news that Ford had officially retired from the series with the Holman & Moody car and their own Kar Kraft car filtered through, but so did the news that Hall was working on a new ultra-lightweight 7-litre engine with large amounts of horsepower, and Parnelli Jones was reported to be entered in a Lola powered by a 5-litre version of the Indy Ford four-cam V8. We had tested a four-cam Ford engine against one of our Chevrolets last year and, since it had shown up slightly better, we had almost decided to use it for this series. While we were getting ready for this race we weren't sleeping quite so easily as we had been. . . .

Our headquarters here in California are in Long Beach, just outside Los Angeles. We have rented quite a good modern workshop for the two months that we will be in the sunshine state. Champion Spark Plugs' engine dynamometer facility is close at hand, and the airport isn't too far away. The big prize money on this series is a good thing—running two cars in this sort of racing so far from Colnbrook can be expensive. Even allowing for our two tons of spares, we still seem to be on the telephone to London once a day and then out to the airport to pick up the latest shipment. First it was bigger brakes, then stronger fuel bags, now heavier driveshafts, and the next crate will be stronger rear wheels.

The cars were taken completely apart. Denny's car needed a good look at the chassis structure where he had hit a bank fairly hard at Mosport, but as far as we could tell apart from the front substructure folding up (it had been designed to do just that and we had a spare) the basic tub was fine. Or at least it looked as if it was. We had to throw away the axles because the big Goodyears put bigger load on them

Bruce McLaren
FROM THE COCKPIT

than we have had before. We crack-tested everything that wasn't actually riveted down and then put the whole lot back together just as carefully as we knew how. On the engine side we had four freshly built motors. Denny's had 514 bhp and mine had 516 bhp, but we didn't have time to run the two spares.

Laguna Seca is about 100 miles south of San Francisco in one of the prettiest areas of the Californian coast, but unfortunately it was a hot and dusty track for us all weekend, and we had to give the surf and the Pebble Beach golf course a miss. Practice started on Friday the Thirteenth, and it was certainly Denny's unlucky day—in fact it wasn't really his weekend at all. First his fuel injection metering unit seized up, putting everything out of time; then his brake pedal bent (although it didn't quite break), and he was starting to get a little apprehensive. We were worried about some little cracks we had found in the wheel, and they seemed to be spreading. When we got Denny's car back to the workshop we found the chassis had started to fold up in front of the engine mounts where it should have gone after the Mosport incident. Probably Black Friday was just too much for it. In the meantime my car couldn't have been running better. During practice sessions I'd even had time to get

into a machine-shop in nearby Salinas to have some steel crosses made to brace up the suspect wheels. I ended up with fastest practice lap, half a second ahead of Gurney and Denny, and Hall and Parnelli Jones were close behind them. My time was 3 secs faster than last year, and altogether 13 cars were inside last year's lap record.

Race day was so hot that I knew we would have some sort of problem. It was a rolling start, as is usual in this series, and Gurney in his Lola-Ford out-dragged me into the first corner. I glanced in my mirror to see that Parnelli had done the same to Denny, but the order settled down after about 10 laps. Dan and Parnelli were out; I was about 10 secs ahead of Denny, and he was a similar distance ahead of Hall's Chaparral. If they had stopped the race then it would have saved a considerable amount of agony. It wasn't a race against the other cars as much as a race against the sun and heat. After 20 laps I'd had enough. I pulled my face-mask down and gulped big mouthfuls of air. When that hurt too much I closed my mouth and pulled air up through my nose. It just didn't seem possible to get enough air.

There is a very slow hairpin in front of the pits, and fortunately Denny had thought of a "water stop" sometime during the race. I hung on until about half distance, then gave the signal; and the next lap round I pulled over against the pit wall, slowing down to about 15 mph, whereupon my crew sloshed a bucket of water into the cockpit. That was just about the best thing that happened to me all day. For about 10 laps I was almost comfortable again. Then I just couldn't wait for the chequered flag. Denny's engine had blown up and he was out. That track for a 200-mile race is hard. There is no straight to speak of, and not only was it hot, but I could hardly hold my head up. I was barely able to get excited that I had won my first CanAm race, and that our team had tied up the CanAm title. Maybe when the blisters go down I'll feel happier about it. . . .

DURING the second round of the CanAm Series, the Chevron GP at Bridgehampton, Bruce's McLaren leads George Follmer's Lola, which finished third behind the two M6As (left). NOT ONLY F1 World Champion but also winner of three CanAm rounds, Denny Hulme on his way to his first victory, in the Canadian GP at Elkhart Lake (right).

THE CAN-AM SERIES: WHAT EVER HAPPENED TO FORD?

Ford was all set to take the Can-Am series by storm. Here's a report on their progress so far.

By FORREST BOND

The United States Auto Club's Group 7 racing is to this country's sports car buffs what Grand Prix is to Europeans. It's the fastest, most brutal racing to be found on the road circuits in the U. S. Dominating the entry list for years has been the Chevrolet V-8 engine in a variety of cars.

So, fresh from two straight wins at the LeMans (France) endurance classic, Ford Motor Co. decided to take a piece of the action. Its big seven litre monster motor was deemed fit for competition because of its LeMans triumphs and the Ford Mark IV (formerly the J Car), could easily be revamped to suit the U. S. road courses.

Then came the first race of the Canadian-American Challenge Cup series for Group 7 cars at Elkhart Lake, Wisconsin. Ford was expected to field six cars: two from stock car aces Holman & Moody, two from Shelby American and two from Ford itself. Mario Andretti, Ford's drive-anything-fast ace, was the only one to make it, showed up in a Holman & Moody "Honker" and made a couple of disappointing laps before packing it in and becoming a spectator.

Only threat from Ford was Dan Gurney, who drove his English-built Lola with Ford engine. He was third qualifier, dropped out with transmission troubles and was awarded 26th place. Ford looked the other way since the Ford engine had Gurney-Weslake cylinder heads, a product of Gurney's industrious All American Racers shop in Southern California.

Came the second race of the season and Ford was at it again. Only trouble lay in the fact that the Ford action was at Riverside Raceway in California while the races were in Bridgehampton, N. Y. Shelby American spent the week before the race testing cars that weren't race-worthy at Riverside while those who were

Mark Donohue, driving for Roger Penske, is typical of car/driver/engine combinations Ford, and now Ferrari, must face in Can-Am racing. Driver is experienced, car is by Lola and engine is by Chevrolet.

Can-Am racing can get exciting. Potent Group 7 cars (maximum displacement limited to seven litres) are handful for any driver, even best can get out of shape.

prepared were qualifying at Bridgehampton.

Again, Andretti was the lone Ford entrant, managed to qualify and ended up in eighth place on driving skill alone as the car simply refused to handle. Gurney again finished 26th.

But the Ford, even managing to finish eighth, had the limelight stolen twice. Denis Hulme won his second straight Can-Am in a team McLaren with Chevy engine. Ferrari, long rumored to be preparing for the Can-Am series, sent Ludovico Scarfiotti to the U. S. and the factory team driver justified the expense by finishing seventh, one place ahead of Ford's Andretti. It was clearly a case of being better prepared before unleashing cars and an advertising campaign.

Ford played second fiddle to Ferrari at LeMans for awhile before winning because the cars simply weren't ready to compete. The same may be true in this year's Can-Am series.

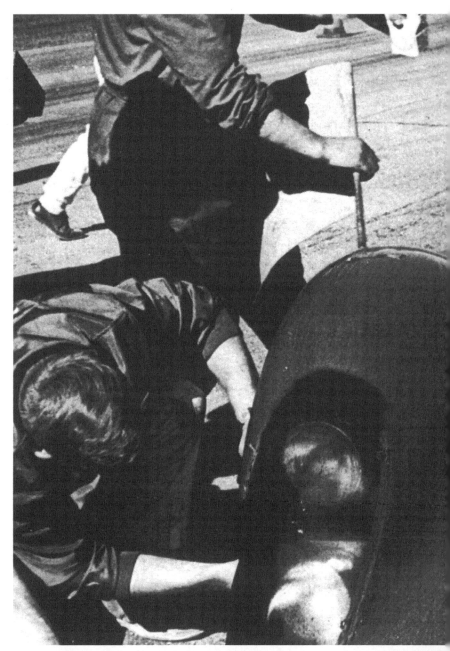

Chris Amon sits out a pit stop at the Daytona endurance race. Ferrari P3 shown has been modified for Can-Am series, uses 4.2 litre engine. Ludovico Scarfiotti drove single P3 entered at second Can-Am race to seventh place, one better than Ford.

Like "Old Man River," the Porsche
multitude keeps rolling along in the
under two litre division, winning
race after race after race.

Blunsden goes all transatlantic in 'Cro-Sal' crash helmet with the big McKee-Oldsmobile.

GROUP 7 McKEE-OLDSMOBILE

MOTOR RACING TRACK TEST No. 67

by John Blunsden

ANYONE driving a racing car for the first time at Las Vegas needs a piece of special equipment—someone else sitting alongside, reading out the pace notes. Come to think of it maybe that's not the answer after all, because for pace notes to be of any value the 'reader-outer' has to know where he is. At Las Vegas you never know where you are—at least, I didn't!

Sited a few miles out in the desert scrub from the world's most famous gambling citadel, the circuit winds its way between dried-out bushes, small rocks and an abundance of sand and dirt for a distance of three miles. Here and there you find a comforting landmark, like the pedestrian bridge entering the final straight, or the grandstands lining turns two and six, but for the most part all you see ahead is a sea of white-painted half-tyres which line all the curves. Finding which of them are supposed to be on your left and which should be on your right is the tricky bit. From the cockpit of a race car it's the nearest thing to driving a slalom in a go-kart.

All of which means that it pays to be wide awake, which is also a bit of a problem in Las Vegas, where to talk of sleep is tantamount to treason. Most nights you are entitled to two or three hours of non-activity, just so as to rest those right-arm muscles, but this dispensation is withdrawn for the night after the Stardust Grand Prix, which starts with the Can-Am victory banquet, and ends with a depleted bankroll at breakfast time.

It is, perhaps, superfluous to mention that

the track test of the McKee-Oldsmobile, which the genial and talented Charlie Hayes drove into fourth place in that final Can-Am race, was scheduled for the morning after that long, long night before. Fortunately, I was too numb to be scared, but—also fortunately—sufficiently awake to recognise the need to take it easy. It came as no surprise at the end of the test, therefore, to discover that my fastest time would have given me the undisputed right to line up all on my own at the back of the grid for the previous day's race . . . by a considerable margin! Charlie Hayes was happy enough to get the car back in one piece.

The McKee-Olds was the most successful all-American car in the recent Can-Am series after Jim Hall's Chaparral-Chev, and its appearance in the series has considerably boosted the reputation of 32-year-old Bob McKee, its designer and builder, who began building transaxles from Ford and Corvette parts in a converted dog kennel in 1960. McKee Engineering now operates from more palatial premises in Palatine, Illinois, where the twentieth McKee racing car will soon be leaving the workshops, the first having been completed just over four years ago.

The Can-Am car is known as a McKee Mark 7, and is owned by Ralph Salyer, who drives it himself in National events, and who in fact became one of the Group 7 SCCA National Champions in 1966. The meticulous turn-out and enviable record of reliability achieved by the car is to the credit of Gene Crowe, a former stock car racing mechanic, who looks after the

car and builds and develops the Oldsmobile engines for it at the Cro-Sal headquarters alongside Salyer's plumbing business in Hammond, Indiana. The car is entered as part of the Smothers Brothers Racing Team, Dick Smothers (one half of a variety act) being a great racing fan who has just taken up driving himself—he has bought a Formula 2 Repco Brabham BT21. Charlie Hayes is the team's number-one driver, and Hugh Powell has been running a Lola-Chev under the same team banner.

Basically a three-year-old design, the McKee Mark 7 is a spaceframe-chassis design, conceived at a time when private owners were the nucleus of Group 7 racing, and therefore McKee's main customers. A reasonable initial cost and low maintenance costs were, therefore, major design requirements. But though the basic design is pretty straight-forward, some of the materials used in it are not, thanks to a close liaison between McKee and the ARMCO Steel Corporation, who supply a number of space-age alloys for the chassis.

The fully-triangulated spaceframe has $1\frac{3}{4}$ inch x .065 inch main tubes, the top tubes carrying the water to and from the radiator, and 1 inch x .065 or .049 inch diagonals. Transverse bulkheads stiffen the structure front and rear, the front suspension links being mounted direct to the forward bulkhead to feed the suspension loads into the main chassis structures. A separate magnesium plate is provided in front of the first bulkhead to carry the steering rack, master cylinders, etc.

The front suspension is somewhat Brabham-ish in conception, with upper and lower leading and trailing links, and the rear suspension is equally conventional in basic layout, with single top links and lower wishbones, the latter incorporating toe-in adjustment. The rear dampers are angled at 41 degrees on the centre lines of the pivot point, so that any looseness has no effect on rear-wheel toe. Everything is left and right threaded for easy adjustment. The front spindles and rear hub carriers are in a special heat-treated aluminium alloy, and the final drive from the Hewland HD500 transaxle is through shafts with Ford GT universal joints at the inboard ends and Corvette u/js at the outer ends, the hub bearings and seals also being Corvette parts. The steering rack is a modified Triumph Herald part and is mounted parallel to the top wishbones to eliminate any bump-steer effect.

American mag five-stud wheels have 9 inch and $13\frac{1}{2}$ inch rims, front and rear, carrying Goodyear 10.40 and 12.35 x 15 inch wheels respectively. Kelsey-Hayes brakes with $11\frac{1}{2}$ inch ventilated discs are mounted outboard all round.

One of the car's limiting factors has been its glass-fibre body, which not only offers considerable wind resistance, but is also excessively heavy—220 pounds with the twin engine oil coolers mounted in the rear spoiler. This contributes considerably to the car's weight of 1,690 pounds with five gallons of fuel on board. The total capacity of the two main side tanks, which have Goodyear rubber bladders, is 48 US gallons, with a further 4 US gallons available from an auxiliary tank on the left side. The body is secured by Dzus fasteners, and the doors are left hollow for the passage of air through from the front wheel wells to exits behind the cockpit.

The aluminium Olds engine has a displacement of 389 cubic inches, and is based on the iron 350 CID block used for the Oldsmobile Cutlass range of cars. The crankshaft is machined from a chrome-alloy billet, and Crowe's 'treatment' includes the use of aluminium instead of steel roller tappets, special valves, springs and retainers, and a clever anti-surge arrangement in the sump incorporating a rotating 360-degree pick-up, which swings around in unison with the oil under the influence of centrifugal force, and is therefore never starved.

The engine up to the time of the test had been running with 48 mm downdraught Weber carburettors, and with jets and manifolds intended for the engine in 350 CID form, although it was about to be bench-tested with 58 mm sidedraught Webers. But even in its existing form the Olds engine was probably giving in excess of 500 bhp, and had an excellent rev span from about 3,800 to 6,500 rpm, although 6,300 is Hayes' normal maximum, and 6,000 rpm was the limit used in the test. An electrical cut-out prevents accidental over-revving.

Charlie being a good 6 feet 2 inches tall, there was ample room in the cockpit, and a convenient foot rest to the left of the clutch. A full harness kept me well located, and the small-diameter steering wheel, with its thick, soft-padded rim, was nicely placed and comfortable to hold. I can't say I went much for the instrument layout, with the fuel pressure and water temperature gauges way over to the left, and even the rev counter placed sufficiently far left to call for a conscious effort to read it, although in this car your ears were a pretty reliable tachometer. Only the oil pressure and temperature dials were straight ahead.

The sharp angle of the screen may not have been the best shape aerodynamically, but at least it provided excellent air protection in the cockpit, and the McKee turned out to be a very comfortable car to drive. Apart from a clout from another competitor against the right rear wheel (subsequent examination disclosed a cracked upright) and a faulty rear damper, the car had come through the 210-mile Las Vegas race unscathed, and apart from a defective starter seemed about ready to do it all over again.

With 500 bhp on tap you get kick-in-the-back-type acceleration, even in top gear, and you have to be sure which way the front wheels are pointing before you press the right pedal too hard. The throttle response, I thought, was a bit too sudden, and especially with heavier-than-normal shoes, I had some trouble in finding the small amount of extra throttle I wanted for downshifts. After the initial burst

of power, the pedal response seemed to get more progressive.

The steering was really excellent, with a uniformly light action, and sufficiently high gearing to cope with the 180-degrees turn six without getting excessively crossed-up. The brakes, also, were in very good shape, calling for only a moderate pressure, and being so effective that I was consistently using them far too early (probably because I was subconsciously thinking that Mv^2 at over 150 mph adds up to a pretty spectacular shunt if it gets out of hand!).

The Achilles' heel of this car, while I was aboard, was undoubtedly the gearbox. It had seen a lot of service, and was overdue for a complete overhaul, but even so Charlie Hayes was able to whip through the cogs like lightning. Unfortunately, I didn't master the slightly unnatural movements required during the brief duration of the test, with the result that I was never completely sure of getting a gear first time.

First had to be man-handled in with both hands, but as this was only ever used for starting

Right: *The McKee's Achilles heel, its well-used and much in need of an overhaul Hewland LG 500 gearbox. Visible here are the massive drive shafts which transmit something like 500 bhp from the 389 cubic inch Olds V8 engine. The notice on the transaxle reads, 'Motor gently in the grease-mud for there lurk the skid demons'.*

it didn't matter. The first-to-second shift had to be taken slowly to resist the box's temptation to select fourth, and thereafter the main problem was the shift from third to fourth, which called for a long movement sideways followed by a very slight movement forwards. The normal slight side movement followed by a push forwards would half the time find second instead, a fact which encouraged me to make this particular up-shift at reasonably low revs! Of course, when you 'live' with a box long enough you gradually adapt to its peculiarities, but in the short term this one was far from idiot-proof!

This apart, the McKee could be driven reasonably fast without any rare skill at all. Fundamentally a modest under-steerer, it would go where it was pointed with a fair amount of certainty, the under-steer only becoming excessive on the mixture of oil and rubber which invariably coats slow corners at the end of a long race. At these places, inevitably, the transition to a power-induced over-steer is quite rapid, but with delicate throttle control the McKee would respond instantly to

a steering correction.

There are one or two vicious bumps on the Las Vegas circuit (just to prove that it is not completely featureless!), and although I was taking these reasonably carefully for obvious reasons, the car took them very well indeed. During the race I watched Charlie Hayes tackle the worst bump of all, after a series of esses, and the McKee even at the speed at which he was driving it, seemed more stable than the vast majority of the cars at that point.

For the 1968 season, this particular McKee will probably be used for National racing only and as a back-up car for the USRRC and Can-Am series. Its replacement will be the McKee Mark 10, a monocoque sports-racing car which apparently will be more than usually exciting and possibly unconventional. All involved in the Smothers Brothers Racing Team are very excited about the new design (details of which are still shrouded in secrecy) because they think it could really ring the bell.

It would be interesting to find out, a year from now, just how different the two cars feel to drive. For a chance like that I'd really steer clear of the 'champers', the one-armed bandits, and the Black Jack tables on 'victory' night. It would be worth it . . . cheaper, too!

Blunsden at speed with the McKee. He found the steering and brakes good features, and was impressed with its cockpit comfort. A good looking car, one of the McKee's limiting factors is the weight of its glass-fibre body.

REIGNING CHAMPION of the Can-Am series, winning the first five events, is the McLaren-Chevy driven by Hulme or McLaren.

GROUP 7 COMPETITION

Two-Seat Road Racing With No Holds Barred

BY JON McKIBBEN

Group 7 is a rather cryptic designation for a class of road racing vehicles representing the ultimate in 2-seat automotive performance over a road racing circuit. Current Group 7 vehicles are an extension of what used to be called C Modified Sports Cars. Whatever the class designation, these automobiles are the least restricted, fastest type of road racing machinery extant.

The term Group 7 refers to a code established by the FIA, chief ruling body for road racing throughout the world. The Group 7 classification is intended for, "Two-seater competition vehicles built exclusively for speed races on closed circuit." There are actually seven divisions of Group 7, with engine displacement classes from 850 cc (52 cid) to over-5000 cc (306 cid).

In the U.S., professional races are currently limited to over- and under-2000 cc (122 cid), with the majority of prize money and participation involved in the over-2000 cc division. Other rules in the FIA Group 7 category include regulations governing self-starting (required, no push-starts permitted), brakes (dual hydraulic system required), seating space (definite limitations on minimum driver and passenger accommodation), and several other safety requirements.

In other important criteria, particularly those affecting performance. Group 7 vehicles are essentially unlimited. No limits are placed on maximum engine displacement, drive train specifications, body contours, tire or wheel size, overall vehicle dimensions, total weight, or engine type. It is this freedom from excessive restrictions that has attracted some of the world's

TYPICAL START of the "big iron" in Group 7 racing is this field at Canada's Mosport Park. Winner Hulme is at left in No. 5. McLaren followed by, left to right, Gurney (No. 36 Lola-Ford), Surtees (No. 8 Lola-Chevy), Spence (No. 22 McLaren-Chevy).

A 1966 MC LAREN MK. II, driven by Chuck Parsons here, shows a few modifications performed by owners and mechanics after taking delivery of the car from the factory in England; spoilers front and rear to combat lift, and a plethora of sponsors' decals.

DISTINGUISHING FEATURES of Pacesetter Lola-Chevy is lack of spoiler in front, and bright paint job.

MC KEE SPECIAL has outward similarity to Lola, but many internal differences. Both are U.S. powered.

most talented and competent designers to Group 7 competition. In the U.S., such men as Jim Hall (Chaparral), Len Terry (formerly with Lotus and designer of Gurney's Formula I Eagles, now with Shelby), and Bob McKee (McKee Racing cars) have entered into competition with such top foreign designers as Colin Chapman (Lotus), Eric Broadley (Lola) and Bruce McLaren (McLaren cars). These men are responsible for design and development of the most sophisticated, best-performing automobiles in the history of the sport. Currently, the latest McLaren appears to be the car to beat, closely followed by Lola and a bit further back, McKee. So competitive is this type of racing, however, that a new design may be introduced before this article reaches the newsstand. And, as has happened before in Group 7

racing, this new design may be so superior in overall performance that all existing designs will instantly be obsoleted.

Although a multitude of detail differences distinguish various Group 7 competition vehicles, a loosely defined stereotype may be formulated as follows: independent suspension all around, with coil spring/shock absorber units at all four corners; 475-550 bhp modified American production engine, usually of Chevrolet derivation, equipped with Weber carburetion, tuned exhausts into two large-diameter collectors, and high-performance valve train; 4- or 5-speed transaxle, mounted for mid-engine layout; very large tires and wheels, usually 12 to 15 in. wide at the rear and 8 to 10 in. wide in front; very low body, less than 3 ft. high, with highly

aerodynamic contours; total vehicle weight of 1500–1800 lb., with 55–60% of weight on rear wheels; and semi-reclining driving position, with driver on the right side of the car.

This stereotype Group 7 car would have a top speed near 200 mph, perhaps slightly higher, and would accelerate at a tremendous rate. With suitable gearing, the car would traverse the standing start quarter-mile in 10–11 sec., with a terminal speed of approximately 140 mph. Braking performance, with large-diameter disc brakes on all four wheels, would be phenomenal, with deceleration rates well above 1 G (-32.2 ft./sec.^{2}). Handling would be exemplary, with cornering speeds that were considered unattainable a few years ago. Suspension geometry and tire size would be selected to give substantial oversteer on

HALL'S CHAPARRALS pioneered use of automatic transmission, movable wing "spoiler" and plastic body/frame in Group 7 competition.

GROUP 7

slow turns and aerodynamic pressure would alter this to provide slight understeer on high speed, large-radius curves.

Most *CAR LIFE* readers are familiar with the Chaparral race cars of Jim Hall. These cars feature a high-mounted airfoil "wing" section, automatic transmission, and other innovations which, although not yet accepted as essential, or even desirable for racing, have provided principles that may well dictate automotive configuration in the future.

This is perhaps the most important contribution of Group 7 racing. Because Group 7 cars are required to go, stop, and handle impeccably over all types of road surface and through all types of curves, Group 7 cars are more closely related to normal passenger vehicles than are race cars used in more specialized competition. Group 7 competition is a proving ground for chassis developments that *can* be applied to passenger cars as

the need for higher performance becomes evident. Suspension techniques learned in Group 7 racing will provide future automobiles with improved handling, increased adhesion and even superior ride quality. Brakes developed for Group 7 cars will enhance safety on the high-speed thoroughfares of the future. Aerodynamics will contribute to increased stability at high cruising speeds. It's long been claimed that "racing improves the breed." This statement is perhaps more true as applied to Group 7 competition than to any other form of auto racing.

Group 7 racing has really "come of age" in the U.S. in the past two years. Popularity has increased at a tremendous rate, bringing with it some factors which are unquestionably good, and some that are unfortunate. Benefits of growing popularity include increased participation by top professional drivers, builders and crews, and increased financial backing from major sponsors. Financial backing has

LOLA-CHEVY (John Surtees' car shown) won six out of eight USRRC races, finished third in another, all driven by Mark Donohue.

NEWEST DESIGN is the Caldwell-Posey car (CL, Nov. '67) which also has movable spoiler.

ANOTHER VARIATION of the movable wing, on the PAM Special, places it just behind the driver's head.

largely come from tire, petroleum and spark plug manufacturers. Any large race will see representatives from major manufacturers running about trying to entice top competitors into using their particular product, hoping to see a decal advertising their produce roll into the winner's circle after the big race.

For using such products, top competitors are often paid a flat sum in addition to qualifying for contingency prize money. Contingency prizes are awarded to a winning car displaying decals advertising its use of a particular product. Prize money, contingency awards and endorsement fees comprise a substantial income for successful Group 7 competitors. The Canadian-American Challenge Cup Series, major Group 7 racing series in North America, offers nearly $500,000 to racers. The Can-Am winner can expect to pocket approximately $200,000 in assured winnings, plus an inestimable amount in subsequent endorsement

fees. This is big business, and the caliber of 1967 Can-Am competition reflects the size of this pot of gold.

Just as increased popularity has improved competition, it has further removed Group 7 racing from the realm of the "little man," a long-sought Utopia that has proven unobtainable in actual practice anyway. No longer can an individual construct a race car in his garage and go out and dice with the best of the competition. Current Group 7 technology is far beyond the abilities of most hobby-racers. Not only are these cars very expensive to build and maintain, but the initial design is a scientific achievement. Simply exercising good craftsmanship and preparation is no longer sufficient to garner a high finishing position.

The men engaged in Group 7 construction are professionals, with all the skills and facilities that the term implies. A private driver, one not sponsored by a large manufacturer, must be prepared to spend $25,000 to field a

competitive Group 7 car, and must be able to invest a similar amount in the maintenance and operation of this vehicle. This sum includes purchase of the best currently available basic car (Lola, McLaren, McKee, etc.), equipping it with a powerful, reliable engine, and outfitting it with the best available tires, wheels and auxiliary pieces. Then, a stock of spare parts must be established. Finally, transporter, crew and garage facilities must be obtained and supported.

Why is Group 7 racing becoming more popular? The answer lies, at least partially, in re-examining basic vehicle specifications. Group 7 cars are noisy, extremely fast, and visually exciting. In addition, these cars are driven by some of the finest drivers in the world, and competition is fierce and close. These are the ingredients for outstanding spectator appeal. Group 7 racing offers a show that is sure to attract more followers in the future. ■

The brains of McLaren Racing Ltd: from left, designer Robin Herd, boss Bruce McLaren, manager Teddy Mayer.

DESIGN & DEVELOPMENT OF THE McLAREN M6A

BY ROBIN HERD, Designer, Bruce McLaren Motor Racing Ltd.

THAT THE 1967 M6A McLaren Can-Am sports cars were so fantastically successful was in no small way the result of a very UNsuccessful Can-Am season in 1966. The team returned determined to do much better the following year and the fact that Bruce McLaren won the Can-Am Championship with teammate Denny Hulme close behind in second place (winning five out of the six races with fastest laps everywhere they went) is some measure of the McLaren team's determination!

We were fortunate in being able to draw on a fair amount of experience from within the organization and during March 1967 there was debate about the various features to be incorporated in the new cars. As well as designing a new chassis, we had decided to do our own engine work. The engines were basically Bartz-modified Chevrolets assembled by us and incorporating a few of our own ideas. Lucas fuel injection was fitted to the 6-liter engines, with much of the work being done by Gary Knutson and Bruce himself.

The choice of transmission lay between the ZF 5DS-25 gearbox and the then-new 5-speed Hewland LG gearbox. For several reasons the LG box was very attractive and it was

selected. This was a decision we never regretted, for it proved to be a reliable transmission and gave the driver a satisfactory gearchange movement.

Our tire suppliers were Goodyear and our liaison with them during the design and development of the car was very close. Both British and American Goodyears were available and it is interesting that the British tires proved ideal for formula racing while the American tires were best for Can-Am racing. These latter tires were based on the 1967 Indy-winning Goodyears. The rear tires we used were immense and initially created a sensation, but by the end of the series they looked quite normal!

Having defined the engine, transmission and tires and obtained the services of world champion-elect Denny Hulme, in addition to Bruce, it remained to combine all these items together with a chassis and we decided to forsake the simple spaceframe and go monocoque.

The basic features of a good racing car are straightforward. It must accelerate quickly to a high top speed with braking and cornering power to match performance. Further, the car should be in every way pleasant to drive as well as being simple to construct and maintain. It should also stay in one piece. Laying down these ideals is the easy bit—their realization in terms of engineering are rather more difficult. One presumes that all designers are seeking the same ends but a glance at the various cars in any form of racing indicates the wide divergence of opinion on how these same ends should be reached.

It is also obviously worth putting in a lot of effort to make a car as light as possible, but the compromise between lightness and strength is about the most difficult factor in racing car design. If one errs toward high strength the car becomes heavy and uncompetitive. Equally, if one errs toward lightness the consequences can be dangerous. To complicate matters, it is frequently impossible to calculate accurately the loads encountered by some of the components. What, for example, is the load on a lower front transverse suspension link as a car understeers into a curb under braking at Monaco? It is possible to get some idea of the forces involved, but in no way as accurately as one might like.

The optimum compromise of the several aerodynamic requirements for a Group 7 car is difficult to achieve. The factors involved are numerous and frequently tend to contradict one another. It is far from being a question of building a low-drag body and then eliminating the snags. However, it is interesting that the quicker Can-Am cars are beginning to show a similarity of body shape, suggesting that the same discoveries are being made and the same ideas put forward independently in several places. Progress in tire technology has been so great in recent years that suspension systems which were fine a few years ago are now undesirable. With the great wide tires now in use, one might think it sensible to keep the tires upright at all times, and the conventional independent system is quite incapable of doing that under normal circumstances. A De Dion axle does keep them upright and might prove to be the suspension system of the future. However, the singular reluctance of the major racing car manufacturers to adopt it suggests that it has some inherent disadvantages and that the conventional system has some less-obvious advantages.

After March's thinking and talking we started to design and build the cars in April, the process from a clean sheet of paper to the first test run taking 11 weeks.

The fiberglass body was built by Peter Jackson and his men at Specialized Mouldings. A quarter-scale clay model was first made and then modified until it was the shape we wanted. Templates were taken at intervals along the model and converted to full scale. A wooden mock-up of the chassis was built, the body sections fitted to it, and the full-size body constructed in clay. From this the body molds were taken.

A fair amount of comment was aroused by the distinctive orange color scheme. This in fact was a crib from Jackie Epstein's T70 Lola which clearly impressed McLaren Racing's team manager, Teddy Mayer, whose choice the color scheme was. It had one unforseen advantage—apparently it showed up very clearly in a racing car mirror and as a result slower drivers moved out of the way fairly rapidly as they spotted the bright orange flash.

On completion of M6A-1, which was to be Bruce's race car, the car was handed over to Tyler Alexander, who was to be in charge of it through its development and also while it was raced. We decided to run the car first at Goodwood. This is a popular test track in England because it presents many difficulties to the car; a driver who knows Goodwood well can cover many aspects of the car's performance there. In general, it is a fairly safe place to have a "moment."

The official lap record was held by Clark and Stewart at 1 min 20.2 sec, in 1500cc Lotus-Climax and BRM Formula 1 cars respectively. In the multi-tubular McLaren 1B with the Oldsmobile engine, a fastest lap of 1:17.2 had been set. The unofficial lap record belonged to Gurney and Brabham at 1:15.4 in their 1967 Formula 1 cars, although the number behind the decimal point varied with the person giving the information! By a little extrapolation (i.e. guesswork), we felt that to be competitive in the Can-Am series we would have to get down to 1:13.5. We reckoned other people might be able to if we couldn't.

Our deadline for the first run of the car from the beginning had been Monday, June 19th. Somewhat to our surprise and pleasure we were able to spend a gloriously sunny June 18th lounging on Bruce's lawn—most of us had almost forgotten what the sun looked like in the previous weeks!

We had decided to run the car initially without the body in order to avoid interference of too many aerodynamic phenomena. In fact we had built one aerodynamic factor into the car and so in one direction Bruce was unable to utilize the car's potential to the full. On that first Monday Bruce recorded a lap at 1:16.2 while running in the car and carrying out a 200-mile regularity run to try and break the chassis.

During the second week of testing, the body was added

Comparison of ¼-scale pre-production model with winning car at Riverside shows how nearly "on" the design was for aerodynamics as no changes were required in body shape and there are no "second-guess" tabs or spoilers tacked on.

McLAREN DESIGN

and Bruce lapped consistently around 1:14.5. Toward the end of the development program, with Bruce and Denny driving the car, both got below 1:14, with Denny marginally quicker at 1:13.4.

Early in the car's life we also ran it for 200 miles on the roughest track we could find—Snetterton—and nothing broke.

A fair amount of research was devoted to the car's body—our level of aerodynamic ignorance was remarkable. We had several ideas for closing our flow system at the tail, and therefore carried out a systematic series of experiments with wings, spoilers, and tabs. Suffice it to say that we ended up with a fairly conventional rear spoiler with an adjustable twin tab.

In our aerodynamic work so far, we have found existing theory and both scale and full-size wind-tunnel work unsatisfactory in many ways. In order to obtain some data which would be fairly realistic, we set up a series of pressure tappings over the internal and external surfaces of the car. Bruce drove the car at about 150 mph while I recorded the appropriate pressure readings in the passenger's seat together with their variation with speed, and under acceleration, braking and cornering. The first lesson to be learned was that all future McLaren racing cars will have to be a great deal more comfortable! On the first day along I racked up 23 individual bruises. . .

From the passenger's seat I also took readings of suspension behavior. When I was studying the rear suspension I had to lie on my stomach facing backwards in order to peer at the wheel and links. I used the roll hoop to the left hand and the filler cap to the right to counter the 1.2g lateral acceleration. Bruce had been experiencing a handling characteristic through one of Goodwood's quick right-handers which we were at a loss to understand without more evidence. Approaching the corner in question Bruce shouted above the wind roar that he was really going to pitch it in. He did! As the car's back end began to break away, I felt a great thump on mine. This seemed odd until I realized that Bruce was trying to apply opposite lock to correct the slide only to find my back side blocking the movement of his hands!

Looking back on this incident I am surprised to recall, as the car got steadily more out of shape, a feeling of calmness rather than terror, and having enough time to argue that if Bruce couldn't get us out of this problem, nobody could. It was fascinating to see the complex combination of throttle bursts, steering movements, and brake applications that sent us spinning harmlessly down the center of the track.

While we were running the car, Gary Knutson was carrying out his engine development work at the factory, except for those occasions when we were examining the engine under race conditions. Tests included back-to-back comparison of carburetion versus fuel injection, as well as the usual engine system proving. The most severe problem encountered was making the oil cooler work. Initially, the cooler received air from the left-hand inlet at the front of the tail section with the hot air exhausted to the rear of the engine bay. Structurally and aerodynamically this was a very convenient system, but unfortunately it didn't work. Eventually we relocated the oil cooler in the tail spoiler, thereby insuring a high-pressure supply of cold air on the inlet side and low pressure on the outlet.

Looking back on the testing it seems to me that two objects were achieved: The first was to subject the car to about 2000 miles of hard running in the hope that any inherent weakness would show up . . . since our main Can-Am competitors would have well proven chassis.

The second object was to make the car more pleasant to drive which, besides its humanitarian aspect, enables the driver to drive the car nearer to its ultimate limit and to maintain that level of performance for a longer period. It is interesting that the ultimate limit of the car has remained unchanged since its inception.

We have always maintained that it is necessary to keep a full and accurate written record of all testing. Before leaving the factory on each test day, the car's various settings were recorded: toe-in, camber, casters, ride height, springs, damper settings, etc. At the track each lap was timed, together with the driver's comments on each of these laps and any changes carried out in consequence.

Inevitably, it was going to be a great reckoning to us when Denny Hulme came to drive the car. His background of Brabham single-seaters and Lola sports cars and GTs—all cars renowned for their handling—would make him a most critical judge. Denny's car (M6A-2) was to be maintained when raced by Don Beresford and Barry Crowe. It was not possible to run the car to its limit during its first outing at Silverstone, but Denny was still well under his own lap record in a Group 7 Lola-Chevy. With the car fully set up he drove it next at Goodwood. After a few laps he said "Leave it alone, I'll race it like that," and that summed up our development. This, to my mind, throws considerable credit on Bruce's shoulders, for his task had been to develop the car to a raceworthy condition and this, in Denny's eyes at least, he had achieved.

The duties of the test driver of a new race car are in many ways similar to those of a test pilot in a new airplane, and they are just as crucial to the success of the project—although this fact is seldom appreciated. Unfortunately there is no recognized training for a test driver, and it is therefore not surprising that those who are very good are also very rare. The driver must be sensitive to the car's behavior, although there are several factors which make this difficult. It is amazing, for instance, how easy it is to become accustomed to owen the most unpleasant faults in a car if one drives it for some time. You encounter this when someone new drives your own road car. Further, for each driver, there appear to be certain aspects of the car's performance to which he is almost blind. To some extent, therefore, the more people you can persuade to drive your race car the better, for you will usually learn something from each one.

The Mk II Ford GT is commonly held to be a pleasant car to drive and I feel that a major reason for this has been the large number of drivers who have tested it and raced it. Each added his own criticisms and suggestions until no major problems remained—at least not from the driving angle. In any case it is necessary for drivers to express the car's characteristics in words that will convey to the engineer what is taking place. In addition to his other abilities, it really would be an advantage to have a driver with a degree in English!

There are so many factors in the performance of a car which cannot be measured, either because measurement would be too complex or because the parameter is as subjective as, say, steering feel. One day we will be able to read these quantities off tapes; Ford and Chaparral are already working this way, but until then we must rely on our test driver. Consequently, the findings of the driver are of great importance, for upon them we base so much of the car's development program.

These, then, are some of the requirements and difficulties of a test driver with a brand-new racing car. It is in addition to his tasks as company director, design consultant and race driver that Bruce undertakes the test driving for McLaren Racing, and the overwhelming success of our M6A Can-Am car reflects very closely how well he carried out his various and complicated tasks.

Broadley's big banger

A new Lola for the Can-Am series by James Tosen

IT takes at least a year to develop a competitive sports or GT car and probably another six months or a year before it can begin to fulfil some of its designer's aims. When you consider that at present the CSI sees fit to effect major changes to its championship regulations at least annually and the rules for one season are not fixed until the previous June, it is not difficult to see why several manufacturers have tired of getting fingers burnt over Groups 4 and 6. And with Porsche having already mopped up Daytona and Sebring, Le Mans looks like ending up as a battle between the durable sophistication of the little Porsches and the brute force of the front-engined 7 litre Chevvy Corvettes: no serious works entries from Chaparral, Ford, Ferrari or Lola. One reason for the present set of rules was undoubtedly to counteract some of the might of Ford but it has left Ferrari with at least a quarter of a million pounds worth of redundant 4-litre engine. Small wonder they have decided to concentrate on FI where at least three years freedom from change is guaranteed.

Most of Eric Broadley's considerable energies at Lola are now concentrated on his new single-seater for the SCCA's 5-litre Formula A and a new car to contest the Can-Am series, all very encouraging for the British Export Council and the Back Britain movement but rather depressing for enthusiasts who have to watch most of their motor racing on this side of the Atlantic. Broadley's predicament is rather similar to that of Enzo Ferrari though his stock of redundant engines is worth rather less.

The body is being made by Specialised Mouldings Limited. Standing behind the car are Peter (left) and David Jackson of SM, and Lola designer Eric Broadley (right).

The tail ends in a neat fixed spoiler with two holes for the exhaust pipes and triangular slots to ventilate the wheel arches in the rear panel. The oil cooler snorkel intake will be added later.

When the present Championship regulations were announced last year, reducing the Group 6 prototypes to a maximum of 3-litres capacity and Group 4 sports cars to 5-litres with a minimum homologation quantity of 50 built, Broadley managed to get the T70 homologated with a 5-litre engine. He has actually made about 90 open and closed cars and the 5-litre T70 Mk 3 is still a force to reckon with in GT racing, even though the simplest means to meet the limit — sleeving

down the more easily acquired 5½ litre unit — gives the engine somewhat irregular dimensions. But Broadley feels that Group 4 will never produce its full potential until regulations governing engine size, by far the most difficult factor for the manufacturer to adjust, are allowed to remain fixed for much longer periods. Changes to Appendix J which controls body dimensions, cockpit width, windscreen height, luggage capacity, etc., are minor irritants but usually met without too much difficulty. The engine capacities of the classes within each group are decided by the Championship Regulations which are issued each spring and guaranteed *only* for the season immediately following. The 1969 regulations have just been released, actually two months earlier than usual, and retain the 3-litre and 5-litre limits, but 1970 is anybody's guess. Hence a brand new car, the T160, for Can-Am where a reasonable life free from official interference is assured.

Though the T70 coupé will continue to be developed for GT racing, the growth in tyre sizes and the enormous power outputs obtainable from the 7-litre engines permitted under Can-Am regulations have put this category a little beyond its capabilities. It was originally designed in 1964 to the previous Appendix C when its 9-in. rims were considered huge. Progress since then, including raising rear wheel rim sizes to 14 in., has increased cornering forces and hence loading on suspension anchorage points while at the same time the amount of available material has had to be reduced in making room to get them in. Eventually a new chassis

Broadley's big banger *continued*

becomes more expedient than continued modification.

About 12 T160s are to be built at present, two for the official Team Surtees entries; the US agent Carl Haas has already sold the other 10. The general layout follows the lines set by the T70, and indeed most other Can-Am cars, with a punt type monocoque chassis of aluminium sheet braced with steel fabrications.

With anything up to 600 b.h.p. to push the car along, strength is at least as important as weight, though at 130 lb. for the chassis complete, it is not exactly heavy – about the same as the T70. But with most of the sheet being 16 gauge it is immensely rigid; 7,500 lb.ft. per degree is claimed, a very high torsional stiffness for a racing car and about two and a half times stiffer than the T70. The amount of steel has been greatly reduced in the interests of simplicity although manufacture is made a little more difficult by the need to clip almost the entire structure together and rivet it in one operation.

The chassis consists basically of two side sponsons roughly quarter circular in section (containing the bag fuel tanks) and these extend rearwards to form forks which cradle the engine. They are joined by the floor and a substantial cross member which forms the back of the seat in front of the engine bay; by a wide bracing member recessed for the battery box under the driver's knees; and by a square section hoop forming the scuttle and instrument panel mounting. A rectangular tunnel extends forward of this to end in a sheet bulkhead and two steel fabricated cross members, one supporting the pedals and the forward pivots of the lower front suspension arms and another, above, bearing the steering gear and the forward pivots of the upper wishbones. Ahead of this is ducting to carry the water-only radiator which is inclined forward exhausting air upwards just forward of the front bulkhead.

The rear pivots of the front suspension members are carried well back into the monocoque, the lower ones into a reinforced section of the cockpit bracing-member on each side of the battery and the others along the top of the forward tunnel into the scuttle hoop, which is similarly strengthened around the mounting. The suspension members themselves follow normal Lola practice with steel wishbone tubes brazed to the sockets of the lower ball joints with both balls in the uprights and Rose joints at the front upper and rear lower inboard mountings to permit camber and castor adjustment.

The engine bay is big enough to take any of the current V-8s including the new aluminium 427 cu.in. engine which Chevrolet are expected to introduce soon. The front mounting is formed by a steel fabrication rivetted into the inside rear corners of the main sponsons. From here the forks extend rearward to end in a further pair of steel fabrications. These are joined by two magnesium alloy castings, one above the gearbox supporting its two mounting lugs and the inboard ends of the single upper transverse rear suspension links, and the lower supporting the points of the reversed lower A-arms. There are two pairs of radius arms in the usual way, the lower pair extending forwards through a hole into the chassis member and the upper pair along the top of the chassis to brackets attached to the roll-over bar; when Brian Hatton made his drawing, the actual detail of the mountings had not been finalised.

Coaxial coil spring damper units are

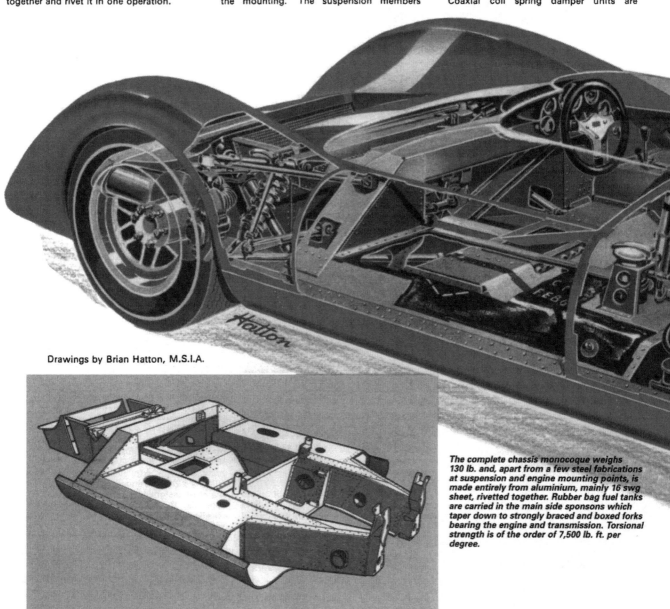

Drawings by Brian Hatton, M.S.I.A.

The complete chassis monocoque weighs 130 lb. and, apart from a few steel fabrications at suspension and engine mounting points, is made entirely from aluminium, mainly 16 swg sheet, rivetted together. Rubber bag fuel tanks are carried in the main side sponsons which taper down to strongly braced and boxed forks bearing the engine and transmission. Torsional strength is of the order of 7,500 lb. ft. per degree.

mounted outboard all round, the dampers being the Koni double adjustable type, and there are adjustable anti-roll bars front and rear, the latter passing under the gearbox. Wheels are 15-in. diameter with 14-in. rims at the rear and 9-in. at the front. Eric Broadley stressed that these are provisional sizes pending tyre developments. Obviously he anticipates that rims are going to get even wider, probably up to 17 in. at the rear, though their accommodation becomes increasingly difficult. Total wheel movement of 6 in. front and $7\frac{1}{2}$ in. rear has been allowed on the T160 which means quite a large wheel arch. If rims do get any wider, the uprights are going to project so far into the wheels that any cooling effect gained by mounting brake discs inboard of the uprights will be lost. So unlike the Formula A T140, which has inboard rear discs, the 160 has all four discs outboard and well inside the wheels, relying on cooling through flexible ducts. The discs themselves are ventilated, 12-in. diameter and 1·1-in. wide with a serrated inner diameter which locates on splines in the rim of a cast bell member projecting from the hub. A locking ring is secured by screws to complete the fixing, called a Redmayne coupling after the Girling development engineer responsible. Alloy calipers are made in four pieces with four pads each and a friction material area equivalent to a two pot calipers of $2\frac{3}{8}$-in. diameter.

Two rubber bag fuel tanks hold 25 gallons each and feed a common collector tank, just ahead of the left rear wheel arch, through one-way valves. With the aluminium engine, which has dry sump lubrication, the corresponding space on the other side of the engine would be occupied by the oil tank. To keep the front radiator area to a minimum and reduce the length of oil piping, two engine oil coolers are arranged horizontally at the back one above the other over the gearbox, with air ducted in through a snorkel. Beside the top one is a gearbox oil cooler with about half the surface area. The gearbox is a Hewland five-speed with the latest modified crown wheel and pinion and the clutch operating cylinder mounted more accessibly from bosses on the gearbox casing instead of on the bell housing.

The T160 has a wheelbase of 7 ft. 10 in. and a track approximately 4 ft. 8 in. front and 4 ft. 3 in. rear, depending on rim size. Weight will be around 1,450 lb. with slight variations for the 427 or 365 cu.in. engines, and distribution about 40/60 front to rear. The body is in glass fibre by Specialised Mouldings Limited. As our drawing shows it is not revolutionary in shape, drag being considered secondary to minimum lift and a sturdy structure. It fits compactly over the works and is designed to withstand the buffeting imposed by the rather rough Can-Am circuits. The maximum speed likely to be reached by these cars is in the region of 180 m.p.h. and to cope with this the body rises gently from the nose to form a wedge with a maximum height of $32\frac{1}{2}$ in. at the point of the spoiler.

The Can-Am series (or Canadian-American Challenge Cup to give its full title) is organised by the Sports Car Club of America (SCCA) and has been in existence for three years. Last year's winner was Bruce McLaren with Denny Hulme as runner-up, both in McLarens. This series and the US Road Racing Championship for Sports racing cars, run since 1962, are now the only remaining major competition outlets for the cars built to Appendix J Group 7 (SCCA actually wrote the Group 7 rules for the FIA). This year the Can-Am series will be run over six events in the US and Canada with prizes of up to $140,000 and total awards expected to reach $600,000.

M

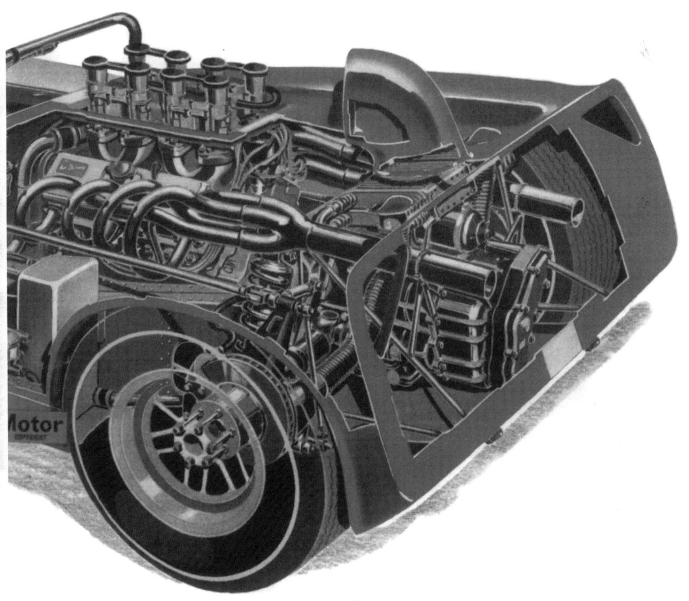

Big stuff: wide tyres, fat exhaust pipes, lofty injection stacks and a hefty Hewland box distinguish the back of the M8A.

THE McLAREN M8A
Colnbrook's new CanAm contender
By SIMON TAYLOR

MODERN motor racing is a most pro-fessional business, with large sums of money involved, and a successful racing programme at any level demands an efficient, single-minded approach. Perhaps the best example of this is the way McLaren Motor Racing went about last year's CanAm Series: they built two cars well enough ahead of the first race in the Series to get in over 2000 miles of prerace testing; the

cars were lighter and handled better than the opposition, and had two top Formula 1 drivers at the helm. Of the six rounds, the team won five, scooping the CanAm Cham-pionship and an estimated £65,000 in prize money—quite apart from turning in a nice little sales campaign for the virtually identi-cal production version of this car, the M6B, quite a few of which have been sold State-side this year.

Bruce and Denny sorting out a throttle linkage problem as the second car—Denny's—is completed on Monday afternoon. At 9 am on Tuesday it was lapping Goodwood.

This year McLaren Motor Racing are out to do it again. With an infinitely fuller Formula 1 programme than last year, they have not been able to do nearly so much advance work on the pair of M8As, the new CanAm cars that Bruce and Denny will drive in the 1968 series that starts on Sun-day week. When I visited Colnbrook last Monday—just five days before the cars were due to be airfreighted to the USA—neither was complete; the bodies were still to be fitted, and the F1 cars sat neglected in the corners of the neat, compact McLaren work-shops as all hands worked on the two big orange two-seaters—including the hands of Bruce McLaren (wearing an old pair of *Firestone* racing overalls!) and Denny Hulme. However, the first car, which Bruce will drive, had already done about 500 miles of testing at Goodwood, in chassis form and also with an old hack body from last year (including a long, long moment on the grass after the rain came down when Bruce was on dry tyres); even in this preliminary form Bruce got down to 1 m 13.1 s without trouble (as compared to his best lap with last year's fully-sorted car of 1 m 13.4 s, 117.71 mph), and when everything is right Bruce expects to be into the 1 m 12 s bracket with no trouble.

Basis of the M8A is a monocoque of L72 alloy with a magnesium bottom sheet, and from the cockpit forwards it is pretty similar to last year's; behind the driver the similar-ity ends—so does the monocoque, for the engine is hung directly onto the ¾ in magne-sium sheet rear cockpit bulkhead, as on the Formula 1 car, which saves weight and also makes the car simpler to work on.

The engine is a very impressive lump, but will be fairly common wear in this year's series; says Phil Kerr, "CanAm this year will be won on reliability and handling." It's an all-alloy dry-sump 7-litre Chevrolet, built at McLaren's Californian engine division by Gary Knutson, who prepared last year's engines. With Lucas fuel injection—complete with enormous 2-ft tall intake stacks—power output is around 620 bhp. All this is fed through a Hewland LG600 five-speed gearbox and BRD frictionless roller spline driveshafts to the phenomenally wide (15 in rim) knock-off alloy McLaren wheels, shod with equally enormous Goodyear tyres. At the front either 9¼ or 10 in rims will be used.

The suspension is conventional, and again pretty similar to last year's cars, although of course at the rear it is carried on a bearer mounted on the gearbox, and further supported by triangulated tubes running forward to the engine—so that if the bell-housing were to break the rear suspension and wheels would not suddenly depart. Lockheed 12 in ventilated discs with twin-piston calipers take care of the braking department. The workmanship throughout is superb, with all the complex piping for the fuel injection and dry sumping neatly thought out and displaying no sign of being rushed, although the McLaren boys have been at it day and night to get the cars ready for a couple of days' testing before they leave the country.

The body, another beautifully finished product from Specialised Mouldings, is nearly identical at the front to the M6A; at the rear it is a little different to accommodate the big engine and its lofty fuel injection. The colour is the familiar orange, with effective blue-tinted perspex screen. Rather surprisingly, despite modern Formula 1 trends and the example set in Group 7 by the Chaparral, the M8A boasts no wings or aerofoils; instead, it is delightly clean, with just a shallow full-width lip at the rear, which will be adjusted only during pre-race tests to find the optimum angle. Bruce McLaren hopes that the shape will do the rest and that no further spoilers will be necessary. The front-mounted radiator is fully ducted, and a large oil cooler is mounted on each side just ahead of the rear wheels. Fuel is carried in rubber bags within the monocoque on each side between the wheels. Despite the bigger engine, which is appreciably heavier than last year's 5.8-litre unit, the M8A weighs only 1450 lb, some 70 lb lighter than last year's car—which was extremely light.

The 7-litre engine is hung directly onto the monocoque, with bearers on the gearbox to carry the rear suspension. Note the centre-fixing wheels.

All the design work was done by the Swiss Jo Marquart, who used to be with Lotus, and Bruce himself. Going round with Bruce, Denny and Teddy Meyer during the series will be six mechanics: three from the engine division in California and three from Colnbrook, including Tyler Alexander and Kerry Taylor, who was Denny's Formula 1 mechanic with Brabham in 1967 and has been back in his native New Zealand since.

The CanAm opposition is going to be pretty tough: most people will be using the same 7-litre alloy Chevrolet and wielding the same 620 bhp, but there is no capacity limit (apart from a minimum one of 2500 cc), and Jim Hall's latest Chaparral is rumoured to have a new 8-litre Chevy lump. Phil Kerr reckons that if Ferrari's dark Prancing Horse, the lightweight Group 7 machine, materialises as a serious contender it could well have 700 bhp from its four-cam

6.6-litre V12, and the known rivals are pretty fearsome, too. There'll be about a dozen McLaren M6Bs—Carroll Shelby is entering two with alloy 7-litre Ford engines, and there's also Mark Donohue's USRRC-conquering Roger Penske M6A, which is Bruce's car of last year with a 7-litre Chevy installed. Dan Gurney will probably use 6-litre Gurney-Weslake Ford units and is entering a McLaren M6B and a new Lola T160; he will drive one and his young protégé Swede Savage the other. John Surtees, of course, will drive his new T160 works Lola.

All in all, it's going to be quite a series, and once again Bruce McLaren Motor Racing have a pretty businesslike setup. With light weight, good handling and two of the best drivers around, they have a fair chance of picking up more than their fair share of the dollars again this year.

The doors carry ducting for the twin oil coolers (left); the little cooler at the back is for the gearbox. Bruce McLaren and Teddy Meyer look pleased with the new machine (right); beside the radiator ducting are scoops directing air to the front brakes.

The British are

● Here they are Ladies and Gentlemen: lightweight, superfast projectiles; tailor-made to order by British (Commonwealth) craftsmen for the Great American Formula. Major components of the most exciting spectacle in racing—Group 7's unlimited displacement sports racing cars. Guaranteed to get results. Drilled for lightness and tuned for ultimate speed. They'll suck the eyeballs out of your sockets. They'll flick over the pages in your program as they pass. They'll fill your ears with over 100 decibels of stock-block roar. See them shoot from zero to 100 mph and back to zero in under 10 seconds! They'll run rings around Grand Prix and Indianapolis cars on any road course in the country. (. . . Er, sorry madam, the one on the right isn't for sale.) Abandoned by the Europeans, ladies and gentlemen—too fast and too dangerous *they* said— but *championed* by America, where we let it all hang out. See these cars, and many, many more, race for over a half-million dollars in Sports Car Club of America's exclusive Canadian-American Challenge Cup races this fall! Six big races, ladies and gentlemen, with $126,000 going to the series' winner! Six big races jammed into just 10 action-packed weeks. *See* Dan Gurney, Jim Hall, Mario Andretti; *your* favorite American all-star trying to become the first *American* to win the World Championship for unlimited displacement sports/racing cars! *See* Bruce McLaren defending his title against the Americans plus European Grand Prix stars like John Surtees and Denis Hulme! Watch him fend off the blood-red Ferraris from Italy. There'll be a race coming up near you soon, so be sure and get out there early and catch *all* the action.

(What's that lady? No you can't buy the one on the right. That's Bruce McLaren's personal car, lady. It's the one he's going to drive *this* year. Why don't you take the new Lola there on the left? It's specially designed for this year's series. Practically crash-proof. Crash-it, bash it and it'll still keep running. Yes, Ma'am, Bruce McLaren *did* win the championship last

McLaren M8A

BY CHARLES FOX

The Can-Am is the fastest, richest, most exciting series in the world but the British have a stranglehold on building winning cars that doesn't look like it's going to be broken this year.

coming The Br

Lola T-160

year, and he'll sell you a car just like the one he drove then. If you want one lady, you'll have to stand in that line over there. . . . er, they're about $15,000 each. Less engine. I don't know where you're going to get an engine, lady. When you get up to the counter just ask for Traco. They'll sell you an engine . . . $5000, lady. You'll need three at least. Tell them I sent you. No, of course you're not going to win with a setup like that, lady. Don't you have any friends at General Motors? Well Ford maybe? Well, how do you stand with the tire companies? Nothing there either, eh? Well listen lady, take my advice and leave it in the savings account. No? Well, go buy a race horse or a Rock Group or something, because Bruce McLaren's going to win the whole thing again this year anyway . . . Yes Ma'am. That's right. I mean if Jim Hall and John Surtees aren't going to stop him . . . That's what I said Ma'am . . . You're welcome lady.)

It's just like the pundit predicts, fellow crystal-ball gazers. We fed all the rumors, propaganda, optimism, evasiveness and facts into our electric aspidistra and it said that if McLaren didn't do it to them all again this year it'd throw itself into an electronic froth.

If you don't believe it just look at what's been going on over there in the U.K. since McLaren and Hulme went back to London last November, after they'd won five out of six in the 1967 series. McLaren subcontracts out the building of a dozen replicas of the McLaren M6A and calls them M6Bs. They're sold directly to McLaren's top competitors in the series to race in 1968, and all the while McLaren is home building a *new* model, the M8B, to blow them off again.

The ones who aren't buying M6Bs are out buying Lola T160s—which isn't a bad way to go either. All except Dan Gurney that is, who leaves no stone unturned. He buys a McLaren and then buys a Lola to keep it company.

itish are coming

Bruce McLaren, who races and builds, has his counterpart in Eric Broadley, who designs and builds the Lola and doesn't race. Broadley builds a new car strictly with the customer in mind. "It's awfully orthodox I'm afraid. Not very exciting at all. Just a simple, immensely strong car. Easy to work on because you can see all the bits." Broadley is English too. He says he sells the same basic car to everyone. Well, almost. The snag is that he has Surtees, the 1966 series' winner, do all the test and development driving for him—Surtees is no longer involved with Broadley financially, but he still likes to have a couple of new Lolas for the series himself. Surtees started sorting the Lola for Broadley in early June. The people who have ordered the 14 new Lolas don't get theirs until August, and you don't want to give Surtees two seconds start in any race, let alone two months.

The only person who builds Group 7 cars for sale in the U.S. is Bob McKee. But Ralph Salyer, a Hoosier plumber, and Oldsmobile, are about the only people who think he's fashionable.

Why can't Americans make a business out of building winning Group 7 cars? Why the dearth of builders in the one country that fosters the breed? According to McLaren, "There aren't many basic thinking engineers in the country. They won't get down to the basics and test. I don't know, maybe it's their training. But there aren't even many basic thinking automotive people in the motor companies. But then I suppose there aren't many Keith Duckworths or Colin Chapmans anywhere." All of which may be perfectly true but leads to the dilemma of why neither Lotus nor Cosworth is involved in the Can-Am, while McLaren is.

Surtees in the Lola

Besides which, McLaren obviously wasn't leveling his charge at Chaparral-builder Jim Hall, and he certainly couldn't accuse Ray Caldwell —who built Sam Posey's Caldwell D7—of not being a basic *thinker*, though Hall and Posey have both sunk fortunes into their cars, and neither has come up with Cam-Am paydirt yet. Posey has literally struggled with the D7 and its solid axles for two years. Now even he's starting to bend in the wind. This year Posey bought a Lola T160. "We're experimenting **Continued on next page** with an independent front end on the Caldwell, but we'll run whichever is quickest." Is nothing sacred?

For Hall, 1967 was a bad year. The Texan has been ominously quiet this year, emerging from guarded quarters in the desert outside Midland, Texas to run two U.S. Road Racing Championship events early in the season and then dropping out of sight. But now comes the 2H—an all-new Chaparral, designed to restore confidence in the American breed— and McLaren had better realize he's got something very serious to worry about.

The Can-Am series has only been going for two years, but it has already developed into one of the most politically complicated, grossly competitive and absurdly expensive exercises in international racing. To win you need a pluperfect organization behind a graded driver. Not to say the right chassis, not to mention the right engineer, and the right tires. After *that* you wrap the whole thing up in at least $100,000 and you're on your way.

This is true of going racing in any major branch of the sports, but in the Can-Am it's even more to the point because there are only six races—starting at Elkhart Lake, Wisc., on Sept. 1 and ending at Las Vegas, Nev., Nov. 10 with intermediate stops at: Bridgehampton, N.Y., Sept. 15; Edmonton, Alberta, Sept. 28; Monterey, Calif., Oct. 13; and Riverside, Calif., Oct. 27. Once you've committed yourself there's no time to make anything but the most minor changes. Underestimate the competition or come unprepared and the Can-Am series will fleece you in very short order; ask Texas millionaire John Mecom, or Ford speed merchants Holman and Moody, or Carroll Shelby— all of whom have been humiliated in varying degrees. And so, unless you're actually Bruce McLaren or John Surtees or Jim Hall, the plan is to sit on the fence as long as possible before you commit yourself to any definite combination—a fine art in itself. Decide too early and suddenly the other camp comes out with something that'll simply blow you off. Leave it too late and you don't get the equipment you ordered in time to do anything with it.

That's the foundation, and that's the plan. But nothing is going to do you any good unless you have the drivers—and they are very few. There's McLaren and Hulme, of course; and Surtees, Hall and Gurney. There's Mark Donohue backed up by Roger Penske's organization, and maybe, just maybe, Parnelli Jones and Mario Andretti have a look in. And that's all. Absolutely all. You might love and cherish local heroes of the Skip Scott variety, or international stars of the Chris Amon ilk—but this is the *Can-Am.*

Come March the rumors start circulating in the independent camp. They sit around scaring each other half to death with stories of a McLaren turbine with dual rears. Or Broadley's four-wheel-drive V-16 Honda-powered Lola. Or a complete armada of 850-hp Ford cars. This year even Porsche got into the act with an 800-lb., 3-liter car (and tiny, hand-picked, volunteer drivers?).

What eventually comes out of all this imaginative churning is usually pretty simple —well, at least by unlimited fantasy standards. The two great leaps forward for this year are in tire and engine sizes. First Chevrolet has, as if by magic, produced a job lot of all-aluminum "427" fuel injected, drysump engines—for the elite. Second placers need not apply. It seems likely that what General Motors has done is take the patterns for the L88 427, cast it in aluminum and bored and stroked it to 480 cu. in. (retaining the "427" designation, nevertheless). A giant mother. As Mark Donohue, who'll have two new Roger Penske McLarens at his disposal for the series, said, "If you don't have 600 hp this year you're just not going to be in the ballpark." The teams which *are* going to have these engines, apart from Penske, are McLaren's and Surtees'. Hall had aluminum 427s last year. He won't admit it but, by all reports, this year he's been trying a 427 Chevy with an ultralight magnesium block. Hall covers his tracks carefully. Especially any between himself and General Motors. "We've been doing some experimenting, but the old aluminum setup (a 625–650 hp Rochester fuel injected 480 cu. in. Chevy) seems the reliable way to go," is all he'll say.

It's a formidable line-up. For GM that is. With the exception of Lothar Motschenbacher (McLaren M6B-Ford) and Charlie Hayes (Cro-Sal McKee-Olds), every independent on the track will likely be running either the smaller 358 and 365 Chevrolet stock-block V-8s which dominated the series last year, or Chevrolet's iron 427—some of them chem-milled (a polite industry term meaning acid dipped) for lightness. Yes, Virginia; engine blocks too.

Of the factory and factory-backed teams that leaves only two Ferraris, which will apparently use 5.5-liter Ferrari V-12s. The rest belongs to Ford.

To be as kind as possible, Ford had a rough series last year. Of the three muchheralded Ford-powered teams one didn't make it at all, and the other two would have been better off if they'd gone to the Falkland Islands for a little boat anchoring. *This* year new Ford President Bunkie Knudsen, who feels the series is very worthwhile from a manufacturer's standpoint, took a long look and *officially* decided that Dearborn didn't have anything competitive enough to face Chevrolet—and he should know—and that Ford should stay out of it in 1968.

But unofficially, the rumors were that Ford did have an aluminum 427 in the works, and Ford's few racing stalwarts hung on grimly in the hope that it did exist, and that it would be ready in time for the series. Their hopes seemed crushed however when racing boss Jacque Passino said: "We *don't* have an engine that'll do the job. Certainly nothing that'll face up to Chevrolet. Mr. Knudsen is a firm believer in 'race what you sell and sell what you race'—a policy which has always been a strong point with Chevy and General Motors racing activities. But if we can't get there this year," he added fairly grimly, "we should be ready for next."

Curiously, even as Passino spoke, 2000 miles away in Los Angeles, Phil Remington, Carroll Shelby's chief mechanic, was stuffing an aluminum 427 fuel-injected Ford into a test car for Peter Revson to drive at Kent, Washington. Shelby has two new McLaren M6Bs on order to take Ford power into the series, but the state of his union with FoMoCo seems rocky. His minions are constantly complaining that Ford has been balking the Shelby Mustang Trans-Am sedan racing program. And that it has been dragging its heels in preparing the 427. With this on the one hand, and Passino busily back-peddling Ford out of the Can-Am program before it gets underway on the other, the Ford Motor Company/Carroll Shelby Racing marriage seems deeply periled.

If Ford's 427 doesn't show, Shelby will presumably drop out also, and Ford's only remaining big guns—Dan Gurney and master mechanic and team-owner George Bignotti—will have to switch to alternate power plants.

Both have potentially strong 2-car teams. For AAR, Gurney will drive one car, and will either line up a top-flight road racer for the other, or—if he feels that he's ready —hand it over to his prodigy,—Swede Savage. AAR's alternate engine will probably be a 377 cu. in. version of the 351 stock-block Ford with Gurney's own heads. But he's also talking about running a 325 cu. in. Ford V-8, which he calculates will deliver 550 hp.

At his shop in Indianapolis, Bignotti has the Lola he ran with Parnelli Jones last year, and a new Lola on order. He talks of either getting Jones or Andretti to run one car, and has a very able road racer, in the form of Al Unser, to put in the other. He ran a 306 cu. in. 4-cam Ford in Jones' Lola last year, and if he can't get hold of the lightweight Ford, may use the oversized Indy engine again. It's strong and Bignotti expects 540–550 hp out of it with a wide range of torque. But strong as it is, the 4-cammer will be no match in torque for the 427s—and he knows it. "I'm sitting here sweating it out right now. The sad thing is that I can just lift up the phone and have a couple of the big Chevys down here in a minute. But I'd rather stay with Ford if I can."

The only other engine in the competition will be a very special Olds V-8 in the Bob McKee-Ralph Salyer-Charlie Hayes car. Salyer's chief mechanic and engine designer, Gene Crowe, has been working with Oldsmobile engineers since last fall on a new 455 cu. in. V-8—presumably an aluminum version of the Toronado engine. Salyer swears it will develop 650 hp. "All I can say about it is that we've done some very radical work on the breathing," he says—

which, apart from black-magic, would seem to at least mean all-new heads.

Whatever the Can-Am teams use though, the big thing is that it means more power than ever, and this has had its effect on the design of the new cars—whether you can buy them or not. "We would have gone to four-wheel-drive," McLaren said, "But there simply wasn't time." Without four-wheel-drive the only way to get all this extra power into use is through the widest tires in the world. And that's what's happening.

Last year, wide tire fans blew their minds when Goodyear showed up for the opener at Elkhart Lake with really obese donuts: 12.5 inches wide at the back and eight at the front. But they haven't seen anything yet. This year they're talking about going to 18 inchers on the rear and 11s on the front.

"We haven't decided what we'll use but it will be somewhere between 13 and 18 inches at the rear—on 15-inch solid rim wheels," said McLaren. "I reckon though that this year will see the optimum tread width reached so that next year we'll not really have any alternative *but* to go to four-wheel-drive."

Broadley is supplying the Lola with 15-inch wheels—14-inch rim widths at the front, 9 on the rear—and he estimates that tires will go out to 17-inch rears and 10-inch

fronts later in the season.

Since Goodyear is the only company still in the full-subsidy business, most Can-Am cars will run on them. But Firestone—with Ferrari, Surtees and Hall—is not exactly bereft.

Wide tires and 600-hp engines have been matched by some firsts in car design. Neither Hall nor McLaren will use a full chassis, both have resorted to semi-monocoques, with the engine as the rear structural member. The McKee is the only car left in the series with a tubular chassis (both last year's Lola and McLaren were monocoque cars).

Looking at the new cars in turn, Broadley's is by far the most conservative. The T160 has a full monocoque tub made almost entirely from 16-gauge aluminum sheet. Steel is used only at engine mounting and suspension pick-up points. The structure is immensely rigid and the whole chassis weighs only 130 lbs. It is basically two main tanks extending back into a pair of boxed arms which embrace the engine, transmission and rear suspension. The driver sits between the tanks, with room for a passenger beside him. Well, a figurative passenger anyway. At the driver's back is a steel bulkhead, and an inch behind that the engine begins. There's another bulkhead, which also acts as the dashboard, over the driver's thighs, and one

under his knees. Together with the floor, these bulkheads give the chassis its essential rigidity. The driver's feet stick into a box beyond the dash. At the end of the box is another steel fabricated bulkhead on which the upper and lower front control arms for the suspension, the steering box, and the foot pedals are all mounted.

The only thing ahead of this is the water radiator (oil radiators are mounted over the 5-speed Hewland transaxle at the back) and the air scoops for cooling the front brakes, which are mounted outboard.

Rear suspension is by reversed lower A-arms, upper links, and two pairs of trailing arms running clear up to the roll bar. Broadley has used double adjustable, coil spring-encased Koni shock absorbers, mounted inboard, all round.

Ventilated 12-inch Girling disc brakes (1.1 inches wide) are mounted outboard—well inside the wheels—because, as Broadley points out, as the rims get wider, the uprights move into the wheels and effectively block any cooling gained by mounting the discs inboard of the uprights. In the outboard position the brakes rely on ram-air ducts, emerging into the airstream just ahead of the rear spoiler and in the nose of the car, for cooling.

The Lola's wheelbase is 94 inches, front track is 56 and the rear 51. The car is six inches narrower than last year's T-70 and 15 inches shorter. With the aluminum 427, the dry weight will be about 1650 lbs., distributed 40/60 front to rear.

"We designed the body shape around the wheel widths really," said Broadley, referring to the fiberglass body which looks much like last year's McLaren M6A. "The leading edge of the body is lower to give it more of a wedge shape, but we haven't reclined the driver any more than last year. If we did he just wouldn't be able to see where he's going. They have bad enough tunnel vision in these cars as it is."

Broadley was effusive compared to Hall and McLaren. But then neither the new McLaren nor the Chaparral is for sale. Still, the general layout of their cars isn't difficult to follow.

McLaren's M8A is a daring and very original sports car, based around its semi-monocoque feature. "We went to this in the interests of saving weight (the car will weigh under 1500 lbs. with the aluminum 427 installed). It's also easier to build a chassis, and makes everything much more accessible. But one of the biggest advantages is that we had much more freedom in placing the radius rods exactly where we wanted them, without having to worry about a chassis or exhaust pipes getting in the way.

"We could also run the exhausts down and out alongside the engine, which sits four inches lower now—and *that* lowers the center of gravity." The rear suspension is similar to the Lola's. "We kept the same basic layout we had last year, just built in a little more anti-squat to absorb the additional power the 427 will give us." The rear suspension is carried on a sub-frame around

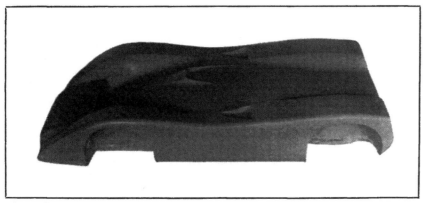

The wooden mock-up of Bruce McLaren's M8A: lower, lighter, and a lot less drag.

Hall's 2H Chaparral in clay form: 20% cleaner. A spoiler is unlikely.

(Continued from previous page)
the Hewland transaxle.

The center section is made up of two pontoons carrying 30 gallons of fuel apiece in FTP foam-filled tanks, held together by steel front and rear bulkheads and the floor. But the innovating McLaren has banished the mid-front bulkhead around the dashboard area. The stresses are fed through the sides of the tanks to the front bulkhead via angled panels—which saves a lot of weight.

The foot pedals and leading control arms for the front suspension are located on the forward bulkhead, and the steering box has been moved behind the centerline of the front spindles. Lockheed made McLaren a special set of 11.9-inch ventilated disc brakes with aluminum calipers, and these are mounted outboard. Needle roller bearings are used on the front spindles.

The fiberglass body is not only lower than before, it's flatter. "We did a great deal of experimenting with body shapes early in the year and came up with a shape that reduces drag considerably. By lowering the engine we were able to lower the tail three inches. Last year the tail was high and flat, but with the new car the tail droops down between the fenders, so that the spoiler doesn't come up above them." He does these things by feel rather than design. "We've consulted dozens of engineers and aerodynamists. But nine times out of 10 when you bring them into racing they just don't understand your world at all. Tell them you've got high drag and they jump up and down, suggest all kinds of things. Do what they say and you end up with a 1960 Vanwall.

"We've found that a week of running the car is worth six months on the drawing board moving the roll center half-an-inch."

And then there's Jim Hall—the recluse, who doesn't normally tell a soul a word about any car he ever made before it rolls off the trailer at its first race. He didn't tell us much about the Chaparral 2H, but that he told us anything at all was almost unprecedented.

The Chaparral 2H is the first totally new car Hall has built since 1963. It is semi-monocoque with 90% of all body panels stressed. Most of the car, including the chassis, is made out of fiberglass, with some aluminum and a very little magnesium. Hall's famous automatic transmission is still there, with perhaps more manual control than before. He has modified the wing but doesn't know yet whether he'll run it or not. "One of the real problems with the wing was getting it to stay on. When we built it we didn't realize that side force on the structure, due to the bump travel of the wheel (the wing is mounted directly onto the rear axle), was terrific, and we built the assembly without taking this into account. We've got it so that it'll stay on all right, but the additional weight it took to do it makes the whole wing concept not as good as I thought it was.

"Another problem last year was we just weren't quick enough down the straights.

So we've made the 2H much smaller and given it a 20% cleaner shape to start." (The car is six inches lower and reduced in width from 72 to 68 inches.) The flatter shape has allowed Hall to recline the driver's seat even closer to the horizontal. Brake scoops at the side and front cool his own brand of single-caliper disc-brakes. The combined oil-water radiator is fed by a full width scoop running right across the rear of the fiberglass body.

Apart from saying that he'll use coil-spring shock units all the way round—and magnesium hub carriers—Hall will not discuss his suspension. "It's something very new. I don't think it's been tried on a race car before." Rumor-mongers have had a field day with this one, saying that Hall is using fiberglass to make up the suspension components to reduce unsprung weight. This much is certain, he will be using 15-inch magnesium spoke wheels and super low-profile Firestone tires.

It might seem at first as though Ferrari guards its secrets as closely as Hall, but that's not entirely true. There's a difference in operating technique. Hall *won't* show anyone his new car until the first race. The Italians *can't*—because they don't actually work more than about 30 days ahead. But they certainly do a lot of advance-planning. At last word the plan was to build two cars—slightly smaller than the Dino 2-liter prototype—with Chris Amon and Jackie Ickx the probable drivers. Enzo Ferrari has dipped into one of his various parts' bins, and the cars will use F/1 suspension, brakes, steering, wheels, tires, and transmission.

Gambling-house owner Bill Harrah of Stateline, Nevada, will fund and equip the campaign. Ferrari sent over an exploratory expedition last year: two 4-liter P4s with the late Ludovico Scarfiotti, Jonathon Williams and Chris Amon driving. The team showed up at Bridgehampton with a car for Scarfiotti, but he quit after Mosport and Amon and Williams ran the second half. Amon, if he is joined by Ickx, coupled by Ferrari's menacing reliability in a series where the average dnf (did not finish) factor is about 65%, would make a formidable team. Amon, 24, and Ickx, 23, are two of the finest and youngest drivers on the Grand Prix circuit. Lee Jellison, Harrah's Transportation Manager, said that they hadn't heard anything about the cars at Harrah's yet. "But they (Ferrari) will call us when the cars are on the plane coming over. We can mobilize here in a few hours and be on the road. That's how they like to operate.

"But if you hear anything more I'd certainly appreciate it if you'd call me."

If the casual approach is what it takes to win the Can-Am, Ferrari's got it. But we're betting against it all the way. Like we said, Hall, maybe; Gurney, maybe; Surtees, maybe; Donohue, maybe.

Everybody else is out.

Except McLaren, who's going to win again. ●

65

1000 bhp per ton

The new McLaren Can-Am car

by James Tosen

THE power weight ratio of an average family saloon is about 60 to 80 b.h.p. per ton, of a sports car like the E-type Jaguar nearly 200 b.h.p. per ton, and a modern GP car packs about 450 b.h.p. into a car weighing 1,200 lb. (almost the same as a Fiat 500), a ratio of close on 850 b.h.p. per ton. For his latest 7-litre Can-Am car, Bruce McLaren will have well over 600 b.h.p. in a car only slightly heavier than a GP car. It weighs in at 1,400 lb. dry, a few pounds more than a Fiat 600, equivalent to the staggering power and weight ratio of 1,000 b.h.p. per ton, the first time four figures have been achieved in a car intended to go round corners.

The new car, the M8A, has been developed from the M6A in which Bruce McLaren and Denny Hulme took the first two places in the Can-Am series last year, and the same two drivers will contest all six races in the Championship which starts at Elkart Lake, Milwaukee, on September 1. At the moment, the last of three cars, a spare team model, is nearing completion at McLaren's Colnbrook headquarters but, if successful, it is likely that more will be built for sale under the McLaren-Elva link-up with Lambretta-Trojan at Croydon. More than a dozen M6As were produced this way last year.

The new car has the same wheelbase as the M6A, 7 ft. 10 in., but the overall width, 6 ft., and the track, 4 ft. 10 in. are both 4 in. wider. The overall height to the top of the roll bar, 2 ft. 9 in., is the same but the general build of the car is some 4 in. lower, partly because the M6A was designed when tyre profile ratios were rather higher than they are now—the new car takes full advantage of the latest doughnuts. Altogether about 100 lb. of weight has been saved, mainly in the body and chassis as the new all-alloy 7-litre Chevrolet engine weighs almost exactly the same as last year's iron block 6-litre, though it produces 100 b.h.p. more.

The main structural difference between this and last year's car is that the monocoque is now braced by only two instead of four fabricated steel bulkheads and it ends abruptly behind the cockpit, leaving the engine as the main stressed member at the back in the manner of Ford engined F1 cars. It is unlikely that Chevrolet intended the engine to serve as a part of chassis in the same way as Cosworth did at the design stage but it seems to work quite well with the aid of a light tubular sub-frame extending rearwards from the bulkhead.

The main hull is a fairly conventional monocoque, made mainly of 20 s.w.g. sheet, aluminium for the inside members and magnesium for the outer skins of the pontoons surrounding the fuel tanks, the proportion of aluminium to magnesium being about 50/50. The sheets are both rivetted and bonded with a cold setting epoxy adhesive made in Germany, called Agomex U3. The idea is to take

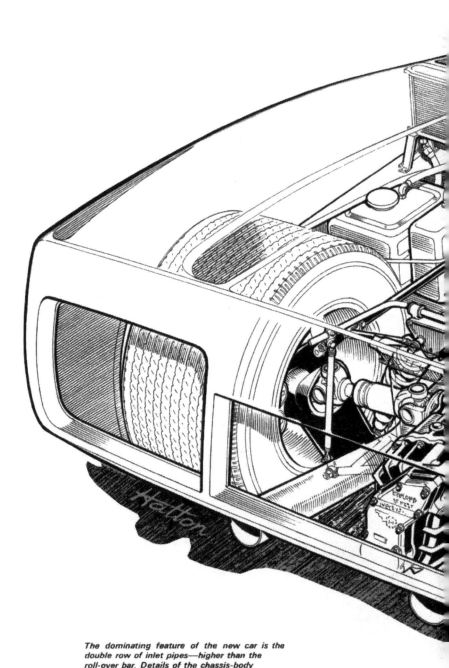

The dominating feature of the new car is the double row of inlet pipes—higher than the roll-over bar. Details of the chassis-body construction and the disposition of the main elements are discussed in the text.

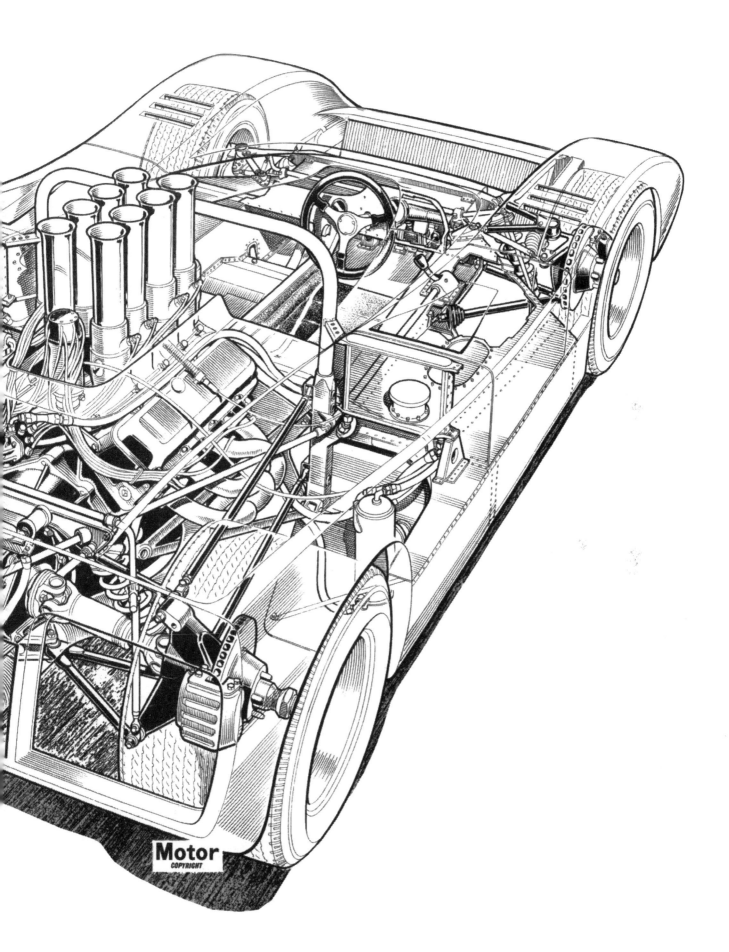

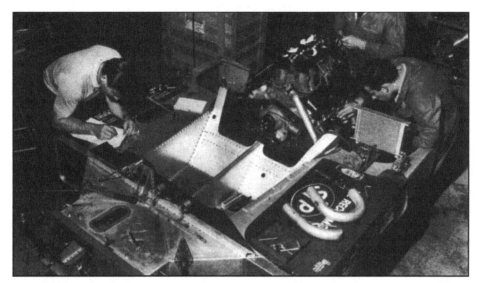

Almost like a small hovercraft in shape—the chassis in its sheet-metal glory. Bruce McLaren on left.

1000 bhp per ton

most of the shear loading off the rivets, to prevent the fretting which often occurs at rivet holes in light gauge materials and thus increase fatigue life, another example of the growing trend towards the techniques used in the production of high speed aircraft. The monocoque weighs only 80 lb. complete and has a torsional stiffener in excess of 3,000 lb. ft. per degree.

The monocoque ends at the front bulkhead, a 20 s.w.g. steel fabrication, bearing the pivots for the floor-mounted pedals, the inboard mounts of the forward arms of the upper and lower front suspension links and the top mounts of the coil spring/damper struts. Behind this, the monocoque is reinforced with stainless steel brackets which pick up the rear upper suspension links and the steering rack, which bolts into vertically slotted holes to provide adjustment to minimize bump steering. The rear lower links extend back into the side sponsons and are attached to stainless steel brackets mounted just inside the cockpit at the front of the seat formers.

Stainless steel is used for most brackets and structural stiffeners for its resistance to corrosion and good fatigue life. The suspension all round is practically identical to the M6A geometry and the spring/damper rates are very similar. The set-up has much in common with the M7A F1 car but the sports cars have more anti-dive and at the front the steering rack is set behind the suspension with rearward facing steering arms. The rack in the F1 car is mounted ahead of the front suspension.

The driver sits almost centrally in the narrow cockpit, which is braced by the scuttle and instrument panel and a spine between the seat formers. The battery is carried immediately behind the driver's back-rest with the button of the starter solenoid projecting through the sheet just behind his right shoulder. Immediately behind the cockpit is the second steel bulkhead, a square section fabrication with each side extending upwards into a tubular hoop to form the roll-over bar. Most of the rear section of the car is hung from this section. A magnesium cross plate attached at two points each side carries the front engine mounts and the tubular A-brackets extend rearward down each side of the crankcase to pick up more mounts just in front of the bell housing. Two rear suspension radius rods are

attached to brackets projecting from points just above the front cross plate mounts and, like on the F1 car, form the only link between the rear suspension and the main structure. The rest of the rear suspension, single upper and reversed lower wishbones, with full rose joint adjustment, is attached to the gearbox by a fabricated beam at the top which also mounts the anti-roll bar bushes and the top of the springs, and a triangular bracket projecting from each side of the gearbox casing to pick up the points of the wishbones. Dampers are Koni aluminium double adjustable all round.

The engine is a new all aluminium Chevrolet unit with the "porcupine" heads produced for the 1963 stock car engine just before GM pulled out of racing. It gets its name from the layout of the valves with inlets and exhausts splayed away from each in two planes so they appear to emerge from the heads in rather random fashion like the spines of a porcupine. Otherwise it is a conventional pushrod layout with wedge shaped combustion chambers and a single camshaft between the banks but most of the internals are reworked by McLaren's California based engine man, Gary Knutson, before being shipped over to Slough. Towering above the engine are eight very long tuned intake trumpets (which project well above the roll bar) into which fuel is injected downstream of butterfly throttles by a Lucas PI system. Fuel is carried in two bag tanks with a capacity of 30 gallons each, the nearside one draining across the car to the other through a one-way valve and then to a collector tank mounted in an extension of the monocoque just ahead of the offside rear wheel arch. Supply is by a single mechanical pump with an electric auxiliary unit for starting. Lubrication is dry sump, with $2\frac{1}{2}$ gallons of oil carried in the space ahead of the nearside wheel arch. There are two oil coolers drawing through vents let into the top of the wing line, the radiator at the front being for water only. The output of the engine is said to be well in excess of 600 b.h.p. at 7,000 r.p.m. with a torque figure which was not disclosed because the McLaren dynamometer reads up to "only" 550 lb. ft. and the needle was hard against the stop. It is certainly in excess of *two* GP engines and the power curve is comfortably above a good F1 peak figure down to 4,000 r.p.m.

All this goes through a triple-plate Borg and Beck clutch to a Hewland LG 500 gearbox —a four-speed box because Can-Am races have rolling starts and there is no need for the very low first gear of the five-speed LG 600

unit which weighs 12 lb more. There will be an infinite variety of ratios but they will be gearing for 190 m.p.h. at Riverside. Drive shafts are BRD pattern roller splined but actually made by McLaren, and have a Hooke joint at each end. Uprights front and rear are practically the same as on the single seater but the axles, common to front and rear, are hollow, machined from solid, and designed for centre-lock wheels with four-stud drive. The brakes, outboard all round, have ventilated discs, like the single-seater pattern, 12-in. diameter and 1.1-in. thick. As is usual with this type of disc now, the inner diameter is serrated to mate with splines in the rim of a cast bell member fitting over the axle spindle. A locking ring is secured by screws to complete the fixing which allows the disc to expand laterally without being subjected to stresses which might crack or distort it. Single piece Lockheed calipers have four pistons and two pads each with a total area of 16 sq. in. per wheel.

The wheels are an interesting new design, cast in magnesium but in two pieces with the rim riveted to the centre section. A variety of rim sizes will be fitted to suit different circuits—all are of 15-in. diameter but with rim widths of 9, 10 and 11 in. at the front and 14, 15 and 16 in. at the rear. Goodyear tyres will be used with a tread width of $14\frac{1}{2}$ in. at the rear, $2\frac{1}{2}$ in. wider than the M6A but with the same diameter of 26.8 in. Front tyre tread width is 9 in., 1 in. wider than the M6A, and the diameter $1\frac{1}{4}$ in. less at 23.8 in.

The glass-fibre body has been made by Specialised Mouldings and is much cleaner in appearance than the M6A, having less rise to the wheel arches and recessed intakes for the oil coolers. The gently rising wedge shape is clearly shown in Brian Hatton's drawing although some of the details had not been finalized when this was made. Not shown are the brake cooling ducts which share the main radiator opening at the front and the oil cooler ducts for the rear. Each front corner will carry a very small additional intake, blowing cool air into the cockpit. With enclosed wheels and a much larger body, a sports car can be shaped to produce far more anti-lift than a single seater but there is nothing like an aerofoil for pressing it down on the road, as Chaparral have shown. At the moment McLaren deny that the M8A will be winged though there is a wing hanging up in the Slough workshop which is much too big for the GP car: but a lip spoiler seems probable which, unlike that on the M6A, will be separate from the body and adjustable, but not during "flight".

FROM THE COCKPIT

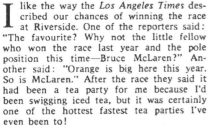

"When you are sitting out in front with the chequered flag and $20,000 waiting, you start to hear all sorts of strange noises."

Bruce McLaren on the Riverside CanAm

I like the way the *Los Angeles Times* described our chances of winning the race at Riverside. One of the reporters said: "The favourite? Why not the little fellow who won the race last year and the pole position this time—Bruce McLaren?" Another said: "Orange is big here this year. So is McLaren." After the race they said it had been a tea party for me because I'd been swigging iced tea, but it was certainly one of the hottest fastest tea parties I've even been to!

We went to Riverside early, more to make sure that we were ready than anything else. We had intended to tyre-test on the Wednesday prior to the race, but Goodyear were fairly confident that they had a good compound for Riverside. They wanted to do any comparisons during practice when conditions were a bit more representative, so on Wednesday I drove Denny's car, got the gear ratios established, and found out just how little rear spoiler we could get away with and still be stable down through the Esses that are so important on this track.

While I'd been back in England working on next year's designs, Gary Knutson and the three others that comprise what we proudly call our engine division had been finding some more horsepower from our 7-litre Chevrolet engines. Back in June on the development engine we had over 600 bhp, but during the Series we'd had one or two problems and lost some of those horses. When I got back to California the encouraging news was that we now had a power curve the best part of 30 horsepower fatter than anything previous. Top speed on the straight we found was up a bit from last year, and according to our gear ratios and tyre sizes we were doing 190 mph.

There was no official practice on Thursday, so I ran my car for only a few laps. Last year Dan Gurney had qualified fastest in 1 m 39.3 s and, since we have had an average improvement of about 3 per cent on lap times on most circuits, we expected a similar improvement this time, but it didn't happen. As it turned out my fastest lap, which was good enough for pole position, was only 1 m 38.5 s—not quite 1 sec faster than last year; but the rest of the field were relatively slower, so the track couldn't have been as fast as last year.

After practice I was reasonably confident that we were in a position to put up a good showing. I could lap fairly fast without trying too hard, the engine was strong and the brakes were just beautiful and showing no signs of fade. From 190 mph at the end of the straight we could pull down to 100 mph to enter Riverside's famous horseshoe Turn 9 in a little over 200 yards, and down through the Esses we found we got a slight improvement right at the end of practice by putting on some slightly wider rear wheels.

Apart from the engine bothers earlier in the series, we had only two other little problems with the car, which were both associated with the rear hubs. There was a tendency for a thrust race to loosen itself up a little, mainly because its push-fit was light in the casting, but we had taken care of that by flying new castings out from England. The other problem was a bearing sleeve that occasionally tended to shift, and the night before the race we decided to make a permanent fix on that by pinning them; so for the first time, as far as I was concerned, we went into a race with no real feeling of what could go wrong. Normally you worry about something. There's sometimes a weak spot, but this time I felt there wasn't an apparent one.

We'd made first and second on the grid again, and as the flag fell I beat Denny to the first corner and decided then to run just as hard as I could. The car felt just great. After about 10 laps I had around 5 secs on Denny and he was a similar distance ahead of Jim Hall's Chaparral. After 20 laps it had opened up to 10 secs, and a further 10 secs to Hall, with Mark Donohue running behind him in Penske's McLaren.

The fantastic middle-range power of our 7-litre engines made passing the slower traffic comparatively easy. We now had a performance edge on everyone in the race—even Jim Hall. I enjoyed it. I was surprised when they hung out a signal saying "30 laps to go." There's nothing like trying hard to make a race go quickly. It was so uneventful it was ridiculous. The only thing that really worried me was whether I would run out of iced tea! We had a quarter Thermos flask of tea packed with ice in the cockpit. It was fully set up with a breather system and a pipe taped onto the shoulder strap of my seat harness, so all I needed to do for a refreshing drink was to hook the end of the hose round and suck. Beautiful.

The temperature wasn't as high as it can be at Riverside, but it was still 95 deg F, and that's not exactly ideal conditions for a motor race. As it happened my iced tea lasted right to the last lap.

The only drama came when Denny got involved with some slower cars and spun out across the inside of a corner, which unfortunately had the half-tyre markers which are a treacherous feature of some American tracks. This completely wiped out the right front corner of the body—it was almost a repeat of last year, except that this incident was at the end of the race instead of at the start. Denny had been lying a comfortable 15 secs behind and if he had finished second it would almost certainly have won the CanAm Championship for him, but a couple of pitstops to check and repair the damage, and the slow laps from then on with the torn fibreglass flapping, dropped him back to fifth.

Jim Hall had pitted to mend a broken brake line which moved Mark Donohue up to second place, about 50 secs behind me. Over the last 10 laps I crossed my fingers and eased off. All the gauges said everything was Okay, but when you are sitting out in front with the chequered flag and $20,000 waiting, you start to hear all sorts of strange noises that could spell trouble. But that big aluminium Chevvy thundered on, and I won Riverside for the second year running to be the only two-time winner of the race. We had proved that when it mattered we could run either Denny's car or mine fast enough to win. Roger Penske's crew were under the impression that Mark Donohue could race with me but not with Denny, so I guess we proved a point at Riverside. John Cannon had won the race at Laguna Seca in pouring rain and I had great satisfaction lapping him this time. Every time I went by I thought, "John, those rain tyres aren't going to help you here today!"

As the CanAm Championship points now stand, Denny leads with 26 points and Donohue and I are tied at 23 points each. I guess really we just ought to run carefully at Las Vegas and try and place both cars, which would mean that either Denny or I (or both of us jointly) would win, but that's going to be hard—it's a lot more fun when you know the car can do it, and just run as hard as you can go!

Riverside: "We'd made first and second on the grid again, and as the flag fell I beat Denny to the first corner." Bruce still has the edge five laps on, both M8As ahead of Mark Donohue's M6B and Jim Hall's Chaparral 2G.

CanAm 1968:
THE YEAR OF THE ENGINE

By PETE LYONS

EARLIER this summer Mark Donohue, who is at least as good an engineer as he is a driver, remarked that, while 1967 had been a chassis year, this would be the Year of the Engine. Now, with four CanAm races run, we can see he was right.

Last year there was a reliable 500-plus horsepower available to anyone, and the M6A McLarens scored as much on Grand Prix quality handling as anything. Now almost anyone can buy an M6B, but the "Horsepressure" necessary is at the 600-plus level, and the engines capable of pumping it out are very new. Just watch the worried faces bent over the backs of the cars, and it's clear that the race is between engine developers probing the unknown.

There's no question either that the way for most people lies through the 7-litre mass production block. Firms like Ferrari can contemplate pure racing designs but McLaren, Shelby, even Chaparral to an extent are very small operations who must buy everything they possibly can off somebody's shelf. There are currently two attempts with exotic, high-winding small engines, Dan Gurney's and George Bignotti's (surely it's a reversal of tradition that they're both American?), and the latter is in the process of switching to the big stuff.

The whole point about the big displacement is torque. Even if the little screamer pours out similar peak power, the big thumper cranks out much more low down, and climbs away from the corners more smoothly. Granted, a big screamer might be more effective still, but pending Ferrari's 6.3-litre arrival we aren't at that point yet. And more cylinders, valves, camshafts and revs mean more weight, as motorcycle designers know so well. So now that General Motors, followed half-heartedly by Ford, have cast a batch of aluminium blocks, the way is clear. Throwing away your old 6-litre Chevy and adding an aluminium 7-litre *subtracts* about 50 lbs from your McLaren's weight!

Comparing the two rival brands, we find both Ford and Chevrolet 427s have near enough identical bores and strokes at 4¼ by 3¾ ins. The Ford, however, is poorer by 1/5th ins in between-bores spacing and is right out at the end of its displacement limb. Its valve and porting layout, too, is a little out of date. This is the 427 that has been granted to Shelby for the time being, essentially the Le Mans engine. There are two other 7-litres being sold to the Ford public, the bread and butter 428 and the new 429, which has even more bore space than the GM block and staggered valves as well; doubtless there is plenty of back room work aimed at next year, but that's next year.

This year it's the Chevy, the warmly beloved "Porcupine" or "Semi-Hemi" of the drag racer, with its superb porting that even in a road car gives a snap and a throttle response uncanny for something that big. In fact it will be very interesting to see just how much better the Weslake heads on Surtees' engine breathe once it gets going—there might not be that much advantage.

Whatever the individual builders' pet tricks, the end result is about the same:

something secret over 620 bhp at about 6700 rpm, and it pulls strongly from below 3000. The safe rev limit is regarded as 6800 rpm, although they have been known to hold together at 7500. Compression ratio is around 12.5 to 1, and fuel consumption seems to average 4½ mpg (English).

Maybe it all sounds pretty crude to Formula 1 fans, but then motorcyclists scoff at Formula 1. Look at the rest of the 7-litre package: small size (less than 24 ins square), low weight (supposedly 460 lbs), massive strength and genuinely low price. Those lumps in the back of today's sports-racer are a bit more than a wagon ride away from the gate of the farmyard—there are a lot of million-dollar minds putting 100-hour weeks into them.

As an instance of where some of the hours go, it's been found that a light-metal head gives less power than a cast iron one of identical design because the former conducts heat away too quickly. The obvious answer is some kind of coating, but results so far are vague, and those who do coat their combustion chambers say it's more to seal porosity than anything else.

What about the severe oil-leakage that has been plaguing all the big engines, that lost Bridghampton for the McLarens, and which Jim Hall solved in secret over the winter? McLaren's chief engine genius Gary Knutsen is one who will discuss his work, or some of it, and he says there was never any suspicion that the crankcase itself, used as a semi-stressed member of the M8A chassis, was warping under load. "We run our bearings pretty close and they would have shown any distortion right away." The trouble was high crankcase pressure. With eight huge cylinders above a very small sump which wraps tightly around the crank, a little blowby means a lot. The scavenge pump was designed to handle a reasonable amount, but the rings were obviously passing far too much. Finally it was recalled that the earliest engines, running in Hulme's cut-up M6A which was actually the prototype M8A, hadn't shown the problem. In a flash of reverse-development insight the special racing rings were replaced by a set from a GM parts shelf and *voilà*—at Edmonton Bruce's engine, at least, finished full inside and dry as a bone outside.

This is the sort of story that underlies one of Gary's basic philosophies—if you can possibly get away with it, leave it standard, or buy it from somebody else. Playing around costs too much money and too much time, that 53rd week nobody has. He concentrates on essentials, like cramming as much air and fuel as possible into every revolution.

His fuel injection rig is a stupefying thing, a forest of trunks and fat nozzles rising 18 ins above the head/manifold interface. The result of exhaustive trial and error, it has a mass production finish ("Bruce is big on looks"). The inside diameter of the intakes is a tiny fraction under 3 ins, and the petrol goes in at a semi-downdraught some distance above the butterflies, which are at the bottom in a one piece casting (one of the many hot-rod items) through which the fuel percolates to cool before going to the

Lucas pump.

It is in their injection systems that all these basic engines seem to differ most. If the layout is the same, then the pieces chosen are different. The Shelby version is to have the intakes cross between each other like interlaced fingers to get a straight run at the ports; petrol flows in at a constant rate downstream of the butterflies. Although the manifold has a welded-in provision for passing fuel for cooling Phil Remington hasn't found any need for it. "We don't bypass enough for it to warm up." He adds that the crossover intakes are limited in their diameter, and there is new manifolding in the works which will use vertical tubes like everyone else's.

Surtees' Weslake system follows that on the Gurney engines: short, small tubes (and small diameter exhausts as well) throttled by slides; Lucas injection but no cooling.

Since being described in June 14's AUTO-SPORT neither the Chaparral nor the Traco (Donohue) systems have been changed in essence: the former with high pressure injection high up the stacks with butterflies on top, the latter using the Lucas to squirt it in at the midpoint above the throttles. Both cars now wear big air scoops, but Hall and Donohue agree that the pressurisation effect is minimal, and that rather the idea is simply to clean up the airflow to the intakes at a location of high turbulence. Jim does say his jetting is richer than it otherwise would be, *ie* at low airspeeds the mixture is somewhat too rich, but Mark denies it. When his Lola ran out of petrol at Las Vegas last year it was using scoops for the first time and the mixture was in fact on the rich side, but it was purely as a precaution against overheating.

Bartz, Cro-Sal, Holman-Moody, Jackson, all have yet different ideas. Who is right? Why do some famous engine men feel a steady dribble of fuel is all that's needed, while Hall is so firmly convinced of the opposite view that he uses a very high pressure pump, so high that ordinary plastic hoses bulge and spoil the timing? He uses steel pipelets which he changes every couple of races to forestall their cracking.

These engines are in their first season of real life—it's fair to say so, since Hall is still using last year's car. How much further can they be taken? Displacement increases keep adding speed, so the sizes will creep up. If the little Chevy started life in 1954 at 4.2-litres and grew to over 6-litres, will the sevens eventually get to 10,000 cc? So much of the road racing engines use hot rod gear that it's instructive to look to the drag strips for a guide to possibilities, and there we see revolutions well over 9000 rpm and peak outputs at the 1700 bhp mark, neither for longer than a few moments of total life; but there was a time when 6000 rpm was impossible. It's mostly a question of materials and design refinement.

There is a move afoot to limit the CanAm engines in an attempt to limit costs, but what limit has ever cut costs? As long as two developers are in intense competition their weekly bills will skyrocket. How much more useful for the officials to turn the other way and look for new sources of money.

AAR Gurney-Ford

Bartz Chevrolet

Chaparral Chevrolet

Bignotti Indy Ford

Penske Chevrolet

Shelby Ford

Team Surtees-Weslake Chevrolet

Traco Chevrolet

McLaren Chevrolet

McLAREN M8A

CUTAWAY DRAWING BY MATI PALK

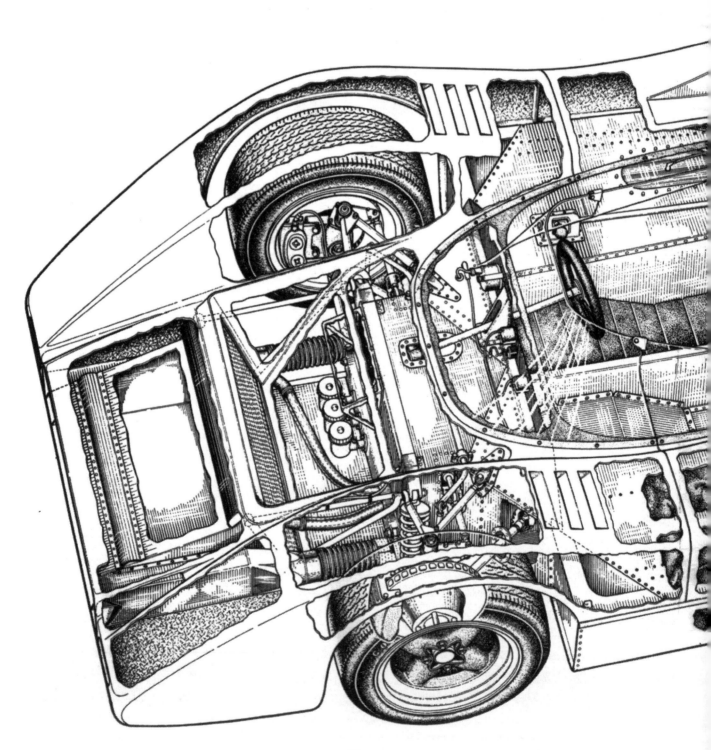

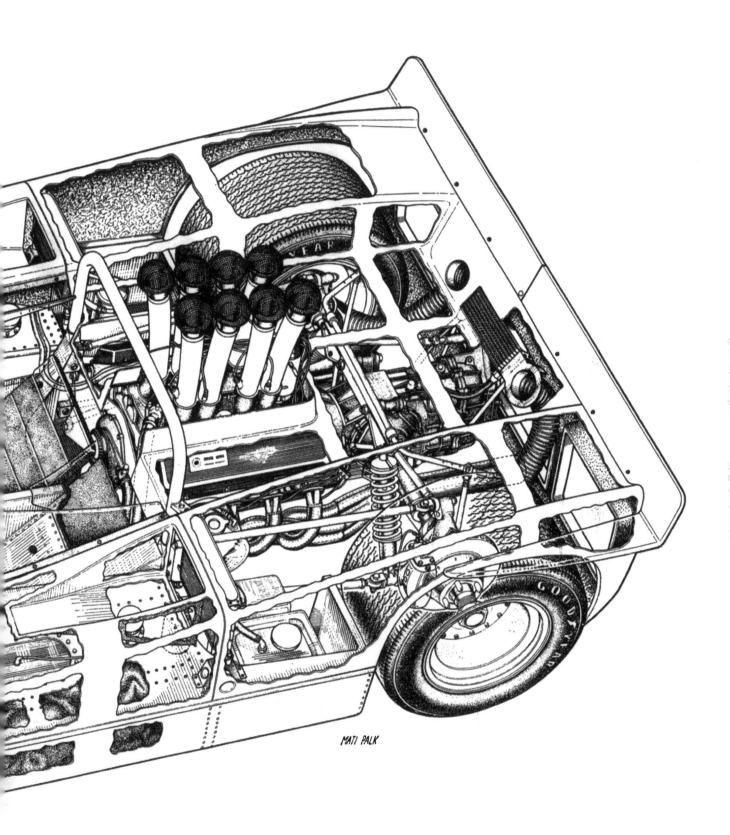

MATI PALK

Bruce McLaren at speed in the M8A which he drove into second place behind team-mate Hulme in the third CanAm series.

Summing up the CanAm

By PETE LYONS

The 6.3-litre Ferrari disappointingly only made one appearance, at the last round at Las Vegas in the hands of Chris Amon; it was eliminated in an early incident, but had qualified ninth fastest. Note the very enclosed cockpit.

WELL, they whipped us again. The Chaparral and the Penske people gave them a good run, but the McLaren boys came with a solid organisation, sound preparation, and the fastest cars. It looks as though they know something the others don't; they're certainly on the next plateau above.

They made the right decisions, and made them early enough to get the machines tested and race-ready (just barely) on time. Maybe the big fact is that McLaren Motor Racing are Motor Racers, that they are at it all year round. This must keep them honed to a permanent fine edge.

When others came with old cars, McLarens came with a fresh design. When others came with new cars which they had to learn to use, McLarens had already discovered every nuance of their own. When others thought to use last year's power, McLarens had new giant engines. When other teams showed up short of spares, McLarens had truckfuls of spares and supply lines reaching across the world. While others might be poor in really top people, the Kiwis were rich in masters. And when some absurd accident came up or an unforeseeable minor breakage eliminated a one-car team, Bruce McLaren had provided himself a duplicate entry and a World Champion driver.

Ray Caldwell, who made a good stab at competing with the winners, understands the structure of the McLaren success. "Look," he says, "when the Air Force wants a new plane it doesn't just order a plane, it orders a complete weapons system. Bruce has set up a racing system."

The machines

There were only four designs of importance in this year's six-race Canadian-American Challenge Cup, and only two were new. The **M8A McLaren** was developed, literally, from the previous year's winner, but scarcely a single part was interchangeable. The car was longer and wider; the weight was slightly less and slung lower, the power much greater, and the aerodynamics more subtle. The machinery looked more complicated but in fact was easier to work on. It was faster and yet more stable at speed, but Bruce admitted the car was a trifle less controllable than the M6 in the tighter corners. "It's hard to say just why this is," he mused. "It's like petting dogs; one will wag its tail and the other will bite your hand." The thought made him laugh.

The private owners running the **M6Bs**, having moved up from older McLarens or Lola T70s, seemed to find them very sound cars, quite race-ready as production racing cars go, much more sophisticated and critical to set up, and to drive "lighter, tighter, you can do more with it." It's just a little curious that so many purchasers of a winning design felt they could improve on it, and changed things drastically. *Sometimes the changes were improvements . . .*

The **T160 Lola** was designed more as a for-sale car than the M6B, and could not help but suffer from the lack of a complete race development season. It showed evidence of rather major rethinking part-way through the design process, in the suspension geometry for instance, and every purchaser found some things that had to be redone before the car would go well. Drivers used to the T70 felt the T160 was definitely a better car, a good car, although trickier to drive as a reverse side to its extra quickness. Toward the end of the series there were several really good performances put in by these cars.

The **2G Chaparral** started as a 2C chassis three seasons ago, and the fact that Jim Hall was able to keep its performance current speaks volumes for his abilities as a designer and a driver. The silly little failures that plagued him were purely bad luck, due probably in some cases to old age. The car pretty clearly had the most power—there is considerable reason to believe that the McLarens started some races with less than 600 bhp. Hall was careful to keep quiet about the design of the never-entered 2H, but had it been an advance on the 2G it surely would have been on the pole more than once. Photographs were circulated of a wind-tunnel model purported to be the 2H; it was small and spindle-shaped, without a wing. How much of this was smokescreen we'll have to wait to find out.

Certainly the wing on the 2G was entirely worthwhile at many points on a race circuit, for instance at Bridgehampton where just before the end of the long uphill straight the road suddenly dips down. Here Hall gave a "touch of wing" and was able to

Jim Hall's Chaparral 2H never appeared, but he put in some consistent performances in the 1967 2G until he wrote it off at Las Vegas.

John Surtees in the Lola T160-based TS-Chevrolet had another unlucky series, although the car obviously has great potential.

One of the most immaculately prepared cars was the Penske McLaren M6B of Mark Donohue, who missed second place in the series by only one point and was consistently the fastest American.

keep hard on the throttle where others had to ease off. Hall has a gift for explaining things colourfully and aptly. Speaking like a boxer, he says that the wing and the left-foot braking and the clutchless gearchanges all "give me more combinations than the other guys have." He has the kind of basic approach to problems which gives him the concept that cars are not simply tyre/road vehicles but tyre/road/aerodynamic machines. Bruce McLaren, speaking in the context of aerodynamics, has said "Every time we try something, we come to find out Jim has been that way about six months before."

The aerodynamics

Aerodynamics are still very much a Black Art, and Ray Caldwell predicts that we haven't seen anything yet. He's very enthusiastic about aerodynamic down-force, particularly for de Dion suspension systems. "You know that the cars can corner harder on the slower turns than the faster ones; the trouble is that it's awkward to design suspensions that will oversteer at high roll angles and understeer at lesser ones. But aerodynamic forces rise with speed and by using them we can get the car to do what we want."

The lay observer can see how much is still Black Art through curious little details, for instance the oil streaks after a race showing that air has flowed and swirled very much counter to the profile of the body, or perhaps on the tail spoiler it has even flowed down from above rather than up over the top. Once, after adding a small side scoop, the McLaren crew checked its effectiveness by pouring a line of engine oil across the body in front of it, and were gratified to see it streaking into the opening after a fast lap. Another team found by chance that the position of a mirror had a noticeable effect on the airflow into the injector intakes, and another briefly had an oil cooler positioned so that hot exhaust got diverted directly into one bank of intakes!

The tyres

Tyres and their behaviour are another only dimly understood phenomenon. It almost comes down to this: wider treads stick better. Goodyear, who supplied tyres for all wins but the rainy Monterey one, had any number of sizes ready, but pretty soon found that 14 ins tread was all anyone could really use at the present, and standardised on that size for the rears and either 9 ins or 10 ins for the fronts. The construction and compounding probably embody secrets that it would take another tyre technician to ferret out; the untrained observer can see the cord angles changing across these wide treads in long S-curves, so that the cords run more parallel to the rotation in the centre. The wider the tyre the less critical is the pressure setting. Stirling Moss was supposed to have adjusted his pressures to the nearest

Dan Gurney campaigned a lowered and highly modified McLaren M6B, dubbed the McLeagle, with limited success.

CanAm cars wear big boots: this is the footwear of the McLaren M8As. Note the depressed crowns on the deflated tyres.

quarter pound, but modern drivers alter it by 3 or 4 lbs at a time. It's interesting to notice that after a tyre is hot it feels sticky to the touch. Indeed, an experienced driver will tell a neophyte to do two or three laps to make sure the rubber is warm before making any decisions about the handling. Also, a cool day upsets the performance of these tyres: they need to run somewhere around 160 deg F.

At Indianapolis the stakes are so high that individual machines can have the tyre men design specifically for them, but the CanAm isn't quite that important yet. As one might expect, they say the de Dion system would be the easiest to design for. There is sometimes a big problem on normal independent suspension systems getting the tread temperatures even enough across the width—15 deg F difference is an ideal spread, 35 deg is tolerable.

The money

Here we come to the heart of the situation. Those involved in design point out that there are any number of ways, theoretically, to make the cars faster: four-wheel drive, fantastic engines, perhaps automatic transmissions. But the expenses are already so high that no one is anxious to go in deeper than the level called for by the rest of the competition. The art, in design as in driving, seems to be to go no further than is absolutely necessary, always bearing in mind the

old adage that there is nothing more expensive than a second-best racing car!

We've now had three seasons of CanAm. There have been dull races, but there have been very high points too. The series must be regarded as a success, and that it should now expand is entirely right. By growing in importance, however, it will take up even more space and time in the motor-racing world, and there will be more of a tendency towards having CanAm specialists who do nothing else. Dan Gurney has just announced that he will no longer do Formula 1, and McLaren Motor Racing will be very busy next summer and autumn keeping a full Formula 1 and CanAm programme going, often on alternating weekends.

For next year the straws in the wind promise a lot of terrific racing. The Ford Motor Co were held back by a crippling strike, but should have suffered enough humiliation in the past two years at the hand of Chevrolet to give it a real try: a new 7-litre-plus engine is on the way. Donohue and the Penske organisation are allying themselves directly with the Lola factory. It's too early in Jim Hall's convalescence to predict the future of Chaparral Cars, but there are signs of a lot of interest from many other quarters. Interest doesn't always or even often promise success, but the CanAm is getting to be a very big prize indeed. As for how to go about capturing it, the McLaren Way is there for all to study.

Background to victory

Round the Can-Am with the McLarens

by Michael Bowler

WITH a gross purse of around £70,000, including a couple of prize cars, and various other less easily defined benefits, McLaren Cars look as though they've made another huge profit out of the six-race Can-Am series of 1968. But such success needs great organization particularly when races are only two weeks apart; that usually means about nine days for repairs, preparation and an average crow-fly mileage of about 1,500 between the far-flung circuits. Mix in four Grands Prix, one of them in Italy, during the same six weeks and that's an awful lot of flying for Hulme and McLaren. Organization costs money; add in the cost of the cars themselves (unassessable), engines (approximately five complete units at £30,000 the lot), travelling for all those involved (around £7,500), and the paid out salaries of those same people, and the project begins to look like a normal commercial proposition—an adequate return on money invested. But then there were useful contributions from the main sponsors, Gulf and Goodyear, so for McLarens, Can-Am racing is a worthwhile proposition; what it must cost those who aren't successful one dreads to think.

Preparation for the 1968 Can-Am series really started at Las Vegas as the 1967 series finished, and has occupied a major proportion of McLaren thinking ever since, and they still find time to run a Grand Prix team as well! The M8As were a direct development of the M6As with more power and a bit more road-holding to give a potential lap time reduction of about 3%. In fact they proved no faster initially in a straight line than the Penske entered M6A (one of last year's team cars) powered by a Traco prepared 7-litre Chevrolet unit, but the 3% came from cornering power.

McLaren's engine division with four people occupied 1,000 sq.ft. in a corner of the Bartz Engine Development Shop at Van Nuys, just down the road from Los Angeles, a convenient centre for the final three races in California and Nevada. Getting a reliable 600-plus development horses wasn't quite as quick a job as scheduled and it was only about three months before the series started that the first engines came over to McLaren's works at Slough. First track test sessions were then compressed into the fortnight before the cars were due to leave the country and, in fact, by the time the two cars were ready to fly they went with a broken engine apiece.

The nerve centre of the movement schedule of McLarens is divided between Phil Kerr and Teddy Mayer, with Phil handling the Formula 1 side and Teddy, an American, covering all

the Can-Am organization. The resulting schedule is an absolute masterpiece with everyone's movements clearly plotted, mechanics, drivers, cars and the various other personnel joining in from the American side; this is all covered in a nine-page day-to-day diary for the 2½ months starting from the moment the Can-Am cars left England. In the last week one of McLaren's men scheduled to go to America, Colin Beanland, had a grinding-wheel burst in his face so the instant replacement had to get an equally instant visa the day before departure.

One of the advantages of the McLaren works position at Colnbrook near Slough is that the airport is very handy, but despite this they admit that they never get there on time. However, four tons of McLaren machinery set off from London Airport on Saturday, August 24, comprising two cars and 2½ tons of spares. At the other end, chief mechanic Tyler Alexander had hired three ¾-ton Chevrolet trucks, the two for towing the cars having 6½-litre V-8s coupled to Hydromatic transmission. The third engine parts truck complete with radio telephone was setting off from Bartz on the other side of the American continent to converge on the first round at Elkhart Lake, half way up the west side of Lake Michigan, on the following Wednesday: Gary Knutson, in charge of engine development, and Lee Muir were with that one. Tyler Alexander and Don Beresford had joined Cary Taylor and Chris Charles in Boston, manning the other two trucks.

As planned, the lot converged on Elkhart Lake, with McLaren, Hulme and Mayer having

Map of Canada and the USA showing the distances involved travelling from one Can-Am race to the next with the occasional Grand Prix thrown in. Even on crow-fly mileage the Can-Am cars have to travel over 8,000 miles!

Had enough; Denny Hulme gets out of the car having coasted to the pits after engine failure at Riverside.

driven over from Chicago, and took over about a third of the main hanger, spreading out all four tons, including four engines. America was certainly as impressed with the set-up as last year but really hardly seemed to have learned by example; Penske with his Sunoco Special—a highly modified M6B—seemed to have the only other organization which could compete on efficiency. Penske, with Mark Donohue driving, had used the Chevvy engine throughout the USRRC series and was hoping that the McLarens were going to need the whole Can-Am series to sort them out; in fact they were going to need two races but if it hadn't rained at Elkhart Lake, the engine would have had a bigger thrashing and probably not have survived.

Preparation at Colnbrook. Bruce McLaren hard at work assembling an M8A chassis.

Background to victory

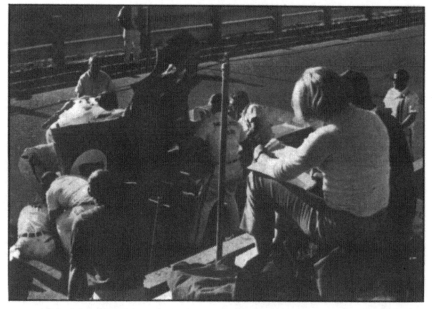

Despite the vast load of bits coming across, McLaren and Hulme didn't come empty handed; some more conventional cast and riveted wheels (as against the new over-light spun aluminium ones) and a spoiler came over in the Boeing's hold. Once there McLaren sat down at the machine shop and fabricated some new engine mounts; he is just as much at home in the workshop, the design office or the cockpit and correspondingly respected by all who work for him. Wheel rims needed hand filing too.

In the first practice session Bruce's engine holed a piston and suffered a cracked throttle bracket, and both had general oil leaks. All was well for the second practice which was used for suspension and spoiler settings; last year both cars were identically set up, but Hulme preferred a higher spoiler this year for greater stability in corners on the tighter circuits where high maximum speed was less important.

The two cars started as they were to go on for just about every meeting of the six—1 and 2 on the grid—with McLaren fastest by 1/10th second. The only time this didn't happen was at Laguna Seca where Jim Hall managed to displace Hulme to the second row. Hulme won the race comfortably despite breaking a rocker five laps from the end, and running out of oil at the beginning of the last lap, and McLaren had a trouble-free second place.

It would have meant about 3,000 miles less travelling if the first two rounds had been transposed, because the three McLaren trucks had to head back to Norwich, New York for the next round at Bridgehampton, Long

Island. That was a trouble-free run and the mechanics had to change an engine for Hulme and change over both cars from multi-stud to centre lock front wheels; all the cars are checked over anyway, but particularly closely on the night before a race. Mechanics don't really reckon to have much sleep that night even if there isn't an engine change; there is a vast eight-page check list of every item to be looked at and sometimes crack tested—suspension, engine and gearbox parts are tested for every race. Meanwhile, McLaren and Hulme had to dash over to Monza for the Italian GP. . . .

Bridgehampton was a disaster for the McLarens. Both engines were still dripping

oil, particularly around the sump joint, which was subsequently shown to be caused by pressurization from piston ring blow-by. The first of the cracked heads had to be changed on Hulme's car, a trouble traced to faulty core-plugs which resulted in nine cracked heads from five engines. (These were later salvaged by McLaren's ingenious modification to a TiG wire feed welder to permit the use of a soft aluminium rod to build up material round the thin spots.) With new, as yet unmodified heads, Hulme's engine still wasn't quite right, so that was changed overnight before the race, but still the M8As were 1, 2 on the grid ahead of Revson and Donohue in an M6B and M6A respectively. Both Hulme

Hulme in full cry on the way to winning the last race of the series at Las Vegas.

Pit stop at Las Vegas. McLaren mechanics rip the nose section from McLaren's car after his first corner touch with Andretti; they put a new nose on and McLaren finished sixth.

and McLaren had a spell of leading but the pressure exerted by Jim Hall and Mark Donohue forced both engines to use oil rather too fast, and Hulme's suffered a rod through the crankcase when the oil ran out, while Bruce caught his almost in time although the virtually seized bearings managed to bend the crankshaft. So that was Bridgehampton, and Donohue moved into the lead of the Championship, 4 points ahead of Hulme.

With so few engines left and the possibility of running out before the end of the series, the organization had to make its first departure from schedule, sending the engine truck back to Los Angeles with three broken units, while the rest set off to Edmonton in the middle of the left hand half of Canada, going more or less past Elkhart Lake again. This journey was something of a marathon.

Up to this point the trucks had given no trouble, being quite happy to tow along at 70 m.p.h. or so without being too tiring to drive; but then on the long slog up to Edmonton, things started to go wrong. The two trucks were going in convoy when a tyre blew, due really to overloading since they had relieved the engine truck of some of its bits; pulling off the highway one truck sank to its axles and had to be pulled out by a highway patrol wagon. Having changed the tyre they then had only one spare between them and convoying was even more important; however despite protestations of unceasing mirror watching the leading truck disappeared into the distance when the second truck broke a prop-shaft, even more embarrassing, because the spare tyre was in the second one. With a repair cobbled up from racing bits, Cary Taylor and Don Beresford limped into Wisconsin to try to get a replacement. It was then that they found these trucks were rather special and no standard replacement was available; so with the help of a local machine shop a new one was built up with racing UJs. It was nearly 24 hours later that they were able to continue, having also refurbished the exhaust system which had given trouble on both trucks.

Meanwhile the leading truck had arrived at a prearranged meeting place at the Can-Am border, with no punctures fortunately, and began to wonder what had happened to their mates. Since the team had been staying at Holiday Inns wherever possible, they persuaded the manager to Telex all the group's hotels throughout America, the work of an instant; and they all replied too, one saying that they were once again on the way, so truck 1 continued to Edmonton and truck 2, after a non-stop 1,750 miles, caught them up 12 hours later still more or less on the originally plotted schedule. With such vast mileages the trucks came up to their service intervals fairly frequently; where possible they called at Chevvy dealers who were ever ready to help the racing team, and even seemed to know what the Can-Am was all about.

It may seem that with 10 days between one meeting and the first practice session of the next that mechanics get a relatively easy time once they are abroad on a series like this, but the first duty is always to the cars and if there is any time for sightseeing afterwards . . . well, they're just lucky; it isn't in the schedule. With two blown-up engines, and a diminished quantity of both mechanics and parts, there was quite a lot to do at Edmonton; the result was two complete engines and only one spare. Since the first two races when oil seemed to disappear awfully fast, Gary Knutson had been working overtime down in Los Angeles and came up with a revised piston ring package; however, before this was proved to be effective, a reserve oil tank was rigged up to retain oil under pressure so that the oil could be directed into the main dry sump reservoir just by pulling a cable, the idea being that the mechanics would see how dirty the back of the car was getting and signal the driver when to pull the plunger just in case he hadn't seen any telltale pressure drops, which don't in theory happen with dry sumps unless through temperature rise.

Edmonton, Alberta is pretty far north and was bitterly cold for the first session, so cold that a fuel injection metering unit seized and sheared its drive pin, something which had happened down at Goodwood on an equally cold day. It took a little time to trace this despite prior experience. Denny Hulme did a few laps and came in for a tyre change but

Background to victory

found the wheel seized on its hub, and it was the end of practice before this was sorted out. Hulme missed a gearchange during the second session, so the engine was stripped to check for any damage; with Edmonton being a new circuit, practice was very much an occasion for sorting suspension and gearing. However, it must have worked out well because this time Bruce and Denny were fastest equal on the front of the grid and, once again won, with Hulme first, making his fourth victory in five international races—two Can-Ams, Canadian and Italian GPs. He led from start to finish, while McLaren had to dispose of the Chaparral to finish second. The piston ring mods certainly worked and the engines were perfectly clean, but the belt and braces spare oil tank worked too because Hulme's car developed a separate oil leak and the reserve had to be tapped. Mark Donohue has finished third so the points situation was a little fraught, with Denny first at 18 points, Donohue second at 17, and McLaren third at 12, so the next round at Laguna Seca looked like being very important to the team. Bruce had had his first Can-Am win there last year, the engines were now sorted, and confidence was running fairly high. The engines incidentally had found more power particularly in the middle range, not that this was going to be much use at Laguna Seca as it turned out.

Apart from one burst tyre, once again necessitating close convoying, the two trucks had a good run down the west coast to Los Angeles and the Bartz headquarters, taking about $2\frac{1}{2}$ days for the 2,000 plus miles. Development on the cars in general hadn't stood still during the first half of the series; such work doesn't necessarily produce an improvement but at least things last a little longer. Design of the new brakes had been behind schedule before the series and the pad design had to be changed twice to prevent cracking. A stiffer anti-roll bar had also been incorporated; this isn't adjustable on the sports models as it is on the F1 cars and you have to change the complete bar. McLaren had also decided that the springs were too highly stressed, and new ones with thicker wire were flown out; bigger wheels were also sent—10in. width at front and 16 at the rear—an inch wider than the originals.

After a thorough checking over the cars were in good shape for the Monterey Grand Prix at Laguna Seca. McLaren had a tyre testing session before official practice, but this was cut short by a sudden loss of oil pressure; a screw holding a sump splash panel had found its way into the oil pump, the subsequent starvation nearly seizing the engine. This meant missing most of the first official practice session waiting for another engine to come along from Los Angeles. Then during the second session Hulme's engine gave up with water where oil should have been in sole occupation, so it was another night's hard work with an engine rebuild on top of the normal check list. This was the race at which one of the orange cars suffered the indignity of having to start on the second row of the grid with Hulme behind Jim Hall; however the Chaparral seized a starter pinion on the line, but it was Revson directly behind who got the advantage after the rolling start pace laps. This was the *wet* race, so wet that many stopped for new goggles, including both Hulme and McLaren; it was won by John Cannon in an M1B who set a fastest lap

about 3 seconds quicker than Denny Hulme, who was aquaplaning round on very big tyres and too much power; Hulme came second and McLaren salvaged a couple of points in fifth place to keep Donohue in sight in the points table.

Just before this of course, came the Watkins Glen US Grand Prix when Hulme's car had been written off after a gearbox output shaft had broken; the way the Formula 1 mechanics flew back to England, made up another car and got it back to Dallas before the convoy to Mexico is another story; documents got lost twice and even the car disappeared until it was located at San Francisco after a fog diversion, but they made it. Anyway this shaft breakage threw some doubt on the strength of the Can-Am ones, so new, stronger ones were made up at Colnbrook, and flown out to be changed before Riverside. With little travelling involved between these last three there was a little more time for relaxation and preparation; but even on these short trips there were still occasional troubles with the trucks which had by now done well over 15,000 high-speed, overladen, towing miles. One burnt out its rear brakes when a handbrake stuck partially, another hit a sudden left-turner, and even the relatively unladen engine truck burst a tyre, too.

After the sodden Laguna Seca, McLaren's car had a minor dent in the stressed, tank-carrying area, and during preliminary practice at Riverside he wiped off a corner of one of the tanks on Hulme's car. Don Beresford, who stayed out there for the whole series, fixed both these, but that was the only chassis damage throughout the six races. A couple of minor changes had been made to the rear hubs, involving new castings being flown from England, one to give a tighter fit to the wheel bearings, and another to pin the bearing sleeve.

In practice McLaren was a little worried by not getting the 3% improvement he had expected and achieved at other circuits which had a reasonable comparison with last year. He was getting only about 1%, but since most people were slower than previously the track itself must have become slower. To get maximum speed but still retain controllability through the Esses at Riverside, they had cut down on spoiler height and replaced the lost downward thrust with bigger wheels at the rear. As if on cue, Hulme's car sheared an output shaft; they had survived four races and conveniently didn't exhibit their weaknesses until new ones were actually there to be fitted. Both cars had them by the second session and once again the two M8As were sharing the front row and again Donohue and Hall were the nearest contenders.

McLaren leapt into the lead and really used the new-found power which hadn't helped at all at Laguna Seca; Bruce had a trouble-free win, his second successive at Riverside. It was Hulme who had the trouble; an involvement with a backmarker slid him across the half-tyre markers that the Americans use to define corners, and lost one corner of the nose section. He had been second at the time which would have clinched the Championship, but he needed two stops to have it taped back together, and then couldn't go really fast afterwards, dropping back to fifth place. So Hulme had 26 points, with McLaren and Donohue sharing 23.

This time, body panels had to be flown out; there was also a complete monocoque structure sitting back at Colnbrook just in case, but that wasn't needed, so two complete bodies were flown out, the presence of the second one being almost prophetic. By now the cars were getting completely reliable and not a lot

of work was needed between races. Helping the Formula 1 boys in getting the M7A to Mexico provided a temporary diversion; it's quite something when you need four people running round one corner of America trying to find a racing car. Normally the Americans are pretty efficient; instant air travel, credit telephoning, freeways, quick customs all help the business man to get things done, but occasionally things happen which make you realise just how efficient the place normally is.

This time everything was absolutely ready, and had to be, too, with Donohue and McLaren sharing second place. Las Vegas is one of the faster Can-Am circuits, with a 120 m.p.h. lap speed; both cars raised their spoilers and Hulme got through brake pads rather faster than McLaren. Again the two cars occupied the front row with McLaren in pole spot over a second faster than Hall and Donohue and about 2 seconds faster than Andretti driving a Lola 70. Just in case there was any last minute drama a spare engine was waiting on the crane, and in the pits the complete body shell was waiting with yards of tape and handfuls of rubber bungee straps. Denny Hulme cantered away from the start and won, comfortably clinching the Championship, but McLaren was less fortunate; a first-corner tiff with Andretti brought him straight back to the pits to check for damage to the fuel tanks. From the cockpit he couldn't see that the nose had been damaged and roared back into the race; he soon found it wanting to lift at speed and came straight back to the pits.

Meanwhile the mechanics had seen what was necessary and had the bonnet all ready to tape and strap into position; at this point Bruce learned that Donohue's engine had never got going on the dummy grid, so he had to get sixth to get just one point; a coil wire had broken on the Penske car, a bitter last-minute blow for the only team whose preparation was anything like the McLarens. Back into the field went McLaren determined to get his point, but then he was blackflagged—the one thing the team had forgotten was to put a mirror on the spare body panel; no recriminations . . . you just can't think of everything. It only took 17 seconds to drill four holes and pop-rivet a mirror in place, pointing presumably in roughly the right direction.

Anyway, Bruce got up to about fifth, which really does show the superiority of these cars over the rest of the field that after three pit stops he could make up that many places. But then a brake seal gave up and McLaren completed the last five laps without any stopping power, finally being dragged to a halt by mechanics spragging themselves into the ground; he had lost a place in the last few laps but still got that vital point to take the Championship second spot.

So that was the end of the second highly successful Can-Am series for the orange McLarens. Pole position every time with McLaren getting four of them to Hulme's one and one tied, four wins and only Donohue in the Penske entered McLaren anywhere near, with one win and several places. After that it was the long flog back to Boston, about 2,500 miles; the trucks, which had really performed yeoman service apart from the Briigehampton-Edmonton run, experienced a little brake fade down the Appalachians on the final run in to Boston, but that was all.

And that really is the background to victory. Not just the story of a succession of races, but the story of the bits that have to be put right behind the scenes with just a mechanic's-eye-view of the race: "Which of our men is winning?"

The McLaren Offensive
THEY CAME TO RACE

And that's how the McLaren team made it look easy at the 1968 Can-Am series

BY EOIN S. YOUNG

Bruce McLaren is a nice enough little guy, and Denny Hulme shrugs his shoulders at most things including cleaning up the Can-Am championship, but the big question is: How did the two New Zealanders manage to walk away with the races so easily?

You know how it went for them, winning four of the six races and, if you'll excuse me for saying so, only failing to win the other two because of freak things like both cars breaking at Bridge-hampton and the untimely arrival of the winter monsoon at Laguna Seca. At every race it seemed as though they had come to the track ready to go out and race whereas the other famous hotshoes were using practice as a test session to find out what they should have already known before the series started. I saw the last two races in this year's series and the superiority of the McLarens was almost embarrassing.

Early in the series the two McLarens were in oiling troubles that were cured when they junked their tweaky arrangement in favor of some more standard GM equipment in the piston ring department. Then they were back up to power par and it was an achievement to keep them in sight, never mind dice with them. Jim Hall and the Chaparral was the combination they feared most, although they knew the canny Penske would ensure Donohue was climbing the championship points ladder without risking his reputation or the motorcar in a track battle. The Penske policy paid off as Mark got 3rd-place points money. Andretti, Gurney and Revson, three men who might have fielded a challenge to the McLarens, changed engines halfway through the series when Ford made a last-ditch attempt to foil the Chevy-powered walk-over. But the aluminum 427 Ford was an oiler and the teams who accepted Ford's help must have wished they hadn't.

Bruce McLaren is a New Zealander, he's 32 and while he isn't the fastest driver in the world, he makes up for any lack of natural talent with tremendous energy and engineering ability. He's a cheerful stocky charger who looks like the boy next door, but he has been in the racing business longer than most people. He was racing an Austin 7 special in New Zealand when he was 15 and he was Grand Prix racing in Europe when he was 21. He has also been racing in American events longer than most drivers. In 1960 he drove Briggs Cunningham's prototype E-type Jaguar at Laguna Seca, and in 1961 he almost won Riverside in a Cooper Monaco. The following year he and Roger Penske shared

a Monaco fitted with a Maserati engine at Sebring. "After that race I came back to England and asked Charlie Cooper if I could run the sports car side of the Cooper Car Company because I felt sure there was a tremendous market for this type of car to use an American engine for American racing. I was convinced at that stage that sports car racing was going to really boom providing there were cars available, and that it would be a great market for an English manufacturer. Charlie turned me down flat."

Two years later McLaren bought the ex-Penske Zerex Special from John Mecom. The car had been sitting in the corner of the Mecom workshops under a dust sheet, along with an aluminum Oldsmobile engine that nobody had gotten around to fitting. After a couple of races in its original Climax-engined form, McLaren and his mechanics, Tyler Alexander and Wally Willmott, switched the engines in McLaren Racing's first workshop—an unbelievably grimy shed that they shared with an earthmoving grader! McLaren won first time out at Mosport.

The Zerex's chassis was a willowy affair, so McLaren decided to design a stiffer one. This tubular frame was completed and ready for painting one Sunday, but the only paint that could be found in sleepy England on a Sunday morning was a tin of garden gate green. So the car was christened the Jolly Green Giant. Because Bruce was still with Cooper in Formula 1 the car hadn't really been called anything, nobody daring to call it a McLaren after the rumpus there had been when Jack Brabham started to build his own cars while still at Coopers! But there was no holding McLaren now. If he could build a chassis, he could build a whole car, so he did. He was convinced that a lightweight engine with a reasonable amount of power would be the equal of a cast iron engine with more power, the equalling coming through a superior power-to-weight ratio. It took two seasons for McLaren to realize that nothing beats cubic inches, and he switched to 6-liter Chevys for 1967. The M6As with their cast iron Chevys were conventional motorcars that won because they were well sorted, reliable and had impeccable attention to detail.

The M8A by comparison was an exotic motorcar with the aluminum 7-liter Chevy V-8 hanging off the back of the monocoque. "We started running a prototype car in March this year. It was really one of last year's cars with lower profile tires and the body cut down. Then we tried a cast iron 427 engine in it, a liter bigger than the engine we ran last year. When we first offered the engine up to the chassis, it looked like an engineering impossibility, but bearing in mind

TYLER ALEXANDER PHOTOS

McLaren Offensive

our Formula 1 construction with the stressed Ford engine, our Can-Am solution was obvious. The old chassis was cut in half and the engine became the rear of the car with the rear suspension hanging off a subframe. With this mobile test rig we tried a dry-sump setup, wings, new brakes, and all the while the new M8A was taking shape on the drawing board."

The initial test with the first of the new cars was on July 16th, but England's traditionally showery summer weather interrupted continuous concentrated development. Bruce crashed one wet morning at Goodwood knocking a corner off the car and setting progress back even further. While development on the first chassis and the construction of Denny's chassis was coming along in England, Gary Knutson, an ex-Chaparral man from away back, and Colin Beanland, a Kiwi who had been McLaren's racing mechanic in 1958, were pressing on with dry sump development on an aluminum 7-liter Chevy V-8. Initially they worked on the engines in a shop in Capistrano Beach, Calif., but later they shifted in with Al Bartz when he moved to bigger premises in Van Nuys. By now McLaren's Engine Division also employed American Lee Muir.

Back at the ranch, Don Beresford (ex-Aston Martin and Lola) was supervising the chassis construction and was later to take over Denny's car working with Kiwi ex-Brabham mechanic Cary Taylor. Tyler Alexander was crew chief on Bruce's car, Bill Eaton was sheet metal bender par excellence, Haig Alltounian came in from Shelby, and Frank Zimmerman was taken on as a Gopher. "The best gopher we've ever had," comments McLaren.

Teddy Mayer as team manager was generally trying to be in three places at once with a worried frown and his yellow legal pad on which he painstakingly recorded all details of testing and development. Phil Kerr (Brabham's ex-manager) looked after Formula 1 operations back in England.

In the drawing office, Jo Marquart was a new face. Of Swiss birth, he was immediately christened "The Foreigner" by a bunch of Americans and New Zealanders working in England. Marquart had left Switzerland to become assistant to the chief engineer of the Scottish Omnibus Company in Edinburgh, leaving there to go to Lotus and moving on to

McLaren Racing when Robin Herd joined Cosworth. "Hanging the engine off the back of the monocoque was pretty much my idea," says McLaren. "Gordon Coppuck and I worked out the rear bulkhead, the suspension detail was a group effort, the front half of the chassis was largely Jo's work, and I worked out the body shape and general layout with Jim Clark of Specialised Mouldings."

Team Manager Mayer burst in on one design huddle over new hubs, blustering that he had to have cars to ship out in August and he couldn't race just hubs and wheelbearings! The Foreigner won instant fame and affection on the factory floor when he replied, "Better we race hubs and wheelbearings than drawings only . . ."

McLaren reckons his Can-Am offensive—it was planned like a military campaign, let's face it—cost around $180,000. "It cost us about $80,000 to run the engine division, and we'll probably recover about $25,000 on the sale of engines we have left. The cars cost us something in the region of $50,000 each and these will remain on the books as assets worth probably $25,000. We won about $180,000 altogether, so if we were able to sell the cars and all the engines we would have a profit of about $100,000."

McLaren illustrates his escalation into the successful big time with a story from early in this year's series when one

McLaren Offensive

of Shelby's crew borrowed McLaren's portable engine hoist. "I was reminded that it used to be us who did the borrowing and it used to be us who ran the little setup with one car. This time we had five chassis men, five engine men, three spare engines, two cars, three trucks, 4500 lb of spares and even a radio telephone!"

It appeared in the final races of the series that the works McLarens were running against very weak opposition. "We were very surprised. Our actual improvement over last year's car had been slight, working on our testing yardstick at Goodwood. I eventually managed to get the new car down to 1 min, 12.7 sec, in a Banzai effort which at the time was calculated by me as an attempt to instill confidence in the new car. We'd had the old car with the cast iron engine and everything just jury-rigged on it down to 1:13 regularly, and the previous year we'd done 1:13.4 with the 6-liter engine, so our actual improvement was under 1.5 percent and this was the sort of improvement in lap times we saw at Riverside and Las Vegas. On other circuits we had almost a 3 percent improvement and yet it wasn't until the final races that we were back up to power after solving our piston ring problems.

"We expected Gurney and Shelby to give us much more opposition. Gurney had proved that his Weslake-headed Ford was capable of producing more than 550 horsepower for 500 miles at Indy and we felt sure that he would get 580 bhp out of his fairly light engine over 200 miles with relatively little effort. In the standard McLaren chassis this engine would have been very quick. We figured Dan in his combination would be a big threat but it didn't materialize. I suppose during our development season we were more worried about what Hall was doing than anyone else. I must say I was surprised—surprised and delighted— at the lack of competition."

McLaren was also rather surprised at the low standard of preparation. "There is *no* standard of preparation other than in the Penske area. In my opinion there is a regrettable tendency for the average American mechanic with very little background to feel he knows it all and never be worried," says McLaren. "Our chief mechanic Tyler Alexander is fond of saying 'Hell, I'm worried all the time—anything could go wrong with the damned thing' and he doesn't presume to have an answer at his fingertips to every situation like some other crews pretend to have. Penske's people are good because of Penske. There are some good mechanics on the series, but there are also some who think they are very good—they could take lessons from any of two dozen Formula 1 racing mechanics who wouldn't presume to know everything . . ."

Talking about improvements he would like to see in the Can-Am series, McLaren mentions standardization of starting procedure. "I'd like to see minute boards before the start with a 5-min board, 2-min and then 1-min so that drivers can start their engines sometime between the 2-min

and 1-min boards and then at 1-min everyone is cleared off the grid and at zero the pace car pulls away. Las Vegas was a shambles. Nobody knew when to start engines, in fact Moss took off in the pace car a couple of times and then stopped. But that's only a detail thing. Taken overall the Can-Am series is definitely on its way to being the greatest thing that has ever happened to motor racing. I think we should continue to have no limitations on engine size and as few rules and regulations as possible. The fact that the cars have all-enveloping bodies has led to relatively safe racing. If we had all been in single seaters in Turn 1 at Las Vegas, it would have been terrifying. Of course there is always the possibility that it wouldn't have happened then because people wouldn't have been game to tangle, but I reckon sports cars are generally safer in the event of the odd fracas. Sports cars are more spectacular, and more important, there's room on which to put decals and other messages from your sponsor!" grins McLaren.

McLaren Racing enjoyed financial backing from Gulf and Goodyear on the series and both Hulme and McLaren basked in yards of prime print publicity as the series progressed. Features in *Time* and *Sports Illustrated* plus local press helped to make the two New Zealanders better known in the United States than they are in England. McLaren has certainly been on television more often on the West Coast than he has in either England or New Zealand!

The McLaren team finished the series in good shape with the drivers reversing last year's positions, Hulme winning and McLaren taking second place. "In a way we did a little better than last year. First and second was what we had hoped for but we weren't very confident about it. We had

pole position at every race this year, whereas Gurney beat us once last year in the final couple of races, but this year we had completely licked our engine problems and we were both in top form as the series ended. So at the moment we're feeling good, but I hasten to add we're not complacent. We're well aware that this season was probably our last easy one. That big Ferrari didn't get a chance to show its race pace, but I followed it in practice and its power-to-weight seemed pretty close to ours. Chris could run down the straight with almost identical acceleration and top speed to us. Brabham was at Vegas nosing around so you can reckon he'll be chasing greenies next year with a new car and Gurney has quit Formula 1 to concentrate on Can-Am and Indy racing, so he isn't going to be hanging about. I even hear talk that Honda is considering trying its hand at Can-Am. Then there's the new 2H Chaparral. So you see what I meant about having had our last easy season. . ."

The Chevy domination of Can-Am has become an embarrassment to Ford since General Motors is supposedly out of racing and Ford is supposedly very much in, and rumor said that McLaren might be tempted to use new aluminum 429 Fords in his cars next year. I asked McLaren if he planned to can his engine development program on the lightweight Chevies in favor of the new Ford. "No. No and no comment." When McLaren doesn't have anything to say on any given subject you can assume that the issue is fraught with deep political and financial undertones, and Brucie isn't about to be drawn into discussion about it. Getting information about 1969 plans was like pulling teeth. Jim Hall and John Surtees are conversationalists by comparison with McLaren when he wants to clam up. "Plans are being made. I'm sure if I told you at the moment, you'd say 'v-e-r-y interesting.' We don't intend to expand our California operation, in fact we are bringing everything back to England to set up shop with our own dyno and test house."

Mixing Can-Am and Formula 1 is nigh on impossible as Gurney, Surtees and Ferrari discovered. McLaren was able to avoid disaster by flooding the projects alternately with staff, but even he had problems. At one stage only one mechanic was working on the Formula 1 cars while the others slaved to complete the Can-Am cars for shipment.

Did McLaren plan to favor the extended Can-Am series next year at the expense of his Formula 1 effort? "We're going to work it 50/50 right down the line except that we plan to do our own engine development in Can-Am which means that in total we'll have more people on the Can-Am project."

Denny Hulme, fellow countryman and Formula 1 world champion in 1967, plans to drive for McLaren again next year. The pair get on well together, Hulme respecting McLaren's urge to design and build his own cars while reckoning himself to be a better driver than Bruce, and Bruce happy to acknowledge the point if it makes for a smooth running operation and lets him concentrate on new ideas.

Team manager Mayer is a 24-hour-a-day operator seemingly pledged to transfer McLaren sketches and scrawled notes into race-winning reality. McLaren puts as many hours in at his 10,000-sq-ft Colnbrook factory near London Airport as his staff does. His work day starts at around 8:30 a.m. and seldom finishes before 8 p.m. in the evening.

For McLaren the actual races are just the top of the iceberg—but he's beginning to notice that his efforts are making the berg turn green. Dollar green.

Left, the M8A chassis with 427 V-8 Chev engine hanging off the back of the monocoque tub. Above, Tyler Alexander, McLaren's chief sports car mechanic, has also found it helps to pray a little. Right, Gary Knutson with the help of Lee Muir was responsible for the McLaren 427 Chev engines. Below, the boss at work.

Ferrari

ENGINE rear, 4 stroke; cylinders: 12, Vee-slanted at 60°; bore and stroke: 3.62 × 3.07 in, 92 × 78 mm; engine capacity: 379.66 cu in, 6,222 cu cm; compression ratio: 10.5; max power: 620 hp at 7,000 rpm; specific power: 100 hp/l; cylinder block: light alloy, wet liners; cylinder head: light alloy, flat combustion chambers; crankshaft bearings: 7; valves: 4 per cylinder, overhead, slanted in sharp Vee; camshafts: 2 per cylinder block, overhead; lubrication: gear pump, dry sump, oil cooler; carburation: Lucas indirect injection; fuel feed: electric pumps; cooling system: water.

TRANSMISSION driving wheels: rear; clutch: dry multi-plates; gearbox: mechanical; gears: 4 + reverse; gear lever: side; final drive: cylindrical bevel, limited slip.

CHASSIS mixed tubular trellis frame, reinforced with riveted and bonded light sheet, parts of body in fibreglass; front suspension; independent, wishbones, coil springs, hydraulic telescopic dampers; rear suspension: transverse leading arms, torque arms, coil springs, anti-roll bar, hydraulic telescopic dampers.

STEERING rack-and-pinion.

BRAKES disc, dual circuit.

ELECTRICAL EQUIPMENT voltage: 12 V; alternator; ignition distributor: Marelli; headlamps: 2.

DIMENSIONS AND WEIGHT wheel base: 96.46 in, 2,450 mm; front track: 63.11 in, 1,603 mm; rear track: 62.63 in, 1,591 mm; overall length: 165.35 in, 4,200 mm; overall width: 88.19 in, 2,240 mm; overall height: 35.04 in, 890 mm; weight: 1,543 lb, 700 kg; tyres: 4.90/13.90 × 15 front, 6.00/15.50 × 15 rear; fuel tank capacities: 35.20 imp gal, 42.24 US gal, 160 l.

PERFORMANCE max speed: 211.3 mph, 340 km/h.

As a result of the well-known controversy over the regulations which fixed a limit of 3 litres for the engine capacity of prototypes, while engines of up to 5 litres were permitted for sports cars (which were practically the same but with the added condition that at least 50 had to be built), in 1968 Ferrari did not take part in prototype racing, and therefore the experimental P 5 shown at the Geneva Motor Show was nothing more than an exercise in coachbuilding. On the other hand, when the racing season was already well-advanced, a really exceptional car was constructed – the 612, which is powered by the largest engine Ferrari have ever made, both in engine capacity and power. This car, which is still in the experimental stage, has taken part in various races in the Can Am series, and the construction of this large engine is certainly the forerunner of further developments in the field of the manufacture of GT cars.
It is interesting to note how well this engine illustrates the technical progress that has been made for, although it is not much larger than the F 1 three-litre and no larger than the old five-litre, it can produce much greater power, with a decidedly improved power-weight ratio.

THE BIGGEST FERRARI OF THEM ALL

The 612 Can-Am's short but promising debut at Las Vegas

BY JONATHAN THOMPSON

FINALLY KEEPING FAITH with the thousands of Can-Am fans who had expected it at every race since Edmonton in late September, the Ferrari 612 reached Las Vegas on November 8, the Friday before the Stardust GP. At the eleventh hour, Scuderia Ferrari fielded the largest, most powerful and fastest racing car it had ever built.

Team manager Franco Gozzi, racing engineer Mauro Forghieri, chief mechanic Giulio Borsari and three assistants, backed up by several of Bill Harrah's automotive crew, had two days to make a dent in the world's most lucrative road racing series. The engine was no problem. The 6.2-liter V-12, based on the 3-liter Formula 1 unit, was proven and strong. Starting it up was as simple as turning on a switch, it idled like a boulevard unit, and driver Chris Amon was able to blast out of the pits on successive practice outings with no apparent warm-up. Gone was the high-pitched howl of the smaller engines, but the 612's angry bellow was still the most distinctive sound at the track.

Running less than 30 laps during the Saturday and Sunday-morning practice sessions, the 612 showed excellent acceleration, a top speed of about 185 mph and fairly good handling, although it was not completely stable in braking. This was a real problem in Turn 8, where a lot of time was lost to the more competitive cars. After the Saturday qualifying sessions, Amon had placed the car ninth on the grid, not earth-shaking, but ahead of 28 other cars, including such respected season-long campaigners as Titus, Motschenbacher, Parsons, Hayes and Cannon. Gozzi felt another two days of sorting would have made the Ferrari fully competitive. As it was, Forghieri only had time for minor adjustments to the suspension, new ducting to the rear brakes, the addition of six spoiler tabs—two on each front fender, two on the tail—and pep talks with Chris Amon.

The race need not be described. After coming 8000 miles the Ferrari, through no fault of its own, covered less than a quarter-mile of the first lap. The tangling of McLaren and Andretti in Turn 1 sent most of the pack off in the desert. Amon skillfully avoided hitting anybody, but the Ferrari, with dirt in the throttle slides, was one of two cars which would not restart.

Aside from Ferrari's preoccupation with the Formula 1 and 2 cars, the main reason the 612 did not appear earlier in the series was the failure of the German maker of its head gaskets to deliver them on time. The first track tests took place at Monza where the reputed 620 bhp seemed to be fully in evidence. The final shakedowns were performed at Modena; the 612 did not break the 50-sec barrier as predicted but came close with 50.8. Much cleaner than most Can-Am cars, the Ferrari is notable for its great width—nearly seven feet—and its mid-positioned wing, which incorporates two pedal-operated braking flaps working in conjunction with a single perforated flap in front.

During a very elegant Saturday-night dinner hosted by Gozzi and Harrah's automotive chief Lee Jellison, Forghieri told me that two Can-Am cars would be campaigned in 1969. The present weight of 1750 lb will be reduced 200 lb by fiberglass body panels and lighter engine castings. *Aspettiamo e vediamo!*

Chris Amon waits while mechanic adjusts rear anti-roll bar and shock absorbers.

Rear suspension, above, has single upper and lower arms, radius rods, coil spring/shock units, anti-roll bar. Upper A-arms are used in front. Radiator air goes through body past tire.

Wing, above, resembles F1 type but incorporates brake flaps at rear edge (see also opposite page). Below, at Modena, aerodynamicist Caliri and Ing. Forghieri supervise bleeding.

88

FERRARI 612 CAN-AM

PETE COLTRIN PHOTO

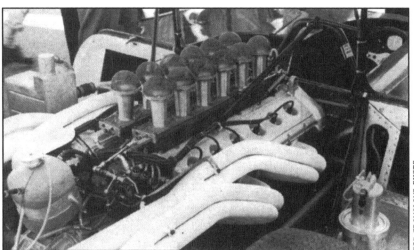

BOB TRONOLONE PHOTO

PETE COLTRIN PHOTO

SPECIFICATIONS (UNOFFICIAL)—FERRARI 612 CAN-AM

Engine...............60° V-12, dohc
Bore x stroke, mm............92 x 78
Displacement, cc................6222
Compression ratio.............10.5:1
Bhp @ rpm..............620 @ 7000
Carburetion....Lucas indirect injection
Ignition................single Marelli
Transmission......4-speed in unit with differential
Brakes.......Girling disc, outboard f/r
Wheels............Ferrari 15-in alloy
Tires.....Firestone, 6.00/13.50-15 front 6.00/15.50-15 rear
Wing.....mid-mounted, w/brake flaps

Front suspension: independent by upper A-arms, single lower arms, coil springs w/telescopic shock absorbers, anti-roll bar
Rear suspension: independent by single upper and lower arms, radius rods, coil springs w/telescopic shock absorbers, anti-roll bar
Weight, lb.....................1750
Wheelbase, in...................96.4
Track, front/rear...........59.8/61.1
Length........................160.5
Width.........................82.6
Height.......roll bar, 35.0; wing, 48.4

The 1969 CanAm champion?

John Bolster visits McLaren's Colnbrook factory to look at Bruce's latest Group 7 machinery

THE CanAm Series this year is greatly increased in scope and the season begins much earlier. Instead of the first race being in September, the battle starts at Mosport this Sunday. For the McLaren team, who are also running two Formula 1 cars in the World Championship, this will mean a fantastic programme of airline bookings as Bruce and Denny commute between one circus and the other, especially as new grand prix cars with four-wheel-drive are about to appear. I therefore went along to the factory at Colnbrook last week to see the CanAm cars on the eve of their departure, and to find out something about the organisation behind this onslaught.

With the earlier start and many more races —11 instead of six this year—it was decided that there was hardly time to build new cars and develop them, especially as the existing ones are more than competitive. Nevertheless, the opportunity has been taken to make some important changes and the machines have been reconstructed throughout, using the knowledge gained in their last extremely successful season.

The chassis is a two-bulkhead monocoque, using the engine as a stressed member, with glass-fibre body panels. It is of the type sometimes referred to as a semi-monocoque, because it does not extend right over the top but forms a pair of fuselages united by the undershield, the construction being in aluminium sheet with steel bulkheads. Auxiliary tubular members reinforce the engine and transmission assembly, ensuring in particular that a cracked bell housing would not result in the car having a broken back—an important safety precaution.

The independent four-wheel suspension resembles that of a grand prix car, with wishbones and helical springs in front, the big anti-roll torsion bar being tubular to save weight. Behind, there are lower reversed wishbones and short upper tubular members, fore and aft location being by the usual long paired radius arms which feed their loads into the rear bulkhead. The helical springs are reinforced by a lighter torsion bar, solid in this case. The hefty tube which forms the roll-over bar is much lighter than it looks, being of titanium, and the same material is used for a small tubular structure behind the gearbox which carries the stoplights. It goes without saying that the steering is by rack and pinion.

The brakes are 12 ins Lockheeds with ventilated discs and no servo, each one having four pistons to apply two pads. Cooling air is fed into the eyes of the discs and exhausted through the spokes of the road wheels by turbo action. In front the air is picked up at the nose of the car on either side of the radiator, feeding to the discs through flexible hoses that describe a U-shape. At the rear the air enters a couple of holes in the spoiler, feeding down through hoses to the centre of the discs. The centre-locking peg-drive wheels are cast in L127 magnesium, carrying 15-ins Goodyear tyres. The rim widths are 10 ins at the front and 17 ins at the rear.

Goodyear also manufacture the rubber fuel tanks, which are carried in the side sponsons of the chassis and contain a total of 62 gallons. McLarens have always had an elaborate system of pipes to prevent the fuel from being thrown from one tank to the other by centrifugal force on corners. Even greater elaboration of pipes and valves now ensures that every drop of petrol, to the last half pint, can be used up.

The top panels, which give the body its shape, are of glass fibre strengthened with carbon filaments. The whole car is in the form of a wedge, with a built-in spoiler at the back. A wing just above the body will be used if permitted, but if not an extra spoiler can be added, at the cost of 5 mph or so. The engine radiator is mounted in the nose, leaning forward, with a small header tank to the left front of the power unit. The body is now cut away behind the front wheels for better air extraction. The engine oil radiators are on each side of the rear bulkhead, with channels in the body to give them air. The transmission oil radiator is in the centre of the rear spoiler, with the brake cooling ducts on either side of it. The windscreen is of Plexidor, a yellowish German plastic which is almost unbreakable, unlike the usual material, which cracks easily under tough racing conditions.

The V8 engines are light alloy Chevrolets of 7-litres capacity. They are now built in England at the McLaren works, to avoid administrative problems. To achieve reliability, every component is examined and tested exhaus-

The front suspension (left) with massive four-pot calipers for the ventilated disc brakes, and the rear suspension (right), with giant BRD drive shafts.

tively. For example, each connecting rod is hardness tested on receipt, which means scrapping 5 to 10 per cent of them, and then magnafluxed, which entails the loss of another 5 to 10 per cent. It is then polished, shot peened and straightened, every other component, including nuts and bolts, having to undergo a similar series of tests and treatments. It will be understood that this is an immensely lengthy process, and as 10 engines are required for the CanAm series, the work and expense can be imagined.

A little more power has been obtained since last year, with an even wider usable rev range. A slightly reduced stroke has been countered with a bigger bore, the dimensions being of the order of 4¼ ins x 3¾ ins, neglecting decimals. The power output is 635 bhp at 7000 rpm, an immense speed for an engine with pistons like bloody great flower pots and valves like small umbrellas, but in spite of the single camshaft, pushrods and rockers, it will safely go up to 7500 rpm and the ignition is arranged to cut out at 7600 rpm. A vertical magneto is still used, but a pulse system on the front of the crankshaft feeds into a transistor box, which earths the mag if the revs go too high.

Fuel injection is by Lucas, feeding downstream just above the butterflies of the McLaren magnesium manifold. Butterflies are used because slides sometimes stick, and what is 1 bhp when you have 635 already? The injector pump is driven by gears from the magneto driveshaft. There are three scavenge pumps and one pressure pump for the dry sump lubrication system, assembled as one unit and driven by a toothed belt. Two very large and powerful warning lights blaze forth from the instrument panel if the oil pressure ever drops below 40 lbs per sq in. The water pump is also driven by a toothed belt. The light alloy sump itself, like the rocker covers, is a McLaren production, with two scavenge pump outlets at the rear and one at the front.

There is only a 10 ins flywheel, which means a very small starter ring. Therefore, a spur-gear reduction is mounted on the starter motor. CanAm cars are not driven in the dark and magneto ignition supplies its own current, so there is no electrical system, apart from a battery for the starter, though it is permitted to plug in a lead from the pits for all starts off the circuit. Although the cars are technically two-seater sports cars, they are actually less "civilised" than Formula 1 single-seaters, but there is far less to go wrong, of course.

The vast V8 develops an unbelievable 560 ft/lbs of torque, so the transmission must be rugged. A Borg and Beck triple-plate clutch copes easily, and the gearbox is the big Hewland LG500, giving four speeds. There is no need to have five speeds because CanAm races have rolling starts. A typical set of ratios is : 1st 115 mph, 2nd 142 mph, 3rd 161 mph and 4th 184 mph. Most of the circuits used have short straights, the fastest probably being Riverside with a maximum approaching 195 mph. A terminal speed of 215 mph would probably be the limit, as the body is shaped to give downward thrust rather than for maximum penetration. From the gearbox, the power is transmitted through BRD roller spline shafts, no problem being experienced here in spite of the immense torque. It has been found that F1 cars are just as hard on driveshafts with only half the torque, presumably because they have an inferior ratio of sprung to unsprung weights, causing wheel bouncing and shock loading.

Nevertheless, it seems odd that these 7-litre machines have absolutely no wheelspin problem and could even do with more power, yet four-wheel-drive is to be adopted for the 3-litre Formula 1 McLaren. Evidently the less favourable ratio of sprung to unsprung weight of the single seater, and the absence of any downward thrust from an open-wheeled unstreamlined racing car, ensures that the extra traction will be worthwhile, though the ad-

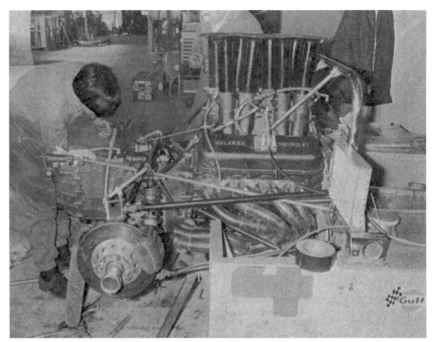

The 7-litre lump breathes out 635 bhp and 560 lbs/ft of torque, and has a Hewland LG500 to cope with it all.

The front brake cooling hoses are U-shaped round the front suspension to feed into the eyes of the discs.

vantage may be fairly marginal. Details of the new F1 car cannot be published yet, but the design is 100 per cent McLaren, and it appears likely that enough weight can be saved by improved techniques to incorporate four-wheel-drive without making the machine any heavier. At the present moment, it seems more than possible that the team will have a four-wheel-drive car at Zandvoort.

I was most impressed with my visit to the McLaren factory and I am very grateful to Bruce McLaren, Phil Kerr and Teddy Mayer for all the trouble they took on my behalf. In spite of the rush to get the cars finished they were beautiful engineering jobs, and I am so glad that Bruce has banned chromium plating, using stainless steel for all bright parts. Naturally, the body panels are in the famous orange yellow.

The 8000 rpm tachometer is no affectation, for with its new short stroke the big V8 is safe to 7500 rpm.

91

PETE LYONS examines THE CHAPARRAL 2H

AT long last Jim Hall has allowed his latest Supercar out for a run. The Chaparral 2H has gone through nearly two years of tortuous development; in all likelihood, had all the interim versions received letters we would be working on another alphabet by now!

Very broadly, the Chaparral 2H is conventional in layout; mid-engined, two-wheel drive, wishbone front suspension, and, like a true Chaparral, the transmission is a three-speed clutchless affair, and there is a flipper at the back. Its two most startling features are its chassis, which is a full monocoque of glassfibre whose outer surface is the body shape, and its rear suspension, which in principle is a de Dion axle pivoted in the middle to allow toe-in changes as the suspension flexes.

Starting from the fact of the great aerodynamic "dirtiness" of conventional Group 7 cars, Jim Hall laid out for the 2H a very slick, clean envelope in a spindle shape. Nothing non-essential pokes into the airstream, and where there is an unavoidable break in the body line, as at the cockpit or wheel arches, the body picks up again behind the interruption in a gentle curve to try to re-establish laminar flow. Growing from the sloping floor of the duct into the rear-mounted radiator are little vanes; these are Vortex Generators, and their function is to reach up out of the sluggish boundary layer into fast moving air, swirl some of it down toward the surface and help the sluggish air move into the radiator. As Hall puts it, "they energise the boundary layer." The net result is to keep the duct itself as small as possible. The same result could be achieved with a scoop, but this way offers less drag and is more "elegant."

The inlets in the driver's head fairing do no more than add air to the radiator flow, those on either side of the top of the engine cover feed the lay-down fuel injectors, those on the side simply open into the engine bay, while the rear brakes (outboard) are cooled from either side of the main radiator duct. The two unmatched Naca inlets on the sloping nose cool the driver, while hidden under the nose is a scooping inlet which exhausts above through a hinged flap—or rather, it is intended to, but the flap, which is designed to act in concert with the tail flipper, was left unconnected for Edmonton. This tail flipper works like previous Chaparral wings, that is pressure of the driver's left foot levels it for less drag. Jim Hall pioneered the idea of mounting a wing directly onto the rear hub carriers; now that everyone else has gone that route the 2H appears with the wing firmly strutted to the body, and hung out over the back where it will have most leverage. Up front are two canard fins, evidently additions to the original design as they are riveted on.

The full monocoque hull is an assembly of glassfibre structures to which everything is bolted and which itself forms the body shape. Hatches here and there provide necessary access, and the large engine cover is completely unstressed and removable. The engine

itself is stressed in compression to help make up the chassis, with a big aluminium strut coming down from each "shoulder" area to the engine at the bellhousing region. While the monocoque stops behind the driver on the upper side, on the bottom it continues as a belly pan which takes lateral loadings at the back of the chassis. Behind the very bulky rear suspension the chassis flares out and up, where a structure of panels and tubes laces the suspension links and wing struts to the transmission case.

The glassfibre is something from the space industry. Called "Pre-Preg," it comes as cloth with the resin already worked into the fibre. Hall describes its raw state as being sticky, and enthuses about the ease of laying it up into moulds. The lay-up is next put into a large curing oven (a recent addition to the Chaparral Cars compound in Midland) and emerges as an immensely strong, light structure. The big advantage of all this is, of course, the close control possible of resin/cloth ratio.

The 2H's giant jointed de Dion beam.

The front suspension is essentially conventional; the wishbone pivot points are canted aft to coincide with the centre-of-pitch and give anti-dive. The one wrinkle is that the coil spring hangs the chassis weight not directly onto the lower wishbone but onto a strut that angles down from the middle of the steering upright, thus allowing wishbone and balljoint to be lighter. The bottom of this strut also picks up the forged end of the anti-roll bar, and there is a third small member which keeps all this in line. Besides allowing an all-up unsprung weight a bit lower than a conventional layout, Hall recounts two further benefits: there is a bit more room for the wheel (for the track of this machine is very narrow) and, since the strut on which the spring hangs is adjustable for length, the ride height of the chassis can be altered without disturbing the spring.

At the back is the difficult bit. We see first a large box structure of aluminium plate which arches from the wheel hubs over the transmission, a "C" with cusps down. This is a de Dion beam, located in two planes by Watt's linkages. The lateral Watts linkage is at the very bottom, and the small central pivot

of this bolts to the bottom of the transmission, thus establishing the chassis roll centre at that point some 4 ins above the ground. Halfshafts run out to the hubs and brakes, but the track is so narrow that the outer universal joints are right in the centre of the brake discs, well outside the hub bearings. The springs go up from the bottom of the "C" to machined brackets on the cylinder heads; here also are brought links to the anti-roll bar, which runs between the heads and is scarcely a foot long.

Now for the wild part. The axle beam is split in the middle, hinged by a massive pivot in a vertical axis, thus allowing the wheels to change their toe-angle. The motion is controlled by a link which runs from the pivot point over a carefully calculated distance and angle down and aft to the chassis extension behind the gearbox. Hall calls this "the steering arm," and it is so arranged that as the chassis squats or rolls the pivot moves aft and the wheels toe in. On the front side of the pivot is a small cylindrical travel limiter. This whole system is called by Hall a Semi-axle. An important feature is that, to a considerable extent, the car's behaviour in roll is independent from its behaviour in bump. It rolls in a corner rather more than a conventional chassis, but even at maximum cornering force there is, Hall says, some considerable bump travel left.

To the 15-ins wheels are fitted Firestone Indy tyres, a "directional" tyre by virtue of having a somewhat harder compound in the outside shoulder—but curiously Hall mounts these with the hard shoulder inboard. Typical tread widths are 11 ins front, 15½ ins rear. The exhaust system curls around and exits sideways, thus avoiding the bulky rear suspension. In the cockpit Surtees sits with the steering rack under his knees.

The first thing everyone notices about the car is the window let into each body side. Closer inspection reveals these to be doors—after all, the FIA requires doors—but why are they transparent? Look at the top of the cockpit. There is no opening for the passenger. Now you and I know there is no point in worrying about a passenger in these machines, but the FIA cherishes a dream.

Around came the Scrutineers, led eagerly by McLaren's Teddy Mayer, and said, but Jim, there is no hole for the passenger's head. Well, why should there be, said Jim, this isn't a roadster, it's a coupe. Franz, enter the car and show the gentlemen that this is a coupe. See, gentlemen, Franz has plenty of room in the passenger seat, he is very comfortable, he even has windows to look out of, like in any coupe. Now, you may notice that our particular driver has expressed that he would rather sit somewhat higher than the passenger, a peculiarity of his, and so we have generously cut a hole in the roof of our coupe so that he may put his head out.

Teddy Mayer was mumbling something about a windscreen wiper, but the scrutineers had already affixed a Passed sticker, and it was too late.

ABOUT THE SPORT
BY JAMES T. CROW

SOME GOOD NEWS so far as this year's Can-Am series is concerned is the announcement by Porsche that they will be fielding a contender in the balance of this year's series.

The car, basically, is the 12-cyl, 4.5-liter Porsche 917 built for Le Mans but now fitted with roadster rather than coupe bodywork and called the 917 PA.

The car will be campaigned by the John von Neumann racing organization from California and the team will be managed by Richie Ginther. The effort will be coordinated by Porsche's director of racing, Rico Steinemann, and the Porsche-Audi Division will be the sponsor.

With about 580 bhp at 8500 rpm and weighing about 1640 lb, the 917 PA will be a bit short of power compared to the 7-liter Chevrolet-engined cars used by the McLaren team but it should have good reliability and a batch of consistent seconds, thirds and fourths could very well result in a very decent overall record in the final tabulation of points.

The 917 PA is scheduled to appear at the next Can-Am race—Mid-Ohio—and the driver will be Jo Siffert.

Hulme's Riverside Can Am

Lined up in the California sunshine are the works McLaren M8Bs which have won Bruce McLaren Motor Racing their third CanAm Series running this year. At Riverside Bruce was out of luck and crashed, but Denny lapped the whole field to keep the record straight.

Porsche 917 PA. Roadster version of the 4.5-liter, 12-cyl Le Mans car with 580 bhp at 8500 rpm will run in this year's Can-Am series.

Bruce McLaren is currently enjoying his third astonishingly successful season in CanAm racing with the M8B.

Background to success —

George Bolthoff, CanAm engine builder

By DOUG NYE

A CE engine builders are few and far between, but one such unsung hero is the man behind this year's McLaren domination of the CanAm series—George Bolthoff. His interest in performance cars and in extracting the utmost from otherwise stock power units began in high school back in California in the early 'fifties. There he built his version of the traditional "flat-head Ford roadster" hotrod, and took it out once a month to the dry lakes to pit his preparation and driving skill against others of the *genre*.

Service in the US Army intervened from 1954 to 1956, and on his "release" he went to work as a rocket engineer for North American aircraft. Engine tuning and car preparation were still a consuming interest, but George soon found that drag race meet-

ings every weekend in the centre of town offered more interest than salt lake record runs once a month 200 miles out in the desert. Rocketry continued as bread-and-butter employment, and from '59 to '63 the amateur drag-racer worked on the beginnings of the Apollo lunar landing project at Lockheeds. So successful was he becoming at blasting along quarter-mile strips that his winnings began to top his basic salary, and so he left Lockheed to concentrate on professional drag-racing. George had built his own sling-shot chassis, and prepared 800-plus bhp Chevrolet and Chrysler gas-class engines to propel it. His rocket experience seems to have come in useful, for the name George Bolthoff began to appear in national gasser record lists as he set "seven-ninety seven ee-tees for a one-

ninety-seven terminal."

He was making his drag-racing pay particularly well by preparing and maintaining his own car and engines, driving his own transporter-*cum*-caravan to meetings all over the nation and generally holding expenses down to a minimum. But when George married, some certain security became vital and so he retired from driving and went to work for Jim Travers at Traco Engineering, preparing and building race engines. There he spent three years doing all the engine assembly work for Roger Penske's TransAm Camaro and USRRC Group 7 championship contenders as well as for Traco's other, less august, customers. At the beginning of this year he heard that Gary Knutson was returning to Chaparral after a very successful spell with McLaren,

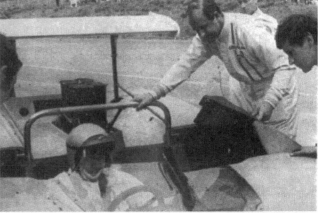

Bruce looks on as the 7-litre McLaren Chevvy is prepared for testing in the Colnbrook factory before the 1969 series (left). Bruce warms up the M8B for practice at the first of the 1969 Can-Ams, at Mosport Park, while Denny looks on (right).

George Bolthoff, man behind the stock-block CanAm conversions for McLarens, offers up a finished cylinder head to the de-burred ZL-1 7-litre block.

John Nicholson carries out a compression test on one of the recent Mid-Ohio CanAm engines; optimum compression is 12:1.

and February 1969 saw the family Bolthoff moving lock, stock and barrel to England, and George taking overall responsibility for the team's CanAm motive power.

McLaren Racing's Colnbrook base lies under the west-bound flight-path from Heathrow Airport and there a small engine assembly shop is staffed by Bolthoff and his Kiwi assistan John Nicholson. Basis for the Can-Am mills is the Chevrolet ZL-1 427 cu ins (7-litre) high-performance option. This is an all-aluminium unit offered as the ultimate in Corvette goodies and selling over the counter for around $3000 in the States. For the CanAm programme, eight of these were purchased, and the modifications made are surprisingly minor in view of the successes they have achieved.

Starting with the block, the castings are generally cleaned up and "de-burred" to remove casting flashes and any other possible cracking sources. The stock heads have their exhaust ports smoothed a little, and the intakes are carefully matched to the specially made McLaren manifolding. The intake ports are straightened and polished, but evidently the basic design leaves little room for drastic improvement. Finally the combustion chambers, which are "semi-hemi" in form, are matched to the bores and to each other for volume, with an optimum 12:1 compression ratio.

Reciprocating parts are surprisingly stock items in the main, starting with Chevrolet's standard ZL-1 crankshaft. This runs in high-performance Chev main bearings but the bearing caps are secured by specially-made high-grade bolts. Another optional item used is a high performance crankshaft damper carefully scribed with timing marks to make final tuning easier. The conrods are stock items again, being de-burred and shot-peened to strengthen them. All these stock items are Magnaflux-tested before final preparation to detect flaws and only perfect components are built into the finished units. The aluminium pistons are specially made by Mahle in Germany, reproducing the basic Chevvy design to McLaren order. Some alterations have been made to the stock shape, but George wasn't too specific on these. . . . Three rings are carried, two 1/16th compression rings and a single $\frac{3}{16}$th for oil control. Stock pistons have been used, in the engine which Bruce raced at Watkins Glen, but cracks were found in one of them before the race started. The team took a calculated risk in running the unit, but it seems their calculations were wrong for the piston did break up, putting Bruce out. George is still keen to run the Chevrolet pistons again, however.

The single central camshaft, running in the vee between the cylinder banks, is another high-performance stock item, as are the pushrods, but stock rockers are replaced by beautifully-made Iskenderian components. These proprietary Californian hotrod parts are cast in aluminium and pivot on needle-roller bearings, and as with all other hotrod items used are supplied by Reath Auto of Longbeach, California. High-grade valve springs made by Engle Cams are another expensive imported goody, but the enormous valves themselves are stock Chevvy hi-performance parts.

McLaren's own induction system is used, this stemming from an original injection set-up produced in California two years ago by Crower Cams, another of the specialist hotrod equipment manufacturers. This comprises a bulky but extremely light magnesium manifold with tall big-bore intake trumpets and Lucas electronic metering unit and upstream injection nozzles. Other specially-cast mag parts are the dry sump and the rocker covers, which have "McLaren-Chevrolet" lettering cast in. A Weaver Bros large capacity hotrod oil pump is fitted, and the M8Bs have an oil tank of about 4 gallons (US) capacity carrying 2 gallons of Gulf oil. Only other mods to the engine concern the tapping of two large diameter bolt holes to attach a chassis A-bracket, through which the unit is semi-stressed when mounted in the M8B chassis. Ignition is by Vertex magneto and Bosch plugs.

When the standard ZL-1 engines arrive at Colnbrook they produce around 475 bhp, a Chevrolet figure which George reckons is probably under-rated. When they leave his shop, output is up to around 600 to 650 bhp, but he can't be sure of exact figures because McLarens do not have their own dynamometer. Early in the development cycle, units were run up on Cosworth's brake in Northampton, and Lucas Engineering's in Huntingdon, but, like Rolls-Royce, output is obviously "sufficient."

A logistical problem exists in building and preparing engines one side of the Atlantic to support a racing programme on the other, and for the three M8Bs at any CanAm round there are five engines present—three in the cars and two spares. The other three mills are then either at Colnbrook being stripped and rebuilt or somewhere in transit between home base and works team. George reckons to take three days to build a completely new engine, three hours to strip a raced one and anything from 12 to 16 hours to rebuild it. In each strip all reciprocating parts are Magnafluxed and rods, bolts and rings replaced as a matter of course. The stock bearings are replaced as standard practice after two races, and even then look fit enough for several more. After a lot of trouble finding a company competent and well-equipped enough to do large-capacity V8 balancing over here, George came up with Hilthorne Engineering, of Hanwell, and they do quite a bit of other contract work on the units, such as head-levelling and so on.

McLaren's own small machine shop at Colnbrook does quite a bit of work on the engines, and George and John are sometimes joined in their clinically clean workshop by John Dornay from the F1 team. They found he had experience in cylinder head work and when there's a porting job to be done he is co-opted to do it.

But perhaps the most surprising feature of McLarens' engines is the fact that they are so stock in specification; it makes one wonder what kind of road car the optional ZL-1 powered Corvette must be like! Apparently it goes like stink and gulps gas at about 6 mpg, and when Bolthoff-prepared it goes even better and still with 4 to 4.5 mpg "economy," which for a racing 7-litre engine can't be bad. George hastens to point out that "It's not what we do, it's the way that we do it that gets results," and it is patently obvious that painstaking care goes into preparing these engines fit for a champion. The only question remaining is, who will it be this year—Bruce or Denny?

Heavy guns but not heavy metal: the surprisingly light aluminium Chevy block and pistons.

Friendly CanAm spirit: At Edmonton, two of the McLaren mechanics and a Chaparral man give Chuck Parsons' Haas-Simoniz Lola mechanic a hand to trace engine trouble.

Bits and pieces: Stock crank, rods, Mahle pistons and mag manifold. One of Colnbrook's problems has been the supply of hot-rod parts from California (left). McLaren goodies: from nearest the camera, mag dry sump, Vertex magneto, mag injection manifold, Iskenderian rockers, mag rocker covers, cylinder heads and Lucas metering unit.

McLaren magic?

No—the secret of the 'Bruce and Denny Show' was a sensible approach, good actors and a lot of rehearsing . . .

Photographs by Edward Deaux, Mel Lloyd

The McLaren record in the Can-Am series is simply staggering. Surely no other team in motor racing history has achieved such a triumph in a major championship.

After scooping the championship in 1967 and 1968, they made it a hat-trick this year with a quite stupendous record of eleven victories in the eleven qualifying events.

Of these, Bruce McLaren won six of the races and Denny Hulme picked up the other five. On eight occasions they were first *and* second, while in one of these Dan Gurney drove the spare team car to make it one-two-three.

No wonder the series came to be known as the Bruce and Denny Show !

With such rich sponsorship, the series inevitably attracted dollar-hungry entrants, yet no-one was able to provide any sort of real opposition to the bright orange M8Bs, which regularly set the fastest training times and then toyed with all rivals to the chequered flag.

To quite a few observers this looked like some sort of McLaren magic, as though the New Zealander had found a fairy godmother to wave a wand and grant him huge bags of dollars. But this was no fairy story, and Bruce is no Merlin. The answer is far more prosaic, for the overwhelming McLaren domination in the series depended on no tricks and no deep secrets. The essential ingredients of success were sensible design, good long-term planning and the choice of just the right sort of people to carry out all the various tasks.

You can be sure that Bruce intends, if he can, to repeat his 1969 whitewash this year, too, and to that end the first car for the 1970 series—designated the M8C—was being tested from the middle of December. (They are building three M8Cs at McLaren's headquarters at Colnbrook, and will probably keep one of the M8Bs as a 'museum piece'.)

This careful programme of development testing is the real answer, according to Bruce. The 1969 Can-Am attack began in November of the previous year, and by December the first M8B was being run at Goodwood, followed by a very intensive test programme in January and February. The M8B was an improved version of the M8A of the year before, which was the result of a design hammered out by Bruce himself, Jo Marquart and Gordon Coppuck.

The tests at Goodwood revealed a higher percentage gain in performance than in previous years, which the team found surprising but very comforting because they anticipated far more serious opposition. The reasons for this gain were many—a little tweak here and a little touch there—though the car was still basically the same as the M8A and was only slightly lighter. But when the series began it was immediately clear that providing the M8Bs were reliable there was nothing to prevent them from sweeping the board.

And they were amazingly reliable. The team depended on eight Chevrolet V8s and during the series they had only four major blow-ups (some of them recoverable).

Champion at work. Bruce McLaren made up for a rather disappointing Formula 1 season by winning the Can-Am Championship by 5 points from teammate Denny Hulme.

Bruce had a broken piston at Edmonton and lost a couple of engines in practice at Riverside, while Denny had engine failure in the last race in Texas.

The domination was so great that Bruce and Denny were able to control the races despite lapping three to four seconds slower than in practice, and on at least one occasion they were driving the race a whole eight seconds slower than their best training times. (So perhaps it was no wonder they had such a reliability record !)

Did Bruce and Denny find it somewhat embarrassing ? 'Yes.' says Bruce. 'At times I am lost for an answer when people ask me questions about dominating the Can-Am. But you know, it isn't really for us to answer such questions. All we've been doing is getting on with the job of going racing. We're not doing it more efficiently or scientifically or any better than it should be done. After all, we provided virtually the same amount of effort with basically the same bunch of people in Formula 1 and only pulled off one Grand Prix win during 1969.'

What of the reaction of spectators ? Was Bruce aware of this ? He certainly was, and at the beginning of the series, particularly at Mosport and St Jovite, he and Denny drove at a pace to make things more interesting for the crowd. They realised that the work they had done, and particularly the development testing over the Winter, had put them well and truly ahead of the opposition, and they also realised that their

Once again Bruce McLaren and Denny Hulme won the Johnson Wax Trophy for the Can-Am series. The presentation was made by Stirling Moss, Johnson's racing director, after the final round at Texas International Raceway.

The 1969 M8B, though very different in detail, was basically the same design that had won the Can-Am in 1968. Outward differences from the M8A included the aerofoil, cut-away front wings and additional brake cooling scoops on the rear body sides.

private worry about the new Chaparral was not going to materialise. (Bruce admits quite frankly that much of the tremendous effort prior to the series was because they were scared of the Chaparral.)

So Bruce and Denny decided to give the spectators something to interest them, by deliberately going slowly and mixing it with some of the opposition. 'We knew it was a little bit dangerous,' says Bruce, 'because you don't normally race that way. I got caught out at St Jovite, where I ran into John Surtees. John went wide and slow on one corner because a yellow flag was being waved, but I was watching John and missed the flag, and so I rammed him. This cost me a pit stop which could have meant losing second place, but in fact I managed to recover. But after that we decided to stop fooling around so much, though Denny and I did play with Chris Amon a little at Edmonton.'

What about the opposition? Well, the Chaparral 2H was way out, and was never anything of a rival. And why was this? Bruce explains his view: 'One of the things which I think has helped me is that while my experience and background is sufficient for me to be able to design a car, I have always made a point of getting the best possible people around me before I make a final decision. I ask them what they would do about a particular point, and having listened to the argument I am then prepared to accept a better idea if one is put forward. I may be wrong, but I get the feeling that Jim Hall is perhaps too much of a dictator in deciding the design of his cars. The 2H was never really on as a competitive machine.

'I think that the other thing that has helped us is that we have never had a surplus of money. We have always had to go racing in order to make money, and being hungry is the best way to have a chance of success.'

The Porsche foray was interesting, but Bruce feels that the 917PA's engine was huge, yet failed to provide sufficient power to make it a menace. He thinks the Porsche

didn't handle very well, either, and attributes this to perhaps a lack of expertise in the test-driving programme.

As for the Ferrari which Chris Amon drove, Bruce describes it as 'not a bad car, not bad at all,' but adds, 'however, it was still not as up-to-date as it could have been.' He came to the view that its worst feature was probably in the aerodynamic department. 'Surprisingly enough,' he says, 'there wasn't all that amount of power out of the V12 engine. We had the Ferrari beaten on power. The Chevrolet engine is quite remarkable. Not only is it a push-rod unit but it pushes out virtually the same output, on a pro rata capacity basis, as the old Coventry Climax 2½ litre engine. The Chevvy probably

produces about the same power per litre as the Climax did, but it probably has a better power range—it will run usefully all the way up from 3,000 rpm to 7,000 rpm. This makes the cars very quick around a circuit. When you have a powerful car which will spin the wheels in each gear you just don't want to have to change down for a corner unless it is vitally necessary, and the Chevvy enabled us to keep our hands away from the gear lever and concentrate on other problems in a corner.'

The engines which Bruce and Denny used were a happy blend of European and American experience. The McLaren team was the first to adopt Lucas fuel injection and European pistons for their V8s. The engines

Somehow a tortoise didn't seem like an appropriate mascot for the team, but it too was Gulf-sponsored and, of course, had a wing!

were prepared and maintained at Colnbrook, with valuable experience provided by George Bolthoff, an American with a lot of V8 know-how learned from the drag racing scene. For the majority of the races the engines were turning out 630-640 brake horsepower.

Inevitably, with the M8Bs going so well, some of the McLaren rivals were prepared to concede them victory and concentrate on picking up places. The exception to this was Chris Amon, who was certainly not prepared to be over-awed and was very willing to have a go. He tried hard, and in Bruce's view he nearly gave them a run for their money. He felt that Porsche thought they might surprise the McLaren effort. He recalls two or three years ago talking to John Wyer, before the Can-Am series became the important championship it is today. 'John congratulated me on our sports car efforts, but pointed out that of course that there was no factory participation. I think that this was probably Porsche and Ferrari's feeling about it this season. After all, we're pretty small, nothing like a factory effort, yet I feel that both Porsche and Ferrari changed their mind before the season ended.'

There was one other rival that impressed Bruce—the Autocoast car which was driven by Jack Oliver. He thinks this was a good, basic straightforward design incorporating a lot of European know-how. It was a car built from hard experience, and Bruce thinks Peter Bryant did a good job with it.

But Bruce does feel that in America at the moment there is quite a good bunch of fabricators and builders—people like Bill Eaton, Ron Butler, Max Kelly and Phil Remington—who with good leadership could be building good cars.

At the moment, though, he feels there are no American teams with all the necessary experience and leadership when it comes to building road racing cars. 'The American race-car industry,' he says, 'is tiny and very inexperienced when compared to the motor racing industry in Britain. They haven't had the benefit of people like John Cooper and Colin Chapman, whose knowledge and experience has been spread around in Britain. In this country, for example, we have people in the 750 Motor Club who have done some good pioneer work and gained a lot of experience. It is this sort of thing, providing a reservoir of talent, which is so valuable.'

But while the young enthusiast in the 750 Motor Club was learning to make a car handle well, the American keen type was concentrating on tuning V8 engines. So in general the Americans have more experience in the business of extracting useful power from V8s, while—and this was demonstrated in the early stages of Formula 5000—the British are superior in the chassis department.

'But I think we could take over in the engine business,' Bruce suggests, 'because in Britain we have an upper strata of engine experts, such as Keith Duckworth, and I am sure that if they apply themselves to the big American V8 they could show how it should be done.'

The McLaren operation in the Can-Am is a formidable affair. The full list of personnel makes interesting reading: two designer-draughtsmen, five car builders, six mechanics to assemble the cars, a parts inspection man, a parts programme man, an engine parts programme man, three engine builders, manager Teddy Mayer, and of course Bruce and Denny. When the series is on there are five mechanics, an engine man and two chaps who drive the tow trucks. (The trucks each covered 30,000 miles during the 1969 series.)

This sounds a lot of people, but Bruce feels it is important to have enough people to do the job properly (and this becomes more important in the later stages of the series).

It is also an expensive operation. A careful breakdown of all the figures shows that, counting everything in, it cost 14,000 dollars per car for each race of the 1969 series. So when you goggle over the dollar earnings in the prize lists it is as well to remember that the McLaren operation cost roughly the same as the money Bruce and Denny won in their fantastic record run. Without the help of their sponsors, McLaren Racing simply couldn't have afforded to do the Can-Am. And that despite winning every race! Make you think?

It certainly makes Bruce think. Which is why the 1970 Can-Am effort began at least a couple of months ago in the McLaren headquarters. And also why even the most prudent punter would surely be prepared to place a modest wager on the M8Cs pulling off the 1970 series to add to an already lustrous record.

The day that the works McLarens finished 1, 2 and 3. Dan Gurney drove the spare M8B in the Michigan race and finished a respectful 0.6 second behind Bruce and Denny. Jack Brabham also drove the third car in practice and Chris Amon later raced it.

Porsche — 1970 plans, 1969 in retrospect

NO BRAND NEW racing cars were unveiled by Porsche at their annual meeting with the Press at Hockenheim last week, the only hitherto unseen model being the 914/6 Rallye, a more powerful better-equipped version of the normal 914/6, which is to be homologated as a Group 4 special GT car in the 2-litre category. Also on show: the latest version of the 4½-litre 917 with revised bodywork, the Can-Am 917PA Spyder, 3-litre 908/02 Spyder, long-tailed 908, Tour de France-winning 911R and a 911/20, which is the rally version of the 911S.

Although snow had fallen all round Hockenheim the circuit had escaped any major fall, but a coating of thawing sleet made it incredibly slippery at first.

Before the demonstration runs, competitions manager Rico Steinemann outlined Porsche plans for 1970, their 20th racing season. Their chief effort will be an attempt at winning the Manufacturer's Championship for sports cars for the second consecutive year. Their cars will be operating from the Slough HQ of the JW-Gulf team. The cars will be the

latest 917s and the drivers will be Jo "Seppi" Siffert, Brian Redman, Pedro Rodriguez, who joins the team after driving for Ferrari in 1969, and a fourth driver who has yet to be signed. Another 917 team will be run by Porsche of Austria with Kurt Ahrens, Vic Elford, Rudi Lins and Hans Herrmann as drivers. This team is to compete in many World Championship events. Several successful private teams will run 917s including David Piper who recently won the South African 9-hours race in a 917, partnered by Richard Attwood.

Porsche will contest the Monte-Carlo Rally with three of the latest 2.2-litre 911S cars driven by last year's winner, Bjoern Waldegaard; Gerard Larrousse, who won the Tour de France and the Tour of Corsica; and a newcomer to the team, Aake Andersson. The 914 will not be rallied until next April.

Steinemann told me that no final decision has yet been taken as to whether Porsche will build a Can-Am car for their US organization, Porsche-Audi, to run or enter a works team. He also announced that Porsche would be

offering a Porsche Cup plus £5,680 in cash for the most successful Porsche private owner.

Porsche Engineer Peter Falk surveyed Porsche's 1969 racing season with commendable frankness, dealing not only with their successes but also their failures and the reasons for them. In December 1968 Porsche went to Monza to run a car for 24 hours, the primary objective being to test the new five-speed transmission that replaced the heavier six-speed gearbox, and also to see whether the new position for the generator had cured the troubles which were their undoing in the 1968 Le Mans. The test ended abruptly after 18 hours when the car crashed and burnt out.

It had run with complete reliability until then and the engine and gearbox, when rescued from the wreckage, showed no signs of failure. However, in the first championship race, the Daytona 24 hours, the light alloy gearwheel which acts on the intermediate shaft that conveys the drive from the crankshaft and drives the camshafts via chains and the oil pump failed. Replacement by a steel gearwheel cured this trouble. At the next race, the Sebring 12 hours, cracked frames eliminated four of the five works cars, all of which were the new 908 Spyders whose preliminary testing on the Porsche circuit at Weissach had been curtailed by heavy snow falls. The rear frame of the Spyders was reinforced with a pyramid-type structure, which increased the weight by 2 kg.

In the next race, the BOAC 500 at Brands Hatch, the works' Spyders were 1st, 2nd and 3rd. Porsche were also 1st, 2nd and 3rd in the next race, the Monza 1,000 kilometres. The Porsche team were upset that the long-tailed 908 Coupés were only slightly faster on the straights than the open Ferrari P312s, and were slower through the bends.

This led Porsche to design a new body for their Spyder which reduced the drag factor to 0.37. The new cars had less downward pressure on the front—the pressure being regulated by spoilers—and were 10 m.p.h. faster on the straight. Unfortunately, at their first appearance, the Nurburgring 1,000 kilometres, two of the new cars were written-

A slight dusting of sleet on the track made the opening laps of the Press session very dicey, above. Before the off Porsche's mighty line-up of point-chasing cars, left

of the big 917 at the Ring had failed to develop it to a state where it could equal the times of the 908 Spyders. However, in spite of unsatisfactory roadholding and overheating of the fuel pumps the 917 won the last race of the season, the Austrian GP on the new Zeltweg circuit.

John Horsman, who was representing JW Automotive Engineering Ltd, at the meeting, told me the 917's roadholding problems had been solved at a subsequent joint Porsche-JW test session at Zeltweg last October. At the suggestion of the JW engineers, the rear of the body above the wheel arches was built up with aluminium sheet and an adjustable spoiler was fitted. This transformed the cars, which now handle quite well.

The cause of the previous trouble was the failure of the air flow to follow the long, downswept tail. In rain, the spray could be seen streaming aft well above the rear fins, and on corners the air flowed across the rear windows and struck the top of the outer fin, thereby producing an oversteer effect. The driver would correct, the pressure on the fin would vanish and he would then have to correct the other way. As a result, the cars went through bends in a series of twitches.

The Porsche-JW link-up stems from a Porsche meeting in October, 1968, when it was decided that some means must be found of reducing their expenditure on racing. It was decided to seek some alternative arrangement. JW's first sign was the appearance of Rico Steinemann in the JW trailer caravan at Sebring last March talking very enthusiastically about the just announced 917.

Porsche will deliver seven 917s to Slough at the beginning of the season. Thereafter the cars will be prepared at Slough between races returning to the factory, possibly, between two Continental events if this is more convenient. The team will take three cars to Daytona and Sebring, the spare car not used at Daytona being included in the team for Sebring, but for most Continental races they will take only two cars with a stand-by at the factory.

Development of the 917 will continue at the factory, and a 5-litre engine will be available later if more power is needed to deal with the new Ferraris.

off during practising and only one started; it finished well down after troubles. However, three of the older type 908 Spyders were again 1st, 2nd and 3rd.

The Nurburgring 1,000 kilometres saw the first appearance of the big 917, which proved so difficult to drive that the works team opted for 908s, and the car was given to Piper and Gardner who finished eighth.

At Le Mans the two 917s were both eliminated by clutch trouble, clutch slip occurring after moderate wear of the friction surface owing to the operating springs being too weak. The heat caused by clutch slip melted the adhesive securing the friction linings to the clutch plates and that was that.

Siffert led the race for some time in a new long-tailed version of the 908 Spyder which had been improved aerodynamically. This proved nearly as fast as the long-tailed

coupés down the straights and was faster through the bends. Unfortunately the extended tail denied ventilation to the gearbox so the plastic pipes from the transmission oil pump to the supply points melted, letting out all the oil.

One long-tailed coupé went out with a dry pinion bearing in the transmission, and after the race it was found that the Herrmann/Larrousse car, which finished second, was also suffering from this trouble, plus a leaking front hub bearing. It was not, however, in brake trouble as Herrmann thought for although the brake warning light lit up as he took over for his last stint, this comes into operation when there is still 3 mm of brake pad left.

After the Le Mans set back, the 908 Spyders were 1st, 2nd and 3rd in the Watkins Glen Six Hours. Meanwhile intensive testing

The 1970 cars in action

DURING THE DEMONSTRATION runs on the short Hockenheim circuit I rode first with Seppi Siffert in the coupe 917 and later with Brian Redman in the Can-Am 917 Spyder. Getting into the coupe is no mean operation and involves a great deal of wriggling and sliding until at last one's feet have got as far as they will go. They finish up cramped into a minute space just clear of the driver's feet. Projecting portions of my anatomy were prodded in and the gull wing door was swung down like a coffin lid and there I was: wedged into place.

Seppi opened the throttle and we stormed away with a tremendous blare of sound, kicking up a great cloud of spray, the tail twitching as the rear wheels spun. This was the first lap of the day for the 917 and Siffert's efforts at keeping the car pointing more or less straight were not helped by the engine getting occasional attacks of the splutters. The first long right-hand bend pressed my head hard against the door, which was okay. What worried me were the left-handers, which had me furiously seeking a secure hand grip with my left hand to prevent myself from sitting on Mr. Siffert's lap. I

could find only a finger hold. However adhesion was so low that the g. forces never became too excessive. Even so, the acceleration away from a corner was fantastic. The noise once under way was by no means as deafening as I had expected and the ride was surprisingly good; on the second lap I could use a camera on the right-hand bends, then concentrate on staying put on the left-handers. At the end of the second lap we came into the pits and willing hands helped extricate me.

Sports Editor Philip Turner partners Jo Seppi Siffert in the 917 coupe for a trip round Hockenheim

Someone else took my place and on the very next lap the big car spun twice, showing just how slippery the surface was.

The open Can-Am 917 Spyder was far easier to get into and there was much more room inside, even after the metal hatch had been dropped into place. But as Brian Redman and I rushed away from the pits it was at once evident the Can-Am car was sheer hell for the passenger.

Tremendous blasts of spray-laden air swirled around my head and came up through the floor, getting under the peak of my crash helmet, trying to tear it off. The circuit had dried slightly by now, and I was thankful to find a body strut on which to take a firm grip with my left hand, for the g. on left-hand bends was quite something. Right-hand bends thrust one against the body side so violently that there was no question of using a camera, which in any case would have received a lens full of spray. It was a really violent experience, with the driver having to concentrate to keep the car on the road as he fed in the power. It was generally agreed among those who tried it, that two laps were quite enough.

Nevertheless an experience I would not have missed.

The March 707 and three
of its adversaries

"Shall we do a drive shaft test?" asked Chris Amon. His mechanic nodded agreement: "You might as well give the clutch a good workout as well." Chris grinned and climbed into the new March CanAm car beside a pale looking Robin Herd who was strapped into the passenger seat. With the fearsome thunder that only a highly tuned American V8 can give the March hurtled down the Silverstone pit lane, bottomed with a thump going down the ramp and rocketed into Copse corner. Less than 1½ minutes later the March slithered through Woodcote, going on to do a flying lap in 1 m 26.8 s before Chris cut the engine and coasted up the pit lane.

The reason for Robin Herd's presence in the passenger seat (apart from the fact that he actually appears to enjoy it) was that Chris Amon was complaining of slight front end instability. What better way for a driver to prove to the designer that something's wrong than by submitting him to a fast lap or two? With a single seater the designer has to take the driver's word for it, but with a real two-seater like the March 707 sceptical designers can soon be proved wrong.

Robin Herd's reason for making his CanAm car wide enough to take a passenger in comfort is that he has had to accommodate some extraordinarily wide tyres, but his mechanics are quite convinced he did it just so that he could take the occasional ride. In fact Robin is something of a frustrated racing driver, and would like nothing better than to buy a Chevron or something and have a quiet go in club racing, or in minor long distance races with his retired co-director Alan Rees. It looks as if this must remain a dream because the March team is busy turning out racing cars as fast as they can go, and putting new designs on the drawing board ready for next season already.

The CanAm car was designed initially at the instigation of Chris Amon, who planned to run in the 1970 series in a similar way to his 1969 effort with Ferrari, by having the cars on loan and close co-operation from the factory, but doing all the administrative work and maintenance himself. However he decided not to do it this way after all, and the March factory are now entering a car on their own behalf with Chris doing the driving. The first car was finished and tested in chassis form in mid-May, but the body was not ready until the end of the month. Two more cars are being built, one as a spare for Chris and one for possible sale if a customer comes along. Robin Herd has no illusions about winning the series or even one of the races this year because, as former McLaren designer, he knows only too well the thorough preparation and long testing experience that is needed to win CanAm races. This year will be treated purely as a shakedown run, and if things look promising they will have a really serious go in 1971.

Nothing sensational

Robin Herd modestly insists that there is nothing sensational about the 707, and is almost apologetic for not being able to reveal details of fantastic novelties in the machinery. It is, however, the first March which he has been able to design in his own time without having to rush, and he hopes the secrets of the March are locked away in such invisible items as roll centres and polar moments of inertia.

By christening the car with the number 707 they expected, and got, lots of cracks about "It'll never get off the ground" and "It should be a flier," and in fact officially the

car is known as the 70C to avoid these comments, but Robin Herd knows that as far as the press is concerned it's a 707.

The March is designed round a set of fearsome new Firestone tyres which are 23 ins wide at the rear. The problem of accommodating ever-growing tyres is perhaps the biggest one a designer faces now, and Herd for one would not object too strongly to a restriction of rim width as is now being advocated by the circuit owners. He feels that a sensible restriction would bring the skill of individual designers and drivers back to the fore.

The chassis is of course a monocoque in 20-gauge aluminium alloy with magnesium bulkhead castings front and rear, the front one being cleverly designed so that two identical half-castings can be bolted together, the only difference being holes in the lower edge for brake and clutch master cylinders on the driver's side and larger holes for the water pipes on the passenger's side. The magnesium bulkhead which terminates the chassis in front of the engine is in fact two half castings joined by a thick Duralumin engine mounting plate.

Fuel is contained in the side pontoons of the monocoque which lie between the wheels, each side containing 35 gallons of fuel. Marston Excelsior rubberised fabric fuel cells filled with foam are currently being used, but a switch will be made to Firestone tanks later on. There are two tanks on each side with flap valves between them to control surge, the fuel passing to a collector pot behind the driver before being pumped to the engine.

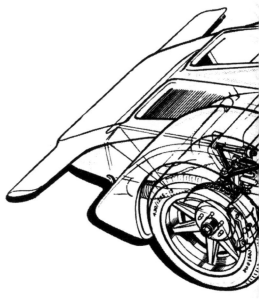

720 bhp engine

The engine is bolted to the rear of the monocoque, but additional bracing is provided by steel tubes which run from the rear of the magnesium bulkheads to the normal engine mounting bosses on the side of the engine. As Jan Hall's Chaparral team may not compete in this year's CanAm series because they are concentrating on TransAm racing, they are supplying CanAm engines to customers. The Chaparral engines, built up by ex-McLaren man Gary Knudsen, are based on the all-aluminium Chevrolet V8 unit, and the full 8-litre (494 cu in) engine now fitted to the March gives a claimed 720 bhp at 6500 rpm! While this seems a trifle optimistic it is almost frightening to stand next to one of them while it is being warmed up. Power goes through a Hewland LG600 gearbox with four speeds, drive to the wheels being taken by BRD roller spline shafts.

The suspension layout is similar to that of the latest Formula 1 March with double wishbones and outboard Koni coil-spring/damper units at the front, and transverse parallel lower arms with a single top link and radius arms at the rear. New magnesium hub carriers are fitted all round, and the Girling 12 ins diameter discs are outboard mounted on all four wheels. The rear suspension is attached to a yoke bolted to the top of the gearbox and to an aluminium plate bolted to the base of the differential.

Aerodynamics play an important part in CanAm racing, and Robin Herd has evolved a new look in all-enveloping sports cars because the car has a narrow, almost formula 1 width nose in the centre of the car, with spoilers attached to each side just as on single seaters. The radiator, which is canted forward, sits in this nose section, large ducts behind it taking hot air over the top of the bodywork. The front wheels are covered in with wheel arches very reminiscent of the M8B

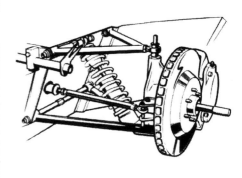

McLaren. The rest of the body section is fairly conventional at present, with a small aluminium spoiler tacked on to the glassfibre body (which has been moulded by Specialised Mouldings), but a variety of aerodynamic appendages will be tried during the CanAm series.

Although little is expected of the March 707 this season, there could be a surprise in store for one or two people.

March 707 specification: Chassis: Aluminium alloy monocoque with magnesium bulkheads. Engine: Chaparral modified Chevrolet all-aluminium V8; 494 cu. in (8-litre), 720 bhp at 6500 rpm. Gear box: Hewland LG600 four-speed. Fuel tanks: Four Firestone rubberised fabric cells; 70 gallons capacity. Brakes: Girling disc, outboard mounted, 12 ins diameter. Suspension: front: Double wishbone and Koni outboard coil spring/dampers; rear: Lower parallel arms, single top links and radius arms. Wheelbase: 96 ins. Track: front: 68 ins. rear: 64 ins. Overall length: 156 ins. Overall width: 93 ins. Weight: 1460 lbs, less fuel.

Despite Bruce McLaren's tragic fatal accident while testing one of the new CanAm McLaren M8Ds, McLaren Cars will be sending one car out for the series. It will be driven by Denny Hulme and he hopes that his burns will be sufficiently healed for him

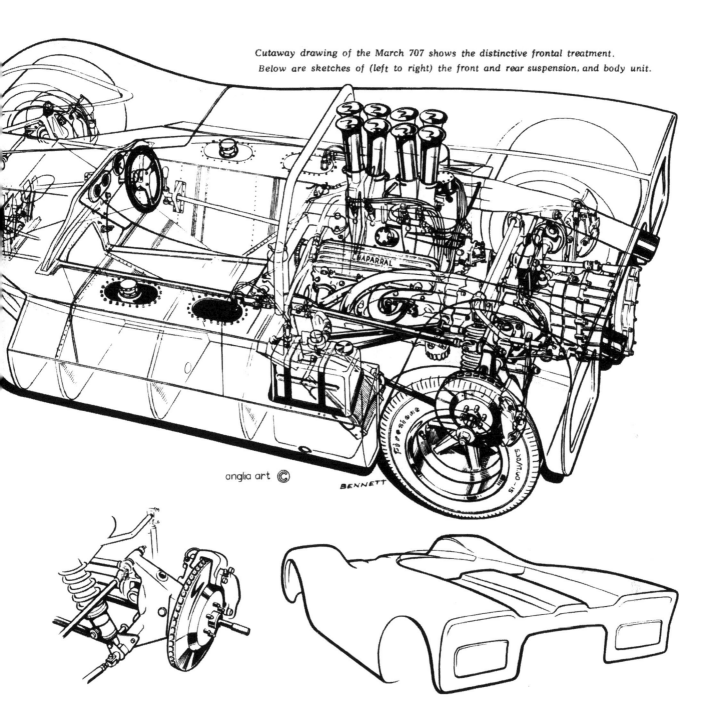

Cutaway drawing of the March 707 shows the distinctive frontal treatment.
Below are sketches of (left to right) the front and rear suspension, and body unit.

anglia art ©

BENNETT

to make the first race.

The new M8D will use the 7.5-litre, 670 bhp version of the lightweight Chevrolet V8 as, in testing under engine man George Bolthoff, McLaren Cars have found the 8-litre, 700 bhp unit to be too unreliable. The M8D itself is based closely on the successful M8A/B series with a very similar monocoque. The track has been increased by 4 ins all round, while the major change is, of course, the swept-up bodywork at the rear which acts as a downthrust force.

McLaren M8D Specification : Reynolds aluminium monocoque with engine acting as integral member. Engine 465 cu ins, 7.5 litre Chevrolet V8, 670 bhp at 7,000 rpm. Front track : 62.30 ins. Rear track : 58.50 ins. Weight : 1,420 lbs. Wheelbase : 94 ins. Length : 164 ins. Fuel Capacity : 64 galls. Brakes : Lockheed 12 ins. discs. Transmission : Hewland LG500.

The second half of BRM's rejuvenation programme, along with their much revamped Formula 1 team, is their entry into the CanAm series. This was largely prompted by the joining of successful McLaren CanAm driver George Eaton to the F1 team. Sponsorship from Castrol ensued, and for the races the

BRM outfit will be fielding two of the new P154s for Eaton and a second driver, probably Pedro Rodriguez. There will be a third spare chassis; all three will be turned out in white with red and green stripes, and the cars will probably be entered under the Castrol-Team BRM banner.

The first car, which Eaton hopes will be ready for the opening round this weekend, is almost complete, while the second is well advanced, and work on the final assembly of the third is due to begin soon. Designed by F1 P153 designer Tony Southgate, the P154 will use a semi-monocoque light-alloy chassis to which will be attached a light alloy 7.62-litre V8 Chevrolet engine. The car is pretty conventional in the chassis and suspension areas, with such items as oil tanks, steering gear and suspension components made by BRM themselves. Specialised Moulding will be responsible for the bodies.

The Chevvy engine has been developed by Aubrey Woods, who expects over 600 bhp with 585 ft/lbs of torque. It will use Lucas

fuel injection and magneto ignition. The cost of making their own CanAm gearbox in such small quantity has been decided to be prohibitive, so the P154 will use the normal Hewland LG500.

BRM P154 dimensions: Length: 146.6 ins. Wheelbase: 93 ins. Front track: 60 ins. Rear track: 59 ins. Width at front: 75 ins. Width at rear: 83 ins. Height of body: 35 ins. Height of engine: 41 ins. Weight: 1425 lbs. 465 cu ins (7.62-litre) aluminium Chevrolet V8 with fuel Injection, giving over 600 bhp and 585 ft/lbs torque.

After several seasons of taking second place to the McLaren team, Lola Cars have come up with an all-new monocoque for the series. Designated the T220, the new car is a very simple and conventional car which is most compact. The first T220, which will be run under the Carl Haas banner with full works Lola backing including the presence of two factory mechanics and Eric Broadley himself, is sponsored by L & M Cigarettes and will be driven by Peter Revson. The T220 will probably use a Chaparral 8-litre Chevvy V8.

Lola T220 Specification : Aluminium monocoque. Engine : 8-litre Chevrolet V8. Fuel capacity : 68 gals. Brakes : Girling 12 ins discs.

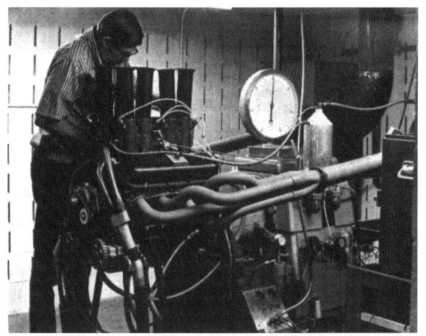

George Bolthoff with one of the 7½-litre Chevrolet CanAm engines on the test bed.

A Chevy cylinder head after receiving the McLaren treatment (above), and the crankshaft used on the 7½-litre engine (below).

McLaren's American Operation

By BILL GAVIN

The major successes of McLaren Cars have mostly been in North America, and it was here that they established their reputation as one of the very best racing organisations in the world. So it was no surprise that last year the late Bruce McLaren and his co-director Teddy Mayer decided to establish a permanent base in the United States.

Detroit was the logical site for a number of reasons. It is central for the seven CanAm races that are held in the East and Mid-West, and also for Indianapolis. There are daily freight flights from London to Detroit, so that anything shipped from the Colnbrook headquarters can be at the Detroit workshop in less than 24 hours. And of course Detroit is the centre of the American motor industry —the Chevrolet engines McLarens use in their CanAm programmes are made here, and the specialist machining and treatment services required to build racing engines are available.

After the final CanAm race of 1969 at College Station, Teddy Mayer and McLaren engine project engineer George Boltoff flew to Detroit seeking suitable premises. They located them in the City of Livonia, a Detroit suburb, and a few days later Colin Beanland flew from England to take up his post as General Manager of McLaren Engines Inc, as the American operation is known.

The workshop covers some 4500 square feet and includes space for the administrative offices. At the moment the working area is divided in half, the engine building shop, dynamometer cell and stores occupying one side, while on the other the CanAm cars are prepared.

The first project undertaken at the new shop was the assembly and subsequent rebuilds of the Offenhauser Indianapolis engines. George Boltoff did most of this single-handed while Lee Muir and John Nicholson started to build the CanAm engines. After Indianapolis George switched his attentions to the completion of the dynamometer cell and the installation of the Heenan & Froude Type G 490, which will take engines of up to 1000 bhp revving at 10,000 rpm. The dyno was first run at the beginning of June, and now George tests every CanAm engine that is built or rebuilt before it is installed in a race car.

With the exception of the specially cast blocks, the McLaren-Chevrolet racing engines are built up almost entirely from standard Chevrolet parts. The 465 cubic inch versions used in the opening races consist of the big-bore 430 cubic inch block fitted with a crankshaft from the standard 427 cubic inch engine which powers Corvettes and other Chevrolet models. The standard crank has to be nitrided, and likewise other components like the camshafts have to be specially treated so the whole unit becomes a very expensive item by the time it's assembled. Both standard Chevrolet pistons and others specially forged by Mahle in Germany are used, and nobody seems to be sure that one type is better than the other.

While George, Lee and John are building engines on one side of the shop, at the other side of the partition the CanAm cars are prepared. Carey Taylor and Jim Stone look after Denny Hulme's car, while Alec Greaves and Tony Attard take care of the other. Both cars are completely stripped after each race and then rebuilt. With only two weeks between most races, and at least two of these spent on the road, there's never more than nine days to prepare for the next race, and sometimes as few as six. The race mechanics put in 11 or 12 hours' work almost every day, and have had only one day off since the building of the cars started at

Colnbrook in March. Strangely enough they spent their solitary day off watching the USAC Championship races at Michigan International Speedway. Jim Stone expressed their self-inflicted policy: "You just don't stop until the job is finished." They adhere to the same policy at races, and often work until the early hours of the morning. It's not that they have troubles; they are just making sure they don't have any.

After the engine in Hulme's car inexplicably overheated at Mosport they devised a remedy for any like occurences in the future. With typical Kiwi ingenuity Jim and Carey bought a Sears Roebuck garden sprayer, and converted it to be pressurised by an air line which could be plugged into one of Goodyear's cylinders at the track. They then fitted a plug-in valve to the water system, so that when the outlet line is plugged in, water is forced into the system at a controlled 30 psi. This kept Gurney going at Watkins Glen although the engine had lost nearly all its water. Recent thinking on the overheating of the 465 cubic inch engines is that the longer crank is dipping into the sump and causing the oil to overheat, which in turn soon raises the water temperature. Both cars started out with 430 cubic inch engines at Watkins Glen, but Gurney chose to use the bigger unit for the race, and once again had overheating problems.

The Watkins Glen victory was the 16th successive win for McLaren Racing in CanAm events. Despite the tragic death of their leader the team continues to be a major force in whatever type of racing it undertakes. The establishment of an American base with their own engine development and building shop can only assist in their maintaining their position as one of motor racing's most successful teams of all time.

John Nicholson at work on one of the alloy Chevy blocks (above right). Each car is completely stripped and rebuilt between races (below).

105

CanAm aerodynamics

By PETE LYONS

It must seem to the AUTOSPORT reader that Lyons is forever apologising for the CanAm. How great it all *could* be, he enthuses, then goes on week by week to chronicle another non-race. Particularly in this year of fantastic Formula 1 tension, the high-priced sports-car shows overseas must seem to be taking up a bit too much press space. And yet, for whatever the reasons it's not, it *could* be great. The actual race days, so far, have been only marginally interesting; the story on the other days of the week is fascinating. Group 7 is by its very definition the advance thrust of high-performance road vehicle design. It is the medium a designer most naturally selects when he wants to try some totally new ideas. Trying wild new ideas may not be the way to win races, especially when the ideas are not backed up by the patient testing that has put McLaren Cars on top, but it does stir things up and, eventually, moves the Art forward.

Each year one aspect of the cars seems to have the most importance. This year the problem of aerodynamics stands out. Even before the introduction of the Chaparral 2J, which uses air in a new way, before Jackie Oliver's wild ride through the sky in the Autocoast at St Jovite, even in fact before the first race, the designers were faced with the necessity to better understand the airflow around their creations. The enforced removal of wings (which were pioneered on a G7 car) removed the lid from a Pandora's box of chassis problems. Suddenly lap times were up by a couple of seconds as the wilful vehicles felt their aerodynamic restraints lifted. "We'd forgotten," remarks one driver, "how many handling faults a wing covered up. We just bolted one on and forgot them, but now we have to get back down to all the little details and work them out." Now only the body-shape, independent of the wheels, may generate downforce. With everyone nevertheless trying to generate as much of it as possible, an effect, just coming into prominence two years ago but then shelved, hits them all the harder: the faster a negative-lift body goes the deeper it sinks on its springs. Thus the tuning of a car for a given circuit, always a collection of compromises, becomes very much harder.

Constant chassis height

On last year's Chaparral, the 2H, Jim Hall attached an hydraulic system to keep the height of the chassis constant regardless of downforce. On the Indianapolis McLarens this year there was a simpler system aimed at adjusting the handling as fuel weight burned off. That team are known to be developing a way, about halfway between in complexity, to do those two jobs, which should appear first on their F1 cars. (It should be noted in passing that the latest Chaparral avoids the aerodynamic portion of this problem, but as it carries a total of 90 US gallons of fuel for its two motors it might well appreciate attention to the second portion !)

A typical G7 body may be 80 or more inches wide (thus one-third more effective from the downforce point of view than anything possible with a single-seater), and about double that in length. Thus regarded as an aerofoil it is grotesquely inefficient, having an aspect ratio of 1:2. High performance sailplane wings have ratios on the order of 20:1 or more, while wings developed for racing cars are perhaps 5:1. A wing becomes less efficient when the air it pressurises spills sideways from its tips; the less the aspect ratio the more spillage. A way to counter that is by "end plates," or "fences,"

The Chaparral 2J has this linkage supporting the Lexan "skirt" to keep its height from the ground constant under all conditions (above). The two-stroke motor driving the fans sits over the automatic gearbox (below).

The Lola T220 of Peter Revson has several alternative suspension pickup points to give a wide range of adjustment (below).

The McLaren M12 driven by the late Jerry Titus and now David Hobbs displays its fully " fenced " body ; aerodynamicist Paul Lamar is on the left.

Fences on other CanAm contenders include the small ones on the works McLarens (above : Peter Gethin climbing aboard) ; and the high reinforced ones on the Lola T220 (below).

which force the air to flow off the back of the wing instead and thus make the most of what area the designer is allowed. If he isn't careful, however, his fences may generate more turbulence and drag than he suspects. The ideal shape has about double the depth on the convex surface (because that surface does about two-thirds of the work) of the wing's form, which on a racing car is the bottom, and the junction of wing and fence is carefully faired to eliminate vortices.

The leading edge-to-trailing edge of a wing, the " chord," determines how much free air-space should be around it to work well. A wing with a chord worthwhile on a racing car should be mounted three or more feet above the body. Now that such heights are restricted by the regulations, there is real doubt that any aerofoil at all is worthwhile. During exhaustive testing on the Autocoast car it was found by aerodynamicist Paul Lamar (to whom we are indebted for much of this information) that any legal aerofoil mounted on the tail of the body was in such unclean air flow that, by the time it was tilted at an attack angle steep enough to be effective, it might just as well have been a simple dam. His solution was to make out of the body-top of the Autocoast one big " tray-spoiler," with fences along the entire length. At one point the car was developing over 700 pounds of squash on the engine cover alone, and this value had to be cut back because the nose was unable to balance it. On the ex-Surtees M12 driven by the late Jerry Titus the existing body had full-length fences built on to it.

McLaren approach

The approach taken by the McLaren team on the M8D was to mount a proper aero-foil between fins on the engine cover, and the fins serve both as fences and as ducts to deliver air to the wing. That this works well is shown by the fact that the drivers take pains to adjust the angle of the wing during practice, to quite minute degrees. Other cars, such as the works Lola T220 and the Mot-schebacher M8B, carry wings mounted on struts with no benefit of ducts. Neither car has by its performance demonstrated superior aerodynamics; on the privately owned, ex-works machine the prime consideration was using pieces that already existed. On the Lola the wing is designed to work in conjunction with the last foot of the body shape; there are air outlets in the suddenly down-turning body line (cutely done in the dark portions of the twin " 26 " number discs, which are mesh-covered openings), and the end plates of the wing do not extend below the wing. All this is a little puzzling, but seems to be on purpose. The 220 also has plenty of airspace in its wheel wells, with the idea of relieving any possible build up of air pressure there.

The Autocoast was the first car actually to run with the works McLarens for any length of time. That does not prove anything either way about aerodynamics, but it is an indication that the two different approaches might work equally well. The drivers of the two types of car have interesting stories to tell. Hulme during practice at Mosport found an opportunity to trail Oliver in the Auto-coast, and found the air in its wake was extremely turbulent. It must fairly boil off the top of the body. An aerodynamically oriented body works best in still air; when Hulme attempted to catch Oliver in a corner the M8D lost all adhesion at the front and understeered nearly off the edge of the road. Oliver in his turn had a wake-experience of his own at St Jovite. The problem of The Jump was well known to him ; he had discussed it with several people and was prepared to keep it in mind during the race. He said later, after his horrifying nose-up flip, that he had settled into a position about three car lengths behind Hulme, thinking that a safe distance. As he crested the rise and his car went light, the M8D dropped away on the other side of the rise. A fresh blast of air as the slipstream vanished—there have been suggestions that the McLaren's wing *accentuated* this blast—caught the underside of the wedge-shaped Autocoast and lifted it.

Rear wings: the Lola 220's (above) is rather an afterthought, with high end plates, while the McLaren M8D's (below) is a triumph of neatly conceived design.

In wind tunnels wedge-shapes have shown just this property of flipping over backwards if tilted up, in some cases to angles as small as 2 degrees.

This is not the first such incident at St Jovite (the first was in 1965, a year before Dibley and Hawkins did it). But it seems to be a problem particular to full-bodied cars at St Jovite, for drivers of single seaters are innocent of it. (Oliver was caught out by air turbulence in a Formula 1 Lotus at Rouen in 1968.) What lessons can be learned from it revolve around the fact that the big, unlimited CanAm car is taking us ever more deeply into unknown regions.

There is no call for a rush to eliminate wedge-shapes. Using the entire width of the body to generate downforce must inevitably require something chisel-shaped. Lamar has remarked: "It seems that every time I test a curvy, sexy body it turns out to generate lift." The 220 Lola has a pretty body, and before its first race a small dam had to be added to the top of the nose to kill lift; this dam was removed when the nose was given fences for Edmonton. Such details have been seen on F1 Lotuses as well; a better place for them, if they are needed and there is room, is under the nose, as on a TransAm saloon or John Cannon's FA M10B. It is intriguing that such ugly devices may not automatically slow the car down; in fact they may actually help it to go faster—lift generates drag, and if you kill the one you may well kill the other! Thus the deep chin of the Aston Martin DBS-V8 may not only improve stability but improve speed as well.

Dams appear, from time to time, on the noses of the McLarens, just ahead of the radiator-outlets. When fitted they act to increase airflow through the radiator duct, not to improve cooling but to add to the downforce effect. At other times small fences go onto the front bodywork; these have less effect than the dam on the duct. (On the Indy McLaren M15s, provision was made for canard fins, but in practice the airflow from the radiator duct was all the car could use, even when the rear aerofoils were fitted.) Cooling improvement is attacked by the careful dimensioning of the duct itself. Panels were added at Edmonton, to the "floor" of the duct above the driver's feet, which did not reduce the size of the duct by as much as an inch. It has come out that the specialised makers of the bodies did not precisely follow the plans, so that the ducts were slightly too large, and the engines overheated.

CanAm Championship positions after seven rounds: 1, Denny Hulme, 72; 2, Dan Gurney 42; 3, Lothar Motschenbacher, 39; 4, Peter Gethin, 37; 5, Bob Brown, 29; 6, Dave Causey, 26; 7, Roger McCaig, 25, 8, Gary Wilson, 24; 9, Tony Dean, 18; 10, Peter Revson, Jack Oliver, and Jo Siffert, 15.

The BRM's body is meant to do its own aerodynamic work, and has neither aerofoils nor fences (below).

THE SUMMER RERUNS

As Ferrari team manager I was told, "You guys have just got to beat those McLarens."

BY BILL GAVIN

Chris Amon in the Ferrari 612: the horsepower came too late.

RICHARD GEORGE

The fourth series for the Canadian-American Challenge Cup was bigger and richer than any that had gone before, but for all that the outcome was an echo of 1967 and 1968.

At the end of the series, expanded from six to eleven races, the lion's share of the $1 million of posted prize money and bonuses went to Bruce McLaren and Denis Hulme who won respectively six and five races apiece, and who predetermined not only the finishing order race by race, but the Can-Am Championship itself, which went this year to McLaren together with $158,750 in prize money.

From the start of the season the press, jaded by years gone by, predicted that the McLaren team's continued domination of the series would ruin it. But race by race the crowds went back in bigger numbers than ever before. At season's end the championship's sponsor, Johnson's Wax, had already decided to plow back another $200,000 into the 1970 fund, satisfied that they were getting their money's worth, while the Sports Car Club of America was already successfully persuading the race organizers that the minimum purse for the '70 series should be upped to $75,000 per race. Everybody who had contested the 1969 series declared they would be back, Porsche and Ferrari with more competitive cars, Eric Broadley with a

"works" Lola effort, plus new designs from Team Surtees and March Engineering, and possibly Lotus. Even the Japanese, with Toyota winning the final but unofficial Can-Am in November, threatened to enter the competition. Toyota has gone so far as to gather complete information on every track in the series, but the morning line has them making a debut in 1971. So it was pretty clear that the domination of the McLaren M8Bs had frightened nobody, and least of all the spectators. If people went to the races to see the McLarens get beaten, they were disappointed, but they will almost certainly go again for the same reason and the outcome for 1970 is by no means an unclouded issue.

Their very invincibility brought the McLaren team into the headlines and brought Can-Am racing more publicity than ever. From that point of view, had the honors been more evenly shared the Series would have lost impetus in much the same way that the PGA golf tour has—now that every time you pick up a newspaper a bunch of entirely new names have finished strokes ahead of Arnold Palmer and Jack Nicklaus.

As Ferrari team manager I was constantly told both by spectators and by people who had never been to a motor race "you guys have just got to beat those McLarens."

Unfortunately it takes a lot more than a strong rooting section and a band of cheerleaders to win a motor race. For a start it takes a lot of time and a lot of money. The fact is that there are a number of teams more than capable of defeating the McLarens—there are better designers, better engine builders, better drivers, but until now they just haven't invested either the time or the money. Ferrari was, and is, eminently capable of building a winning Can-Am car, but in 1969 the Can-Am was just one of six different types of racing that Ferrari engaged in. Quite apart from its Can-Am effort, the company contested the Tasman Series, the Manufacturers' Championship, Formula One and Formula Two, and the Mountain Championship. To add to the problem, the Can-Am was the last of the programs to get started and consequently the car was given testing sessions in Italy that lasted exactly 1½ days and less than 400 miles. About all that this "development program" did was to reveal a basic oil cooling problem that was not cured until the first three races had been run and Chris Amon had been obliged to pussyfoot the 612 into third places at Watkins Glen and Mid-Ohio, and second place at Edmonton. The "cure" for the oil cooling problem brought to light an inherent design fault in the 6.2-liter engine, but it wasn't detected until four engines had been destroyed and Keith Duckworth, designer of the Cosworth Ford engines, had donned a pair of Ferrari overalls and crawled into the oily mess under the 612 during practice at Riverside. Fortunately by then the 7-liter V-12, much delayed by a series of strikes in Italy, had finally arrived, just in time to be fitted to the car for the race. It fired on the starter button on the grid, and was warmed up, then shut off for the national anthem. But our troubles still weren't over. As the last strains of the anthem died away, Amon tried in vain to re-start the new engine. The organizers okayed a push start and then changed their minds and disqualified the car just when Amon was really pressing Bruce McLaren, confident that he could nail him at any time. The 7-liter did about a hundred miles of tire tests at Riverside the day after the race but blew up during practice for the final race of the series at Texas. So the 6.2-liter was put back in the car for the race but a piston let go after only seven laps when Amon was lying in his usual third place.

If the Ferrari supplied little competition for the McLarens, the rest of the field supplied even less. Things had looked hopeful at the outset of the series, but that in itself is beginning to sound like a broken record. There was Chaparral, with a new car, the 2-I, which had been under development for over a year. Jim Hall was still convalescing from his accident at Las Vegas the year before, so he signed John Surtees to drive. When it became apparent to him that the new car was still not ready, Hall went out and bought a new McLaren M12, the 1969 production model, and fitted it with one of his giant aluminum Chevys.

Surtees found himself racing for third in the opening rounds at Mosport, St. Jovite and Watkins Glen but when the new car made its debut at Edmonton, Surtees was lucky to finish fourth, behind George Eaton's M12 McLaren. Hall had gambled with a very radical design, an ultrasmooth envelope shape which almost made a coupe out of the car, and had done away with the wing concept entirely. It didn't work and to add to his troubles he and Surtees seemed to agree on very few things and fell out so completely by the end of the series that Surtees didn't even run the last race at College Station in Texas.

Apart from the Chaparral there were high hopes that Dan Gurney and All American Racers might come up with a trump card. Gurney arrived at Mosport for the opener with much-modified McLaren-Chevy for power, but it wasn't enough. After the engine failed at St. Jovite AAR temporarily vanished from the scene. When Gurney did reappear halfway through the season he was still plagued by engine trouble which never allowed him to make much of an impression.

Charlie Parsons was entered by Carl Haas in what was essentially the works Lola, a T163 with a Chaparral-prepared Chevy for power. Parsons was his consistent self throughout the championship. He picked up three thirds and a second place at Riverside, which gave him a creditable third overall in the point standings, but the Lola was too heavy and lacked development time.

The Porsche appeared first at Mid-Ohio for the fifth round. The car was a re-worked, open 917 with a 4.5-liter flat eight and about the only thing going for it was reliability and Jo Siffert in the cockpit. Siffert finished fourth with the car in its debut and the highest he climbed was third in the seventh race of the series at Bridgehampton, but the Germans weren't worried. This was merely a reconnaissance season in preparation for the future. In spite of this, Siffert managed to finish fourth in the point standings, edging out Eaton who had a very creditable series finishing

with a second place to Bruce McLaren in Texas, the only car on the same lap.

For Ferrari the Can-Am effort had proved a classic example of how not to go motor racing. If the effort had any merit at all it was simply that it was made.

Enzo Ferrari himself is not particularly interested in Can-Am racing and the fact that a Ferrari showed up on the entry lists at all last year was due only to the enthusiasm which Amon has for this kind of racing. Amon had his first taste of excessive power (at least by latter day standards) when he raced a 250F Maserati in New Zealand when he was only 17. But he's been in love with it ever since and he's not alone in this respect—witness the popularity of Group 7 racing among the other top drivers of today. Not that the drivers are the only people turned on by the thought of 700 horsepower in a 1500-lb. car, which is what the fans can expect to see at the races this year.

There is also the question of money of course. The mere presence of a dozen or more factory-sponsored teams lined up for this season, which is about the same number of works entries you can expect to see at a Grand Prix these days, is a pretty clear indication that Bruce McLaren is no longer the only constructor who views Can-Am as a real rival to Formula One.

Undoubtedly, the success of the purse system in Can-Am has played a major role in the decision of the Grand Prix organizers to consider replacing the old starting money gambit with an all-prize money setup. But the North American series still doesn't seem likely to lose its draw-power because the Europeans haven't been slow to realize that the Can-Am has much greater growth potential, as far as the purses are concerned, than any other form of racing.

There are other sides to the commercial aspect too. Porsche for one has seen Can-Am as the kind of racing most likely to have the greatest effect on the sale of production cars in the U.S. and Fiat's Giovanni Agnelli, who now in essence controls Ferrari, is also aware of it—last year he sent an envoy all the way from Milan to report on the Ferrari performance. The man arrived 10 minutes after the start of the Bridgehampton race only to find that the Ferrari had already been retired. He promptly went back to Italy and returned on the eve of the Michigan race to learn that the only Ferrari Can-Am engine we had in the States had blown in practice. Having not much to report he disobeyed his orders and made himself known to us, and once acquainted with our many problems, he sent off a Telex to Agnelli's office suggesting ways they might help. The Telex machine quickly clattered back its reply—the poor man was fired on the spot, 4000 miles from home! Whether or not Fiat

RICHARD GEORGE

110

McLaren and Hulme
(in the practice
car): the M8Bs
were invincible.
(Inset)—Parsons
drove the Lola T162
consistently well
and finished third
in the standings.

(Top)—Siffert in the Porsche: strictly a reconnaissance mission.
(Right)—Hall and Surtees: a falling out. (Bottom)—Parsons in the
"works" Lola and Motschenbacher's McLaren M12.

will back the 1970 Ferrari Can-Am effort is not known, but success here could really help them in this market. Which makes it more surprising that Colin Chapman seems uncertain as to plans for Lotus participation in 1970.

Sponsorship for racing is hard to find anywhere in the world, but it's less difficult to come up with in the United States than anywhere else. The iniquitous thing about sponsorship is that the more successful your team is the more the money rolls in. It's a vicious circle, creating a balance of power that tends to be loaded in favor of last season's winners.

Before the end of 1969 Bruce McLaren had probably lined up more than $300,000 in sponsorship for the 1970 Can-Am series. His test program began in December when he started trying out 1970 modifications on his 1969 car, and at that time his engine development program was already well under way. The sponsorship money alone should comfortably pay all his development

and racing costs, and with that kind of a bankroll, the prize money is merely icing on the cake. But it's doubtful that McLaren Racing will pocket such a big share of the take in 1970. For a start, at least five other teams will have engines based on the 430 cu. in. aluminum Chevrolet blocks that were supplied to McLaren and Chaparral alone last year and these will be raced in 464 or 494 cu. in. form this year which should even out things a little on that score at least. Porsche is variously reported to be considering turbocharged 4.5-liter units, a normally aspirated 16-cylinder, 6-liters or the 6.9-liter Mercedes V-8. Ferrari is applying to the 7-liter engine all the lessons it learned with the highly reliable 5-liter V-12, which has the same block and cylinder heads, so the magic figure of 700-hp should be well within its grasp.

After the Ferrari was declared a non-starter at Laguna Seca last year, Amon was invited to race the McLaren team's M8B back-up car (as Gurney had been

at Michigan earlier in the series). He was very impressed with it, but said afterwards that he was certain that the right man could design a better chassis. The right man as far as Amon is concerned is Robin Herd. As a designer for McLaren, Herd was responsible for the McLaren M6B, which first brought McLaren the Can-Am Championship in 1967. Amon's confidence in Herd will be put to the test this season, because Herd, one of the founding members of the new March organization, designed the new Group 7 car which Amon will drive for the team in this year's series. And March is one of those teams which will be using the new aluminum Chevy, being prepared for them by Chaparral.

Whether or not 1970 is going to be the year in which the Bruce and Denny show loses its top rating one thing is certain. The success of the season past has laid to rest the notion that their monopoly would kill the series altogether. Ironically, it seems to have done just the opposite.

EOIN YOUNG talks to

Vic Elford on driving the Chaparral

Currently the most controversial car on the CanAm sports car scene, the Chaparral 2J ground effect car—or the "super sucker" or "vacuum cleaner" as it has been christened—has yet to finish a race. The controversy has been sparked off in CanAm by the alarming potential of the new car, which uses an auxiliary engine to drive suction fans which help to create a partial vacuum under the car, thereby "sucking" it down on to the road.

The car first appeared at Watkins Glen in July with the then world champion, Jackie Stewart, at the wheel for his only appearance in the CanAm series. He set fastest lap in the race before the auxiliary 750 cc JLO two-stroke engine failed. With the exception of Laguna Seca, where the 8-litre Chevy engine blew up at the end of practice, the little JLO has always been the main problem with the complex new car. In the final race at Riverside, with the threat of protests and official SCCA banning hanging over the Chaparral, Elford qualified the car 2.2 secs faster than Denny Hulme's title-winning M8D McLaren. Through Riverside's Turn 9 loop at the end of the long straight the Chaparral was a clear half-second faster than the McLaren.

"The big difference between the Chaparral and a conventional sports car like a 917 Porsche or anything else I've driven before, is this unreal sensation of being glued to the road," says Vic Elford. "Just to explain that a little, the partial vacuum that is created underneath allows the air pressure to work a little harder on the car, so that in effect the car has a down-force or loading on it of something like 1000 lbs over the weight of the car. Driving through a corner it has this much extra weight acting on the wheels.

"As you start to approach the limit of adhesion on braking or cornering with a conventional racing car, whether it's a single-seater or a sports car, it starts to get a little bit out of shape. It will start to twitch a bit. The back starts to go from side to side, and the driver is kept busy at the wheel. With the Chaparral—at least at the stage I've reached with it—this just doesn't happen. When you want to go through a corner you simply turn the wheel and the car goes round as though it's on rails.

"I'm now beginning to get to the stage on

Vic Elford prepares to take to the track in the 2J "super sucker."

some corners where I am reaching the limit, but even when this happens it's quite undramatic compared with a normal car. It just starts to slide out a little. In a faster corner the back starts to come out, but it really floats rather than slides, and I don't have to start twitching the wheel to hold it. I take off perhaps half an inch of lock, and the car remains in its smooth line through the corner.

"The same thing is true under braking. I can brake considerably later than most cars on the way into corners because the car is so very firm and stable on the road. If I make a mistake, as I have done once or twice with the car on the approach to a corner and I enter it too fast, I can put the brakes on and start to slow it down when I'm on the way in or halfway through a corner. With a normal car if you started to do something like that, the chances are that you would lock a wheel instantly, if only for a fraction of a second, and slide off the road."

This season CanAm fields have averaged 27 cars, and with only perhaps half a dozen

competitive machines there is a definite problem with slow traffic. Denny Hulme complained earlier in the season that the leaders were having to set their pace to that of the slowest car to avoid being run off the road while negotiating the tail-enders.

In this respect, Elford was fortunate with the Chaparral. "The car is just so good in traffic. In any race you encounter slower cars as you get on through the event, and passing them with any normal car is often quite a problem because they tend to stick to the line and we have to go round the outside of them. This is where the 2J shines, because it is so much better than conventional cars when you get it off the accepted line for a corner."

Ask Vic about horsepower from the aluminium Chevy built down in the Midland, Texas, engine workshops by Gary Knutson, and Vic casts an anxious eye at Chaparral boss Jim Hall. Hall tells him to say the car has 700 horsepower and that it's on a par with the rest of the front runners. As with the McLaren

Elford expounding a point (left), and proving it setting pole position at Riverside (right).

Vic finds the sensation of being "glued to the ground" very strong when driving the 2J.

team, there is always a doubt hanging over the CanAm races that perhaps the Chaparral team are running larger engines than they claim. This makes it easy for the slower drivers to excuse their lack of pace.

Before Vic drove the car for the first time at Atlanta in mid-September, he went down to Midland to try the 2J round Rattlesnake Raceway, Hall's private test track near his racing workshops. His main preoccupation then was learning to drive the automatic transmission car and braking with his left foot since there wasn't a clutch to worry about. Anticipating when he would race an automatic car, Elford had practised left-foot braking from the day he took delivery of his automatic Ford Zodiac, but in moments of stress he tended to forget. "It was a bit dramatic occasionally because I would tramp on the wrong pedal coming up to traffic lights! When I drove the 2J at Midland I did have a bit of a problem once or twice as I went to change gear with the selector lever, particularly changing up. I would tend to stamp on the brake pedal just as I flicked the lever through. This happened at Atlanta the first time I drove it in practice, but I soon got used to it." At Atlanta Elford qualified on pole position, 1.26 secs faster than Hulme in the McLaren.

Like the Chaparral he drives, "Quick Vic" tends to be a controversial personality, speaking the truth as he sees and understands it rather than playing the motor racing diplomat which seems to be vital these days. The facts are often not as important as how they are presented. Through personal determination and drive, Elford has graduated from a rally navigator to a Monte Carlo-winning rally driver with Porsche, and thence into top-line international motor racing. His appearances in Formula 1 to date have not been remarkable because the cars have tended to overshadow the driver's ability. Elford's plans for 1971 include the full CanAm Series, perhaps the three major speedway races at Indianapolis, Ontario and Pokeno, and the chance of a Grand Prix drive as well. He has been talking with Ron Tauranac about a Brabham ride.

Elford is 35, wiry at 11 stone, and lives with his wife and family at Heston, only seven minutes from London Airport, which is an important consideration. His blonde wife Mary accompanies him to all his races. To gain a foothold in CanAm he drove less than competitive cars, flirted with the way-out knee-high AVS Shadow, and then suddenly appeared on top with the Chaparral at Atlanta.

"I enjoy CanAm racing. These two-hour 200-mile sprint races are ideal for the driver, because you keep going pretty well flat out and you can have a good race for that time. The only criticism I've got about the CanAm Series is that there is so little competition. I don't mean for us, but with or without the Chaparral there are still only four or five cars that are really competitive. The two McLarens, the L&M Lola, the Autocoast, and that's about where it stops. After that it tends to become a bit of a procession and people trundle round knowing that they're going to finish somewhere in the money. In many cases when you get below the top six or seven they don't race anyway—they're quite happy to drive around just to finish. The racing would certainly be a lot better if there were more factory entries either from America or from Europe. From that point of view, ignoring the controversial side of it, the Chaparral must have increased the value of the CanAm Series as a public performance because it gives the public another competitive car."

The Chaparral controversy is a dangerous one to get involved in without appearing to take sides. As Jim Hall says, if the issue was black or white there would be no problem. The Chaparral would be either legal or illegal, and he gives you to understand that he wouldn't have built the car if it was going to be illegal. The Sports Car Club of America regulations banned wings acting on the suspension at the end of last season, but their definitions in the specific area of aerodynamic aids were not as clear as they might have been and this is where the problem has arisen. The issue is grey round the borders, rather than a clear-cut black or white. Everyone wants the SCCA to clarify their regulations, and it appears that every team with the exception of Chaparral would like to see the 2J banned.

The McLaren team sees the sucker system increasing the cost of CanAm racing, which is already expensive when the same amount of extra pace could be obtained by allowing suspension-mounted wings back on CanAm cars. As Denny Hulme points out, wings were banned by the FIA because the wing structures were breaking only on some Grand Prix cars. There had been no breakages on CanAm wings.

Peter Bryant, once a racing mechanic in Formula 1 with Reg Parnell, and designer and builder of the Autocoast Ti22 titanium car sponsored by Norris Industries until his recent controversial dismissal, points out that even though they have fitted a bigger 494 cu in engine, their times are slower than in 1969 when they ran with a wing. There would be astronomical development costs if others had to fit a sucker system of skirts and fans to their cars. "It took them two years to sort out the Chaparral and they have their own race track. It cost me $500 a day to hire Riverside. We could have built a car like the 2J, but it would have meant asking more money from our sponsors, and good sponsors are hard to get."

March designer Robin Herd estimates that the Chaparral is currently using only about 2 per cent of the suction that is theoretically available. "There are practical difficulties about getting more, but this figure can obviously be improved," says Herd, who has been studying the system in America with a view to incorporating a similar arrangement on the Formula 1 March.

"I personally don't think the car is illegal because I don't think it conflicts with the regulation about moving aerodynamic devices," says Elford. "However I prefer not to get too involved with the technical side of it—it's my job to drive it."

Hall maintains that aerodynamics are concerned with air moving over a surface. The Chaparral sucker system "does its thing" sitting still on the grid, so how does it get to be an "aerodynamic device"?

"If they ban the 2J in CanAm racing I might as well go into Formula Vee or USAC or some sort of tight formula, which I didn't think CanAm was supposed to be," says Hall, having the last word.

The 2J naked, showing the Lexar skirt and two-cylinder, two-stroke JLO fan motor.

PETE LYONS discusses

Technicalities of the 2J

The 2J Chaparral was described in essence at the time of its introduction. It is quite a simple vehicle in concept, using as many proven components as possible in the interests of allowing development to concentrate on the one "trick," the extractor-fan and articulated skirt system which makes the vehicle cling to the road like a limpet. That the idea works is now proven. Whether it *is* the way of the future will depend on other factors. But the feeling of the engineer whose child it is, Don Gates, is this: "Our car is in the same relation to conventional race cars as the first steam boats were to the clipper ship. The clippers were finely developed, efficient, well proven, well understood, and they were very beautiful. The first steamers were crude, heavy, unreliable, inefficient, and they were ugly. They even threw soot all over everybody. But look around—where are the clippers now?"

The actual figures describing the 2J's operation are difficult to extract, Jim Hall quite reasonably feeling that to learn them cost him a lot of money and time. In point of fact the actual figures are probably not important, because the car is only on the bottom floor of what it could become. But the characteristics of its twin fans are available; they can each pass over 9000 cubic feet of air per minute and, given the claimed horsepower of 45 bhp from the JLO "little motor" they could maintain a steady pressure differential of about one-third atmosphere. As the skirts enclose an area of about 7400 square inches, there is a potential "suction" of over 2000 pounds, which must be very close to the grid weight of the car. The chassis and suspension members were designed to carry 2G (multiplied by a safety factor of three). The car has not as yet quite achieved 2G on a circuit, but it has come very close. Don Gates says that he could right now build a car which would operate at 3G—and it would do that under both braking and cornering, which operations use up perhaps 25 per cent and 55 per cent respectively of a typical CanAm circuit lap. Only the power of the engine would govern the G-forces of acceleration.

When the car first appeared, a member of the McLaren team remarked that there was a British gas-turbine available which would make a nice way to extract air from the interior of a " sucker." But the Chaparral has fans driven by a piston motor, and a little delving into the subject shows it to be a cunning combination. The characteristics of the "vane-axial" fans are such that a certain level of pressure-differential is maintained at a certain rate of airflow, but that as the rate of flow rises there is suddenly a point at which the pressure-differential drops off. Now, if the car as a whole should aviate over a jump, or drop an edge into a depression, and the clearance between skirts and ground should increase from the normal ½-inch, the drag on the fans would suddenly reduce and they would over-speed. But as the revs of the little motor rise, its power curve drops off, and the result is to keep the over-speeding to a minimum. Thus the driver is presented with as little complication as possible. In

any case, the proper pressure level would re-establish in as little as half a second, once the skirts were at their designed height.

Another problem facing a turbine would be the high quantity of dirt and track debris sucked up from the surface; after a run of any duration the engine compartment of the 2J is filthy.

The potential of the concept is illustrated by the fact that, if one could double the horsepower of the fan-drive, one could achieve *quadruple* the downforce. But the corolary is that a little loss of fan horsepower has a large effect on the downforce. In its *début* the two-stroke gave trouble with fuel vapour-locking, and Stewart started the race and set fastest lap with only 30 per cent suction available.

The story has been published that the 2J was built in its basic form by Chevrolet in Michigan. The Chaparral men say that Chevrolet did indeed have a test-vehicle using the principle, but the 2J is entirely their own work. In the first plan (see photo of clay model), the car would have been very conventional in shape, with a low wedge nose and exposed wheels all round, the skirting enclosing only a space between the wheels. But at another stage it was intended to have the *entire body shell* ride with the suspension and act as a skirt. The final form leaves the front wheels exposed, and the skirts have their centre-of-pressure about two-thirds back on the wheelbase.

The final nose shape is something new, and Gates is very enthusiastic about it. The idea is to split the airflow sideways, because any air that goes over the car *must* create lift; he says that if he could have built the nose like the prow of a ship he would have.

It was not intended to use rear spoilers of any kind, but they were found necessary to balance the effect of what downforce is generated by radiator airflow. Fences on the body top would greatly increase downforce; in fact they would cause the body to collapse. It's been tried.

Obviously what happens to air going under the car is the important thing. The three visible skirts are simple stage-curtains, but the fourth that runs across behind the front wheels cannot ride up and down because of the driver's legs. It is in the form of a panel which trails from a hinge and drags on the ground, and is separated into a dozen separate pieces to allow for body roll and the occasional stone. Ahead of this, under the radiator, are two rubber flaps running full width. This is one of the non-discussable items *chez* Chaparral, but they must act to block some of the slipstream before it can affect the main skirt. When Tom Dutton left the first thing he did to his McLaren was to add a rubber flap under the nose. . . .

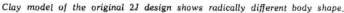

Clay model of the original 2J design shows radically different body shape.

Inevitable favourite : Denny Hulme with the 8.1-litre, 7430 horsepower McLaren-Chevrolet M8F during a lull in recent Goodwood testing.

For several seasons now, at the beginning of each CanAm Series, we've been asking: Is this the year that will see the end of the McLaren stranglehold on North American Group 7 racing? With the opening round of the 1971 series being run at Mosport in Canada this Sunday, it's the same old question. Last year the challenger to the Gulf-orange cars' supremacy was the dramatic Chaparral 2J "sucker" car, the year before it was the 6.3-litre Ferrari. This year it's World Champion elect Jackie Stewart in Eric Broadley's latest creation from the new Lola factory at Huntingdon.

The CanAm Series was inaugurated in 1966, although several of the six rounds had existed as one-off sports car events in their own right in earlier seasons—young Bruce McLaren had even won a few of them in the Zerex Cooper Oldsmobile. But that year John Surtees' works Lola T70 won three of the rounds, with one going to Phil Hill's Chaparral 2E, one to Mark Donohue's Lola and one to Dan Gurney's Lola : Bruce had only a couple of seconds and a couple of thirds, and his Kiwi team-mate Chris Amon had one of each.

But in 1967 it was a different story. McLaren produced a pair of completely new cars, M6As, using 5.6-litre fuel-injected Chevrolet engines. The Chaparral 2G of Jim Hall was very fast, and John Surtees won the last round in his T70 Lola when the others retired, but Denny had three wins and three retirements, and Bruce had two wins, two seconds and two retirements. Bruce was champion, Denny runner-up, and there was really no one else in it.

In 1968 it was the seven-litre M8A. With three wins and a second, Hulme was champion : with a win and two seconds, Bruce was runner-up. The other two races, Bridge-hampton (Donohue in a production M6B) and the very wet Laguna Seca (Cannon in an old M1C) were won by McLarens too. The new Chaparral 2H never appeared ; the works 6.3-litre Ferrari for Chris Amon did appear, right at the end of the series, and was a damp squib.

For 1969 the CanAm Series was expanded from six rounds to 11. The works McLarens, M8Bs now, dominated the series more than ever : Bruce won six of the 11 and was second in three, while Denny won the other five and was second in five. The Chaparral 2H did appear, but unsuccessfully, in John Surtees' hands : he said it was the worst-handling car he'd ever driven. Chris Amon supplied some opposition early on in the 6.3-litre Ferrari, but the next quickest car to the two works McLarens was the third works McLaren. Chris Amon drove it once and Dan Gurney drove it once : both races were a McLaren 1-2-3.

Last year's series started under the shadow of Bruce McLaren's death while testing one of the 1970 7.6-litre M8Ds at Goodwood (the M8C was the 1970 production car), but the two works cars were at every one of the ten rounds. Denny Hulme was having to contend with severely painful hands in the earlier rounds, after his Indy fire, but he ended up Champion again with six wins. The second car was driven by Dan Gurney, who had two wins, and Peter Gethin, who had a win and two seconds.

But it was the most varied and stimulating series so far. Jack Oliver supplied a lot of the fun in a Pete Bryant-designed car which was first called the Autocoast and then, after the project had changed hands and a new car had been built, the Ti22, and he was second to Hulme in the last two rounds. The Chaparral driven by Jackie Stewart and Vic Elford, was tremendously fast when it was going, three times earning pole position, and Peter Revson was also a threat in the works L&M-sponsored Lola T222, bumping Hulme off pole on one occasion. And Tony Dean's little Porsche 908 won one of the rounds when all the other big boys retired ! Two

CanAm cars from British F1 teams, the BRM P154 for George Eaton and occasionally Pedro Rodriguez, and the March 707 for Chris Amon, generally failed to impress.

How will it go this year ? Well, Jackie Stewart is bound to be as fast as the works McLarens if the new Lola works reasonably well, as early testing by Frank Gardner seems to indicate, but his car will also have to match up to the McLarens in another area in which they are very strong : meticulous preparation. Alas, the Chaparral is gone, for Jim Hall has understandably given up the fray now that his ground-effects vehicle has been declared illegal. But there's a new car for Jack Oliver from Pete Bryant, and once again there are strong rumours from Italy of a big, big Ferrari.

This year's production McLaren from Trojan is called the M8E, but the works car is the M8F. The team are now using 8.1-litre Chevrolet V8s, for which their engine specialist Gary Knutson is claiming 740 bhp, using alloy blocks developed by one of their major sponsors, Reynolds Aluminum. Designer Gordon Coppuck has lengthened the wheelbase 3 inches since last year ; the monocoque is stronger and the rear brakes are now inboard. Although the body shape is little changed from last year, fences for added aerodynamic stability run the full length of the car on each side of the body, terminating in tail fins which form the sides of the rear aerofoil. The colour is of course the familiar Gulf orange, for the oil company are once again a major sponsor. Tyres are Goodyear, as they are on Stewart's Lola, and rear wheel rims are 17 inches wide this year.

Denny Hulme, with 17 CanAm wins in 33 starts, is backed up the team by Revlon cosmetics heir **Peter Revson** from New York, who's been around in motor racing a long time but still keeps getting better. Last year he was one of Denny's most serious rivals in the works L&M Lola, and in his first 1971 works McLaren outing—this year's Indiana-polis—he won pole position at record speed and finished second in the race.

To buy one of last year's works McLarens is a catch indeed, and there are usually several bidders for the Colnbrook castoffs. Hulme's M8D has gone to Yorkshireman **Tony Dean**, who was such a feature of last year's series in his Porsche 908, and Gethin's to German-born **Lothar Motschenbacher**, a CanAm regular whose consistency made him runner-up to Hulme in last year's series. Dean is still recovering from his Castle Combe F5000 accident, and until he is better his M8D will be raced by American driver Chuck Parsons : he still has his 908, which **Steve Matchett** will drive.

Among the M8Es which will be contesting the series is the American Racing Associates 8.1-litre car for **Vic Elford**, who impressed a lot of people in CanAm last year with his handling both of the Chaparral 2J and the extraordinary little AVS Shadow. German driver **Franz Pesch** is hoping to field an M8E, as are Canadian **Roger McCaig** and Americans **Bob Bondurant, Gary Wilson** and **Fred Park-hill. Bob Brown** will again be out in his ex-Gurney "McLeagle," a much-modified M6B, and other McLarens will be handled by **Bill Wonder** (M8C), **John Cordts** (M8C), **Oscar Koveleski** (ex-works M8D), **Rainer Brezinka** (M6B), **Cliff Apel** (M6B), **Charles Kemp** (M8C), **George Drolsom** (M8C) and **Tom Dutton** (M6B). Perhaps we may later see some of the European-based M8Es currently being used in the Interserie, like the Sid Taylor/Peter Gethin, Ecurie Evergreen/Chris Craft, Gesipa/Willi Kauhsen, VDS/Teddy Pil-lette and Gelo/Georg Loos cars.

Jackie Stewart's new Lola is fully des-cribed by John Bolster at the foot of this article, so suffice it to say here that the car is a fully works-backed project. It will be run in the series by Carl Haas, who is Lola's North American agent, under sponsorship from L&M cigarettes who similarly backed the Revson T222 last year, and in its white and red colours it looks very purposeful indeed.

Among the other Lolas expected for the series is a T222 from Japan, with 22-year-old **Hiroshi Kazato** at the wheel. **Frank Kahlich, Dave Causey** and **Bob Nagel** will be in Lola T222s also, and **Jo Bonnier** and **Giampero Moretti** may take their T222s over for one or two of the races. In earlier Lolas will be **Peter Ritsos** (T165), **Dick Durant** (T163) and **Jim Place** (T160).

March Engineering have no plans to send a works car to the CanAm Series, although they have already built one example of their 717 for Interserie competitor Helmut Kel-leners: with its blunt nose and mid-mounted radiators it shows similar thinking to the new Lola. However, one of the original 707s is still in North America: it belongs to Canadian March agent Gordon Dewar, who will campaign it in the series.

What of Ferrari? Nothing has been heard officially from Maranello since Enzo Ferrari's pronouncement at his annual press conference last December that "later in the year two Group 7 CanAm cars will be produced," and that "a seven-litre V12 racing engine is now under construction." Certainly the project is happening, but in previous years CanAm Ferraris have had to appear rather half-heartedly towards the end of the series because of Maranello's preoccupation with Formula 1, and the same situation seems to exist this year. Unconfirmed reports in the American press say that four seven-litre V12s have been built, and all four have blown up on the brake. When the car does appear, following current Group 6 Ferrari practice, it will almost certainly have central radiators and a blunt, stubby-nosed shape similar to the new Lola's. With **Mario Andretti** and **Jacky Ickx** as drivers and pro-bably an easy 100 bhp per litre from the four-cam engine, the Prancing Horse should be a real contender—if and when it appears.

Meanwhile American privateers **Jim Adams** and **Greg Young** will be doing their best to uphold the Ferrari name with their 512Ms. Roger Penske abandoned his plans to convert his Sunoco Ferrari 512M into a CanAm Spyder when it became evident that he

CanAm plans for the new BRM, which Rodriguez practised at Zolder last weekend (above), are still unannounced. Beneath the wedge nose is a canted radiator; engine is a BRM-modified 7.6-litre Chevrolet (below), and the car is type-number P167.

couldn't increase the engine size sufficiently to get a power output to put driver Mark Donohue onto a par with the 8-litre pushrod V8s. But he has already shown at Daytona and Sebring that he is more capable of making a Ferrari go well than the works are, and he may be showing the same thing at Le Mans this weekend. Surely Ferrari would be well advised to make one of his new 712P Spyders available for Mr Penske to paint blue. . . .

BRM have also not announced any official CanAm plans—but one of the P154s has been radically rebuilt as the P167, with redesigned bodywork and inboard rear brakes, and it made its *début* at the Zolder Interserie race last weekend with Pedro Rodriguez at the wheel. But BRM can't have gone to all that trouble just for the Interserie, and both Rodriguez and Jo Siffert are very keen to do some CanAm races. Howden Ganley probably is too.

The only all-American car in this year's CanAm Series will have a British driver:

Jack Oliver. This is a sort of marriage of the old Autocoast and AVS Shadow projects, for after the collapse of the former its de-signer Pete Bryant joined the AVS setup. The AVS Shadow, with its tiny wheels and radiator in the rear wing, was too far-out to work last season, but Bryant has rede-signed it completely. It is more conventional now, but still very low and compact, with 12-ins diameter front wheels (for which special tyres are having to be made) and orthodox 15-ins diameter rears. Last year's car had 10-ins diameter fronts and 12-ins diameter rears! The car is sponsored by Universal Oil Products, and will have a full 8.1-litre Chevrolet mill prepared by George Bolthoff.

For the kick-off at Mosport this weekend Oliver and Elford will be busy at Le Mans, but the McLaren/Lola confrontation should be in full swing. God and the transatlantic airlines willing, you'll be able to read Pete Lyons' full report of it all in next week's AUTOSPORT.

Stewart's Lola challenger

The production of Lola T260 prototypes will consist of 2½ cars, after which the T260 will go into full production in finalised form for the customers. An impressive new factory has been opened at Huntingdon, where the construction of 212s is already in full swing. Though the T260 is American-entered in the CanAm, there is total involvement of the Lola works, and the team is 100 per cent British. The prototypes are costing £35,000 to £40,000 each, and Eric Broadley estimates that the production cars will work out at about £15,000 each, with engine.

An entirely new shape has been chosen, as a result of an extensive programme of testing in the wind tunnel of Specialised Mouldings.

Compared with last year's CanAm Lola, the nose is very much shorter. It resembles the shape pioneered by Sir Henry Segrave's Irving-designed Sunbeam, which broke the 200 mph barrier some 45 years ago. It is of great interest that Chevron with the B19, Porsche with the 908/3 and March with the 717 have also espoused this long-forgotten shape recently.

A full monocoque construction in L72 and NS4 light alloys, bonded and riveted together, has been adopted. The fuel bags are contained in the sides of the monocoque and hold 60 gallons, the oil tank being at the rear of the left-hand fuel compartment. Glassfibre covers contain the front wheels and air is admitted

Frank Gardner did some testing with the just-completed Lola T260 at Silverstone before it was flown to the USA this week (above). The Foults-built Chevy, like the McLaren engines, uses staggered-length inlet trumpets (below).

through holes in their top surfaces to the two Serck brass-finned water radiators, which are contained in NACA ducts situated behind the driver's shoulder level and exhaust through large louvres in the rear deck. The two engine oil radiators are behind the water radiators in the same ducts. A small transmission oil radiator lies flat above the gearbox and a hole in the tail communicates with it. The wing is mounted on the glassfibre body structure above the bell-housing.

The cooling ducts were evolved in the wind tunnel and give 15 per cent better cooling with the same radiators than the conventional front location. This is largely because the centre section of the nose of the car has been found to be an area of low pressure. Indeed, the central panel has no bracing and has holes covered with gauze to equalise the pressure in front and behind. Two air ducts at the bottom of the nose feed the front brakes. The cooling air for the rear brakes is collected by horizontal ramming pipes on top of the transmission cover.

The suspension has been designed to permit inboard brakes to be used, but at present the Girling 12 in x 1.1 in discs are outboard mounted, as research is still continuing on the inboard location. The front suspension is by unequal length wishbones, of which the upper ones are triangulated to form bell-cranks. These operate Bilstein telescopic

dampers surrounded by coil springs, which lie almost horizontally across the front of the chassis. The rack and pinion steering is ahead of the front suspension.

At the rear, the monocoque continues to the back of the engine, which is sandwiched between two bulkheads. The bell-housing supports the gearbox and absorbs the suspension loads. At the top there is a short, adjustable link and a long radius arm, which articulates on the bulkhead in front of the engine. At the bottom an elaborate member, which could perhaps be described as a broad-based wishbone, extends backwards to a cross-member bolted to the rear face of the gearbox. The spring-damper units are attached to this bottom wishbone and transmit their load to tubular outriggers on the bell-housing.

The engine is a George Foults-prepared Chevrolet and various specifications are available — indeed, different power units may be chosen according to the circuits which they suit. Round figures would be a capacity of 496 cu in (8.1-litres) and a power output of 650 bhp. Fuel injection is by Lucas and

Rocking triangular wishbones operate horizontal front springs; the original design specified inboard front brakes.

ignition by a Scintilla Vertex magneto. The horsepower is transmitted through a Hewland four-speed gearbox and BRD roller-spline driveshafts. The magnesium wheels are of Lola manufacture and are of the centre-locking, peg-drive type. The rim diameter is 15in, and 10½ in (front) and 17 in (rear) are the widths for the Goodyear tyres.

The wheelbase is 8 ft 2 in, track 4 ft 10 in, overall length 11 ft 7 in, width 6 ft 4 in, and height to top of rollbar 3ft 3 in. The weight is likely to work out around 1600 lb. The battery is in the nose of the car, the Graviner fire extinguisher cylinder is behind the instrument panel, and the small leather-covered steering wheel has a protecting cushion at its centre. Smith's fuel pressure, oil pressure, oil temperature and water temperature gauges are mounted with a Jones rev-counter.

The 260 has already attained 190 mph at Silverstone, and as last year's car touched 196 mph at Riverside it is likely that the magic 200 will be exceeded this year. The stupendous acceleration allows very high speeds to be reached on the shortest straights, so the work demanded of the brakes is greater than in any other type of car.

The rear end is sharply cut off, with radiator exits incorporated in the body.

McLAREN M8F

The latest & greatest Can-Am car & how Denny Hulme drove it at Mosport

BY PETE LYONS

"**B**ALANCE," states Professor Hulme, thumbs tucked comfortably in his Nomex suspenders, "the whole theory of race cars is *balance*. That's all there is to it."

He's just in from practicing Mosport laps. His new Can-Am car, in its first weekend at the front lines, has not been behaving well. The official qualifying times show the Scot Stewart is quicker, but now Denny is confident of holding him off in the race. The McLaren's tail had been loose, but now he's put a set of older, inferior tires on the front. Not a sophisticated solution, but it works. Balance.

Out in the sunlit paddock the Kiwis have pushed the long M8F into their roped-off bay and stripped off its bright ocher panels. Its bare metal structure seems a familiar sight. It looks like Lothar Motschenbacher's ex-factory M8D a few bays away, and really it looks like Roger McCaig's brand new M8E across the path. The F is in fact a direct progression of the M8 series that have served so well these three years past. Back in the Colnbrook drawing office, we know from the stimulating new USAC and Formula 1 cars, there are plenty of fresh ideas. There are plans for a new Can-Am car which, if built, will be the M20. But *probably* the F is going to be enough change for this year.

First, the basic car is longer. Three inches have been added to the middle of the tub and now the wheelbase is 98 in., which should have the effect of shifting a fraction of the weight aft and improving braking stability. But the track, which last year went wider in contravention of long-standing McLaren thinking, is narrower again; 60 in. front, 58.8 rear. The suspension geometries are altered, giving modified camber-change curves at both ends and a bit more anti-squat at the rear. The front upright castings are straight off the Indy car and give slightly different geometry as well as being much more rigid. The weight of the rear brakes has been moved inboard next to the transaxle; the intrusion of the 12-in. discs here has forced replacement of the accustomed reversed A-arms with Surtees-style parallel links, which minimize bump-steer.

The transaxle itself is Hewland's new LG 500 Mk II, distinguishable by its much beefier case and side plates. It follows modifications McLaren made to their own Mk I last year. The big engines have been giving the hapless internals a bad time; this new case should position them more firmly.

The monocoque's fuel-tank sides are made of 0.062-in. sheet to try to prevent shunt-punctures. This is pretty heavy stuff and permits the rivets to be recessed aircraft style. It looks neat, but any effect on streamlining must be negligible. The driver's footwell has been braced with a new hat-section hoop, again with the odd collision (fact of Can-Am life) in mind.

Compared with the M8E customer car, the F has a few things made of more exotic materials, magnesium and titanium, and here and there some pieces may be thinner; but the overall weight cannot be very much less. Empty of all liquids the complete car probably scales close to 1550 lb.

There are two engine options. Gary Knutson, back after two years at Chaparral, builds up normal aluminum-block Chevies displacing 494 cu in. (the 4.44-in. bore of the 430 block with the 4-in. 454 crank) and fits the injection with staggered intake trumpets.

For Mosport he'd developed a torque curve that bulged up to some 600 lb-ft and continued to 700 in a straight line over a 1500-rpm band. Peak horsepower reading was about 740, but with Apollo-booster push like that the actual peak seems academic. The drivers were supposed to hold the revs below 7000, but dyno tests have seen these engines running at 7800.

The other option, not used at Mosport, is "the Reynolds motor" with its Vega-type sleeveless block. Partly because of piston-supply problems McLaren has fixed the bore of this at 4.50 in., and in an effort to make it a free-revving unit has elected to use the "427's" 3.75-in. stroke, which gives 480 cu in. The trusty sliderule calculates that with the 4-in. crank displacement would go out to 512 cu in. It would seem that the 800-bhp Can-Am car is not far away, but whether the current bottom ends could hold it inside for 200 miles is perhaps another thing.

Despite what rulebooks seem to think, the first job of the body is to generate squash. To this end last year's add-on "fences" have been made integral and run the full length of the body. Air shoveled up from the wedge nose is supposed to stay on top of the body, pressing down as it flows past, and on its way out over the stern the wing throws it upward again. Most of the inlets that used to be let into the top of the body have been relocated to interfere as little as possible with this airflow. The rear body line ducks down more sharply than it did last year to give the wing more room to work in. For what it's worth in terms of less drag, the side fins are thinner this year, because they no longer carry the full weight of the wing as they did before Bruce McLaren's crash.

The coolant radiator is still at the front, where the air extracted from it helps generate downforce. A large NACA duct in the left side of the body leads to the doubled-up engine oil coolers; a similar duct in the right flank in early-season testing delivered air through three hoses to the rear brakes and the transmission cooler but now merely offers a light breeze to the engine bay. The transaxle cooler is now fed from the only NACA inlet in the top surface, one back under the wing. The rear brake discs have neat little metal fabrications scooping up air from under the engine.

The Goodyear tires are designed especially for Group 7 and don't work well on anything else. They mount on 15-in. wheels at both ends, the front rims being 11 in. wide and the rears 17. The front "footprint" is about 9½ in. wide, the rear about 14¼. The tire pressures will be set at around 18 psi and the surface compound will run about 180 degrees Fahrenheit. A front wheel and tire, with weights and security

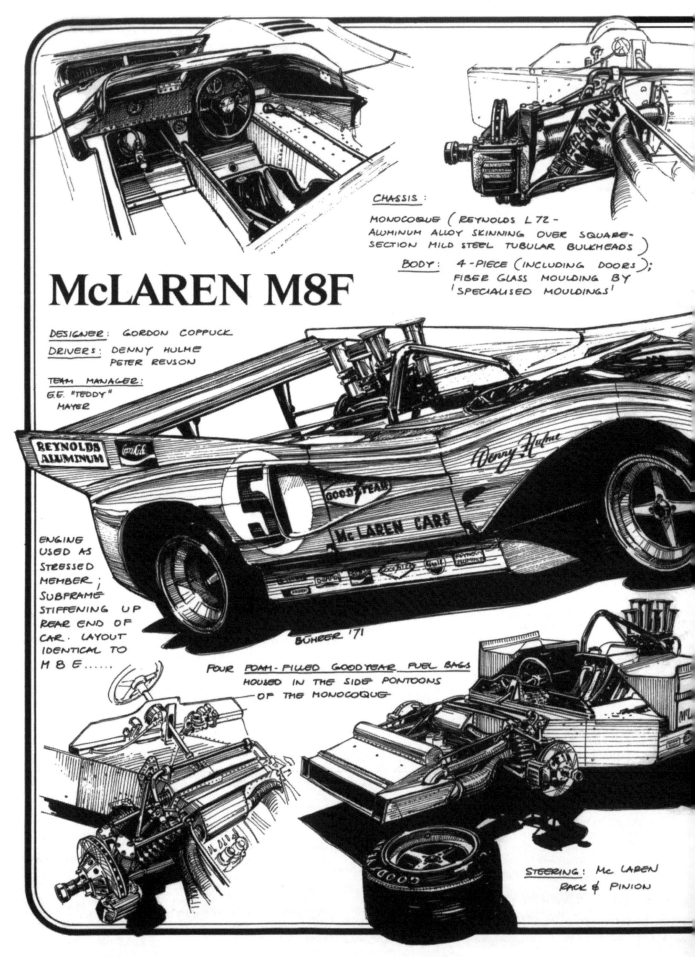

McLAREN M8F

CHASSIS :

MONOCOQUE (REYNOLDS L72 -
ALUMINUM ALLOY SKINNING OVER SQUARE-
SECTION MILD STEEL TUBULAR BULKHEADS)

BODY : 4-PIECE (INCLUDING DOORS);
FIBRE GLASS MOULDING BY
'SPECIALISED MOULDINGS'

DESIGNER : GORDON COPPUCK

DRIVERS : DENNY HULME
PETER REVSON

TEAM MANAGER :
E.E. "TEDDY"
MAYER

REYNOLDS
ALUMINUM

50

Denny Hulme

GOODYEAR

McLAREN CARS

ENGINE
USED AS
STRESSED
MEMBER ;
SUBFRAME
STIFFENING UP
REAR END OF
CAR. LAYOUT
IDENTICAL TO
M8E......

BÜHRER '71

FOUR FOAM-FILLED GOODYEAR FUEL BAGS
HOUSED IN THE SIDE PONTOONS
OF THE MONOCOQUE

STEERING : McLAREN
RACK & PINION

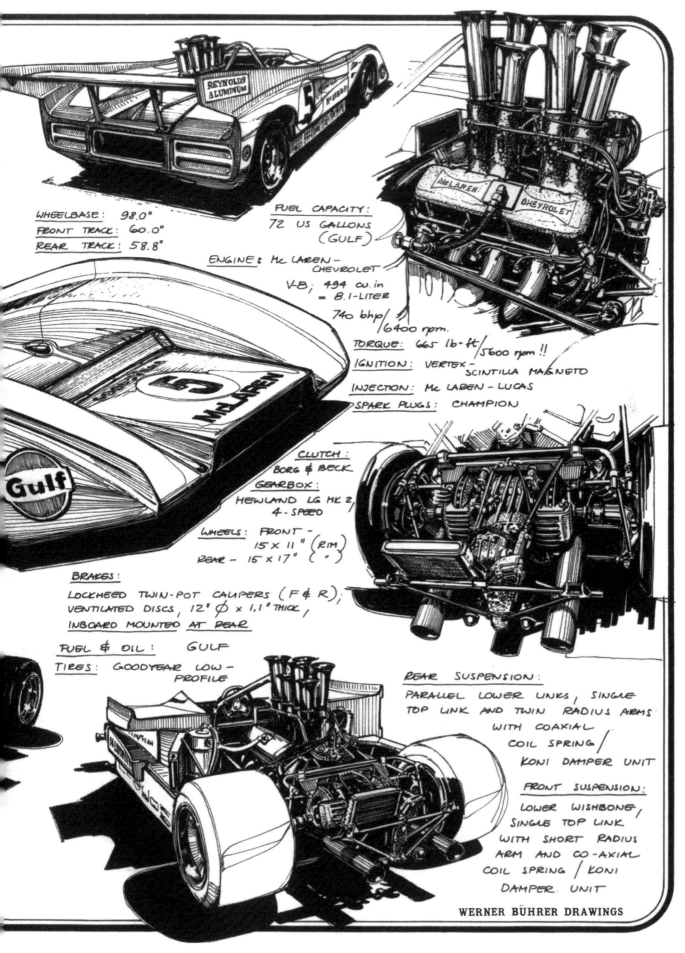

WHEELBASE: 98.0"
FRONT TRACK: 60.0"
REAR TRACK: 58.8"

FUEL CAPACITY:
72 US GALLONS
(GULF)

ENGINE: McLAREN -
CHEVROLET
V-8; 494 cu. in
= 8.1-LITER
740 bhp/6400 rpm.
TORQUE: 665 lb-ft/5600 rpm !!
IGNITION: VERTEX -
SCINTILLA MAGNETO
INJECTION: McLAREN - LUCAS
SPARK PLUGS: CHAMPION

CLUTCH:
BORG & BECK
GEARBOX:
HEWLAND LG MK 2,
4-SPEED
WHEELS: FRONT -
15 × 11" (RIM)
REAR - 15 × 17" (")

BRAKES:
LOCKHEED TWIN-POT CALIPERS (F & R);
VENTILATED DISCS, 12" ∅ × 1.1" THICK,
INBOARD MOUNTED AT REAR

FUEL & OIL: GULF
TIRES: GOODYEAR LOW-
PROFILE

REAR SUSPENSION:
PARALLEL LOWER LINKS, SINGLE
TOP LINK AND TWIN RADIUS ARMS
WITH COAXIAL
COIL SPRING/
KONI DAMPER UNIT

FRONT SUSPENSION:
LOWER WISHBONE,
SINGLE TOP LINK
WITH SHORT RADIUS
ARM AND CO-AXIAL
COIL SPRING/KONI
DAMPER UNIT

WERNER BÜHRER DRAWINGS

121

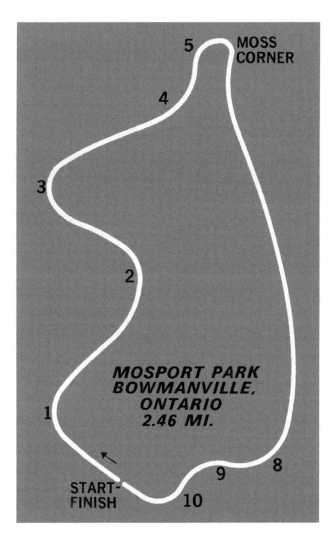

5 MOSS CORNER

4

3

2

1

START-FINISH

10 9 8

MOSPORT PARK
BOWMANVILLE,
ONTARIO
2.46 MI.

McLAREN M8F

bolts fitted, will weigh about 28 lb, a rear wheel about 40 lb.

Every millimeter of the car has been shaped by very careful, very expensive hands. Even a twin parked alongside is slightly different. Both machines will absorb every possible minute, the most painstaking care, the fullest devotion of the swarm of orange-shirted mechanics. After every day of use the cars are stripped for examination. Every critical part, which means nearly every part, is discarded on a strict time schedule and renewed as are cells in the human body.

When the McLaren is clipped together again, it drapes across its wheels with the loose grace of a relaxed athlete. Every line seems to suggest some vaguely evil purpose. The splayed injector horns, tinted light blue, plume from the glistening deck like outrageous irradiated flowers. Says Hulme:

"Shooting up the straight you're going about 175. Right at the crest of the hill you've got to *ease* up on the pedal. You mustn't let the nose get too high, or you'll get air under it and you'll take off. You mustn't touch the brakes, either, because you don't want the tail to get light. You just *ease* over the hump, sort of float. Then once you're down you get all over the brakes, get down to third, for turn eight. It's pretty bumpy through there, the surface is terrible, and I stay over to the inside as I go in. You'll often find me taking a different line to everybody else. Out at Elkhart, especially.

"Once you get into eight the surface is smooth; in fact it's one of the few places here where it *is* smooth. So you

can put a reasonable amount of power on early, and get it all on—or off-and-on—early. You'll find you can put the right front wheel up on the curbing. It doesn't disturb the car.

"You want to stay over toward the right of the road to be placed properly for nine. You come off the gas smooth and easy and sort of roll around nine to the left. I can't seem to get the car right in against the left curb for some reason, it wants to stay a couple of feet out.

"Then you can give it a bit of a squirt if you want to, and get right over to the left; hard braking, get down to second, and then straight across to the apex of ten and out the other side, keeping straight as the road drops off level. You don't want to give it too much power here, get too far sideways; you could if they'd build up the edge of the road."

I interrupt, saying I suppose another reason not to let the car powerslide is that we understand it exaggerates this tire vibration problem everyone's been having.

"Don't seem to have that with these tires we've got fitted today. Can't seem to feel it. But you can go out and tell who has it and who hasn't. You can see it in the marks they lay down coming out of the corners.

"You snatch third past the pits, shoot under the bridge and get set up for one. Don't get too far over to the edge. Touch the brakes. It seems you could take it faster, but there are bumps all down through the first part and they make the car understeer. You mustn't toss the car. You must be smooth, let the car just roll in, or you'll hit the rail like that guy did this morning. It's a bit like Indy, this turn. You think you need to stay right in the groove but you'll find you can get away with leaving it to get around traffic.

"When you get the power on the car goes neutral. You can't actually nail it until you actually get out of the corner. The instant you just *crack* the throttles you've got forty percent of your power. We've got lots more horsepower and torque this year, and it's got just the same holes for the air to go through, and it all happens much more violently."

I say I remember the number of times last year he asked for a "430" because it was smoother to drive.

"Right. In fact it isn't until now I realize just how good the 430 was. Another thing about turn one as I think about it, I just now see why it seems slower this year. At the exit out near the rail the surface is bad. It's always been rough but it's worse now. You can't run on it.

"Up toward two, staying in third—in fact you'll be staying in third all through here until you get to five—you must back off for two at what seems too early. You brake a wee bit and then get right off the brakes and let it roll over the crest. If you let the braking go later and later it disturbs the car too much, because the road drops away from under you. It's like turn seven at Riverside in that respect. Then there's a new bump at the apex, a bloody great patch.

"I notice Jackie's going wide around it and then pinching in tight later on down the hill. This is one of those places I told you about, where I'm apt to take a different line from anyone else. I run across the patch and then let the car go out wide.

"I remember with the high wings a couple years ago it was really keen down through there—you could really nail it. You'd come out the bottom like a rocket.

"Going up into three is another of those bumpy places, where you've got to be smooth. None of this lock-to-lock business. Coming out it's like the other corners; you can't give too much power until you're really out.

"Then heading into four I give the brakes a. wee bit of a pump to make sure the pressure's up, then steady gas down into the valley, all the way down to the bottom. Then maybe I'll give it a squeeze right at the bottom, then hard on the brakes and straight down into first gear. It doesn't seem to matter where you are on the road here, you can be inside or outside. I flick the car in here and give it a big boot and get it sliding up over the crest and heading for the hairpin."

Pete Revson has been leaning into the conversation, and now he interrupts with a puzzled frown. He can't make his F do that. If he tries to get its tail out it gives him warning signals. It wants to bite.

"Yeah," says Denny, "I've been seeing that. We must get that sorted out. Mind, last year Dan was getting through there fabulously, much better than me. He'd come rushing right up to me there. I don't know how he did it. But then he didn't seem to be as good through the next part, the Moss hairpin.

"Here's a funny thing. I can tweak the steering hard over long before I get to the hairpin. I can spin it right over to full lock, and it'll carry straight on for perhaps 20 feet. Then suddenly it digs in and takes me right in to the apex perfectly. Then it's wide-open throttle and we're away. It comes out on a lovely powerslide, right out to the edge and back toward the middle, tail out all the way. Then just as it begins to get straight you must lift off a wee bit and let the back wheels get locked in.

"Then it's up through the gears—second, third, fourth and you're rushing up the straight again."

Where is this kind of car different from F1?

"Oh, there's not too much difference really. You use the same line and much the same reference points for braking and so on. This probably brakes a wee bit better, because of the body. In terms of power-to-weight there isn't really that much difference.

"One thing about driving these cars is you don't realize you're going as quickly as you are because of the sound, the low apparent engine speed. An F1 has got ten on it, it's screaming and roaring, and it really feels like you're covering the ground."

I've heard that with Can-Am cars the wake turbulence from a preceding vehicle can be troublesome.

"It's terrible. You want to stay in clear air with these. If you're overtaking a backmarker and you come into a turn behind him, if you stay over toward the inside of his line you're fine. But gradually he comes in across you, making his apex, and suddenly you're into his draft. Your car just picks up and moves across the road by yards until you come out the other side. Then it grips again and you're all right, and you can run by. Out at Riverside, especially. You know the bend in the back straight, before you get to nine? You're really flying down there, 190 I suppose, and if you get into the bend behind someone your front end goes completely dead and you carry straight on. There's plenty of roadway there so it's all right, and you can carry on and be well placed to get underneath him going into nine. *But* you must be very, very sure not to alter the steering by a fraction while you're in his draft, because if you did, if you'd put more lock on, once you came out it'd grip again and you'd *really* go spinning off.

"It's not just bad in the corners, either. Once last year at Edmonton, you know that long straight past the pits, I got up close behind Motschenbacher, I think it was. Really up close, right on his tail. Suddenly I realized my front wheels were off the ground."

Quickly, so as not to appear to be overly impressed by a wheelstanding Can-Am McLaren, I turn to Revvie. What are his impressions of the M8F?

"It's definitely a car for a high-speed track. On slow turns there isn't any downforce and the back wants to come out—on mine, anyway. Maybe it's just my driving, maybe I'm just not used to it yet.

"One Group 7 car can be as different from another as it is from a Trans-Am car, you know. It's just a matter of how it's set up. Denny thinks this sudden oversteer thing is because of the engine coming on so strong, but I kind of think it's chassis problems.

"It's a car that is very sensitive to changes in things like ride heights. We've been playing with my ride heights and spring rates all over the map. My front end was wallowing and pitching around so we went to stiffer springs to hold it up. But now it has a tendency to 'speedboat' on the straight.

"Compared with my Lola T220 of last year, the steering is much lighter. I'd say that's the major difference. And this car seems to do a better job of keeping level. It's got more front downforce and the aerodynamics are better balanced."

Suppose that right now Hulme were to start laying down a successor to the M8 series. What areas would he try to improve?

"Well . . . I suppose possibly we'd be thinking about a suspension system more like the F1 car. And we might do some looking into aerodynamics. You see the nose on the Lola that Jackie's driving; well, we've been keeping that in mind for some time, it's just that they've done it before we have. One doesn't know just what is ideal for us. You could start in with an exhaustive aerodynamics program to find out—or you could whosh-bonk it! Probably get the same results."

"Whosh-bonk" just about describes the race. Stewart's new Lola, the L&M-supported T260, was taken to Mosport for a private day of testing on Thursday. It proved a valuable advantage for the first day of official qualifying, Friday, for he was fastest at 114.5 mph, or 1 min 17.3 sec. This was 0.9 seconds slower than Gurney's 1970 record but enough to hold off Hulme and Revson at 1:18.0 and 1:18.1. The Gulf-Goodyear-Reynolds McLarens were in their first day on the track and the drivers were confident of doing better the next day. But a combination of factors slowed the track by at least two seconds on Saturday and Stewart retained his pole.

Saturday night the Lola's engine was replaced, and there was something wrong with the throttle linkage Sunday morning. Stewart found it still sticking on the pace lap, so prudently he let Hulme beat him into the first turn. He had to watch the McLaren pull out a lead of six seconds in the first nine laps. But a backmarker, in one fell swoop across his nose, cost Hulme all his advantage and Stewart sneaked by. As soon as he was behind, Denny noticed oil leaking from the Lola's new Mk II transmission, so he relaxed and sat comfortably in second place waiting for the inevitable. It happened just before one-quarter distance and Jackie pulled off course into a stone quarry. As he walked back to the pits he watched Hulme and Revson run easily to another nose-to-tail Orange Elephant win, just the kind of sight everyone had hoped Stewart could prevent. 🔸

MOSPORT CAN-AM   Bowmanville, Ontario—June 13, 1971

	Driver	Car	Laps
1	Denis Hulme	McLaren M8F-494 Chev	80
2	Peter Revson	McLaren M8F-494 Chev	80
3	Lothar Motschenbacher	McLaren M8D-465 Chev	79
4	Bob Bondurant	McLaren M8E-465 Chev	79
5	John Cordts	McLaren M8C-465 Chev	78
6	Bob Brown	McLaren M6B-494 Chev	78
7	Dave Causey	Lola T222-465 Chev	75
8	Jim Adams	Ferrari 512-304 Ferrari	75
9	Hiroshi Kazato	Lola T222-494 Chev	75
10	Roger McCaig	McLaren M8E-465 Chev	74

11 Tom Dutton, McLaren M6B-427 Chev, 71 laps; 12 Dan Hopkins, Lola T160-427 Chev, 70; 13 Stanley Szarkowicz, McLaren M6-454 Chev, 66; 14 Frank Kahlich, McLaren M6B-427 Ford, 62 (not running at finish, blown engine); 15 Rainer Brezinka, McLaren M6B-365 Chev, 57, (not running at finish, battery failure); 16 Bill Wonder, McLaren M8C-427 Chev, 46; 17 Dick Barbour, Porsche 908-183 Porsche, 39.

Distance: 80 laps of 2.459-mi circuit—196.72 miles.

Avg speed: 109.033 mph. (Record: 110.214 mph, Dan Gurney, McLaren M8D-465 Chev, 1970.)

Fastest lap: 1:18.8, 112.343 mph, Denis Hulme. (Record: 1:18.0, 113.492 mph, Dan Gurney, 1970.)

Retirements: Gregory Hodges, Lola T70 3B-360 Chev, 38 laps, dead battery; Dick Durant, Lola T163-427 Chev, unknown; Steve Matchett, Porsche 908-183 Porsche, 26, accident; Oscar Koveleski, McLaren M8B-427 Chev, 28, broken piston; Jackie Stewart, Lola T260-465 Chev, 18, broken crown wheel and pinion; Charles Kemp, McLaren M8C-427 Chev, 16, blown engine; Gordon Dewar, March 707-427 Chev, 15, fuel pump failure; Bob Nagel, Lola T222-465 Chev, 10, clutch failure; Rudi Bartling, McLaren M2B-360 Chev, 9, front pinion.

A kid
who never
grew up

JIM HALL

talking to PETE LYONS

In 1970 the Chaparral 2J "ground effects vehicle" participated in four CanAm races. Each time it proved the fastest car entered, recording the quickest race lap at Watkins Glen and earning the pole at Atlanta, Laguna Seca and Riverside, but each time the elaborate machine was plagued by many detail troubles.

But unsuccessful as it proved in terms of results, its potential so impressed certain of its competitors that they initiated proceedings to have it banned, on the grounds that it violated FIA regulations concerning "movable aerodynamic devices." This ban came to pass, eliminating the car from the CanAm, and USAC later indicated that they would not allow a similar car at Indianapolis. The 2J has nowhere to race, and has been turned out to end its days as an attraction in auto shows.

The Chaparral Cars compound in Texas, once humming with race preparation activity, is quiet and nearly deserted. Two of Jim Hall's oldest employees remain on the payroll, turning out a few engines for customers "to pay the electricty bill" and overhauling street vehicles. In their own spare time the two, Franz Weis and Troy Rogers, are building up a Formula A car for Franz to drive in the Continental Formula 5000 Championship, starting with a monocoque hull designed for an Indianapolis project of four years ago which never saw the light of day.

Jim Hall himself spends little time at the shop. He seems out of touch with the latest developments on the general racing scene—he's even let his subscription to AUTOSPORT lapse There is obviously no new Chaparral on the stocks, and while he is not yet ready to make any announcements about the future one does not get any feeling that there will *inevitably* be another one, ever.

Looking back over his years on the international scene, Jim notes that this is the third time the FIA has shot him down: the 1968 ban on big engines at Le Mans, when he had already spent a lot of time and money on a revamped 2F; the ban of suspension mounted and driver adjustable wings; and now this.

"It's just not any fun anymore," he says. He looks at the question of the 2J's legality this way:

"In my opinion the car is absolutely legal, under both the FIA and SCCA regulations. I don't really see what the point of contention is. The skirts on the 2J are not an aerodynamic device. Aerodynamics implies relative motion of the atmosphere to the car. This device works just as good sitting on the grid as it does anywhere. It's not an aerodynamic device, it's a static pressure device. It doesn't rely on the relative motion of the car at all. They are applying a rule that was written about an aerodynamic device to a device that's not that in fact, it's a completely different thing. It's like trying to apply an aerodynamic regulation to the wheels, or the throttle valves.

"And as far as the fans being moveable aerodynamic devices, well, it's no different

from a brake rotor. It's just a matter of degree. If the fans are no good then brake rotors ought not to be either. Or the fan on a Porsche engine, or on an alternator pulley, or for that matter a water pump pulley—a water pump pulley is going to pump some air, you know ! "

What do you say to the argument that the expense of duplicating the sucker system might hurt racing?

" I don't think this car is all that much more expensive. The first one cost quite a bit, we spent quite a lot of time on it, but once you see what we did the equipment on the car could be built for less than $2000. That just doesn't seem significant compared to what we're doing. We're racing for a million-dollar purse. These are supposed to be high-quality, all-out racing cars, and two thousand dollars just doesn't seem important to me. You know, if any of the major competitors in any of these major series thought they could get another 20 horsepower they wouldn't mind spending $2000. They spend that much on camshaft development. It's just not a big number. Now I agree, *this* car is designed differently, it's heavier, it's stronger. But normally the major competitors build new cars every year anyway."

So you don't buy the argument that it would hurt racing?

" I really think it's got some appeal, from a spectator's standpoint. It's different, it looks pretty spectacular in the corners, it makes funny noises . . . I think it's an appealing car to sell to the public, and we're kind of in that business. I feel it would be a draw for the series. Now, what happens when you've got ten of them, I don't know.

" I'm not quite like these other guys, you know. The opinion seemed to be, ' We'll have to build one of those.' Well, I'm not sure I'd do that, if I saw that car run and its history and its, uh, winning ways. I mean, would *you* want to copy that ? You'd have to be a lot smarter to copy the McLaren at this point. I think if I saw somebody else run that car I'd go back and scratch my head and think, ' Well, gee, he must have made some bad mistakes in there somewhere. I'll figure out a better way to do it.' Your field of view narrows down to your own product, you know ? Maybe I missed a big point, I don't know. I did it the best I could.

" No, I think that type of car would have gotten cheaper, in reality. Anything you do for the first time, you're going to see ways to improve it, make it simpler. Who knows what it might have done in four or five years ? I don't. That's one thing that I think is really

wrong, saying, ' Uh, this adds too much to the price of the car.' We might have been able to do the same thing as cheaply as we can build a body shell, given another couple of years of development."

How about the safety angle? Suppose in five years cars were going through corners 50 per cent faster in terms of miles-per-hour? There is always the point about circuits being outgrown by the cars on them, and the 2J was a major step in speed magnitude.

" Ehh . . . it's a difficult question, isn't it ? Any speed increase tends to make the amount of energy in the collision worse, so . . . yeah, I agree, any speed increase makes racing more dangerous. But that's the name of the game. The whole game is ' Go Faster.' Anybody who's in it thinks the risks are worth the gains. So you're kind of chasing your tail with the question, really. Like, if I build a good race car it's more dangerous, so I ought not do that !

" I'll tell you what I found attractive about the 2J : the principle that automobiles operate on and always have is that they're land-based vehicles that operate from tyre forces, and that's what this thing does. All its cornering power, braking power, control stability, comes from the road, and that's a classic automobile. It's not like adding a rocket or something like that. I think it's a classic automobile, and I think it's the kind of major step in performance that we haven't seen in a hell of a long time. It's like when somebody first put four-wheel brakes on a car—that was a very major step in performance. And I hate to see somebody say ' Gee, that's a pretty big step, you ought not do it.'

" I mean, what have we done in automotive development, race car development, over the past ten years that's going to have the effect on lap times that this did ? We've all gone wide with tyres, and to disc brakes. These kind of things have all been exploited, and everybody says, ' Well, what comes next ?' Obviously, to me, *this* comes next.

" We'd been assured that rules under CanAm would not be changed for two years. You can't go into a programme like this thinking that you're right, that you've got some protection on rules, with a feeling that they're going to say, ' That's too fast, it's illegal.' If you don't have any protection like this there won't be *any* development. You'd just twiddle around and never do anything like this at all.

" If there's going to be a big change, I may not want to be a part of it anymore.

" The ground-effects principle is not all that much of a far-out idea, you know. There is a train in France that uses it, and I should

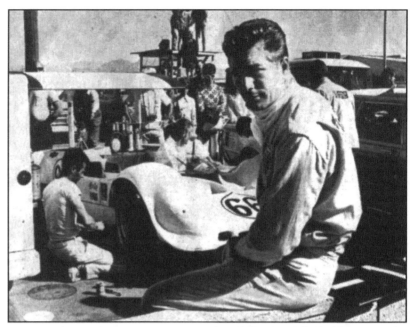

Back in his racing days before his Las Vegas accident, Hall waits while his 2G is prepared.

think it could be reversed as on the 2J to give that train superior braking. There must be a lot of applications like that.

"It seems to me that this business I've been in is the only industry where such an investment as we've made is not rewarded or compensated in some way. If I'd been in aircraft development, for instance, and I'd developed, oh, a new wing-root or something like that, if it proved to be superior, it would have swept through the entire industry."

So what has always attracted you as an engineer to Group 7, and it was Group 9 before that, was this chance to develop the most advanced concepts?

"Yeah. It was always pretty much a free formula racing where pretty much anything went as long as you fit the basic dimensional concepts, and so forth. That's what did attract me to it, the fact that you had a free hand to do what you wanted with it. You know, building a Formula Vee car is not too exciting. What are you going to do with it?"

So you like making big development steps?

"Yeah. It's fun."

I would imagine you wouldn't be particularly interested in running a merely conventional car—you had a taste of that doing the TransAm last year?

"No. I didn't like that very much. You ought to be paid a lot of money to have to do that!"

Jim, looking back, how many cars have you built now?

"Uh . . . up through J? Well, the first cars were Type 1s, they were Troutman and Barnes space-frame cars. I financed the building of the first one and bought the second. I think there were six altogether: Harry Heuer bought two and called them Meister Brausers or something, and there was one that Roger Ward ran at Riverside and dumped off Turn One into the underpass, and then there was one sold in England as a hillclimb car.

"The first rear-engined car was our own work, that was the Type 2, with the glass-fibre chassis. We put a 2 body on a 1 and ran Sebring one time. There were a couple of modifications of the 2 which should have been called 2 A or B or something but weren't. The first of those had a bunch of louvres on the body. Finally we built an aluminium chassis and called that the 2B, and from then on we went with the letters pretty consecutively. Whenever it got too confusing as to which parts went on which car we'd change the name.

"The first 2 had its début at Riverside in 1963. It qualified on the pole, and quit after four laps with an electrical problem. That car was subsequently run in modified forms almost

The 2J with its rear bodywork removed, showing the two-stroke auxiliary motor above the rotors.

to the end of the '65 season. One of those had the first automatic gearbox, at Laguna Seca in '64. I never did run the B in public. That was our first aluminium car and it had some problems. We built another one and called it the C, and that appeared at Seattle in 1965. It had a little flipper on the back body."

When you introduced the automatic, did you already have the flipper in mind?

"No. It was just that with the automatic you weren't doing anything with your left foot, and you wanted something to do with it!"

How far can you look ahead in doing something like this?

"This far!" (touching tip of nose and laughing). "It hasn't normally been that I can look very far ahead. You're so busy developing what you've done that it's not until it gets a little bit old-hat and you have time to sit back and cogitate a little bit that something else occurs to you. Now we've been in a few good situations, like in 1965 with the 2 when it was so reliable and so fast that

we had plenty of time. In fact we built the 2B and scrapped it and came out with the 2C before the 2s were obsolete. We had quite a bit of stuff we could just tack on it if the competition warranted it. And that happened because we were lucky, I guess, and having Hap Sharp involved in part of the work and getting everybody organised and going, and we had the winning spirit going, and everything was going just right. So we had time to get ahead, and kind of pull stuff off the shelf if we had to. And once you do that, boy, it's tough to beat you, because you're reliable already, and you're out there making tests for next week instead of scratching around trying to catch up this week."

Then to continue the line, the fibreglass cars were turned into FIA cars and called 2Ds, and then became the 2Fs. The 2Cs were modified up through 2E and then 2G CanAm cars. The 2H was the fibreglass CanAm car of 1969, and then the 2J came along concurrently. Along this long line of development, what stands out in your mind as high points?

"Well, I think the first real high point

The final Chaparral? The revolutionary 2J, Vic Elford at the wheel, in one of last year's CanAm rounds before it was banned.

First of the rear-engined Chaparral line was the 2, which was run in various forms from 1963 to 1965.

First Chaparral to wear the high flipper—and indeed the first car of any sort to do so, later copied by F1 constructors: the 2E.

Successor to the 2 (the aluminium 2B never appeared in public) was the 2C, with cockpit operated rear spoiler (above). In FIA form this became the Nürburgring 1000 Kms-winning 2D coupé (below).

Only British Chaparral appearance was by the 2F, which won the first BOAC Brands Hatch race in 1967 driven by Phil Hill and Mike Spence (above). The 2G was a wider-wheeled, updated 2E (below).

was when we built the first rear-engined car and set it on the scales, and we realised the car was really going to hold everything and be as light as it was and do everything we said it would do; that was kind of a high point for me."

Was its being made of fibreglass part of that?

"No, it's just that fibreglass looked like being the best material at the time. Then we realised there were some problems involved with the glassfibre cars that we didn't know about before. We're still not sure it isn't better, but it's expensive, for one thing.

"Then the automatic transmission was a real high point, to have it work and be the best car still, that was another plus."

You mentioned last year the transmissions you had on hand had just about reached their limits in ability to cope with the big engines, and you'd probably not invest in a new design, but go to a conventional type. Would you finally be willing to reveal what was inside the automatics?

"Uh . . . No, I don't think so."

OK. Was the flipper, the pivoting aerofoil, a high point?

"The flipper thing seemed so obvious to me that I don't regard it as any kind of major step—unless you're talking about mounting it up on struts on the wheel hubs, yes, that was a major change.

"And I think the concept of the E was, too. You're seeing it as late as now in Formula 1: the Lotus 72 is very similar to the 2E; we did it a long time ago—moving the centre of gravity aft, getting the radiators back there which gives you good penetration. . . . Of course a Formula 1 car can stand a little more weight on the back than we can. It's a question of how much torque you have.

"The G was just an extension of the E and no big deal; it would have been a pretty good car had the engine been reliable, but it wasn't.

"The H was a total failure in my opinion, except that it made me learn something—it was a pretty expensive way to learn!"

Yeah, Jim, why did you keep on and on with it?

"I guess I'm just stubborn. I thought it was a pretty good idea at the time, and it did some things real well. But it turned out to be a very hard car to drive, it wasn't comfortable from a driver's standpoint. It was scary, it didn't give any confidence at all. It was hard to tell when it was at the limit, so therefore it was never driven at the limit because of the individuals involved.

"The idea behind it was that the rubber has gotten to the point where, with independent suspension, the way you have to run it for cornering on the outside you don't use the inside wheels much, you de-camber them. They run on the shoulder and you're really carrying around a lot of extra tyre, as far as cornering is concerned.

"So I figured that a de Dion axle would

The first Chaparrals were these front-engined spaceframe devices which were financed by Hall but built by Troutman and Barnes.

give me increased cornering power. And then I said that if I'm going to have increased cornering power I'm going to make the car narrower. That way I'll have a wider road to go around in, and I'll cut the drag down at the same time; but I'm not going to sacrifice anything in cornering because I'll use the tyres more. In fact I thought I was going to pick up something in cornering. I thought the compromise was such that I was really going to corner faster with a narrower car and be able to go faster on the straight at the same time. I didn't think I was losing anywhere and I thought I was going to gain everywhere. It didn't turn out that way, just because the car was undrivable.

"Now I'm not sure that car was very clean, either. It was the way we designed it but not the way we ran it, with the wings. That car was *not* fast in a straight line, and it should have been. That may have had something to do with having the rubber on the road, that may be something I missed the point of completely. Things like that are awful hard to instrument."

Last year when the J was introduced, there seemed to be a change in your style of dealing with the press and public, things were more open.

"That wasn't forced on me, that was my choice. We'd been in a position where we couldn't apparently command the sponsorship that is necessary to run an operation like ours, and I felt that if we got our name out and spent a little more time on that, maybe it would have an effect on potential sponsors. Now that may not be a permanent thing, the returns aren't in, but we gave it a try."

Do you personally like to beat the opposition by building a car or by driving it?

"That's always been kind of a hard question in my career, because everybody always thought I had a better car. I don't think there's ever a driver who wouldn't like to have a little advantage, no matter how good he thinks he is. I mean he doesn't bother

to change the sway bar, when it lets him go easier on the car and on himself.

"As you know, I came back to driving myself a few times last year in the TransAm. I wasn't fast enough. I was doing the same thing I used to do, but I wasn't going as fast. I sort of felt I'd failed my driver's test. I haven't really made up my mind whether I will continue with it. I'm not going to do it unless I enjoy it, and it's not any fun for me to run tenth, I don't enjoy that. Right now I don't know what my skill level is. I may go back and have another operation on my leg (damaged in the terrible 1968 Las Vegas accident in the 2G which made him give up serious racing), and if I do it might delay me finding my level."

What makes Jim Hall tick? Why did you get into race cars in the first place?

"It's fun. I'm just a kid who never grew up! A big part of it is the challenge of making something work that nobody ever thought of. That was a big part of why I kept on after the H, trying to make it work. I thought it was a good idea and, by God, I was going to find out whether it was or not. It turned out that it wasn't, I'm satisfied of that now. Now I'll get *some* good out of it, there were some things on it that were good."

Would you rather have not put it out into public?

"You've got to race them, you know, that's what they're for. You can't just keep 'em to play with."

A kid who never grew up. Well, one has the impression that some of the recent history of Chaparral Cars has grown Jim Hall up a little, or aged him at least. As he says, three times now one of his central developments has been banned from international racing. He says, "It's just not any fun any more." He is clear in his mind that he introduced his big white Chaparrals in good faith that he was advancing the technical history of the automobile. On one level at least he was playing a big, glorious game. But he just wasn't playing the same game as the other kids were.

The only Chaparral not to have been ultra-competitive was the strange, narrow 2H, seen here with John Surtees at the wheel.

LOLA T260:
THE REIGN-BREAKER

Some Can-Am cars win,
Some Can-Am cars are different,
But only the Lola T260 is both.

BY PETE LYONS
DRAWINGS BY WERNER BÜHRER

"THERE'S A LOT to learn about these—and the more you learn the less you know. It's very frustrating, really. I suppose that's why you keep at it."

For Eric Broadley, entrusted with the provision of a vehicle for Jackie Stewart's first full-scale penetration of the American motor racing market, it would have been *adequate* to simply make up a version of the standard, for which read McLaren, sort of Can-Am car. But nothing which happens around the Scottish Showman is ever allowed to be humdrum, and everyone working on the project (L&M, Goodyear, Carl Haas) was caught up in his carefully generated excitement. So rather than merely follow established lines of thought, Broadley elected to try to advance that thought.

His T260, while it is no Chaparral "sucker," is quite a departure from what four years of McLaren victories have taught us is normal. The new Lola is startlingly blunt to look at, its body obviously shaped to do something other than simply generate downforce. Under the skin the elements are all familiar, but many are arranged differently. Originally the front wheels were to be of smaller diameter and all four brakes were to be mounted inboard on the chassis, but the designer retreated from these features. Overall it is a car which shows evidence of uncertainty on his part, the kind of uncertainty which accompanies probes into unfamiliar zones.

In Stewart's hands it was reasonably successful right from the start, earning pole position at its first race, winning the second, and setting fastest race lap (equal to the best qualifying time of the Chaparral a year before) in the third.

However, these results were very much in spite of the new machine's visibly inferior handling qualities. Stewart at one point said it handled "like a pregnant elephant"; someone else said, "It may be up front but he carried it there on his back."

Between each of these races the car was altered in considerable detail (suspension geometry, rim and tire size, wing placement) and gradually things improved. To follow these changes was to follow an engineer's tortuous advance in understanding.

Eric Broadley is a shy man, very quiet, with a sudden

WING POSITION: ORIGINALLY IMMEDIATELY BEHIND ENGINE.
AT ATLANTA (CAN-AM) WING MOVED MORE TO THE REAR.
HOLES IN FRONT PANELS TO ALLOW AIR ESCAPE FROM INSIDE TO REDUCE LIFT.

"ATLANTA"

LOLA T260

DRIVER: JACKIE STEWART
CHASSIS: MONOCOQUE (SEMI-M.)
BODY: FIBERGLASS MOULDINGS.
TIRES: GOODYEAR.

FRONT WHEELS: RIMS ORIGINALLY OF 13 in. ⌀. NOW INCREASED TO 15 in. ⌀.
'ATLANTA' SEE WIDENED WHEEL ARCH.

RADIATORS: IN THE REAR — BESIDE THE ENGINE (WATER & OIL); AND ABOVE GEAR BOX (TRANSMISSION - OIL).

EXTREMELY LARGE BELL-HOUSING: → ENGINE WEIGHT TOWARDS FRONT

FRONT & REAR BRAKES WERE ONCE MOUNTED INBOARD. NOW FRONTS ARE OUTBOARD LOCATED.

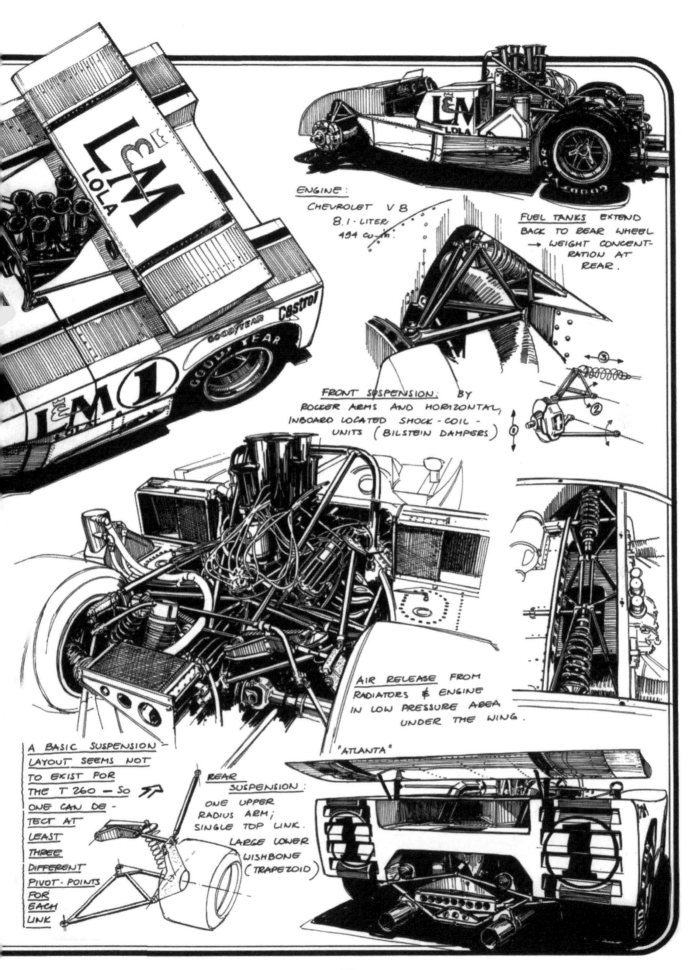

ENGINE:
CHEVROLET V 8
8.1-LITER
494 cu.in.

FUEL TANKS EXTEND
BACK TO REAR WHEEL
→ WEIGHT CONCENT-
RATION AT
REAR.

FRONT SUSPENSION: BY
ROCKER ARMS AND HORIZONTAL,
INBOARD LOCATED SHOCK-COIL-
UNITS (BILSTEIN DAMPERS)

AIR RELEASE FROM
RADIATORS & ENGINE
IN LOW PRESSURE AREA
UNDER THE WING.

"ATLANTA"

A BASIC SUSPENSION-
LAYOUT SEEMS NOT
TO EXIST FOR
THE T 260 — SO
ONE CAN DE-
TECT AT
LEAST
THREE
DIFFERENT
PIVOT-POINTS
FOR
EACH
LINK

REAR
SUSPENSION:
ONE UPPER
RADIUS ARM;
SINGLE TOP LINK.
LARGE LOWER
WISHBONE
(TRAPEZOID)

LOLA T260:
THE REIGN-BREAKER

smile. He can be very reticent about what he thinks of as tricks of his trade; ask him about roll centers, for instance, or camber change curves, and your answer is likely to be a long uneasy silence finally illuminated by that smile. Restrict your prying to broader concepts, though, and he will cooperate. His open face becomes thoughtful and he looks down between his shoes at the long line of Group 7 cars he's fathered: at the T70 which established the modern idea of a sports-racing car and with which Surtees became first Can-Am Champion; and at the list of Lolas which came after but never quite made it as big.

"These cars, these big-engined cars, aren't as quick, in my opinion, as they ought to be. Their cornering speeds are pretty disappointing, really. If you put it all out on a piece of paper they *should* be quicker. It's a fairly compromised sort of design compared to a Formula 1 car, for instance, which is *truer*. It's difficult to get a balance here. The engine tends to take over a bit; not the size or weight of the engine, so much, as the torque reaction, the inertia produced by the internal rotating mass. It's something you have to play around with. We've passed, I think, the optimum point of engine size with these. You can draw curves, which have intersection points, and we've passed those points. It's like a dragster. The front tires will lift right off the road, if you aren't careful . . ."

In his T260 the weight of the engine is carried well forward, with a specially-cast bell housing twice as long as the usual one uniting the Chevy block to the Mk II Hewland transaxle. This in turn places the driver a bit more forward. On the other hand there is no front radiator; there is a pair of water radiators in the sides of the car, fed with inlet ducts in the tops of the door moldings and there is a pair of smaller engine oil coolers directly behind the water ones. (The transmission oil cooler is at the extreme rear of the car, lying down flat.) The fuel load is divided into four cells, two within each monocoque tank, and is normally pumped

from the right front cell just as in a McLaren. However, the center of gravity of the entire load is carried much further aft than in its rival, and the whole visible monocoque between the wheels functions as chassis. The engine hangs on transverse bulkhead plates at either end of its block.

"Of course tire development comes into it. We seem to have run into some kind of barrier here as well. We've tried to use wider tires; we tried tires as wide as 20 inches a year or two ago, but we couldn't keep them sufficiently upright throughout the range of suspension movement."

The rear suspension upright castings are virtually the only parts carried over from the T220 series. The bottom link at the rear is one big wishbone which allows no bump steer, while the motion of the top of the upright is controlled by a transverse link and a trailing radius arm. Every single pivot point on the chassis can be altered, to change roll centers, cambers, anti-squat reactions, etc.

At the front the most interesting feature is the built-up rocker arms which carry the weight of the car to the coil spring/damper units mounted horizontally above the driver's footwell. The dampers can function when tipped over like this because they are gas-pressurized Bilstein units. This arrangement is of course a legacy of the original intention of mounting the front brakes inboard, but Broadley notes that in any case it gives a nice, uncluttered layout. Here again, he has built the chassis so that the geometries can be altered. Does he plan that, once the best movements are decided, he can still adjust the car minutely to each specific race track?

"That might be an advantage if you could have three solid days of testing at each track but you'd run out of engines and out of cars! You're still required to finish the race. The state of the art isn't quite at that point."

The brakes were moved out to the wheels for two different reasons; the rears because of problems with heat (apparently solved on the M8F McLaren, which is constructed

PHOTO BY LARRY GRIFFIN

original body mold which makes them ultra-smooth; they are closed off by metal panels riveted to the outside body surface.

Originally the rear wing was to be mounted just behind the rear axle line, and little pedestals were molded into the body to support it there. For the first two races, however, it had been mounted about a foot farther forward than that. It went to Atlanta, where for the first time Stewart began to say he felt some confidence in the car's behavior, before the wing was moved to its intended supports.

A McLaren's body generates a lot of downforce, chiefly concentrated into two areas ahead of and behind the axles of the car, where exists the most room for large-scale uses of the airflow. What is the thinking behind the blunt Lola shape, which obviously doesn't demand so much work from the air?

"Well, it's experimental, and so I suppose it's still a bit classified. But you know that a wedge-shaped body can generate lift; under certain conditions it can suddenly generate lift instead of downforce. *Any* car will generate some lift; whenever you raise air over a body you cause lift. So you have a conflict. This shape, I suppose you could say, is an attempt to *destroy* lift without using downforce to counteract it. It was developed in the new wind tunnel at Specialised Mouldings by their engineer Peter Wright, who is a very practical sort of chap.

"I don't know what sort of downforce we really do need. It will probably take several races to decide things like that. It's difficult to get a correlation between the tunnel and what happens on the track. With this car we really hadn't enough time to carry out sufficient pre-race testing either, but anyway it's difficult to do satisfactory pre-race testing; the conditions in racing are different. They're really quite different."

One can theorize that the shape is intended to produce a car which will be more stable in a varying aerodynamic environment than a more conventional car, which works very well when things are just right but can be easily upset. It is probably a case of practicality taking over from idealism. There is another case of that sort of thinking in the body: the rows of holes in the nose panel are covered with wire mesh, over which has been sprayed paint forming the bold L&M logo—and the paint closes off most of the airflow through the mesh.

"There are times," smiles Eric, "when engineering considerations are outweighed by commercial considerations."

Jackie Stewart made an honest effort to help develop the T260 before the start of the Can-Am series, but there was some time spent converting to outboard front brakes, and two separate test sessions were spoiled by rain. He actually drove the new machine seriously for the first time on Thursday before the first race at Mosport. He found that the front wheels were just not gripping the road at all, and there was a peculiar "slow roll" effect at the rear as well. The phenomenon that might be called "powerslide vibration," a sort of chatter developed by the inside rear wheel which has been plaguing racing people for about three years now, was quite pronounced. Occasionally, as he changed gear while still bent over into a corner, he felt a baulk in the linkage, as though the chassis might be twisting.

At St Jovite two weeks later the rear geometry had been altered, there were wider wheel rims at the front, and he seemed to feel the car was coming along. He was generous to the men behind the design, pointing out that he himself must require some time to acclimatize himself to this type of car. He also took great pains to point out that these first two tracks in the series were extremely bumpy, and it was always difficult to sort out a car on a bumpy surface because you could never be sure what faults were actually in the car and not common to all cars operated on such a surface. His driving of the unruly white box was very spectacular to watch, as to overcome the lack of adhesion at the front end

more "openly" in that area) and the fronts because of problems with the driver's nerves. Stewart cannot forget that the death of his close friend Jochen Rindt has been attributed to the failure of an inboard front brake shaft. Lola constructed a machine to investigate the dynamic forces involved, but until everything is understood the front brakes of the race car will be outboard.

It is in its shape that the T260 departs most from convention. It has a very blunt, boxy appearance, with a nose that drops sharply down to present an almost vertical face to the air. In the panel between the front wheel wells are cut a number of rows of holes; these were apparently added after the first series of tests in order to allow air to escape from inside and thus kill lift. (The bottom of the area covered by this pierced panel, that is to say the belly pan, is closed off completely; it would have to be open if there were to be any pseudo-Chaparral suction developed by these holes, to press the car onto the ground.) Out from the bottom edge of the nose sticks a horizontal plate, only an inch wide in basic form; at various times mechanics affix extensions whose function is to persuade air to flow over the nose rather than under. Four additional holes are in the lower front of the nose; two feed the front brakes through hoses and two simply let air into the front wheel wells.

The rear edges of the front wheel wells are cut away extremely, serving to help air be extracted from these wells. There are no vents on the top surfaces of the fenders. As an incidental observation, one can see in the line of the wheel arches how they were originally intended to drop lower over the original 13-in. front wheels.

The rear of the body is cut off square, with slatted panels covering the rear but allowing air to escape.

Air from the twin radiator ducts flows together into one duct behind and above the engine and is finally let out into the low-pressure area generated below the wing. These ducts, by a nice tweak of manufacture, are formed in the

LOLA T260

he would get the back loose with power.

For just such "learning" races George Foltz built him engines with very wide, flat torque curves, so there would be no behavior problems which weren't actually in the chassis.

At Mosport Stewart won the pole position on Friday, and was able to keep it because during Saturday's qualification sessions the track was spoiled with rain and spilled oil. In the race he was able to get by Denny Hulme in traffic and take over the lead, but his race came to an end with a blown transmission seal. At St Jovite Hulme won the pole and during the first part of the race the McLaren was clearly faster than the Lola, but then Hulme succumbed to some kind of stomach ailment. Stewart, whose best lap in the race was 1.5 seconds slower, went ahead to win. At Atlanta both factory McLarens qualified faster, Hulme by exactly one second, but on the smooth "driver's" circuit Stewart stormed ahead of both M8Fs. They were both troubled by poor brakes and had the Lola remained sound to the end it might have been a very keen race. But Stewart's spectacular race was interrupted by a flat tire; when that was replaced he drove as hard as he knew how and established the race's fastest lap, 0.3 sec better than Hulme's qualifying time, but then had to retire because a rear shock absorber broke.

So the T260 was getting better all the time; and whatever inadequacies it started with were being methodically erased. It was the first machine in a long, long time to put steady, serious pressure on the McLarens.

No one could be more modest about his new car's success than Eric Broadley. He knows it isn't right yet, and he is one of the few personalities in this egotist's game who will freely admit he doesn't know all the answers. Sometimes, he says, he feels very dumb indeed. He accepted the responsibility of trying to create a new kind of car knowing full well he would be staying up very late on very many nights trying to worry the faults out of it.

"You start off a new design with a lot of experience behind you, and you see lots of 'trends' around you. You try to integrate all these elements. It's difficult to say just *why* you select any specific feature. Everything interacts with everything else. And when there are problems, the same thing is true. When you alter one thing, everything else is affected throughout the whole design. It *is very* frustrating."

But fascinating too, to us onlookers. It is often through watching a designer's tribulations that we learn more than by studying a successful, finished machine. The Lola T260 has already been a winner; whether it will actually establish a new line of Can-Am design remains to be seen, but it serves as a splendid textbook just the same.

ST JOVITE CAN-AM

Mont Tremblant, Quebec—June 27, 1971

Driver	Car	Laps
1 Jackie Stewart	Lola T260-494 Chev	75
2 Denis Hulme	McLaren M8F-494 Chev	75
3 Peter Revson	McLaren M8F-494 Chev	74
4 Chuck Parsons	McLaren M8D-465 Chev	73
5 L. Motschenbacher	McLaren M8D-494 Chev	73
6 Hiroshi Kazato	Lola T222-494 Chev	71
7 Dave Causey	Lola T222-465 Chev	70
8 Milt Minter	Porsche 917-290	70
9 Tom Dutton	McLaren M6B-427 Chev	69
10 Dick Durant	Lola T163-427 Chev	68

Distance: 75 laps of 2.65-mi circuit, 198.75 miles.

Avg speed: 100.95 mph, new record. (Old record: 97.95 mph, Dan Gurney, McLaren M8D-465 Chev, 1970.)

Fastest lap: 1:33.6, 102.92 mph, Denis Hulme, new record. (Old record: 1:33.8, 101.70 mph, Denis Hulme, McLaren M8B, 1969.)

ROAD ATLANTA CAN-AM

Gainesville, Georgia—July 11, 1971

Driver	Car	Laps
1 Peter Revson	McLaren M8F-480 Chev	75
2 Denis Hulme	McLaren M8F-494 Chev	75
3 L. Motschenbacher	McLaren M8D-494 Chev	74
4 Tony Adamowicz	McLaren M8B-465 Chev	72
5 Milt Minter	Porsche 917/8-290	71
6 Dick Durant	Lola T163-427 Chev	68
7 Roger McCaig	McLaren M8E-465 Chev	68
8 Tom Dutton	McLaren M6B-427 Chev	67
9 Charlie Kemp	McLaren M8C-454 Chev	64
10 Jim Adams*	Ferrari 512-305	64

*Not running at finish.

Distance: 75 laps of 2.6-mi circuit, 195 miles.

Avg speed: 111.17 mph, new record. (Old record: 103.45 mph, Tony Dean, Porsche 908, 1970.)

Fastest lap: 1:17.4, 117.35 mph, Jackie Stewart, new record. (Old record: 1:18.05, 116.40 mph, Peter Gethin and Peter Revson, Lola T220-465 Chev, 1970.)

CHAPARRAL

"So, okay, I over-design a little"
--Jim Hall

Jim Hall. Product of New Mexico, Cal Tech and the high, oil rig-pocked plateaus of west Texas. Lean, craggy, burnt old/young man. Road runner. Racer. Intense, secretive, close-mouthed crossroads beholder in the process of self-unravelment. Changes are what he's into. Reflection is his method.

☐ My older brother and Carroll Shelby became friends, and Carroll and Dick opened that sports car dealership in Dallas that Carroll ran. It was partly mine and partly Dick's, too, and it wasn't doing worth a damn. Dick was sick then. He had rheumatic fever when he was a teen-ager and he just got worse and worse. He got arthritis and he couldn't see and he asked me, since I wasn't planning on going on with school, if I'd go down to Dallas and work with Carroll. That's what I did. I spent a year working at that, trying, and finally gave up and went racing with Carroll.

Over the next three years I raced mostly through the Southwest. I went to Nassau and Sebring and California, too, and then I was running pretty much all over the country. In '61, we moved from Odessa to Midland, because of the business. It was really our business by then. Us boys. We were in the oil business and Dick had done most of the work, as far as keeping it together. My dad was killed in an airplane crash when I was 17. And like the government'll do to you, on being ordered up to pay taxes, we had to sell his whole business. So the three of us got back in together. Dick really took over the responsibility of looking after it and the sicker he got the more responsibilities I had to take. I just kind of worked into it, and the main office turned out to be in Odessa. You don't make anything sitting on your ass. Nobody does. It's not something somebody gives you. I admit I had a hell of a start, my dad was successful and I was in a position where I had some equity money and could borrow money, and that's a lot different from being a down-and-outer. I'm damn glad I had it. I'm not knocking it all. But, still, that doesn't make it a success. You could just piss the whole thing off and that'd be it.

Hap Sharp bought an AC Bristol from us when I was running the sports car place. That was his first race car. We maintained that and took it up to the races for him and so forth. Then he

bought a 2-liter Maser. Hap and I were close after that. He's only six or seven years older than me.

Then, the next year, in '62, I ran the Troutman-Barnes car. It had been started, I think, in early '60, although my memory sometimes fails me, and that car was another real test. In other words, that was a car started from scratch and the guys were craftsmen in a sense that, *boy,* they did nice work and the welds didn't fail and that kind of stuff. As far as overall design they were going pretty much on what they saw and what they had seen work before.

It's the difference between Cooper and Lotus, really. Troutman and Barnes built that first rear-engine car over here and they really were the first guys to sort one out and, from a practical standpoint, they did a nice job. Well, Colin Chapman came along and realized what they had done and knew his first rear-engined car was better than anything anyone had ever built, including Cooper. Chapman has a quirk, in that he under-designs everything. It seems like in the number of years he has been at it, that he would quit that, but he still does it. I suppose all designers have flaws like that.

Possibly my flaw is completely opposite from Colin's. Trying to get into too much detail and trying to make sure everything is too right—I'm guilty of that—and I've screwed up quite a few things by saying, "No, that's not exactly the way we want it, we're going to go back and do it again." And then end up screwing it up, you know? It's like you build a $20,000 race car and I've seen a lot of guys argue about a $10 part to go on it. I can't see what difference $10 makes to the project. I want things the way I want them to be and I want it to be the best it can be, and if it costs $10 more, well, I don't think that's significant. Even if it takes another hour, then I think you ought to do it. It makes some of these guys work late as hell sometimes, and I do, too.

If I have confidence in a car, I can run over tires or into potholes or whatever and feel totally confident that it is not going to come apart. But if you have a question in your mind—I've never seen anybody that could just get in and drive hard knowing that the car is not very good. You don't do that, you creep around, you wouldn't want to hit that. Same as there being a vast difference

between testing and racing. The Chaparral 2H, the one they called the "whale." It got a black eye because of the particular position I was in, recuperating from the accident, introducing a new model and then having to have someone else do the race driving. The car wasn't as bad as it looked. Now, the car wasn't a good car, and I'll admit to that. There were some flaws in it. It was not a nice-feeling car and it did not give you confidence—not in its ability to stay together, but in its predictability. It just wasn't a handy car. You always felt, well, this SOB might do something that I'm not expecting. You kind of had to be keyed up to drive it.

I think it was the rear suspension on the 2H. I tried to keep the wheels flat to grab that extra cornering power that's available. I got that all right, but when it turned loose, it all turned loose at the same time. You went from that real good cornering power to nothing.

Where the cars that have the geometry go out of whack, they turn completely loose slower. And give you more warning. They're more forgiving cars to drive, really. You can have a car that corners very fast but is unforgiving and a guy is just not going to drive it around a racetrack very fast. That's what happened to us that year. Our driver, John Surtees, didn't feel well in the car. The corollary is that the damn car ran like hell in testing here at Rattlesnake Raceway. It went good.

Anyway, we called the Troutman-Barnes car the Chaparral and that was the first one, really. That was Chaparral 1. The name came from a guy around here who owns some horses, and Hap always has been horse-crazy, and we were over at this guy's place, looking at polo ponies. We were just building the car and Hap and I were talking about names. This guy said, "How about the road runner" (which is indigenous to the area), and a Mexican hand said, "Ah, Chaparral." That's where it came from. So when Hap and I decided to do another project, I asked Troutman-Barnes if they wanted the name and they said no.

In between, I bought a 2.5-liter

Cooper from John Coombs and a Formula 2 Lotus with a 2.5-liter Climax. I swapped engines and ran the Climax in the Cooper at Riverside for the Formula 1 race that year. I was running fifth right up to the next to last lap and had an axle failure and coasted across seventh. Then I ran a season of Formula 1 racing in Europe, thinking I wanted to be world champion. You know, a lot of people think I put the money up for that deal, but I didn't. I was hired, went over there for Ken Gregory and did it. I didn't get paid much, but still I got a round-trip ticket or 500 pounds of rice or something. God it was a disappointment. They were so disorganized. They were supposed to be the hot setup. To my mind, Formula 1 racers knew it all. Well, I got over there and I listened. I did that for several months trying to learn and not popping off. I finally came to the conclusion that those guys really don't know much about it and, besides, they were a little staid, a little bit class-oriented.

It was easy to make the decision to get out of Formula 1, because Hap and I actually started building that first plastic car in the summer of '62 and had it running by the summer of '63. It had started when I went to Europe. I made a couple of trips back here, just to make sure it was going well. And it was. That first plastic car with the old iron-block engine weighed about 1200 pounds. There was a hell of a savings in building a body-chassis unit that weighed less than 100 pounds.

Then, too, you see, Chapman built the Lotus 25 at the same time. Our designs were concurrent and Hap and I built our car at exactly the same time as Chapman's, except that he was racing his first, because of my doing the Formula 1 thing. The other cars of the time, incidentally, weighed in around 300 to 400 pounds heavier. Still, we copied a lot of Lotus stuff eventually and ended-up heavying it up quite a bit, making it stronger. That was the Chaparral 2. There was an aluminum car that ended up being used for testing only. It finally showed up in our lineage as the 2C and then the 2E. The 2C, the 2E and then the 2G were all aluminum cars. We've done it both ways, aluminum and plastic, and we've vacillated at times as to which is the better medium.

Then I got sidetracked into this Manufacturers Championship thing and, of course, Carroll Shelby was in that and doing well with the Cobras. Hap wanted to go and do that. I didn't really care too much about it because I couldn't see any good things about it from the start. Well, that's a damned expensive series to run and there's no remuneration in it, either. I couldn't see what we'd get out of it. The only thing we did that really helped us over-

all was that we were forced to work on reliability and durability. The 24-hour standpoint, where we learned how hard to run that stuff for that long, was, I think, a good program.

Anyway, Hap quit driving at the end of the '66 season and he was associated with Chaparral Cars as a partner until the end of this last season ('70 – Ed.) when I bought him out. He had just slowly drifted out of activity. Hap went to Le Mans with one of the cars in '66, the C's successor, and I stayed home, working on the E car then.

I guess if I have made any contribution to the state of the art in automotive design it is probably because I realized sometime in the early Sixties that you couldn't just be interested in the negative drawback aspects of the aerodynamic function, but that you ought to use it as a positive influence on the handling of the car. In all the designs since the first one, I have had that in mind. For example, you can go through high-speed turns in a car with wings at 1.5 gs like it was nothing. You're going through slow ones at 1.2, 1.3. I thought, hell, if I can do that good on the high speed turns, why not do it on the slow ones, too? That's where the idea for the sucker came from. I started thinking about it and realized whatever system I used would probably have to be powered. That thought came at a period of time, I guess, when I realized we were in deep trouble on the 2H. Early in '69, I could see that progress was not being made well enough, in terms of man-hours expended on the project, and I began looking around. I still wasn't truly able to drive the thing, although I busted my ass in testing on it. I decided we ought to do something and I was scratching my head at the time and I just felt that the sucker was a really

significant giant step that we ought to make.

I test-drove the 2J somewhere in the latter part of the '69 season and I just instantly knew we were really into something. I personally didn't feel like I was in shape to race the thing in the Can-Am. I was represented by Mark McCormick, and Jackie Stewart was also represented by them. They knew what we had going on and they said, "Christ, Jackie doesn't have a ride in the Can-Am this year and wouldn't it be keen if you guys could...." I could go out and run ten laps, but if it was to be 200 miles I'd never have made it. So on the chance – you feel like it would be a shame to penalize the car on the basis of a driver who can't hold up – and he was available and I knew it wouldn't be the same kind of deal as the year before with Surtees and the H car. And, God, Stewart's a terrific driver. The only thing that really worried me about Jackie was that he is real on about this safety business. I figured anybody that's thinking that hard about it must have some pretty serious questions in his mind. But I'll be damned if he doesn't get into that car and strap it on and he goes "click" and he's all race driver, I'll tell you. I figured that would influence his driving, but it doesn't. I'll guarantee that he got into that car, which was not properly sorted out, and in three laps he was down to record times, you know, and it wasn't even working right.

We're not going to go racing in '71 at all. I'm not even sure about after that. I'm well enough physically to drive myself, but I haven't got the urge. It's like any other sport that you don't practice for awhile. You lose the touch. And everybody else is gaining during the time you're losing. □

Below is the earliest 2E, which we introduced at The Bridge.

The championship-winning Gulf-McLaren team. Left to right are : Denny Hulme, Jim Stone, Tony Attard, Vince Higgins, Alec Greaves and Peter Revson.

THOSE MILLION DOLLAR McLARENS

IN THE EARLY SUMMER of 1964, three men —hell, we must have been boys then, not one of us over 26—sat around a table in the cramped kitchen of a rented house in New Malden that served as the headquarters of the new Bruce McLaren Racing Team. Bruce, fresh from winning the Tasman Championship with a special 2½-litre Cooper, teetered back on one of the chairs and wondered aloud whether to go Formula 2 racing with a Cooper or to try his hand at sports car racing in America. New Zealander Wally Willmott, Bruce's personal mechanic then, opted with Bruce to go for sports cars, but I didn't agree. Looking back I could call it a vote

of caution, but in all honesty, as history has proved, I was quite simply wrong. So Bruce picked up the phone and began a series of transatlantic calls to track down and buy the Zerex Special that Roger Penske had driven to a string of wins in the pre-CanAm series of sports car races in the United States.

The rest is history. Within three years the McLaren team was dominating the richest series of road races in history and in seven years they had won more than a million dollars in prize money and bonuses. Bruce loved CanAm racing and CanAm cars, even though it was the 1970 M8D that was to cost him his life in a crash while he was testing the

car at Goodwood last June. The team tremored at the stunning blow of Bruce's death, but recovered to pick up the ball and run to win again. Bruce's widow Patty inherited Bruce's role as chairman of the company with Teddy Mayer and Phil Kerr as joint managing directors. New to the board was Tyler Alexander in charge of engineering. Tyler had joined the team along with the Zerex Special back in 1964.

This year the McLaren cars took American racing by storm. Their superiority in CanAm racing was by now acknowledged and the fact that even Jackie Stewart in a new and advanced Lola couldn't stem the tide of

CanAm conquerors Peter Revson (left) and Denny Hulme pose with Miss Labatt's Blue CanAm.

EOIN YOUNG gives the background to the CanAm conquerors: the dollar-eating McLaren team

Eoin Young

EOIN YOUNG, aged 32, was a founder director of the McLaren company. He left the team in 1966 to start his own business as a racing consultant and freelance journalist. A frequent contributor to AUTOSPORT, he also has regular columns in Autocar and Car in England, Road & Track in the United States and other magazines abroad. This year he crossed the Atlantic 20 times covering the CanAm series as well as the Grand Prix season in Europe. His wife Sandra used to be John Surtees' secretary.

McLaren race wins merely added to the aura of glory. USAC racing on the big-buck ovals, however, was a new world to conquer for the McLaren men and if you had spoken with just about any of the "rail birds" at Indy last year you would have heard the word that this time the McLaren team was biting off more than it could chew. The McLaren M15 was an unashamed single-seater version of the CanAm sports car and as such a compromise; it didn't have what it took to win the famous "500"—even though the Indiana Chapter of the Society of Automobile Engineers voted it a special award for the advancement of engineering at Indy.

But it had features on it like the inter-link in the rear suspension that were to be copied on the M16, and as a general test-bed it had proved its worth. The wedge-nosed M16 this year re-wrote the record books, and taught the people who regard Indianapolis as the cradle of motor racing that in the Grand Prix world there are people with better ideas. The M16 was an all new car with side-radiators and the wedge nose of the Lotus 72 Formula 1 car, but apart from that concept the rest was all-McLaren. It was the lowest, lightest, slimmest and fastest car that had ever been to the Brickyard and Mark Donohue in the prototype that had been bought by

Denny Hulme's McLaren-Chevrolet M8F leads Jackie Stewart's L&M Lola-Chevrolet T260, a car that promised so much but was not quite the match of the " Orange Elephants."

Roger Penske to run under Sunoco blue colours (the works cars were Gulf-sponsored orange) added a fantastic 10 mph to the record during practice before qualifying started on a 2½-mile oval where annual speed rises are usually measured in hundredths of a mile an hour! Revson took the pole in the works M16 and took second place to Al Unser's Colt-Ford in the race, but Donohue had led going away in the Penske M16 and before he retired on the 66th lap he had set a new record for the Speedway at 174 mph. At Pocono on the new tri-oval he won off the pole, he won the Michigan 200, and added 8 mph to the record at Ontario to sit on the pole at 185.004 mph for the California 500.

It didn't take the Americans long to realise that the McLarens weren't really magic and that their speed was man-made. Bud Poorman, in charge of USAC racing for Goodyear, put it in a nutshell at Pocono when he predicted that the others would soon catch up. "Monkey see, monkey do," was his apt description, and by the end of the season Bobby Unser's Eagle and the Colts driven by Al Unser and Joe Leonard could leg it with the McLarens. But the fact that the McLarens had shown the way in a brand of specialist racing regarded by many as a "closed shop" was particularly significant.

The M16 was designed by Gordon Coppuck, the quiet bespectacled draughtsman who had worked under Robin Herd at the National Gas Turbine Establishment at Farnborough; he eventually followed Herd to the McLaren design office and took over as chief designer when Herd left to join Cosworth and later March Engineering. It's often hard to know whether Coppuck is surprised that his cars go so fast or surprised that they don't go faster. He looks more like a Post Office clerk than the designer of cars that are cur-

Bruce McLaren, CanAm Champion of 1967 and 1969, was tragically killed when testing the 1970 McLaren-Chevrolet M8D at Goodwood in June of that year. His cars continued to dominate the series.

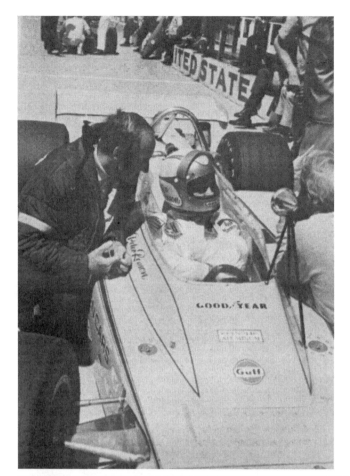

Peter Revson and Denny Hulme talk tactics at Indianapolis with team manager Teddy Mayer (top, left). Revson set new records for the 2½-mile Indianapolis Speedway when he qualified for pole position at an average of 179.696 mph over the four laps. Tyler Alexander strips the fuel-injection on the four-cylinder Offenhauser engine while the car is lined up for qualifying (top, right). Peter Revson on his way to second place in the Team Gulf McLaren M16 at Indianapolis (above).

rently the fastest on the American racing scene, but the results prove it all for him. Even now, Coppuck is working on the nuts-and-bolts area to complete the design of the McLaren M20 which promises to be to CanAm racing what the M16 was to USAC.

Does the McLaren team really need a new supercar in CanAm? With five Championships in five years you might be forgiven for thinking that the team could ride to victory next season on the laurel wreaths, but the team are very much aware that since 1968 they have been updating a basic design that began life as the M8A and won the CanAm title and $93,000 for Denny Hulme that season. In 1969 Bruce took his second turn at the J-Wax Championship in the M8B, Denny won again in 1970 with the M8D, and this season

the team clinched the championship again with three races left to run using the M8F —the final version. . . .

In the palmy days of CanAm racing the McLarens were so superior that they could almost guarantee wins the following season simply by climbing a letter up the alphabet and little else, but their stranglehold on the dollar purses is starting to loosen and the 1971 policy has definitely been "back to the drawing board."

Now don't get me wrong. CanAm racing isn't racing like Grand Prix events. There isn't the same pressures to bear, and the fields are definitely lacking in driver talent and car preparation. But it was Ken Tyrrell who said he wasn t so much impressed at the fact that the McLarens kept winning in CanAm, as by

the fact that they were always there at the finish of the 200-mile races. Their 1-2 finish at Donnybrooke this season was the 18th time that McLaren team cars had crossed the line first and second since the J-Wax CanAm series started.

Other teams were frustrated at the apparently effortless ease with which the McLaren romped through the series, but Tyler Alexander points to the fact that much of their success can be put down to good preparation by a dedicated team of car builders and mechanics, and the fact that the McLaren team tend to do their homework that much better than anyone else. When it was announced that Jackie Stewart planned to compete in the 1971 CanAm series with a new Lola, it looked as though CanAm would

Mighty McLaren Chevy mill (left). Would you believe 740 bhp from 8.1-litres?

at last get the shakeup it so badly needed, and the fact that it was to be televised live only added icing to the prospect. The television coverage lasted only two races. Jackie's challenge to the McLaren domination turned out to be more of a thorn-in-the-side variety than a full-blooded club-wielding smash on the forehead.

The 1971 M8F McLaren was essentially an update on a proven winner, but when the new T260 Lola was rolled out for the first race at Mosport it bristled with new features that made the McLarens look almost old-fashioned and made the McLaren men wonder whether they should hurry on with the new M20 instead of leaving it in the drawing office file for the summer. The Lola was snub-nosed and stumpy-tailed with side radiators to test Eric Broadley's theory that perhaps downforce could be better used directly over the wheels than towards the extremities of the nose and tail overhangs as on the Mc-Larens. The design bore similarities to Broadley's 2-litre sports cars, but in this case it would be fitted with an engine four times as large in capacity and turning out around 740 bhp. The tail was in danger of shaking the dog.

Jackie Stewart is a high-powered combination of businessman, showman, and super-racedriver. You get the impression that if you stuffed a light bulb into his mouth it would flash on. He's a walking dynamo. He isn't an engineer and doesn't pretend to be. At the start of the season the Lola was a real handful simply because there hadn't

Smooth lines of the 1971 McLaren M8F — Hulme driving — are developed from earlier models.

in the series was one reason why McLarens were loath to produce the M20 before the start of 1972 so that the German company would not enjoy the winter building a copy-car or at least borrowing some of the McLaren ideas. Siffert, however, was strongly denying the hints of factory backing. It was a private entry, he said, and Porsche competitions manager Rico Steinemann supported this view, saying that Siffert had been offered a choice of running a factory entry or running as a privateer to earn points for the Porsche Cup which is worth $15,000 to the winner. Siffert took second placings at Mid-Ohio and Elkhart Lake, scoring on reliability from the 5-litre flat-12 while the Behemoths with their 8-litre pushrod V8s did themselves in. Next year the CanAm series is threatened with works Porsche Spyders using either turbo-charged versions of the current air-cooled flat-12 engine, or a mighty flat-16 7-litre turning out 800 bhp guaranteed to strike fear into the hearts of men.

Private competition to the "Orange Elephants" has been negligible, the most consistent coming from Lothar Motschenbacher with a pair of ex-works McLarens, one driven by Lothar and the other put out to rent to various warmshoes during the season.

Money, cold hard cash in the form of dollars, is a major obstacle to would-be CanAm contenders and it is one of the reasons for the McLaren success. With substantial backing from Goodyear, Gulf Oil, Reynolds Aluminium and Coca-Cola, this season the McLaren budget has been adequately covered, although Teddy Mayer maintains that the vast amounts of prize money they earn can only come close to covering their costs, and the sponsorship is very necessary to carry on business as usual back home at the factory in England.

In addition to financial support from Reynolds, the McLaren engineers have worked with the aluminium boffins to perfect a version of the aluminium Chevrolet V8 that does away with the cast iron cylinder liners and therefore aids heat dissipation. Since there are no liners to cool, the water jackets can be reduced in size which in turn means that the cylinder bore can be increased to raise capacity even more than the current 8 litres. The engines are prepared by Gary Knutson, Lee Muir and their team at the McLaren Engines Inc facility in Detroit to give around 740

bhp. And there is plenty more where those came from if the CanAm should turn into a horsepower race.

Gulf and Goodyear have provided track-side technical assistance on fuel and lubricants and tyres, but this season Gulf went one better with a luxury £12,000 Avco motor-home as a hospitality press headquarters and mobile team base. It had twin air conditioners when temperatures were up over 110 as they were at Mid-Ohio, and heaters to cope with a low around freezing point up at Edmonton.

At the Edmonton race the McLaren "homework" consisted of discovering during practice that the cold wheels wouldn't fit the hot axles during a practice tyre-change, so for the duration of the race, one of the team played an acetylene flame over the hubs on a set of rain tyres in case a switch became necessary.

Revson joins Hulme

Denny Hulme started this season as CanAm champion with Peter Revson, the handsome American (who spends part of every press interview denying any affiliation with the Revlon cosmetics empire) as his number two. Revson, ironically, had driven Carl Haas's L&M-sponsored Lola the season before with plenty of ability but a depressing lack of success. Both driver and entrant seemed amicably pleased when they parted company at the end of the season. With a good car at last, Revson has blossomed this season to take five wins in nine races (this was written prior to the tenth [and final] Riverside event which rounded off the series) and overshadow his team leader who has had less than his share of good luck. But as Revson could rightly point out, he has been running against luck for the past 10 years—he has had the ability but seldom the cars to prove it. The McLaren ride this season has been the reward for his tenacity in sticking with the racing programme.

Hulme, dubbed "The Bear" by the press, is truly the king of CanAm, with luck or without it. With one race left in the 1971 series, Hulme's personal total of victories stood at 19, out-stripping by far Bruce's total of nine before his death. Next up came Peter Revson with five, John Surtees on four and Dan Gurney with three.

New Zealander Denny Hulme and New Yorker Peter Revson were Team Gulf McLaren's driving strength both in USAC competition and the 10-race CanAm series.

been time to test and sort it. Jackie was on the pole for the first race at Mosport and he won the second at St Jovite. At Road Atlanta he led until a puncture pitted him, and at Watkins Glen he was in the lead again when the Chevy engine broke its crank. But the credit for these stirring performances were being laid more at Stewart's door than Lola's. It was said that Jackie stood a good chance of giving himself a hernia by carrying the car round on his back at such a pace. For some reason the Watkins Glen performance was Jackie's high point in the season, and at Mid-Ohio, Elkhart Lake and Edmonton he started off the second row of the grid.

Jackie Oliver's appearance in the revised UOP-Shadow was heralded by the press as a challenge, but it appeared to be taking the full season to get the low-profile car sorted out and Oliver himself was presented with the biggest challenge. The car was designed by ex-GP mechanic Peter Bryant, who had designed the Autocoast Ti22 in 1970—a car that showed a lot of promise before it became swamped in a legal tangle and wasn't rescued until late this year.

Porsche threat

Then there was Jo Siffert's privately entered Porsche 917-10 Spyder which was to be regarded as highly significant from a fore-runner point of view, since Porsche were known to be working on factory CanAm cars for 1972 and the Siffert car was strictly fielded as a "feeler." This Porsche interest

Peter Revson won more CanAms than team leader Denny Hulme to clinch the 1971 title.

The million dollars in prize money has been coming into the McLaren coffers steadily since their winning streak began in 1967—the season that Hulme joined the team for the first time. An American statistician worked out that the team has been earning at a steady $23,000 per race ever since!

Any team is only as strong as its morale, its *esprit de corps*, will allow it to to be. With Bruce there was never a question of team loyalty—the "Bruce and Denny Show" was exciting fun, and the team was more of a family. Denny shouldered the "father" rôle after Bruce's accident, and although Denny and Peter are not as close as Denny and Bruce had been in the good old days, there is still a light-hearted off-track approach to the serious on-track business that makes for a close-knit team. Denny's mechanics are Jim Stone and Tony "Smokey" Attard, while Peter's mechanics are Vince Higgins and Alec Greaves. Teddy Mayer team manages the CanAm operation, and Tyler Alexander oversees the technical side at most of the races.

A relaxed atmosphere

Generally speaking the CanAm trail is a lot like the Tasman series used to be, and Jackie Stewart has commented on this several times. Although he has been working a lot harder for less results than in European Grands Prix, he has probably been enjoying himself more because the pressure is off. It's by no means a doddle, but the atmosphere in the pits is much more relaxed.

And so the Gulf-orange McLarens have won their fifth J-Wax CanAm Championship and exceeded a million dollars in team earnings since the series started in 1966—a total domination package, the like of which is seldom seen in road racing.

When Bruce was painting a rosy picture of what American sports car racing could be like if the team was successful as we discussed the pros and cons of his ideas in that New Malden kitchen seven years ago, I'm sure even *he* didn't imagine that his forecasts would be so absolutely correct! The pity of it is that he's not around to see the team he started going from success to even greater success.

McLaren's M16 Indianapolis car shows the influence of the Formula 1 Lotus 72.

Riding with Revvie

By PETE LYONS

Our scribe from America, Pete Lyons, takes a CanAm lesson from Peter Revson, the CanAm headmaster.

Caught in a bad dream. Wedged in an angular bathtub. Its metal thrilled and in my helmet was a heavy throb. I glimpsed a white needle fluttering: 64, 66, 68. Six-eight in third is 158 mph.

It was time to wake up.

The vibration cut off. An instant of calm. Then a great hammer struck my spine, slamming my head back. I forced it down, and stared at the long black roadway between the orange wheel bulges. It was rushing like some demonic torrent frantic to enter the gates of hell. Small markings—stains, patches, pebbles—appeared as flickers and were gone like dust on a cine film. There was no longer any sensation of speed. We were going too fast.

This fantasy had gone too far.

A bridge flashed overhead like an aircraft's shadow. The wide straight kinked to the left. Still absolutely on full bore the McLaren bent into it. The world tilted on edge. To hold myself away from the driver's arms I had to strain every tendon. Just ahead the world ended in a boilerplate wall. The last time I saw the tachometer it had been showing 6600. That had been 184 mph, but Peter Revson's foot had been hard down ever since. I couldn't look at it now. My eyes were stuck on that wall.

I really wanted to wake up.

McLaren's M8F is the greatest sports car in motor racing history. Denny Hulme established that by his record lap at Riverside, when he beat the year-old speed of the 2J Chaparral. No other sports car could go as fast; I believe further that, all conditions being optimum, this Group 7 car would beat any Formula 1 car.

The greatest thing about the F, though, is its passengers space! Thanks to Coca Cola, one of the team's major sponsors, I've had a ride in one: three laps of Riverside with the new CanAm champion, Peter Revson. It was his very first day on the track with the car, the gearing and aerodynamics were only approximately correct, the tyres were workhorses, the track surface was covered more with dust than with rubber, and the engine was a little off. It was only giving about 710 bhp. We only reached about 190 mph on the straight. We did a lap time that would have qualified us 13th on the grid a few days later. But I think I had a pretty good ride, good enough to feel what a G7 car is like.

It's like an insane bull. Whatever you think of the level of competition in your average CanAm, the McLaren record is remarkable. Including the series' first year, when the M1B was not successful, there have been

49 races. A works McLaren has won 37. In the past five years they have met defeat only six times; four due to mechanical failure, once to inferior rain tyres and once to driver illness. These statistics would not mean quite so much if it were not also true that on almost every occasion these highly reliable machines have also been the fastest.

The F is the fourth version of a design which began with 1968's weapon, the first to use the big-block Chevrolet motor. Not very much has been changed from the original layout; what alterations there have been were done to enhance the original characteristics. Everything about the car embodies lessons learnt by Bruce McLaren in a decade at the specialised game of North American sports car racing. It's sturdy. It's simple. It's reasonably light. Its suspension is supple, its brakes very powerful, and it uses the biggest engine available. Its body has downforce as its first concern. Compared to its predecessors, the F is a few inches longer (wheelbase, 98in) but has been kept as narrow as feasible (track front and rear 60 in and 58 in). The

current car has a considerable degree of anti-squat—and the rear springs are progressively wound—but there is almost no anti-dive. Except for some of the engine blocks there is nothing "trick" about the car, it's all perfectly standard practice.

With the parent organisation busy in two other spheres, the G7 car started the season somewhat short of perfection. Hulme's first impression, confirmed by his lap times, was that it was no advance at all on last year's D. He found it difficult to feed in smoothly the power from engines 15 per cent larger than his favourites of 1970. His new team-mate, Revson, spent two races in misery because he'd had no time to sort out his car's handling. During the season there were some embarrassingly public failures: rear subframes due to tyre vibration, U-joints due to bumps, a broken wheel, a set of broken drive pins, all quite apart from some internal engine troubles.

The Kiwis being what they are, though, things improved and the performance levels picked up. Many little pieces were beefed up—

Denny Hulme watches closely as Lee Muir makes suitable adjustments to the engine.

sometimes whether they had demonstrated they needed it or not—and of course the Goodyears were better almost every week. The engine characteristics were, allegedly, not altered, but the drivers began having an easier time with them. The major suspension parameters were, allegedly, not changed, but stiffer springs improved the handling. Whereas at the start of the 10-race series the "orange elephants" were not as fast as the year before, and occasionally not as fast as Stewart's troublesome new Lola, by the end they were as fast and in one case faster than the "sucker" Chaparral. Between them they made 20 race starts, eight times from pole. They won eight races, finished second six times, third twice, and recorded only three DNFs.

Serviced by two separate teams of mechanics, the initially indentical team cars diverged in detail during the season. After his Ohio crash the arch conservative Hulme wanted no more part of inboard rear brakes; Revson was content that more frequent U-joint replacement had solved the problem. In the last two races the latter's car used drilled front brake discs, while earlier it had been fitted with thicker discs and bigger calipers. (Revvie sometimes used an astonishing amount of brake material). His car was more subject to tyre vibration, so his rear subframe crossmember became very strong. Two different solutions to the driver-cooling problem resulted in Hulme getting a modified body shell, which thanks to a sort of "chin-spoiler" affect at the front seemed to improve the handling. Apparently No 7 never handled as well as No 5, Revson sometimes saying he could not safely toss the car around as Hulme seemed able to, but yet he often had too much understeer at the same time. Twice during the year Denny tried the other car, when he gave us to understand it felt peculiar; after the last race Peter tried No 5 and apparently found it more controllable and also that the steering felt lighter. Yet, as far as anyone could discern, the cars were identical in all significant respects.

Hulme started from pole in five races, but rather often there was something wrong with his engines and he won only three times. Revson earned three poles—all in a row—but won five times.

The all-alloy, linerless cylinder blocks were by all accounts a big success. Not for the first reasons that come to mind: the weight saved by elimination of eight iron sleeves is not great, nor is there any great increase available bore diameter, and the internal temperatures are if anything higher, but nevertheless the high-silicon material must be the way of the future. Once a proper "ring package" had been worked out, wear on rings, pistons, and bores was negligible. Indeed, after 2000 miles of hard operation there was no measurable bore wear. Furthermore the one-piece blocks were free to expand with heat evenly in all dimensions; inspection of iron-liner engines after use proved that at working temperature the sleeves were flopping around loose in the case!

But enough of these technicalities. I'd been bothering my head about them all year. After about five thundering minutes my head was going for a ride. Coca Cola had laid this on, renting the Riverside track on the Tuesday before the final CanAm to introduce the subject to the Los Angeles daily press. (I don't qualify in that category, but at a time like this I'm pushy.) Pete Revson, co-operative soul that he is, agreed to give up a free day at home in Redondo Beach to ferry us around. His two personal mechanical geniuses brought No 7 out early to warm it up, Vince Higgens doing this little chore at a tedious hundred mph or so for about 10 laps—he said he had to do that many to run-in a new CWP. Some excuse. With this practical experience it was his duty to show each tyro passenger how to climb in and where to hold on. To Alec Greaves fell the lot of screwing his face up with sympathetic agony every time his precious car struggled out of the pits; this kind of non-racing use is abuse, in his eyes.

The engine fitted was a Reynolds of 509 cu in (8346 cc) which was fresh but for some reason a little soft by perhaps 30 bhp. We'd have

to be content with a mere 710. It was still going to drink its Gulf at the rate of one gallon every 3½ miles.

Before things became hurried I asked permission to sit in Peter's chair. I found it a somewhat tight fit (no surprise there!) with everything so readily to hand it was almost cramped. The pedals are distinctly offset toward the centre of the car, as is the plump steering wheel. The knees are held in place left and right by careful tailoring of the scuttle with no padding. The gear lever is conveniently placed on the vast plain of fuel tank top on the right. Visibility over the top of the broad windscreen is excellent; Revvie can see the ground just about 85 in ahead of the nose, and the 2in high side fences drop out of sight below the wheel covers well aft of any point where they would begin to obstruct vision. This cockpit would never be worth anything in a street car, but for 2 hr racing it would be comfortable. Very comfortable indeed. It would be quite easy to spend two hours driving this.

My dangerous thoughts must have showed on my face for suddenly Alec and Vince were grasping my arms, tugging frantically. I put up a good fight but as it was two against one, they hauled me out eventually. Next time I'll fasten the six-point harness.

The fire bottle in the leftside footwell had been removed to give a bit more space for our soft journalistic bodies, but it was still an inch-by-inch slither to get all the way down. The feet had to be threaded into a space not really big enough for one, and the hips were a press fit between aluminum panels innocent of upholstery. There was plenty of room for the left arm which was best employed hanging on to the outside edge of the broad fuel tank, but to keep the right arm out of the driver's sphere of operations it had to be bent up behind the passenger's head grasping the rollover bar. One does not feel really secure in this position. The thin body shell does not give any feeling of enclosure; rather the impression is of sitting on top of a squat metal sleigh. It would be a good dating car—the driver and passenger are intimately close. The remote battery was plugged into the side of the car, Pete flipped switches, a pump whined, and then. . . .

The engine is a hammer. A great heavy iron sledge hammer, that treats the car like a golf ball. The noise is deep, the beat almost stately, the most intrusive element a kind of dry rattle. This must be generated by the staggered intake horns, for it comes from somewhere above the head as well as behind.

Revson is a gentle driver. He gets us rolling with no feeling of suddenness, until we are fairly around the end of the pits wall and

Riverside gapes before us. Then he nails it. Kicks the bull between the legs. My right hand hurts—it has been crushed by my helmet. I can see nothing but blue California sky. My flesh is melting into every rearward cranny of the cockpit. There is a shattering bellow going on, which I feel as much as hear. I feel it in my chest. Everything behind me seems to be trying to push through to the front of me.

The long bottom gear pulls us up above 90 mph. There is a pause, my spongy body recoils forward, then . . . slam! The great hammer smashes my spine. Again the huge noise. Again the tremendous push. Another pause, another slam. The acceleration feels absolutely as strong as before.

From the pits the first corner is Turn 2, a 120-odd-mph right hander entering a little valley which holds the Esses. From the track you can't see all the way round 2, it vanishes between dun-coloured slopes. The track is a dark grey bend, and on it is a black arc. You know that arc is your life-line. You must hit it precisely. It's all shooting back at you like falling off a mountain. It looks narrow. It's arriving very fast. Too fast really to think about.

The engine's throb eases. Revson's hands press the wheel. The McLaren has darted around. It was over like a lash of a whip. For one instant there was a bucket-on-a-rope sensation, then that huge engine was driving again and we were straight.

That was the only moment in the entire ride I felt any apprehension. That magnificent automobile had shrugged off that curve with such contempt that I surrendered myself completely. No twinge of doubt about the car's abilities ever formed again. I relaxed.

The Esses as a whole are a quick slash-slash with powerful side forces; only one other bend is so acute we must lift for an instant, all the rest is taken with the engine beating hard. Turn 6 is a tight 180 over a hump, which must be entered at 60 mph. The brakes go on before we get to Turn 5, a left-hander immediately before 6, and it turns out the brakes are this car's most phenomenal feature. Revvie's right leg makes one strong pumping movement, and a tremendous force, like a giant octopus, tries to suck me down into the footwell. But almost before I can notice what is happening, it's all over. We have slipped down into second gear and we are whipping up into the first of the two apexes. The line of half-buried white tyres flash under the nose and we're bursting out the far side of the corner. We are a rocket sled. There is that rising machine-gun

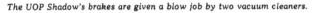
The UOP Shadow's brakes are given a blow job by two vacuum cleaners.

146

rattle, that slight moment of stasis, that heavy slam in the back, the same incredible force thrusting us down the next straight. The straight is nothing before such acceleration, it hurls back at us like a snapped rubber band.

Turns 7 and 8 are as slow as 6. The big McLaren must be hauled down hard for each one, and it does not seem happy at such slow speeds. It does not go through them with the same whiplash alacrity as it does the faster turns. Through 7 especially, which is a descending left-hand 180, there is a place in the middle where nothing happens for a moment. We just coast along for a few yards waiting for the end of this obstacle, without the violent velocity changes we perform everywhere else. There is no force but side-force, which seems rather low, almost down in the everyday-experience category. At this speed, in fact, I found myself thinking, "I could handle this car." Dangerous thought! Driving this car slowly is like pulling back the hammer to cock a revolver; nothing much is happening yet, but you better have it pointing in the right direction. Later Revson explained that in these slow turns he was holding the car just under a serious push condition, that if he tried to go any harder the front wheels would wash out across the road.

On one lap, trundling down through 7 he held up a finger to say, " Watch this." As the turn began to open out and we had begun to pile-drive forward again, he gave the wheel a big wrench to chuck the tail out and in the next instant stamped open the throttles. The whole massive stern of the car went into a severe tremble—tyre vibration. I could feel all the various sprung and unsprung masses joggling against each other rapidly. It was much the sort of feeling you'd expect should an aircraft piston engine suddenly lose a propeller blade. It was so strong a phenomenon that I could easily visualise the whole car shaking apart. As we snapped back straight and blasted away up the next piece of road Peter turned his face to me, and I could see his eyes through his visor asking me if I understood just how serious a problem this tyre vibration

is. I nodded vigorously. Two other times in the ride, at other places, this started to happen spontaneously, and I could feel Peter feathering the throttle to kill it.

At higher speeds—which it reaches before you can draw a breath—the M8F comes into its own. The aerodynamics squash the car to the road and it changes direction like a puma chasing a rabbit. Slashing through the Esses is like being attacked on both sides at once; the strain toward one side is replaced with its opposite before you can brace yourself. That left-hand kink in the back straight comes at you faster than your mind can grasp; it would give you the same bewilderment to replace a tennis ball with a bullet. The sequence beginning with Turn 9 is like a flowing aerobatic manoeuvre: the crushing G-loadings on the banking which are smoothly overlain with the driver's progressive feeding in of power, the white steel rails looming in toward us at the exit, but we just miss them and immediately veer back across the track, a big extravagant sweep which flings us straight under the starter's flying bridge. How could anyone have time to notice any kind of signals, we've just wound out in third gear and, slam, entered fourth. Although we're going hard in top gear there is no need to lift the foot, but the car goes light over the hump of Turn 1 and a shallow transverse depression makes the front wheels slither sideways a foot or so. (A few days latter Revvie said he'd managed to tune that out.)

As we charge up on some of the faster corners I notice an interesting steering effect. Revvie's thick white gloves twirl in the steering lock a split second before anything happens; there is an instant of feeling the front tyres scratching at the road before they seem to bite. I conclude this is the car's basic understeer characteristics showing through.

On the matter of feeding in power through a corner, I can detect no problem at all. Apart from the driver's persistent tendency to put his foot hard down a few yards sooner than I expect, everything seems perfectly smooth. The mass of the tail shifts

into a new position on the road, the big rear tyres settle in firmly, and we are launched out the far side on our way to the Moon. Revvie's hands are in constant twirling motion, but seldom does he need more than about one-sixth steering lock. It seems smoother than I expected.

Downward gear changes are smooth also, just an easy blip of noise but no perceptible jerk of the car. Upward changes are something else. Pete's hand doesn't move the lever very rapidly, and there is a distinct pause between gears when nothing happens, always followed by that terrific bruising slam when he lets the clutch out. The sheer mass of moving parts in a big Hewland apparently discourages " speed shifting."

The braking power remains the most astonishing thing. Even on the long, undulating right hand curve into Turn 8, which is begun on full bore acceleration in third when the brakes are clamped on they are on almost full. The hopeless passenger pitches forward into the footwell, but the car makes not a weave, not a waggle. All it does is stop. In sections where the car is straight while braking, the retardation is incredible. Flying down into Turn 9, aiming squarely at that boiler plate wall at 190 mph, and the driver finally condescends to slow down. We're down to about 125, bending cleanly down into the banking as his right hand tenderly drops into third. When you stop to analyse it, the braking performance of a modern race car is such that the brakes are not really in operation very much time during a lap. They are used hard five times at Riverside, for a total time which cannot exceed 15 sec, from a 92 sec lap. Thus nowadays an improvement in sheer braking power of quite a sizeable percentage would not translate into very greatly shortened lap times. It would probably help a driver in overtaking, though.

One overall impression of my ride remains: a sensation of having entered another world. A first class racing driver allowed me to visit the place where he is home. During those few minutes we were in a capsule, a cocoon, shut away from the familiar values of action, reaction, velocity. The old world was still there all around us, but it had nothing to do with us. We were enclosed in our own world. Different laws applied. Everything was magnified. The most delicate movement on a control produced intense response. A manoeuvre which, from the outside, looks easy and gentle, is a maelstrom of violence from the inside. A place on the road which looks from the outside to be a disturbing bump is not even perceived from within the car; two places at Riverside which look to be shallow elevation changes become to the race car a nasty spank in the bottom and a severe drop—at 185 mph the worst bump on the circuit. The individual lap, made up of seemingly unrelated curves and straights and hummocks, becomes a single long file of problems to be solved, presenting themselves to driver like a stream of tracer bullets. All the passenger is able to do is follow, tardily, a few of the driver's more obvious solutions. When he appreciates that in fact the driver is coping with every problem precisely and punctually and furthermore that he is actively with his right foot trying to make them come at him even faster, then the passenger's admiration rises in his throat. He would cheer, but he knows his voice would be as nothing against the bellow of the car.

Three times we flashed around. The better of the two lap times that were taken—using a point in the back straight—was 1 m 38.5 s. I was pretty impressed with that, as it was a mere 2 sec off last year's best race lap done by Oliver in the Ti22. With all the factors slowing us down that day I felt Revvie had given me a damn fine ride —and I still felt so late in the day when he went out alone to shake off the feeling of being a bus driver and went 5 sec faster. I had been taken up into his world as far as it was seemly for me to go. The farther reaches are his alone.

But I most certainly was sorry to stop !

An eagle-eyed Jackie Oliver watches as a mechanic balances the brakes on his UOP Shadow.

When to suck and when to blow

By Pete Lyons

Penske comes into our friendly old CanAm like a cold north wind. There is lots of business with tarpaulins to cover secrets, lots of shooing away of inquiring busybodies, and some of the crewmen have been programmed to sacrifice their very bodies to block camera lenses. Therefore it has taken me several weeks of furtive observation and careful conversation to arrive at an understanding of the L&M Porsche's turbocharger system, but this is how it works—I think.

We start with the knowledge of how any exhaust-supercharged engine is laid out: exhaust gases are piped to a turbine wheel, attached to which is a compressor wheel which forces air into the inlet manifold. In the exhaust side there has to be a spring-loaded relief valve, because the boost pressure must not exceed a certain value if the engine is to survive. Successful engines have

their fuel injected down at the inlet ports. This describes the basic elements in your standard Indianapolis motor—exhaust manifolding all going down into one pipe, past a "blow-off valve," to a single turbine case; a single compressor casing with single long pipe, or a branched pipe if it's a V8, going to an intake manifold log(s). There has to be a small pressure-sensing line running from intake to blowoff valve, but it s a pretty simple setup. But the Porsche has much more.

There are two complete turbine/blower units, much smaller than the normal Indy units, each fed by and feeding one six-cylinder bank. Both sides are controlled by a single blowoff, mounted on a cross pipe running between the main exhaust pipes just before the turbos. As is normal a large screw-with-locknut, which sticks out of the top of the blowoff valve through the bodywork, con-

trols the maximum exhaust pressure, and hence is the "horsepower screw." One pressure-sensing line runs from one intake manifold log to the blowoff housing; at the front end of the twin logs a half-inch diameter pipe connects them. Down from each log run individual inlet stacks to each cylinder, with a butterfly valve near the middle height and fuel injection nozzles going in—at a steep upward angle—near the bottom. Also near the bottom, each set of three vertical stacks is connected by what appear to be hollow tubes. Up at the butterfly level are what look for all the world like carburetter air screws going into the housing at a downward angle; there is no discernible fuel going into their area. The fuel comes from a Bosche 12-cylinder pump which looks identical to that on a normal 917, except that into the adjoining governing unit goes a pressure line from the nearer manifold log; thus fuel input is governed by manifold pressure as well as engine speed and throttle position.

In the inlet manifolding are the most intriguing bits: a total of 12 valves of three different types. In each main blower-to-log duct, near the blower ends, is a cylindrical device with a screw-with-locknut and a bunch of holes round the base, mounted to angle in and down below body line. I feel certain these two devices are emergency blowoffs, to act when for any reason (perhaps an explosion of fuel mixture in a log?) the main exhaust-side blowoff doesn't cope. I should mention, though, that on one occasion in practise I watched a mechanic adjust one of them, and I haven't developed a theory to account why.

The second type of valve is eight in number, four mounted on top of each log fairly evenly spaced so they don't actually sit directly over more than a few of the 12 inlet stacks. Each of these devices has a black plastic cap which very likely protects an adjustment screw and a spring. Through the holes at

Mark Donohue inspects the blowers during testing before his Atlanta accident.

Eight valves, four mounted on top of each log, are evenly spaced so that they don't actually sit directly over more than a few of the 12 inlet stacks. Each has a black plastic cap which protects an adjustable screw and spring.

148

the base I can see the stem and head of what seems to be a poppet valve, and from its location and the way the stem goes up into the "guide" I am convinced the valve opens downward and is therefore an *inlet*. It could only work should there be any occasion when pressure in the log drops below atmospheric, so as to suck air in.

The third type of valve is one that has caused all the trouble in races so far. There is a pair of them, one in each inlet duct just before (i.e. on the rearward end) of each log. It comprises what in plumbing parlance would be a "T," with the upright of the "T" pointing down and open at the bottom and containing what must be a butterfly controlling whether or not the entire inlet manifold is open to atmosphere. A small spring, exactly like a throttle-return spring (one of these broke at Watkins Glen), holds the butterfly in the closed position. A sliding-yoke linkage connected to the throttle mechanism ensures that at closed throttle these butterflies are *open*; as the driver's foot goes down the tension on the closing springs is released and at some point, perhaps about one-third throttle opening, the butter-flies are fully closed. Therefore these are manifold "pressure-dumps," letting blower pressure out whenever the driver's foot lifts right off or nearly off.

So, the system has the ability to control its own pressure in several ways: its maximum pressure, controlled by two different types of spring loaded valve; it can release its pressure suddenly on closed-throttle through the "dumps"; and it can suck in normal atmosphere on occasion through the eight "steamwhistles" on top. The last two functions are the most interesting, and are obviously called for by the notorious throttle lag problem.

The "dumps" would serve to keep the blower wheels up to speed during closed-throttle periods; without back pressure in the inlet manifold the blower has less resistance to spinning and will be at a higher rpm when the driver once again asks it to go to work. The eight inlet suction valves would operate at very low rpm/throttle-opening, possibly as in starting up and idling (both very simple, drama-free performances on the Porsche) but certainly when the driver first puts his foot down coming out of a corner—or even when blipping the throttle for down-changes. The motor would then be normally-aspirated.

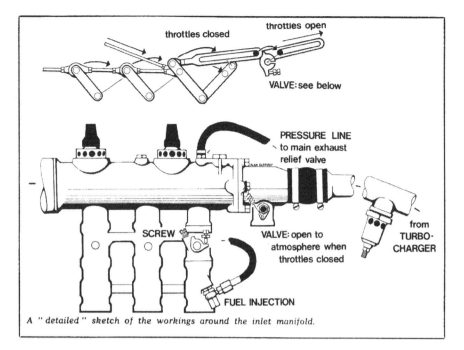

A "detailed" sketch of the workings around the inlet manifold.

What I don't pretend to know are any of the details—pressure values, valve sizes, passage dimensions and profiles—which were so exhaustively developed by the Porsche engineers over the past year or 18 months, and which are the reasons no rival builders could simply copy the external confifuration and expect to beat the Porsche right away.

I suspect the maximum pressure is set at or slightly above one atmosphere, which is about half what an Indy engine operates at; there is what I believe to be a manifold pressure gauge on the Porsche's dash which reads to 1.5 and is marked in red at about 1.3—but I would be prepared to find it was a decoy like the suction-gauge on the old 2J Chaparral. I see no good reason to doubt the usually quoted horsepower figure of 880 at 8000 rpm. There is a throttle lag, one can hear it in the way the blower whistle rises in the middle of a corner a good second before the engine note hardens.

A problem with the engine is spark plugs: there are 24 of them, and because of the chassis construction those in four cylinders are very hard to get at. It reportedly takes two hours to change plugs—and it only takes 1½ hours to change engines! Should the plugs foul, as happened to Gregg at his first race with the engine due to too much low-speed idling and paddock-driving, one is in trouble. For this reason Champion have evolved a platinum plug, which better resists fouling. The ignition voltage for these blown engines must be about 50 per cent higher than for a normally aspirated engine, incidentally.

Certainly the car works, and on that score both Porsche and Penske Racing deserve full admiration. Such a complicated mechanism with such built-in problems could have fallen on its face (but then, of course, we would never have seen it in public) but in fact these men have solved the problems, and it is the first time in the world's history.

George Follmer at Elkhart Lake

Lola T310 CanAm car announced

The 1972 CanAm challenger from Lola Cars left Huntingdon this week bound for the second round in the series, at Road Atlanta this Sunday. The T310 will be entered by US Lola agent Carl Haas, in association with Steed, and will be driven by Britain's David Hobbs.

Lola claim the car has the best downthrust/lowest drag co-efficient of any car currently racing. It has a low, shovel nose and all-enveloping body, which makes it the longest, widest, flattest Lola yet—and a far cry from last year's stubby T260.

The T310 was completed late last week and was tested by Frank Gardner at Silverstone on Friday. Another test session followed at Snetterton on Monday, after which the car was air-freighted to the States.

Lola have been doing a great deal of background design work on the car, which was actually built in about a week. (Lola actually claim the G-for-Guiness

The new Lola T310 which David Hobbs will drive for Carl Haas at Road Atlanta this weekend.

from March !) It is a total Eric Broadley concept, but the shape was finalised using the wind tunnel at SDA, the specialist division of Specialised Mouldings.

Main departure of the T310 is the body style. It is said to give good penetration and plenty of downthrust without any air getting trapped or exerting excess down pressure. Ducts in the bodywork let out any air trapped under the bodywork—air that has been used to cool the radiators and brakes.

Beneath the glassfibre body, by Specialised Mouldings, the car is fairly conventional. It has a full-monocoque chassis, outboard front brakes and inboard rears. The wheelbase is 105 in and the track 62 in. Wheels are 11 x 15 in (front) and 17 x 15 in (rear). The engine, a dry sump unit by Foltz, will be between 8.2- and 8.8-litres.

A spare car may be built for the Haas team but there are no other firm sales at present.

Through the Goodwood chicane the McLaren M20 lifts its inside front wheel as Denny piles on 760 horsepower in bottom gear.

Taken for a ride— at 188 mph

By SIMON TAYLOR

Even though there was no upholstery and I was sitting, or rather lying, in the bare monocoque, it was surprisingly comfortable. When the bodywork was fastened down I found that, by bending my knees sideways, I could squirm down quite low, with my line of vision through rather than over the tinted aeroscreen. McLaren team manager Phil Kerr, who was patiently supervising the insertion of wriggling journalists into his shiny new car, told me to clutch the fuel cell top on the monocoque side with my left hand, although this afforded little grip. To ensure that I didn't break my neck when Denny snapped open the throttles, and also to prevent myself from falling into his lap at an inopportune moment, I curved my right arm behind my neck and grasped the roll bar. Denny nodded to me and punched the starter button.

The huge Chevy engine—all 8.1 litres of it—thundered into life, sending earth-shaking tremors through the car. Denny engaged a gear and motored nonchalantly off down the road. The acceleration felt tremendous, but I knew from his casual gearchanges that this was just a warmup. Out of Madgwick and through the long curve of Fordwater he began to turn on the power, and the sharp left-hander at St Mary's came up very rapidly. Then the double right-hander at Lavant, and on to the straight. I knew we were going very fast, but sheer speed was not the sensation: it was more one of acceleration, noise and extreme brutal power. Woodcote coming up looked very narrow and sharp,

but we were round and Denny was taking bottom gear in the four-speed box for the chicane.

That was the end of the warm-up lap. Now the real thing started. Coming out of the chicane in bottom Denny floored the throttle, and I felt like an insignificant fly that has been swatted by a giant. Our little orange toboggan was catapulted down the narrow ribbon of road to the thunderous sound of eight very big cylinders combining to produce 760 horsepower, and my stomach seemed to have wrapped itself round my spine. Bam, second gear almost immediately, and Bam, third. Madgwick, a narrow, blind apex righthander, and its earth bank were approaching at what was now over 155 mph. This was perhaps the only moment when I actually experienced fear: in my mind I knew that the man sitting next to me knew exactly what he was doing, and that there was no worry he was going to do a silly thing like forget to brake for a corner. But my body didn't for this split second want to believe what my mind was telling it, and as the earth bank rushed towards me, apparently now only a few feet away, I felt myself cringe deeper into the fibreglass.

Then came another giant fly swat, only this time in the chest rather than the back. The CanAm McLaren's big Lockheed ventilated discs are just incredible, and all the giant-hand clichés can't begin to describe the four-square sensation in which the car presses itself into the road, still feeling completely stable.

Climbing aboard (in stockinged feet) is a delicate business. . . .

Now we were in the corner, and the G-forces were pushing my head into my left shoulder as the big Goodyears—their footprint 16 inches across at the back—held us on line at cornering forces way beyond my experience. Top gear now, and round the apparently never-ending Fordwater, the horizon tilting as I struggled to keep my head off the left side bodywork. Just as I had come to terms with this on came the brakes, Denny grabbed third, and I was being thrown to the right: my arm gripping the roll bar behind my head was almost pulled from its socket as we rocketed through St Mary's.

The short straight between St Mary's and Lavant seemed to have disappeared, for just as Denny was accelerating out of the left-hander in third, my head jerked back under the acceleration, on went those astonishing brakes, jerking my head forward. Second gear, throttle open again, head jerked back, and the horizon fell away once more as the McLaren hauled itself round the double apex of Lavant Corner. Under 650 lbs ft of torque even those big back tyres lost their cool and the tail flicked out, but Denny was as un-ruffled as ever and caught it almost before I'd realised it had happened. "I wasn't going to unstick the back end with a passenger on board," he told me later, "but I figured AUTOSPORT needed the full treatment." Thanks, Denny.

Now that bewildering acceleration again, second, third and into fourth. The rev-counter needle climbing rapidly to 6800 rpm. We're doing one hundred and eighty-eight miles an hour: still the car feels steady as a rock, although the Lavant Straight kink has become a sharp curve. Denny takes a pre-cise line through it, foot on the boards. Here comes Woodcote: by now I'm prepared for the late, fierce braking, and I force my body to relax as Denny continues to do 188 mph right up to the corner before hitting the brakes, going straight from fourth to second and powering us through the corner. It's only a short, sharp spurt before the brakes go on again and we're in bottom gear for the chicane. This is so sharp that Denny drives rather than powers the car round, but once he's skimmed the second apex his right foot is firmly planted

on the loud pedal, and we are being flung on down to Madgwick again.

During my first fast lap I was so busy trying to keep my head more or less vertical and my body from hurling itself either into Hulme's lap or out through the left of the car that I had little time to notice how astonishingly smooth Denny Hulme was. But by my third lap I had become even more fully lost in admiration for the man, and the way his rapid yet totally unhurried movements of wrists and ankles controlled the charging, maddened bull of a car calmly and com-petently. And we weren't hanging about: our fastest lap was 1 m 11 s. When Goodwood last had an outright lap record it was in the mid-'20s. Everything's very different now, I know, but that's only six years ago. In fact Denny found this time so easy that he was consistently doing it with journalists large and small on board—he said that most of them made the car feel as though it had plenty of fuel in the tank—and on his own he has motored round Goodwood in 67-odd seconds. That's with *really* late braking. . . .

All too soon my four laps were over and we were coasting into the pit lane. On our last lap Denny changed straight into top from second going on to the straight, and glanced across at me as if to say : " This is

a full-blooded racing engine, but just feel this low-speed torque.'' At very low revs he plonked his foot down and, sounding only slightly more grumbly than usual, the big V8 pushed us off down the straight, coming rapidly on to the cam so that the power built up in a great rush.

As we rolled to a halt Denny switched off and a great hush descended. I clambered out, to mull over a swirling mass of impressions : mainly impressions of immense G-forces, braking, accelerating and cornering, all on a level not dreamt of by the normal motorist and not really aspired to by even the average racing driver. As a machine built for the sole purpose of taking itself plus skilful driver round a road racing circuit as fast as possible, the McLaren M20 is bewilderingly effective: the product of clever designers, painstaking technicians, and season after season of very hard work and very high expenditure, finding half a second here, half a second there. The fruit of Team McLaren's long labours is the M20 and its 67 s laps of Goodwood. Every-body connected with it, from designer Gordon Coppuck, organiser Phil Kerr and driver Denny via the mechanics to the man who sweeps those very clean factory floors at Colnbrook: they all must feel very proud. In any case, I owe them all a big thank-you for five minutes that I shall not forget.

. . . but once aboard, the M20 really is a two-seater, if a rather intimate one.

PORSCHE'S 1000 BHP RACER

In the first round of this year's Can-Am series, a shatteringly fast turbocharged Porsche 917 virtually blew all opposition off the track. Failure of a turbocharger component prevented the car from winning, but its superiority over the hitherto unbeatable McLarens was clearly demonstrated. Peter Anderson brings you the story of the car's evolution, and the man behind it.

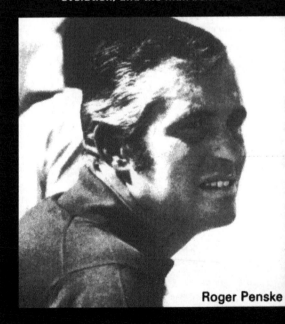

Roger Penske

In the light of the current super car controversy, suggesting that a car have 1000 hp and be able to use it sounds like terminal automotive insanity.

But believe it, the Porsche people in the United States have and use it to very good effect.

It is the output – 1005 bhp actually – of the current Porsche-Audi engine as used in Roger Penske's much modified lightweight Porsche 917 Can Am car.

It is the final result of 18 months' work.

The programme began when Porsche wanted to win the Can Am series against the might of the unbeaten McLarens. They tried a lightened 908/3 while they were winning the Interseries European sports car championship.

The 908 didn't get all that far, barely keeping the McLarens in sight. So experienced American driver Roger Penske was asked to make a Porsche win. That, plus a significantly large budget, is all Penske needs – apart from the driving and sorting our genius of Mark Donohue.

Penske started with the 917 coupe, cut off the roof and began looking at the mechanicals. McLarens were running special aluminium Chevrolet V8s which with their fuel injection looked very hard to toss. They were both powerful and reliable.

Early testing of the 917 engines showed that even with

fuel injection they weren't going to get near the opposition's output.

So another tack was tried. The 917 motor was turbo-charged – a shrewd move for the power to run such a device takes nothing from the crankshaft.

A turbocharger is in fact a two-stage turbine, exhaust gases spinning it on the power side and the driven side working like a conventional supercharger, ramming air and fuel into the cylinders.

Turbochargers can rotate at speeds to 9,000 rpm so they are quite able to produce considerable boost if needed. They also produce more usable power at high rpm than mechanically driven superchargers.

Even more amazing than the 1005 bhp figure is that it comes from just 4.5 litres, little more than half the size of the Chevrolet engine which isn't too far behind on power.

The Le Mans winning 917 Porsche had a five-litre vers-ion of the air-cooled flat 12. As part of his development, Penske looked at a 5.4-litre version of the same unit.

But once turbochargers had been decided upon, the larger engines were eschewed for the smaller 4.5-litre version. This, in its original 1968 form, pumped out 580 bhp – the final power figure determined by Porsche after running an 18-hour non-stop test sequence.

This is the sort of long-term power output Porsche needed to be sure the unit was reliable for long-distance races. The 917 motor was conceived in classic style with centre power take-off for both driving the car and the cooling fan. This meant that in effect there were two 2.2 litre 911S motors joined back to back with a common crankshaft, cooling fan drive and power take-off.

The problem of taking the drive from one end of this rather long motor was the excessive crankshaft whip induced with a single-ended drive.

It was easy to revert to the paired sixes – each of course a horizontally opposed air-cooled type.

The extreme width of this type of motor is one reason it hasn't made its way into Formula One cars although a water-cooled flat 12 has been tried. (It also ingested water down the intakes on wet tracks, dampening performance and development enthusiasm).

The light weight of the air-cooled motor was part of Penske's plan to extract the power from a normally aspirated 5.4-litre 917 motor. It could give away a little power in return for its lighter weight.

In five litre form, the 917 Le Mans motor had 630 bhp so Penske's 5.4 litre motor churned out even more – but it wasn't enough.

So the 4.5 was again brought out for development. Power extraction creates heat from the thermal activity in the cylinders needed to produce the power. The closer cylinder jacket spacing of the larger 917 motors made cooling the turbocharged motor a difficult problem. The wider spacing between the barrels of the 4.5 litre motor solved this.

The plan was to run one turbocharger for each bank of six cylinders, one per side. Eberspacher turbochargers were selected. They make turbochargers for diesels in Germany and have specialist knowledge and research behind them in the field.

Using a turbocharger speed of 88,000 rpm, the boost was around 14.7 psi – one atmosphere, as a Porsche engineer let slip – giving the motor around 30 psi all up.

The problems were only beginning then. The mechanical fuel injection system needed new sensors, for the boosted mixture couldn't be read from straight manifold vacuum.

The bottom end of the engine took the power extremely well with no changes necessary at all. "We have a rather large safety margin even in our racing engines" said a Porsche engineer.

Compression ratio was dropped to 8:1 but the sodium cooled exhaust valves were retained. Titanium inlet valves and spark plugs with platinum electrodes were used.

Practice on Porsche's new Weissach test track near Stuttgart demonstrated that the extra large oil cooler was sufficient for sprint work but a larger output fan was needed to keep cylinder head temperature down.

The bigger than 5-litre fan fitted was also driven at a higher speed. According to factory test engineers, who now seemed to be doing most of the development of both car and engine, the cooling fan took only slightly more than the 17 bhp needed to run the five litre 917's fan.

Dual development now began to take place. Penske in America had one of the 917/10 Can Am engines and cars and Porsche had a duplicate in Germany.

Both had aluminium space frames – there are plans to add more lightness as Colin Chapman advises with magnesium parts later – big fuel tanks and stiffened gearcases carrying tougher gears.

The engines, meanwhile, had been subjected to dynamometer tests but not the usual type. Because Can Am stresses aren't the same as those of European road racing. Porsche only gave the motor six hours instead of the usual 18.

But for four hours, the 917/10 motor pumped out 880 bhp. To see what she'd do, they blipped her on the dyno and got the flash reading of 1005 bhp! Without the four figure power reading, the 917/10 engine and car have a power rating of more than 1000 bhp per ton. (How would that stir super car gripes?).

The car and its handling is a mixture of Penske, Donohue and Porsche test facilities. Donohue flies to Stuttgart, takes the Porsche car out on the Weissach circuit and makes a list of suggestions. These are simultaneously done on both cars in Germany and the United States.

Porsche men work on the aerodynamics and Penske prepares the racing programme.

The car was one second faster around the circuit in practice for the first Can Am than the McLarens and when the flag fell, it sprang to a commanding lead.

It opened this further for 20 laps until a turbocharger component failed. Replacing it cost 3 laps. But the car finished only 55 seconds behind Denis Hulme's ailing McLaren.

The spectre of 1005 bhp frim 4.5 litres sounds like Gotterdammerung, appropriately Wagnerian for a Porsche from Oestreich.

Below: From left: Donohue, Penske, chief Penske engineer Cox and Porsche's Rice Steinemann - 1972 Can-Am victors?

TOWARDS 1000 BHP

Tony Curtis examines Porsche's latest racer — the blown 917 Can-Am car

On either side of the gearbox lie the turbines of the two turbochargers, each one driven by the exhaust from a bank of six cylinders. The third, central and smaller exhaust pipe takes pressure-relief by-pass flow. Outboard of the turbines are the compressors which force additional air into the cylinders

Surrounded by a throng of admiring journalists, this is an experimental hack with the turboblown engine. Improvements developed on this car as transferred to the Roger Penske cars

Right from the beginning Can-Am racing congealed into a set pattern: the McLarens versus a generally very inadequate remainder. But thanks to American Roger Penske (see last week's colour feature) there are signs that this could change. His weapons? Driver Mark Donohue and the fearsome turbo-supercharged 917-10 Spyder which Porsche put on view for the first time at their impressive new Weissach development centre and test track recently — which we'll be describing in a later issue.

In its Le Mans-winning form the aircooled flat-twelve 917 engine reached a capacity of 5 litres, and bigger 5.4-litre versions have since been built, but for the turbocharging exercise Porsche reverted to the layout and capacity of the early 4.5-litre unit because the wide spacing of its cylinders helps to ease cooling problems. In 1969 this engine developed just over 580 bhp at 8400 rpm, but with a turbo-supercharger to each bank of six cylinders the power output is raised to no less than 880 bhp — to convince sceptical visiting journalists a unit on a test bed was momentarily blipped to produce a flash reading on the dynamometer of over 1000 bhp! Afterwards the door of the test cell was opened so that the assembled company could listen reverently to the awesome Wagnerian boom. Even with a measly 880 bhp on tap, the power-to-weight ratio of the Can-Am Spyder will be well over 1000 bhp/ton, since the overall weight is around 750 kg.

The two turbochargers which create all this extra power are assembled from components out of the standard range of Eberspacher, a German company specializing in the manufacture of turbo-blowers for large diesels. On the 917 these blowers reach a top speed of 88,000 rpm, giving a maximum boost pressure of about one atmosphere or 14.7 psi — getting on for 30 psi absolute — and to prevent detonation the compression ratio has been reduced to around 8.0:1. As before there is a mechanical fuel injection system, but with a more complex form of control.

Increasing power by such a large amount in this particular way won't raise the mechanical stresses so very much but must involve a great increase in thermal stress. However the engine components involved had already been developed to withstand the 630 bhp of the 5.0-litre unblown unit — more still for the 5.4-litre engines, also unblown — and Porsche say that they always build-in a big safety margin. Even so, it's not surprising that various modifications have proved necessary. As before, the steel exhaust valves are sodium cooled, but the inlet valves are now made of titanium and the sparking plugs have platinum electrodes. The larger oil cooler used for the shorter circuits is a permanent fitting, and the enlarged fan runs at a higher speed than before, though the Porsche engineers say that nevertheless it absorbs not much more than the 17 bhp needed to cool the 630 bhp 5.0-litre unblown engine.

At first the blown engine was fitted to an ordinary 917 with its top cut off to create an open car, but a new version of the aluminium space-frame chassis has been built — and Porsche are said to be experimenting with a special magnesium alloy. The fuel tank capacity has been increased and the transmission has stronger gears in a stiffer casing.

The new car is the result of an intensive development programme lasting, Porsche say, some six months, and involving much work on matching the turboblowers to the engine for good torque at low revs and minimum throttle lag. Mark Donohue says that the engine develops not far off maximum power from 5500 rpm onwards; there is some throttle lag but he doesn't find it too much of a problem. Normally Porsche expect their racing engines to survive an 18-hour test running at full throttle and different engine speeds, but since the new unit wouldn't last very long if held at maximum power, its acceptance test lasts only four hours. Porsche point out, however, that on hardly any circuits — particularly Can-Am ones — is maximum power held for more than a few seconds. They feel this philosophy is a sound one and expect to develop a race-winning car at least by the end of the season.

THE PENSKE-DONOHUE PORSCHE 917-10

5 liters, 12 cylinders and twin turbochargers add up to 900 bhp— but the Can-Am Porsche Spyder's big advantage is in the corners

BY PETE LYONS

ILLUSTRATION BY WERNER BÜHRER

AMERICANS ARE ADDICTED to The Noble Experiment. For years the SCCA tried to run the Can-Am with as few car rules as possible, a noble experiment dedicated to the proposition that a good spectacle could be achieved with essentially Formula Libre machinery. Unhappily, in six years the series has never really reached its potential. It *is* the premier form of American road racing but it hasn't attained the stature of various oval-track or dragstrip shows. Thus the Can-Am has been open to criticism, and over the past few years several different forces have been chipping away at the original Formula Libre concept. Aerodynamics, for one large instance, are under rigid control, and more and more the movements of an innovative designer's pencil have been laid out for him by one regulation or another.

Still free, though, are two areas: overall weight and engine size and type (except that, to pick nits, you can't use a gas turbine, nor an engine under 2500 cc). To those of us who still wistfully subscribe to free formulae, then, it is gratifying that in finally making their long-anticipated North American assault the Porsche engineers have concentrated on the two free areas. The new Can-Am Porsche 917 is made of elaborate and expensive lightweight materials, and by exhaust-

supercharging their 12-cylinder engine they have made their first solid foray into a new realm of road racing power. The best part, though, is that this complicated, potentially troublesome new concept works. In the car's debut performance at Mosport Park Mark Donohue was fastest.

Naturally, the critical forces bayed like hyenas. Unfair! Too Expensive! Ban It! Write New Rules! Outlaw Turbocharged Aircooled Multicam Engines!

Hold off, pack. Walk out to one of the corners with a stopwatch. Check cornering speeds. That's where Donohue was making it at Mosport. His turbopower—800, 900, whatever—was hustling him up the straights pretty well but he was a lot faster than anybody else in the corners. By a factor of 5%—which is a bunch.

No, the thing about the L&M Penske Porsche is that it is a total automobile. It's not a trick with one good feature, like a dragster. It does the whole job. Banning one aspect of it would be silly, a thoughtless gut reaction.

Porsche's Group 7 project takes the form it does for practical reasons. Even those engineers who are intrigued by the difficulties of developing a turbocharged road circuit engine must recognize that it's not the best way to generate lots of horses.

PHOTO BY RON STEAKLEY

The simplest way, which in this context as in so many others is the best way, is to build big engines. The 500-cu-in. Chevies are the best Can-Am engines because they are simple, light, compact and relatively cheap. The most straightforward way to challenge these attributes would be to design a better Chevy. However, to do that Porsche would have had to start from scratch, and that would have been far from cheap (especially the way they do things). It was much more practical to draw on their roomful of existing 5-liter 917 engines, virtually useless after the end of the 1969-1971 Group 5 regulations. These can be taken out to about 5.4 liters and it might be anticipated that careful development work and higher rev limits could squeeze out something approaching 700 bhp. However, in terms of low-speed performance (torque) such an engine would be left behind by a good Chevy. But if you supercharge an engine, you in effect increase its displacement. In round figures, stuff 50% more air into a 5-liter and you get 7.5 liters. Of course, there will be problems—dissipating 50% more heat, holding 50% more BMEP inside—but solving them should be cheaper than developing a whole new engine.

If you choose what has emerged as the most efficient super-charging method, in which the compressor(s) is (are) driven by exhaust pressure, you introduce the additional problem of a lag between the time the driver's foot asks for more power and the time the engine grants it to him. At Indianapolis the engines are small and the boost pressures are high, so the throttle lag is sizable. Drivers cope with it there because of the relatively simple (which word emphatically does not mean easy) nature of the cornering. Occasionally such engines are tried on road courses but there hasn't been any discernable rush to adopt them. However, if you were to start with a relatively big displacement and didn't ask for too great a boost, maybe the lag could be kept within manageable bounds.

Porsche engineers were developing a turbocharged unit all through last season. Occasionally a driver would come back from a test session with his eyes big and his mouth quavering out stories about giant wheelstands and 1000-horsepower spyders. Yes, but how about the throttle lag? "Well, yes, there is some throttle lag . . ."

Other aspects of the coming Can-Am assault were not being neglected. Jo Siffert brought a new spyder to the series to try out some chassis ideas. This 917-10, lighter than the earlier coupes and the spyders derived from them, had its own space frame and its own aerodynamic peculiarities. It was hearteningly

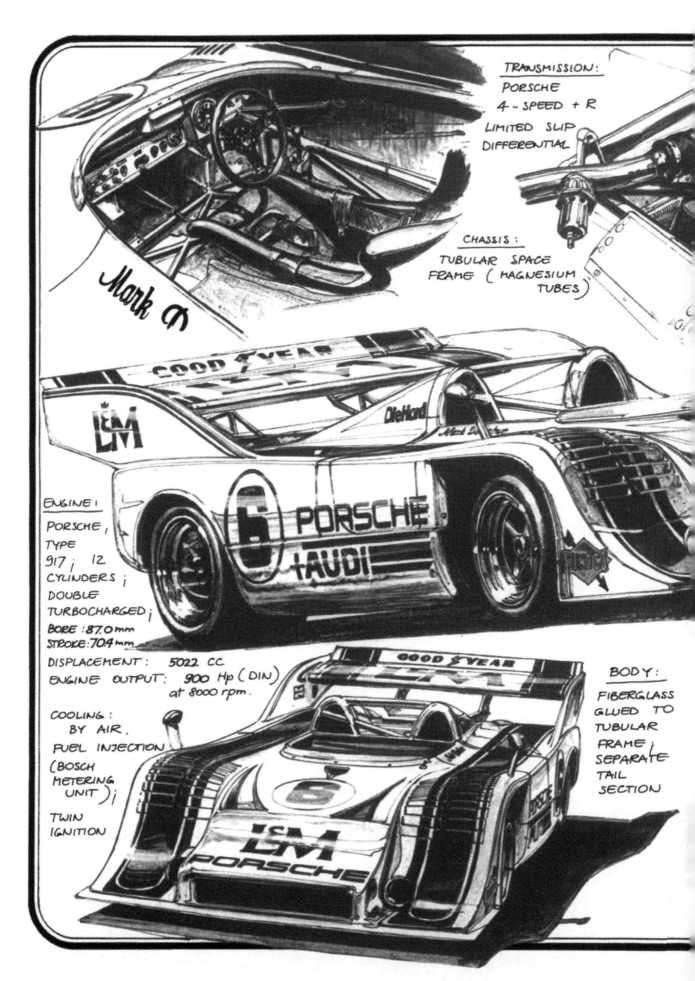

TRANSMISSION:
PORSCHE
4-SPEED + R
LIMITED SLIP
DIFFERENTIAL

CHASSIS:
TUBULAR SPACE
FRAME (MAGNESIUM
TUBES)

Mark D

GOOD ₣YEAR

DieHard

6 PORSCHE +AUDI

ENGINE:
PORSCHE,
TYPE
917; 12
CYLINDERS;
DOUBLE
TURBOCHARGED;
BORE: 87.0 mm
STROKE: 70.4 mm

DISPLACEMENT: 5022 CC
ENGINE OUTPUT: 900 Hp (DIN)
at 8000 rpm.

COOLING:
BY AIR.
FUEL INJECTION
(BOSCH
METERING
UNIT);
TWIN
IGNITION

BODY:
FIBERGLASS
GLUED TO
TUBULAR
FRAME;
SEPARATE
TAIL
SECTION

GOOD ₣YEAR

6

L&M PORSCHE

158

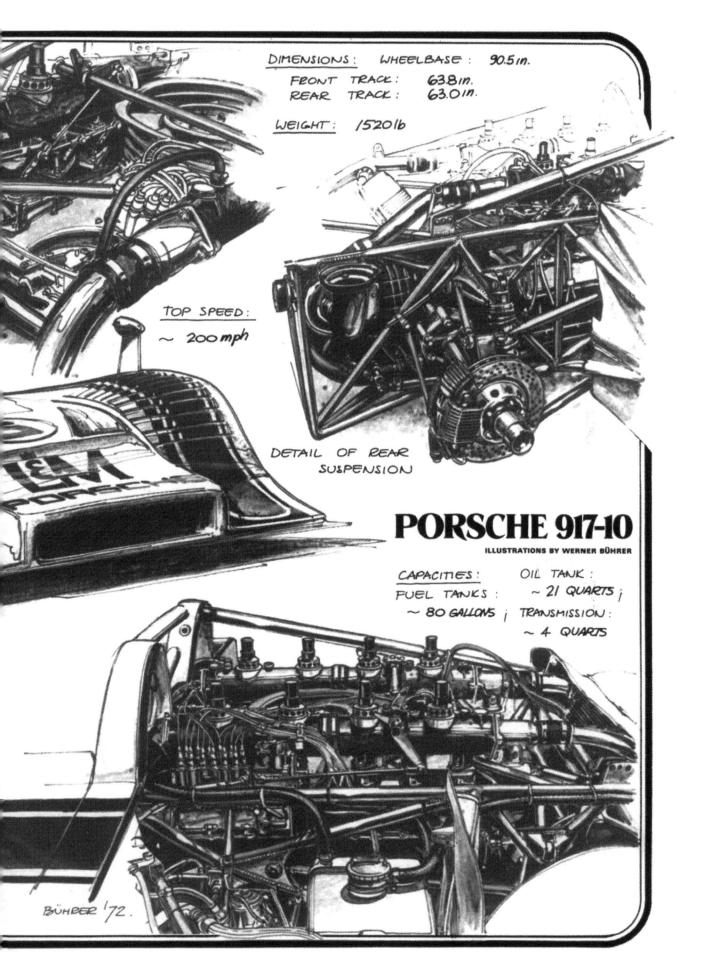

DIMENSIONS: WHEELBASE: 90.5 in.

FRONT TRACK: 63.8 in.
REAR TRACK: 63.0 in.

WEIGHT: 1520 lb

TOP SPEED:
~ 200 mph

DETAIL OF REAR
SUSPENSION

PORSCHE 917-10

ILLUSTRATIONS BY WERNER BÜHRER

CAPACITIES: OIL TANK:
FUEL TANKS: ~ 21 QUARTS;
~ 80 GALLONS;   TRANSMISSION:
                  ~ 4 QUARTS

BÜHRER '72.

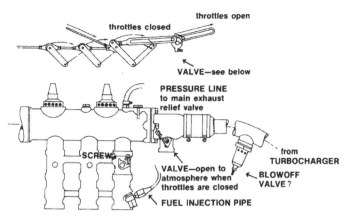

PHOTOS & DRAWING BY THE AUTHOR

throttles open
throttles closed
VALVE—see below

PRESSURE LINE
to main exhaust
relief valve

SCREW

from
TURBOCHARGER

VALVE—open to
atmosphere when
throttles are closed

BLOWOFF
VALVE?

FUEL INJECTION PIPE

Sketch of intake manifold details, many of them unexplained.

Brakes are unusual too. The vented discs are cross-drilled in a pattern similar to the internal ribs shape, and the calipers are elaborately finned to provide that last Btu/min of heat transfer.

reliable, Seppi finishing all five races he entered and in fact scoring two second places.

Meanwhile, the redoubtable Roger Penske Racing organization was itching to get back into something they'd done well enough to tantalize themselves (Donohue won two races, in 1966 and 1968) but which they knew required the resources of full factory backing. After negotiations with three other European factories, they entered into a 3-year liason with Porsche. Mark began to spend week after week in Germany.

"I've got a unique relationship in this project," says Donohue, "a kind of relationship I've never had before. Helmut Flegel is, oh, sort of 'the boss of the 917' and he's a man who is capable in every respect. I can talk to him, I can say things to him and he to me and we understand each other perfectly. We speak the same language, and I've never really had a relationship like that before. I've always been used to doing it all myself. This is fabulous for me. I've really learned a lot."

Good lord, a double Donohue. McLaren took this new threat so seriously they pirated Jackie Stewart away from Lola and laid down their first all-new car since 1967. Their Detroit engine facility began playing with turbocharged Chevies. Can-Am fans, used to spending the winter with crossed fingers, began to have real hope. The 1972 confrontation might be the real thing at last.

Early in the year the chassis sent to America as a development hack allegedly went around Atlanta at record speed but later it wasn't so impressive at Riverside. At this stage it wasn't using the turbo engine; that was still obviously not ready. By April there was no hard evidence that the Porsche was going to be a contender. Visitors to McLaren's Colnbrook plant were given the impression they no longer worried about it very much; their own M20 prototype was going really fast at Goodwood. Apparently their own experiments with blown engines had shown them there were big problems to be solved. They probably wouldn't go that route.

This was all more or less confirmed by Donohue at Mosport when he remarked that only a short time before he'd expected to miss the first event. But then the development team made some big breakthroughs. In the last couple of weeks the car changed a lot, both in the engine compartment and the overall body shape. Pictures that had leaked out into public gaze suddenly looked outdated.

In the week before official Mosport practice Donohue got in some solid testing at the track—at this point the McLarens weren't even in the hemisphere—and cut about three seconds off the existing Group 7 lap record. (That had been Dan Gurney's, from 1970, at 1:16.4.) In fact, he was about 1.5 seconds better than the best F1 time. We'd have to wait for the McLarens to arrive to know, but it looked like they had some real catching up to do at long last.

There's a lot of familiar 917 in the Can-Am car (see the

June 1971 R&T). The basic dimensions are about the same, the suspension layout and pieces are very similar, it retains the space-frame construction concept, and the flat-12 engine and 4-speed transaxle look much the same. A lot of the details are special, though: the frame tubes are of some secret material which is probably a magnesium alloy; the body is not glued to the frame but the metal sheets forming the fuel tank sides are welded into the structure for stiffness (the rubber cells merely rest in these without being enclosed—the inquisitive finger can depress the exposed top of the cells); the suspension links are blue-anodized aluminum alloys; there is lots of magnesium and titanium and honeycomb fiberglass everywhere. Going on the announced weight of the normal-issue 917-10 (driven at Mosport by Minter and Gregg), which is about 1565 lb, the Penske car probably scales about 1520. That makes it very close to what the McLarens weigh.

The body shape breaks ground in that at long last (although this comment also applied to the Chaparral 2J) some aerodynamicist has had the courage to produce an *ugly* shape when his tests showed it to be best. The sharp-bottomed, concave, louvered nose is very short on esthetics—but if you visualize the airflow and pressure distributions over it, you'll see it must work very well. The dished contour produces downforce; then when air reaches the wheel domes and must bend back to horizontal flow, a condition that would otherwise produce lift at that point, the copious venting fills in the low pressure with air from underneath. It goes deeper: since there is in fact no belly pan to this nose section, any low pressure generated below the visible surface is carried right down to the road. Presto, a "sucker" effect.

THE PENSKE-DONOHUE PORSCHE 917-10

It is noticeable that, compared to earlier photos, the new nose has allowed the rear airfoil to be enlarged and mounted farther aft. It may be this "giant-hand" aerodynamic system that accounts for the very high cornering power (at 80 mph on Porsche's Weissach skid pad the car reportedly has generated 1.54g). At Mosport the Porsche was using the identical Goodyears as fitted to the McLarens and the Shadow, so it wasn't just a matter of tires. The high engine power is able to pull the necessarily high-drag shape up the straights as fast as or faster than anything else, too.

Which brings us to the most glamorous, and most secret, part: the blown engine. Each bank of six cylinders has its own blower system, although there are interconnections between the two sides at certain points. The six exhaust pipes per side merge down into one, which feeds a smallish German-made (Ebersbacher) turbine wheel. The two blower units are mounted in available space to either side of the transmission. Just before the turbine the two exhausts are connected by a cross pipe over the top of the transmission. In the middle of the pipe is the single blow-off valve. As on any Indy installation, this is pre-set to relieve pressure at a certain value and is probably the primary "horsepower screw."

The pair of compressors draw air from twin NACA inlets on the body top and force it forward to a pair of log manifolds atop the two cylinder banks. So far so normal, but from here it gets tricky; careful study of earlier photos (see some of the L&M ads in the magazines) indicates the following details are fairly recent additions. Atop each log are four devices which look like spring-loaded relief valves; these "steam whistles" may serve to eliminate the chance of manifold explosions, or they may have to do with equalizing pressure along the length of the log. On the other hand, there is a theory that they are inlets which open when the manifold pressure drops and thereby convert the engine temporarily to normal aspiration. This could reduce throttle lag. There aren't many who know just what these eight things do and those who know aren't talking.

Farther aft, just after the air comes out of the compressors, each pipe has what is pretty certainly a straightforward preset blowoff valve. This is also something Indy engines don't have.

The most intriguing gadgets are between these two blowoffs and the logs. In a T-shaped housing just before each log lives what has to be a little butterfly valve, springloaded to the closed position and located so that when it opens it opens the manifold to outside air. A sliding-link connection to the main throttle linkage allows this butterfly to close when the throttles are opened more than about half way, but when the driver lifts his foot right off *this butterfly is caused to snap open.* Now, what do you think is the purpose of all this? Could it suck air in at low throttle openings, once again to make it normally aspirated? Or does it serve to dump inlet manifold pressure when the driver reaches a braking zone, canceling any tendency of the engine to drive on for an instant? Could it also eliminate most of the back pressure in the intake manifold which might develop on a suddenly closed throttle, "stall" the compressor, slow it down, and therefore create throttle lag when next the driver wants power?

All we know is that in the Mosport race one of these butterflies jammed in the closed position on the 17th lap. The car, which was leading, became "undriveable" in Donohue's word; he lost several seconds on the next lap and came in to the pits to have the mechanics discover what was wrong and free it up. It absolutely cost him the race.

Mark and the other people behind the Porsche are not lighthearted types. They take the whole thing very seriously, they have worked exhaustively to solve their problems, and they are determined to keep their secrets, their "unfair advantage," as long as humanly possible. They discourage prying eyes with tarpaulins, flatly refuse to answer certain questions, and are positively rude to photographers. Fair enough; we survived that sort of attitude in the gruesomely tense Trans-Am of 1970, when six Detroit firms were locked in bitter bloody battle. The Can-Am used to be relaxed and friendly, but if we need glint-eyed enmity to create a good competitive series, fine.

"Besides," admits Mark with a sudden grin, "it's more fun this way!" He really enjoys turning aside sudden rapier questions about his latest toys. He has come right out and told us the name of the secret frame material, though. He's granted us that little.

It's "Unobtainium."

PORSCHE 917-10 SPECIFICATIONS

PRICE
List price $124,000
  (including turbochargers; without turbos approx. $34,000 less)

ENGINE
Type .... dohc flat 12
Bore x stroke, mm .... 87.0 x 70.4
Displacement, cc 5022
Compression ratio 8.5:1
Bhp @ rpm, net .... est. 900 @ 8000
Torque @ rpm, lb-ft .... est. 650 @ 6600
Fuel injection .... Bosch mechanical
Fuel requirement 100-oct
Crankcase material: magnesium alloy with Nickasil cylinder liners
Head material: aluminum alloy
Engine weight, lb 600

DRIVE TRAIN
Transmission: 4-sp manual in unit with differential; 3-plate clutch, Porsche synchronizing

CHASSIS & BODY
Layout .... midship engine/rear drive
Body/frame .... light alloy tube frame with welded lower sheet aluminum & fiberglass skin
Brake system .... 12-in. vented disc front & rear with finned calipers
Swept area, sq in 513
Wheels .. cast alloy; 15 x 12.5 front, 15 x 17 rear
Tires .... Goodyear Blue Streak; 11.30-15 front, 15.70-15 rear
Steering type .... rack & pinion
Overall ratio 13.6:1
Turns, lock-to-lock 1.5
Turning circle, ft 42.5
Front suspension: lower welded A-arm, upper tubular, adjustable A-arm, coil springs, tube shocks, anti-roll bar
Rear suspension: upper & lower wide-base, adjustable A-arms; long trailing arms, coil springs, tube shocks, anti-roll bar.

ACCOMMODATION
Theoretical seating capacity, persons 2
Seat width .... 2 x 18

INSTRUMENTATION
Instruments: 10,000-rpm tach, engine oil pressure & temperature, transmission oil temp
Warning lights: oil pressure, alternator

GENERAL
Race weight, lb 1520
Wheelbase, in 90.5
Track, front/rear 63.8/63.0
Length 155.5
Width 82.0
Height 38.5
Ground clearance 4.0
Fuel capacity, U.S. gal 80
Oil capacity, U.S. qt 21

McLAREN M20

The next stage of evolution as practiced by Can-Am's Establishment

BY PETE LYONS

Aᴌᴛʜᴏᴜɢʜ ᴛʜᴇʏ ᴜsᴜᴀʟʟʏ manage to avoid producing camels, the men at the McLaren establishment operate as a committee when designing new cars. They are a conservative group—racing experience produces conservatism—and don't seem the least bit sorry not to have a reputation for wild innovation. When they do lay down an all-new racer it's apt to draw heavily on what worked before. So it is with the M20. Most of the pieces are familiar and everything is good, sound, sturdy McLaren practice. Yet it is a much better car and seems to have achieved everything the committee wanted after teething troubles were sorted out.

Gordon Coppuck: "We've taken great pains to get the weight distribution about the same as last year's car, but with a lower polar moment of inertia (Isn't that an Eskimo's tea break?) to produce a quicker and more predictable car. We've added two inches to the wheelbase, although there's an 8-in. spacer ahead of the gearbox which moves the engine up more toward the middle of the chassis. The driver has been moved forward as well, while the radiators are back amidship and the fuel is maintained in a more compact mass."

Isn't much of this similar to last year's Lola T260 in layout?

"I feel Eric made a mistake on that, doing it like a Formula 1 car. A slidey, throw-it-around sort of car. Our experience is that a Group 7 driver who throws it around is going to lose it. We prefer to have the car stick right down to the ground."

Tyler Alexander: "The first thing we wanted to fix was a problem we'd had on the earlier cars. . . . I'm not going to say what it was."

"Was it a matter of front-end adhesion?"

"Ah . . . partly."

Teddy Mayer: "The first reason for the radiators in the sides is to lower the cockpit temperature, but it also allowed us to do more with the aerodynamics at the front, create more aerodynamic efficiency. And we got it, we were about 10 mph faster on the straight at Watkins Glen this year—about 192, I think.

"Then we wanted *zero* change in the weight distribution between full and empty, and we've pretty well achieved that. There are some small geometry changes; the track and wheelbase are bigger. The car is about 25 lb lighter than last year's, and it's got a lower polar moment and also the weight distribution is changed; it's a little more toward the front. The roll centers are 'in-the-air'—above ground. There isn't any anti-dive. There is some anti-squat, about the same as last year or maybe a little more. The radiators are something like 25 or 30 percent bigger in area, not because they have to be when you put them on the side but because the M8F's cooling capacity was pretty marginal.

"Gary's improved the engines quite a lot this year—at Mosport our engines weren't good but they are now. There's a little more horsepower and the torque is better, it's flatter, it doesn't drop off so much at high rpm."

Peter Revson's impressions: "It's a better balanced car than the M8F and there's less understeer. Because the balance is better you're able to get out of the turns faster, get the horsepower down to the ground better coming out of the turns. I can't say I can really feel this 'lower polar moment' subjectively. But the cockpit *is* cooler, a lot cooler."

Denny Hulme: "We wanted it to run cooler, that was the main thing—and it made all the difference at the Glen this time, I can tell you! And it's a faster, better balanced car. I don't know about the 'low polar moment' business; it's not something you can feel in the seat of your pants. What makes a race car quick is *balance*. What's happening at one end you want happening at both ends, even-steven. You want *balance*—else you'll fall off the high wire!

"Basically there's no change in weight distribution between the start and finish. It's very good and it stays fairly neutral. Quite often in the F1 car we've got that problem but not in the Can-Am car now.

"And we've got some mighty brakes. That's mainly due to Lockheed; they've spent time with us getting big, light brakes. At first the pedal wasn't good enough, but it's slowly become better. The brakes *are* better, especially when you consider the work they do, the energy they have to absorb; it must be *enormous*, if you calculate it.

"There are some geometry alterations, but I can't really describe what they are—close as I am I don't really take much notice, and an outsider wouldn't have any idea. You never know the effect subjectively of these things, it's just a quicker car or it isn't. Everything we've done has had a slight effect and it all adds up."

So: driver and engine cooling, nimbler handling with more front adhesion, cleaner aerodynamics—all with the same ruggedness and reliability that have paid off before. Motor racing to Teddy Mayer is not to dazzle everyone with technology, it's to balance the books and keep faith with your sponsors by winning races. The M20 is a tool to do that job.

What's old and proven about it are the working bits: engine, transaxle, suspension, brakes, wheels. The engines are all big

FOLTZ PHOTO

STOTT PHOTOS

Reynolds aluminum blocks of 509 cu in. (4.5- by 4-in. bore and stroke) with detail improvements, pistons especially, to give about 750 bhp and a better, flatter torque curve. The gearbox is Hewland's strong big Mk II, as it was last year with the exception that it's the USAC version with a starting-motor shaft sticking out the back. This isn't for use with an external starter like Indy; it's because the new seat-back fuel tank prevents access to the front of the engine when the mechanics want to turn it over. The 8-in. spacer casting between engines and gearbox is hollow and does nothing but fill space, while Porsche on the 908/3 and Alfa Romeo have put their gearboxes in that empty space, and March tried it on the 721X F1 car. Coppuck says the impossibility of changing gear ratios makes the amidships gearbox impractical. The suspension members look as they did before. The geometry changes are due largely to the different arrangement of components, the longer wheelbase and wider track and such details as the chassis being about one inch shallower. The brakes continue trends begun late last season, in that the front discs are larger instead of being equal with the backs. Late last year Revson's car had cross-drilled discs, but now they have found the same job can be done by machining grooves in the disc faces; typically there are three grooves per face running tangentially out from the hub to the edge. Their function is to prevent both pad dust and pad material "out-gassing" from interfering with friction.

The new chassis is bent up out of 16- and 19-gauge aluminum, riveted and bonded to itself as before, but this time the front suspension loads are taken not with a full steel bulkhead but by small steel brackets mounted on the tub. Yet the front of the chassis is designed to be stiffer than before. (There is no front radiator ducting/mounting structure to absorb collisions.) The shape of the tub is largely determined by the new radiator location, as fitting big enough cores takes up all the space right down to the bottom of the chassis. Therefore the outside edge of the fuel tanks had to be cut away at the rear to form a nice (and very carefully drawn) smooth air entry. It is this that produced the F1-style "Coke bottle" shape in plan view. To gain back the lost capacity an 18-gal. tank was put across the

DRIVERS: DENNY HULME, PETER REVSON

MOSPORT

BÜHRER '72

McLAREN M20

SPECIFICATIONS:

WHEELBASE : 100 in.
TRACK FRONT/REAR: 61.8 / 60
WHEELS: 15 x 11   FRONT,
        15 x 17   REAR
CHASSIS: MONOCOQUE , L 72
         ALUMINUM ALLOY SHEET

A SCALE WOODEN MOCK-UP MODEL
OF BASIC M 20 DESIGN WAS
BUILT AT McLAREN WORKS.

BRAKE SCOOP
OPENINGS ———→
WERE MOVED FROM
BODY PANEL (UNDER
FRONT WING) TO
FENDER SURFACE ; AT
ATLANTA AND LATER.

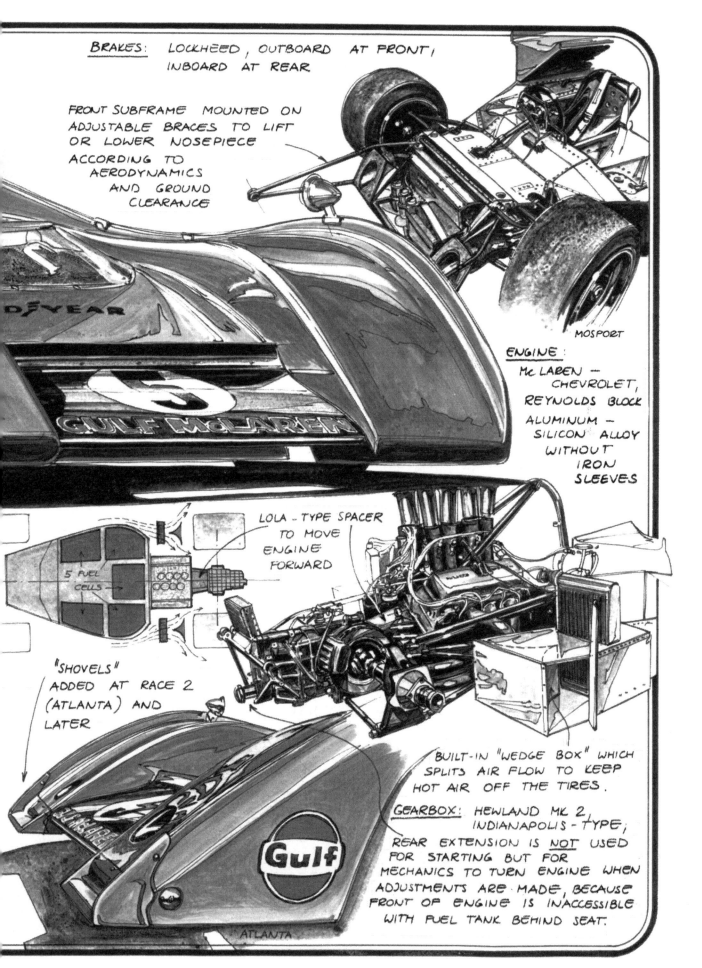

BRAKES: LOCKHEED, OUTBOARD AT FRONT,
INBOARD AT REAR

FRONT SUBFRAME MOUNTED ON
ADJUSTABLE BRACES TO LIFT
OR LOWER NOSEPIECE
ACCORDING TO
AERODYNAMICS
AND GROUND
CLEARANCE

MOSPORT

ENGINE:
McLAREN —
CHEVROLET,
REYNOLDS BLOCK
ALUMINUM —
SILICON ALLOY
WITHOUT
IRON
SLEEVES

LOLA - TYPE SPACER
TO MOVE
ENGINE
FORWARD

5 FUEL
CELLS

"SHOVELS"
ADDED AT RACE 2
(ATLANTA) AND
LATER

BUILT-IN "WEDGE BOX" WHICH
SPLITS AIR FLOW TO KEEP
HOT AIR OFF THE TIRES.

GEARBOX: HEWLAND MK 2,
INDIANAPOLIS - TYPE;
REAR EXTENSION IS NOT USED
FOR STARTING BUT FOR
MECHANICS TO TURN ENGINE WHEN
ADJUSTMENTS ARE MADE, BECAUSE
FRONT OF ENGINE IS INACCESSIBLE
WITH FUEL TANK BEHIND SEAT.

Gulf

ATLANTA

McLAREN M20

width of the car behind the driver's seat; it is actually the 5th fuel cell in the system, into which the other four (two per side) feed, and this new flow system helps position the several hundred pounds of liquid in the middle of the wheelbase as it burns off in a race.

The new car's body shape looks much like the old and in fact descends directly from it: the technique is to make up one more of the old body in extra heavy cloth, cut it into pieces and drape them over the new chassis, and then fill in the gaps to produce a male buck of the new body. The changes on the M20 are at the sides, where air is induced to flow into the radiators, and at the front where an airfoil rides in the gap between the wheel arches where the radiator ducting used to be—the radiator used to throw its exhaust air upward and produce downforce, but the airfoil does it more efficiently and is adjustable. Both drivers, incidentally, say there is no reduction in the buffeting of their heads from this air flow, but since it's cool air pouring over the top the cockpit is much more comfortable. A neat touch about the new nose is that it hinges up for access; furthermore, the struts that mount the hinge are adjustable for length and allow small adjustments in nose-rake angle.

Under the skin probably every piece, familiar or not, has been revised. The "beam," the rear crossmember which carries the top suspension, is much stronger this year and the lower pickup casting is more elaborate to feed the loads into the differential casing more evenly. With stronger U-joints—they measure about 0.75 in. wider—Denny is content to have his rear brakes inboard again this year. One of the maintenance improvements is the method of mounting the front of the engine: as before it's hung on a plate running across the chassis but this time the plate is actually three pieces butted together with "fish-plates." When changing engines the "fish-plates" are disassembled and the central portion of the main plate, complete with all three pumps, comes out with the engine. It saves a little time, yes, but the mechanics say a bigger bonus is that the pump installation has all been dyno-tested with the fresh engine, so they know it all works and doesn't leak.

When testing the prototype M20 a great deal of worry went into getting the radiators to work their best. Several different detail configurations of inlet duct had to be tried before the final arrangements evolved, and the same trouble was caused by getting the air out. Also, the first radiators of aluminum had to be replaced with copper ones—apparently copper can be in thinner sheets and you get more flow through a given size core.

Once out in the world there had to be several significant changes. At Mosport the two new cars did not go well at all. Part of it was engines, part of it was tires: Hulme says Mosport proved to him and to Goodyear that the Porsche and the McLaren need different tires, and part of it was indicated by the changes made for Atlanta a month later. There were modifications to spring rates at both ends and the track was widened about 2 in. To be specific, both cars had spacers of 0.9 in. put under each front wheel, and Hulme's car had longer links to do the same job at the rear, a job so involved that only his car was done at that time. By Watkins Glen both cars had the new track measurements and it was done at both ends by longer links and wishbones. Brake cooling ducts were let into the front slope of the nose, replacing the original inlets which had been obscured behind the front airfoil in the panel ahead of the footwell. Another change was to reposition the rear airfoil

McLAREN M20
SPECIFICATIONS

ENGINE

Type	ohv V-8
Bore x stroke, mm	114.5 x 101.6
Equivalent in	4.50 x 4.00
Displacement, cc/cu in	8369/509
Compression ratio	11.75:1
Bhp @ rpm, net	750 @ 7200
Torque @ rpm, lb-ft	650 @ 5500

Fuel injection: Lucas/McLaren mechanical
Cylinder block and head material: Reynolds high-silicon aluminum alloy

Engine weight, lb	485 lb

DRIVE TRAIN

Transmission: 4-sp manual Hewland LG Mk II, in unit with differential; Borg & Beck 3-plate clutch

CHASSIS & BODY

Layout ...... midship engine/rear drive
Body/frame: monocoque chassis structure in 16swg/19swg L72 aluminum sheet with unstressed fiberglass body panels
Brake system: 11.8-in. grooved disc front and rear

Swept area	na

Wheels: cast alloy; 15 x 11 front, 15 x 17 rear
Tires: Goodyear (sizes vary with race location and conditions)

STEERING / SUSPENSION

Steering type	rack & pinion
Overall ratio	19.4:1
Turns, lock to lock	1.75

Front suspension: lower A-arms, upper tubular adjustable A-arms, coil springs, tube shocks, anti-roll bar
Rear suspension: lower parallel adjustable lateral links, upper single adjustable lateral links, long trailing links, coil springs, tube shocks, anti-roll bar

ACCOMMODATION

Theoretical seating capacity, persons	2
Seat width	2 x 15

INSTRUMENTATION

Instruments: 8000-rpm tach, engine oil temperature and pressure, fuel pressure, water temperature

Warning lights	none

GENERAL

Dry weight, lb	1525
Wheelbase, in	100.0
Track, front/rear	61.8/60.0
Length	155.0
Width	76.0
Ground clearance	3.0
Fuel capacity, U.S. gal	75
Oil capacity, qt	10

some 6 in. more to the rear; this was done at Atlanta on Hulme's car in testing and later transferred to Revson's car to compensate for his not having the wider rear track. The advantage seems to be to get the wing back in cleaner air so it can work at a lower attack angle. In fact it proved a 2-edged foil; Revson kept it at the Glen and found he was indeed able to pull up on Hulme on the straight, but in the corners when following in the "dead air" behind the leading car, which always robs the front of adhesion, the added leverage of the rear wing created even worse understeer than usual. In practice at Ohio he found its leverage increased the "pitch-back" on acceleration out of the slower corners and generated too much understeer. And he removed it for the race.

Another change to the aerodynamics was in two stages and was once again aimed at taming understeer. At Atlanta both cars had little molded lips, or "shovels," riveted to the front edges of the body to prevent air going down from the stagnation point and around the edge under the car. These remained for the Glen race, and at Ohio the same treatment was applied in aluminum to the leading edge of the nose airfoil.

Aerodynamics demonstrated its truly awful power on the 5th lap at Atlanta when Hulme's car flipped backwards like a hydroplane gone amok. Apparently it was a nasty combination of circumstances: he was close behind Follmer in the Porsche, which robbed the McLaren of nose adhesion; he had just gone over the crest of the rise in the back straight and he had just changed into top gear so the nose was pitching up as the clutch gripped. Perhaps, although he doesn't remember anything about it, he was just then darting out of the Porsche's draft and catching a sudden blast of wind. The combination of effects was enough to raise the nose into an angle of attack, giving positive lift rather than negative—several hundred pounds of lift. Ugly, ugly.

Denny has a sturdy New Zealand skull and recovered quickly. Two weeks later with his new car (actually the prototype refur-

bished to the latest specs) he ran away with the Watkins Glen Can-Am flag-to-flag.

THE THIRD AND fourth races in this year's series were fascinating demonstrations of what people like about motor racing: You never know what to expect. The turbocharged Porsche should have been a cannon on the Watkins Glen straights—but it bombed. The McLarens, bounding back from their debacle at Atlanta, absolutely ran away one-two. Two weeks later the Porsche should have been a terrific handful on the tortuous Mid-Ohio track, but it started from the pole, blew the McLarens off, lasted on dry tires through a rainstorm which had the one surviving McLaren in the pits *five times* to change tires, and won very convincingly. *Nothing* is sure about this sport.

At Watkins Glen Revson was on the pole (the only driver under the magic 100-sec lap time) but from the first turn Denny stormed ahead and went all the way to the checker. Revvie hung on as best he could and actually set the race lap record. He had some idea of passing the old man to win himself a motor race for a change, but a couple of things held him back. His brakes faded away badly—nobody seemed to understand why—and also he had an aerodynamic imbalance whenever he came close up into Hulme's turbulence.

Another super show at the Glen was put up by David Hobbs, who put in a brilliant drive in Steed's Lola and passed everyone but the pair of leaders to hold a solid third, before having to drop back from exhaustion caused by heavy steering and high cockpit temperatures. Francois Cevert took Revson's old M8F ahead to make it McLaren one-two-three. The Shadow had another terrible day, brake trouble holding Jackie Oliver down the field before finally pitching him off into the guardrail and retirement. And the Porsche? Simply put, it was a crock. Evidently the handling was down, perhaps because of tire vibration in conjunction with the lagging characteristics of the throttle response, and apparently the engine was duff: Penske had to use the unfreshened Atlanta motor for Watkins Glen too. In the race several minutes were lost with a problem in the inlet-manifold relief vents, the same thing that caused trouble at Mosport although this time it was simply a broken spring. The Porsche factory had chosen this day to fly over a bunch of European journalists to watch their Panzer crush the Kiwis. It'll be a long time before they do that again.

They should have brought them to Ohio instead. Penske took it very seriously, coming early in the week for solid testing with Mark Donohue going around on crutches to help Follmer sort things out. That it all paid off was shown by the Porsche on the pole, a tenth of a second better than Hulme, and by the first lap when Follmer pulled out fully two seconds. He went on from there, spinning twice in the later rainstorm but recovering without losing anything to score L&M's second dark-horse victory on this track. The McLarens were nowhere, Revson having his transmission fail just before the rain and probably being glad of it when he watched his teammate's struggles. Denny finally made five pit stops to change back and forth between wet and dry tires; still he got fastest race lap right at the end and later was able to joke: "After the first stop I reckoned we might as well do some tire testing, Goodyear pays you five bucks a mile for it." The man who won himself some overdue honor was Jackie Oliver, who drove on through the rain like a demon without stopping or even spinning, was electrifyingly fast in the wet, even faster than some people with rain tires, at one stage hauled four or five seconds on a lap in on Follmer, and brought the UOP Shadow home second on the same lap with the winner in Oliver's first finish this year. Milt Minter was almost as fast as Oliver in the rain and even more spectacular, for he spun off twice—demolishing the speed trap the second time!—but he gave Vasek Polak's 917-10 another good finish of third.

So in four races it was McLaren two, Porsche two, and the ups-and-downs of both *marques* have given no convincing idea which is the better car. ◼

McLaren

Would you buy a car if you had to persuade the dealer to put an engine in? Would you wait three years for delivery? Would you accept it without lights of any kind? Would you agree to **no** guarantee whatsoever? If you can answer "yes" to any of these, then you're either an out-and-out nut or a very happy French Canadian named André Fournier, who is the owner of an altogether unique and highly treasured means of transportation—the sole existing M12GT McLaren—a derivative of Bruce McLaren's personal grand touring prototype that almost made it to the world's car marts.

An attitude such as Fournier's is scarcely representative of the masses' choice of motoring media, for a keen interest in cars is not at all a commonplace among North American road users. Indeed, the reaction of virtually the entire car-driving population west of the Grand Banks and east of the Pacific can best be typified by that of a former employer of ours who shall remain nameless: "If I turn the key in the morning and it starts, that's good enough for me!"

The enthusiast minority, on the other hand, has several methods of avoiding assembly-line obsolescence—designing and building their own cars, mortgaging their earthly wealth for a limited-production "classic" or—the ultimate—amputating one's right arm to acquire BMW's Turbo, Coggiola's Volvo, or Vega's project XP-898. Each of these is possible, all require a modicum of knowledge (expertise even), but there is one inescapable common denominator—cash by the carload! Thankfully, there are still a few fortunates left who aspire to the *last* avenue of vehicular "soul."

André Fournier is one member of this elite group. And he would

appear to have all the necessary trappings; youth (he's only 33), married (with two children)—though this is hardly a prerequisite—and varied business interests that include a travel agency, a dry-cleaning establishment, and Automobiles André Fournier Inc., a GM franchise dispensing Chevrolet and Oldsmobile cars, all in the city of Waterloo, about 65 miles south-east of Montreal. We rhetorically asked whether such accoutrements made paying for the upkeep of his pride and joy easier to bear! He laughingly replied: "Well, it does, naturally. But, really, it's the type of thing I like. I love cars, and, as far as *that* baby is concerned, paying for it hasn't been a problem at all, because I've had as we say in French 'beaucoup de plaisir' (kicks, if you will) in having it and owning it. It's been very worth while."

Fournier's involvement with "that baby" began almost four years ago as the result of a trip to the UK. He had heard that Lola were involved in a project to put GT coupes on the road, but a visit to the Slough works found Eric Broadley's offering a bit pricey. Fournier then reasoned that if Lola were doing this sort of thing, perhaps McLaren would be, so a short hop to Colnbrook commenced a bargaining session that was to last almost three years.

The first inkling that Bruce McLaren indeed had the more sporting motorist in mind appeared in the racing press in mid-1968, when it was rumoured that consideration was being given to the homologation of a coupe version of the McLaren-Elva sports racing car to compete with the Lola T70 in Group 4. The M6A had proved eminently successful in the Can-Am Series, so what better test-bed by which to assess the merits of the venture than the production-line M6B?

The Kiwi Maestro had fond hopes of thrashing it out with Porsche, Ferrari, and Alfa, on the circuits of Europe, and, besides, what was wrong with importing the old American "win-on-Sunday-sell-on-Monday" philosophy? Hearing this background story, Fournier promptly put down a deposit, but it was some time before his dream was to become a reality. Revised rules for the FIA Group 5 World Championship for Makes had been altered to require a minimum of 50 identical models before homologation. And they had to be complete cars, unlike McLaren's plans for the M6BGT which left the engine option to the customer. The longed-for homologation papers were, therefore, never to materialise, and the project started to die a slow death with Fournier's deposit being returned. Early in 1970, however, McLaren had a prototype prepared using one of 50 all-enveloping bodies (which had been delivered for homologation purposes) to surround a stock M6B chassis. It soon became his favourite project, and, amid speculation over an unusual vehicle making a hash of traffic in and around Walton-on-Thames, Trojan Cars released the news that they had in fact cobbled up a road-trimmed version "for evaluation purposes, as it is possible that Trojan may market a road-going version of the M6BGT." Back came Fournier's cheque! In his book, "McLaren! The Man, the Cars and the Team," Eoin Young reveals McLaren's thoughts at the time: "Building his own road car was a project that had interested Bruce as an ambition to be achieved when the company was well under way with the racing programme."

But such high hopes soon gave way to disaster when the personable New Zealander met his tragic and untimely end on June 2 while testing the new model M8D Can-Am car at Goodwood. Much ground had been covered in preparing Fournier's car, and, in fact, delivery was imminent (though without an engine, contrary to expectations). But, with Bruce's death, negotiations naturally came to a halt, not to be resumed for almost two years. Finally the eventful day arrived, and it was one happy fella that met a BOAC cargo flight at Montreal's International Airport to take over his charge, in May, 1972, almost three years after he had first broached the subject.

What Fournier got was a far cry from that originally planned. In the first place, the designation "M12GT" is entirely applicable (see table), and it appears that one of the available sets of

COMPARATIVE MODEL SPECIFICATIONS

| | AS ANNOUNCED | | | AS PRODUCED | |
	M6A	M6BGT	M12	M12	*M12GT
Wheelbase:	93½ in.	93½ in.	93½ in.	93½ in.	93½ in.
Track: Front: ...	52 ,,	53½ ,,	53½ ,,	57 ,,	57 ,,
Rear:	52 ,,	53½ ,,	53½ ,,	55 ,,	55 ,,
O-A Length: ...	155 ,,	162 ,,	155 ,,	155 ,,	155 ,,
O-A Width: ...	68 ,,	73 ,,	71 ,,	75 ,,	75 ,,
Height to top of windscreen:	31 ,,	31 ,,	31 ,,	30 ,,	30 ,,
Approx weight less fuel:	1300 lb	1400 lb	1400 lb	1300 lb	1300 lb
Fuel capacity (Imp gals):	54	32	52	52	52

* as delivered to Mr Fournier.

Muscle in Montreal

Happiness is having your own road-going Can-Am car, says Jim Mollitt

M6BGT coachwork was shortened and widened to accommodate the M12 chassis. The M12 had been the 1969 production-line sports racer, and, though basically similar to the M6 series, most thought it a retrograde step. It nevertheless sold a-plenty. Our subject vehicle seems to be the odd-ball of a quartet, and is, therefore, all the more exclusive. The prototype M6BGT was sold to Britisher David Prophet, who raced it for a time then converted it to a roadster. Its present whereabouts are unknown. One was prepared by Trojan for McLaren to undertake his feasibility study, and a third was assembled in Croydon for Trojan to put on exhibition. The chassis number of Fournier's M12GT is 50-04, which would seem to indicate that it is the fourth in a projected run of 50 which ties in nicely, but information is sketchy on the chronology of its predecessors. We learned recently that Bruce's personal car will shortly find a permanent home in a museum in Auckland, N.Z.

Along with his prized possession Fournier received a set of M12 Group 7 coachwork (in case he ever wanted to race it, we expect), a large supply of spares, *and an engine*. This last was victory for the lucky owner, since Teddy Mayer had not been too well disposed toward becoming an engine supplier! But what was received was not as anticipated. Instead of the 302 cu. in. (5-litre) Chevy V8, he found that a Weber-carbed, 350 cu. incher had been substituted. It turned out that this power plant had been built by the Californian Al Bartz and subsequently "McLarenized" at Colnbrook. Included in the specification were dry sump lubrication and a bhp rating of 575 at 8000 rpm—a bit long-legged perhaps, but more in keeping with the more leisurely pace of North American traffic. The whole question of performance is academic really, when you learn that Trojan's John Bennett virtually guaranteed a 0-100 mph time of 8 seconds and a top speed of 225 mph !

Upon arrival at the Waterloo shop, a complete tear-down was dictated, not so much to correct as to examine ! A full complement of legal lighting was fitted—an easy task since almost all the necessary wiring had previously been installed—but no special goodies were added. The services of race driver, Jacques Duval, were then called upon to give the sleek, bright red machine its shake-down cruise. Says Fournier: "The only problem we had of any consequence was in determining the proper oil to use in the differential. But we got hold of Roger Penske and he sent down a special blend that he was using in his Lola and it worked perfectly. We've had no trouble since."

There was a bit of an incident with the rev counter, however, when Duval thought it strange that he was getting only 85 mph at an indicated 12,000 rpm ! Knowing no 350 cubed Chevy *anywhere* ever turned that high, Duval pitted and a faulty tach was soon discovered and quickly replaced.

If Fournier was surprised at the ease with which he obtained a licence for his "baby," he has been more than a little bothered by the highway patrol. "It's funny," he says, "but when you're on the highway, or in the city, or somewhere, they stop you, not because you're making too much noise or speeding, but only to have a look ! Almost everywhere we go, even on the Auto-route, they stop us. All they say is : 'Oh, is *that* a McLaren?' That's all. Then they let us go."

Though close to 700 miles were spent in the making of a special film, Fournier has added little more than 800 in the past year, weather permitting, for he does not drive in the wet, Goodyear "dry" racing tyres being what they are! He has used the car for several promotional schemes associated with his various businesses, and it was a high point of Auto '73, Montreal's fifth annual international auto salon, but he insists that he will only ever drive it for his own amusement. "There is lots of room for a passenger," he says, "and, usually, I drive around my home town with my two kids, or my wife, or a friend, and I have a lot of fun." Heat in the cockpit, no luggage space, and the lack of a spare tyre are the least of Mr Fournier's worries.

How does one place a value on such a conveyance, for the owner preferred not to reveal the purchase price ? What would *you* pay for a thoroughbred, race-proved, road machine ? A well-known American is reported to have once said : "If you have to ask how much it costs, you can't afford it !" We *know* André Fournier didn't ask. And it seemed crass to insist on an answer.

SPECIFICATION
McLaren M12GT

Chassis
Rigid, lightweight aluminium alloy monocoque with steel bulkheads bonded and riveted into the structure.
Body
Reinforced polyester resin moulded body. Built-in ducting for brakes, radiator, and oil coolers. Moulded, tinted acrylic front screen and side screens.
Brakes
Girling ventilated discs, 12in front and rear, 16-3-LA calipers. Twin master cylinders actuated via a restricted movement compensator with adjustment for bias. Air ducting to brakes.
Wheels
Cast magnesium, 15in diameter front and rear. Centre lock fitting with left and right hand nuts. Rim width front 10in rear 15in.
Tyres
Goodyear, front : 10.55in x 15in with 9in tread. Rear : 12.50in x 15in with 14in tread.
Suspension
Front : independent, unequal length, wide-base wishbones. Cast magnesium uprights. Adjustable camber, castor and wheel alignment. Anti-roll bar. Adjustable coil springs and aluminium damper units. Rear : independent. Trailing arms with top link and bottom wishbones. Cast magnesium uprights. Adjustable camber and wheel alignment. Anti-roll bar. Adjustable coil springs and aluminium damper units.
Weight distribution
40-60 front to rear.

Wheel base
93½in.
Overall length
75in.
Track
Front 57in ; rear 55in.
Height
30in to top of screen.
Steering
Rack and pinion. Helical cut in magnesium housing.
Cooling
Forward mounted double pass aluminium radiator. Alloy header tank with bleed system, coolant passed to engine via aluminium pipes through chassis.
Weight
1300lb approx, less fuel.
Fuel capacity
52 Imp gallons.
Engine
Chevrolet iron block V8 with aluminium heads.
Displacement
350 cu in (5.73 litres).
Bore and stroke
4.18 x 3.75in.
BHP
575 at 8000 rpm.
Carburation
4 double throated Weber carburetters.
Fuel
Premium petrol.
Electrics
12 volt positive earth system. Stewart Warner fuel pump.

DRIVE TRAIN
Transmission
Hewland LG500 with limited slip differential. Pressure lubricated. Fitted with cooler.
Gears
Five forward and one reverse.

PORSCHE'S

SINCE 1969, the power output of the Porsche 917 engine has been increased from 520 to about 1000bhp, yet the engine and chassis are basically the same. This in itself is a remarkable feat, but is matched by the success of the car: World Champion Make in 1970 and 1971, and winning car in the 1972 CanAm Series. Mark Donohue seems certain to win the CanAm Series with the latest 917.30 this year, too.

Throughout its life, the Porsche 917 has succeeded because it has had plenty of power and has been reliable. And it came into being when Porsche took advantage of a typically short-sighted set of regulations produced by the CSI. In the late sixties, the CSI messed around no end with sports-racing categories and decided that, from January 1968, 3-litre prototypes would be the premier class, but that 5-litre "production" cars would be permitted.

This ruling was intended to give the Ford GT40s, Lola T70s and other cars with American engines a new lease of life. Since these engines were developing about 400bhp at the time, there was every prospect of interesting racing, with these cars competing against the 3-litre prototypes. But lamenting the fact that Ford was unwilling to develop a real racing version of the 289 engine, Len Bailey remarked to me at the time that one of the manufacturers, either Ferrari or Porsche, would surely take advantage of the regulations to build a batch of 25 sports-racers with new racing engines.

In the event, it was Porsche that found the considerable finance needed to develop a 5-litre sports-racer. The 917 was first shown at the Geneva Motor Show in March 1969, and Porsche lined up the 25 needed for homologation early that year. The car was really a logical development of the 908 3-litre car, and on paper at least seemed to be streets ahead of the opposition, who were relying on aged GT40s or 3-litre prototypes.

Because they did not expect anyone else to develop a 5-litre car, Porsche adopted a 4.5-litre flat-twelve engine, with the 86mm by 66mm bore of the 3-litre unit, and the decision speeded up development. Initially the engine produced about 520bhp at 8000rpm, and it incorporated several novel features. With such an engine, the crankshaft is very long, and care is needed to avoid catastrophic torsional vibrations. To avoid these problems, two connecting rods were mounted on each crankpin, which makes the crankshaft as short as practicable, and the drive to the clutch was taken from the middle of the crankshaft. In fact, this simplified

HARD CHARGER

manufacture as well since, in effect, there are two six-cylinder crankshafts joined together by the take-off gear. The drive for the four camshafts was also taken from the middle of the crankshaft. Other novelties included the use of titanium connecting rods, and the use of chrome-plated aluminium cylinder barrels. As might be expected, many magnesium components, including the crankcase, were used. Initially, a Fichtel and Sachs clutch was installed in conjunction with the Porsche five-speed gearbox. Both the chassis and suspension followed existing Porsche practice, but the frame was unusual by normal standards in that it consisted of an aluminium spaceframe — as did the 908.

Low-drag body

But when the car first appeared, it was the body that stole the show. It had a fairly short nose, a narrow and long cockpit or "glasshouse", and a long tail. At the rear of the tail were a pair of moveable flaps, and these were actuated by a linkage connected to the rear suspension. These were designed to keep the car riding at a constant angle, so if the rear of the car lifted the flaps moved upwards to increase downthrust. (Mobile flaps were all the rage at the time, but were banned during 1969, and after Le Mans the flaps of the 917 were fixed.)

Few racing cars meet with success immediately, and even fewer sports-racing cars. Because the main sports car races are of six to 24 hours duration, reliability is all important, and this usually results mainly from race experience. So it was not to be expected that the 917 would sweep all before it in 1969. In the early races, the car gained a reputation for poor handling, and it was clear that Porsche had not really come to grips with the aerodynamic problems, despite the fact that long and short tails were produced. Porsche cars have always had a reputation for low drag, and it seems likely that Porsche were unwilling to sacrifice the low drag for downthrust and stability at first.

At Le Mans, however, the opposition in the form of Ferrari, Gulf-Mirage and Alfa Romeo saw what they could expect. With the engine now developing 580bhp at 8400rpm, the 917 reached 236mph on the Mulsanne Straight and led for 20 hours before retiring. At the same time, however, John Woolfe's fatal accident on the first lap increased the suspicion that all was not well with the handling.

Development continued apace, and a short-tailed car won the Austrian 1000kms

continued overleaf

PORSCHE'S HARD CHARGER

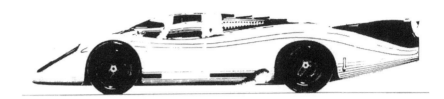

race. Meanwhile, an open version was built for the CanAm Series, and it was driven with some success by Jo Siffert, despite its relatively low power output.

Enter Gulf and JW

For 1970, operation of the 917s was entrusted to John Wyer's JW Automotive and Porsche-Salzburg, both of whom received full support from the factory. Evidently, the experience of Wyer and Horsman led to JW Automotive, who were sponsored by Gulf, making significant improvements to the 917s. The most marked change was the adoption of a wedge-shape short tail, which improved both the stability and the handling, even if it did increase drag. A Borg & Beck triple-plate clutch was adopted, as were Girling calipers (on the Gulf cars only, owing to licensing arrangements) and perforated discs. For all races except Le Mans, a four-speed gearbox was used.

As if that wasn't enough, by the Monza 1000Kms race some cars appeared with 4.9-litre engines! These were almost the same as the 4.5-litre units, except that the stroke had been increased from 66 to 70.4mm, and the power output was raised to 600bhp at 8400rpm. Maximum torque was 415lbs/ft at 6400rpm.

Already, 917s had won at Daytona and Brands Hatch, and one of the 4.5-litre cars won at Monza. Now, they really took over, winning at Spa, Le Mans, Watkins Glen and the Osterreichring. Porsche's dedication to reducing drag dominated the factory development that year, and evidently two cars were destroyed while a satisfactory solution eluded the engineers. However, a successful long tail was produced for Le Mans, but John Wyer preferred his short-tail cars, which had extra rear wings. In fact, it was one of the short-tailed Porsche-Salzburg cars that won, driven by Herrmann and Attwood, while a long-tailed car was second.

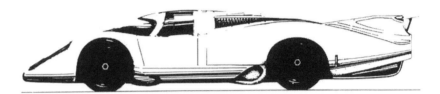

Prototypes again

Once again the regulations were changed for 1971, perhaps with the aim of giving someone other than Porsche a chance. So for that year only, 5-litre prototypes were admitted, but for 1972 a 3-litre class was to be the premier category, anything larger being banned. Therefore, Porsche set about improving the performance of the 917 on a

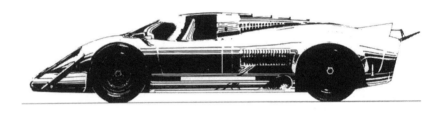

1969 917LH, 4.5 litre

1969 917LH, 4.5 litre

1969 917K, 4.5 litre

1969 917K, 4.5 litre

1969 917PA, 4.5 litre

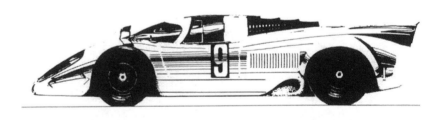

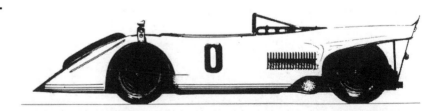

PORSCHE'S HARD CHARGER

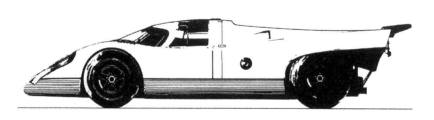

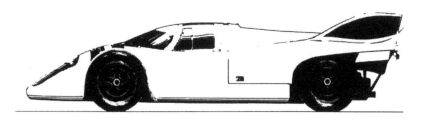

prototype basis for that year, and on a long-term basis for an onslaught on CanAm racing in North America.

As a first step, the engine was enlarged to 4998cc, by the use of a 86.8mm bore instead of the 86mm bore, in conjunction with the 70.4mm stroke of the 4.9litre engine. The cylinder bores were coated with Nikasil, a nickel-silicon material, and these changes improved the durability and allowed the power output to be increased to 630bhp. This increase still left the specific output of 126bhp/litre a little lower than that of the 4.5litre unit, and was expected to be barely enough to compete with the new Ferrari prototypes. At the same time, the gearbox was strengthened, and a lightweight body construction, consisting of a sandwich of thin epoxy resin skins and a foam core, was introduced.

Although the Ferrari 512M was definitely faster than the Porsches at the beginning of 1971, its reliability was poor, so Ferrari decided to use the season to develop the 3-litre car for 1972. Therefore, the Porsche steamroller continued: the 917s won at Buenos Aires, Daytona, Sebring, Monza, Spa, Le Mans, the Osterreichring and Watkins Glen. Perhaps the greatest achievement was at Spa, where Pedro Rodriguez and Jack Oliver averaged 154.7mph. Jo Siffert, who drove with Derek Bell to finish second, was credited with a lap of 3mins 14.6secs — a speed of 162mph! And since Siffert and Rodriguez were circulating the two Gulf-Wyer cars in close company at the time, the record might just as easily stand to Rodriguez.

During 1971, several different body shapes were tried, but most incorporated a concave front deck and a flatter front undershield. The long tail was also revised successfully, and Oliver was timed at 240mph at Le Mans in a car fitted with a long tail. One of the curiosities of Le Mans was the Porsche Big Bertha, an attempt to gain the best from the short and long tail designs. This squat-looking car was developed by the Porsche experimental department and SERA, a French consultancy firm. Evidently, Porsche stylists were asked to paint the car, and they responded by painting it pink, and identifying the various sections as parts of the pig's anatomy! Whether this indicates their excellent sense of humour of profound disgust, I don't know; in any case, the car crashed.

But 1971 saw the transition of the 917 from a long-distance racer to a CanAm car. First, Porsche developed a magnesium chassis

1970 917LH, 4.9 litre

1971 917K, 4.9 litre

1971 917K, 4.9 litre

1971 917/20, 4.9 litre

1971 917LH, 4.9 litre

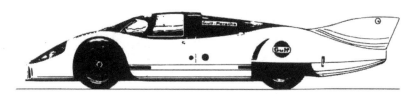

frame, in the search for low weight, and this was incorporated in the Le Mans winning car. Then, a 5-litre open car was built for the 1971 CanAm Series, and was driven with some success by Jo Siffert, who died at Brands Hatch later that year. In addition, a 5.4-litre engine was built, and this had 90mm bores. However, owing to the compromises involved in this design, Porsche started work on the real CanAm development, turbocharging with the smaller engines.

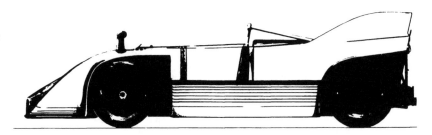

Turbocharging

It was decided to use twin Eberspacher turbochargers on the engine, and most of the development centred around the problem of reducing the lag before the engine responded to throttle opening. With a turbocharged engine, the turbine has to speed up before the engine responds to throttle opening, and it is here that Porsche made most improvements. About 20lbs boost was used, and a by-pass valve prevented this being exceeded. Turbocharged, the 5-litre engine developed about 850-900bhp...

To transmit this power, a new gearbox was designed, stronger titanium driveshafts were used, and Porsche developed their own aluminium brake calipers. One of the two Roger Penske cars had an aluminium frame, the other magnesium. The bodies were designed to produce the maximum amount of downthrust without much care being paid to low drag.

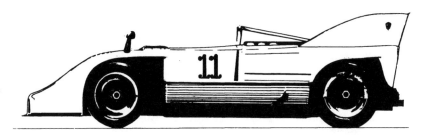

Within a few races, and despite Mark Donohue's serious accident, the 917 had revolutionized CanAm racing. It had shown that sheer power was enough to win, even if the handling and braking did not seem to compare with the McLarens, which struggled to keep up with only 700-750bhp.

For 1973, the 917 was further modified, with a new body and the adoption of the 5.4-litre engine, developing well over 1000bhp. This year there are six turbocharged 917s, and the privately-owned McLarens are lucky if they can get within five seconds of the Porsches' lap times.

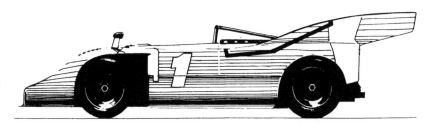

So from 1970 to 1973 the Porsche 917 has dominated each class of racing for which it has been entered seriously. The earliest cars achieved their dominance because Porsche were prepared to take advantage of the regulations, and were able to produce reliable cars, or enough cars so that some always kept going. In CanAm, Porsche were clever enough to exploit turbocharging, without suffering the problems of poor throttle response which dogged other attempts to gain high boost pressures.

Development still continues, of course.

One of the latest developments is the instant power switch. This is an electrically controlled device that varies the boost pressure by operating the relief valve in the turbocharger ducting; if the driver feels the opposition is getting too close, he can increase the boost temporarily and gain more power!

And that really illustrates how far the 917 is ahead; at the flick of a switch it can get further ahead, and the opposition is still trying to make turbochargers work!

JOHN HARTLEY

1971 917/10, 5.0 litre

1972 917/10, 4.5 litre

1972 917/10, 4.5 litre

1972 917/10K, 5.0 litre, turbo

1972 917/10, 5.0 litre, turbo

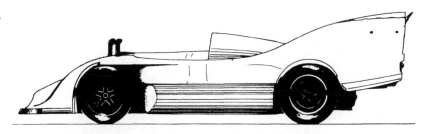

1100 bhp, 240 mph

Mark Donohue, CanAm Champion (Ret'd) talks about the birth, the life and the death of the world's fastest racing car: the Porsche 917/30

By Ray Hutton

Total domination–the works Porsche 917/30 of the Penske team, driven by Mark Donohue (inset) won six out of eight races in the 1973 CanAm series

"AT THIS TIME there is nothing in the world any quicker, any better handling, any more advanced technically, or any more fun to drive. It is to me, the perfect race car." These are the words of Mark Donohue, CanAm champion, and the subject of his unabashed enthusiasm, the Porsche 917/30 that he used to win the 1973 series.

We were talking at Riverside, California, on the eve of his sixth win in the eight-race series. At the time I did not know that 24 hours later, when he was crowned champion, Mark was to announce his retirement from race driving. And neither of us knew until a few weeks later that the Sports Car Club of America were to change the rules of the Canadian-American Challenge Cup so as to outlaw the turbocharged Porsches that had won the championship two years in a row.

With the fuel limit (73 US gallons) applied for 1974 races, the 1.5 mpg 917s will not be able to run in their present form. The critics are pleased, pointing out that no Chevrolet-powered car could compare to the turbo-Porsches, and that the earlier 917/10s could not stay with the Penske-prepared 917/30, replicas of which were to be made available by Porsche for the 1974 season. It had become, they said, a race of investment. Porsche had reputedly spent over a million dollars on the CanAm programme and Donohue's six wins in 1973 netted only 114,533 dollars. Even with generous sponsors, that doesn't make sense, claim the losers–who include some of the private Porsche teams.

But let us leave aside the frightening cost of the project for a moment and consider the development of what is probably the fastest circuit racing car in history — and likely to remain so for some time to come. It is an example of the thorough scientific approach for which Donohue–a highly qualified engineer as well as a super driver—and Roger Penske's team are renowned. They dubbed it "Penske's Unfair Advantage".

The reason I say this car is so good," explains Donohue, "Is that since the inception of the project I've been directly involved. Nothing has been done to that car that I didn't think was right. All the development went in directions that I wanted to go. That's very satisfying for me–I've done something, it works, I have to live with it, and I've won with it.

"I have developed cars before, but this was one that everybody said was impossible. Porsche didn't agree, neither did I. I had faith in them, they had faith in me. It was a tremendous honour to go to a factory like that, and for their engineers to trust what I wanted, to see that what I wanted to do was win."

Regulation trouble

The history of the Porsche 917 is one of continuous clashes with racing's rule-makers. The original coupé appeared at the 1969 Geneva Motor Show and it was something of a shock to realize that the CSI's reduction of the production qualification for the then Group 4 to 25 cars per annum had produced a new breed of super-powerful, super-expensive endurance racing cars. The 4.5-litre 917 was a big jump for Porsche, who only a year before had been racing 2.2-litre 907s. At first it didn't handle well, and there was a row at Le Mans when the organizers wanted the suspension-connected aerofoil flaps removed and Porsche claimed they were essential for the car's stability. In due course the 540bhp 4.5-litre flat-12 engine became a full 5-litre and for two years these magnificent monsters dominated the long distance sports car classics. Then for 1972, much to Porsche's disgust, the 3-litre prototype ruleswere re-introduced and the Porsches rendered ineligible. As early as 1969 they had built an open-bodied version of the 917 for the late Jo Siffert to drive in the CanAm series. Outlawed from the World Championship of Makes, they decided to concentrate on these North American races in 1972 and they chose the Penske team to develop the turbocharged version jointly with the factory engineering department. Donohue recalls their original strategy:

Planning perfection

"We talked for a week before I even got into the car. We all agreed on a basic approach, from which we would not waiver no matter who criticized–and at the

The drawings, published by courtesy of Auto Zeitung emphasize the length of the tail and engine bay of the Porsche 917/30. The 5.4-litre flat-12 engine is air-cooled. It has two valves and two sparking plugs per cylinder and Bosch fuel injection. The twin turbochargers are by Eberspacher with an Airesearch waste-gate (above the tail pipes, centre). The transmission is a Porsche 920 four-speed. There is no differential and the titanium drive-shafts have rubber "doughnut" joints at their inner ends. The multi-tubular chassis frame is aluminium and weighs 133lb

1100 bhp, 240 mph

BRUNO BETTI

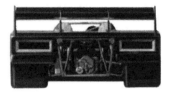

1100 bhp, 240 mph

Mark Donohue tackles a less demanding technical problem

time there were a lot of people who criticized our approaches. A lot of days were wasted in fruitless experiments. But at least we went down the path, saw it was junk, and never went down there again. Other people might have said 'we know that's no good, why go down that road?' We went down to see it was a dead end. To be *sure.*"

The development programme was much more than taking an existing car and making it work with a turbocharged engine. Donohue is guarded about the handling of the 917 when he originally drove it. "Let's say that we would have done it a different way. If you really held your breath, and the track was smooth, it was fast. But Porsche had gone to better shocks (dampers), steering dampers—Band Aids. I think we showed them something else. At Atlanta I demonstrated with lap times some of our ideas. They (Porsche engineers) then improved on them and we started really working together. As soon as that bridge was crossed we were able to get to work on the front, the back, the fuel system, the aerodynamics—the whole car."

Donohue may be diffident about the improvements he made to the 917s roadholding and handling but they were obviously considerable. Vic Elford, who was one of the faster drivers of the early 917 coupés and had one race in the factory's turbo-917 test car last season, says that the change is remarkable and that the CanAm car is *much* better balanced than the coupé.

Cutting the lag

The actual production of power from the turbocharged engine was not a problem once the increases in temperature had been coped with—by increasing the cooler fan speed, making valves and

pistons from special materials, and developing a new type of platinum sparking plug. But making the best use of that power and making the car drivable was another matter. Donohue knew about turbocharged engines (he won at Indianapolis in 1972 with a turbocharged Offenhauser in the Penske McLaren) but road racing with them was something new. The problem, of course, was response, the time that the turbocharger takes to build up to its 90,000 rpm working speed. "Any turbocharged car has some throttle lag," says Mark, "You have to change your driving habits a little, opening the throttle before you want the power. But we have worked really hard to reduce that lag. Now it is between a half and a tenth of a second, depending on rpm. If the motor is running at 5,000 rpm and you open the throttle it takes . . . no I don't want to tell you that . . . let's say it takes x. At 6,000 rpm it takes $\frac{1}{2}x$. So you gear carefully. It has good power from 5,000–8,000 and you can get boost at 4,500. In fact, generally we use the 5,500 to 8,000 range. We shift at 7,800 rpm. The rev limiter is set at 8,300, but 8,500 would be possible. The trouble is that at 8,500 and three quarters with one weak valve spring, a valve can hit a piston—that valve train is very light."

The throttle lag problem has been attacked by sophisticated flap valve systems which release back pressure in the induction manifolds permit and turbocharger speeds to be kept up while the engine breathes "normally" at low speeds. Porsche are tight-lipped about the details of this but Donohue regards this part of the development as critical. "There are times when you cannot anticipate when you need the power. We worked a long time to give the engine some power *without* boost,

so that it could be driven round a slow turn as if it was normally aspirated.

"You can never interest an engine guy in making an engine idle, or start properly, or run at part throttle. They're interested in the figures on the dyno. It took a little while for me to persuade them to develop the uncharged range of the engine—fit mild cams, restricted intakes and so on."

So in its final form the 917 turbo is not so very different to drive from a normally aspirated racing car. Donohue does not believe in left-foot braking, for example, to overcome the throttle lag (except at the start of a race): "In the Porsche the left foot is for

Champion's seat. Gauges on the left are for turbo boost and fuel pressure; switches above them for four separate ignition systems and two fuel pumps. Dials flanking rev counter show oil pressure and temperature

working the clutch. It is very critical, if you miss a shift you can do a lot of damage. I'd get confused if I kept switching." In this respect the driving technique is entirely different from Indianapolis: "In any Indy car you don't need response. You hardly get out of the blower at all, the engine hardly ever backs off. But the engines are unreliable, very sensitive; you never know when they are going to go. It's kinda like driving a hand grenade."

By comparison, Donohue and Penske claim that the Porsche

engine is very reliable in its latest form and have used this as a counter to those who criticize the high (70,000 dollars?) initial cost. The 1973 5.4-litre engine was apparently a big improvement on the previous year's 5-litre. It could rev higher thanks to different cam timing, new camshafts, revised injection calibration and blower arrangements. "The package is now so perfect that anybody can get 800 miles (two races and practice) of trouble-free service. It's because Porsche have such excellence of thinking," says Donohue. The Vasek Polak and Bobby Rinzler teams that ran 917/10s last year might not entirely agree, however.

With the turbochargers set to deliver 1.3 atm. boost, the 5.4 litre engine gives about 1,100 bhp, over 100 bhp more than the 1972 5-litre. Increasing the power further is as simple as turning the screw on the blow-off valve on the cross pipe between the two turbochargers, and several of the Porsches in last year's CanAm had devices to allow the driver to increase boost from the cockpit. "I used mine only once, at the end of a race," says Donohue. It is estimated that the increased boost —to 1.7 atm.—gave more than 1,200 bhp. (At 2.2 atm. on the test bed a figure of 1,560 bhp has been recorded!) To some extent this is a progress to diminishing returns, for very high boosts increase piston blow-by which can pressurize the crankcase and *reduce* power, while temperatures rise tremendously and there is the danger of detonation, which with a petrol-burning engine is very difficult to deal with.

Too much power?

Is this really going too far? Have these cars got too much power, more than they can ever use? Donohue answers that emphatically: "Too much power is defined as when at the end of the straight in top gear the wheels are still spinning, the driver can't cope. We are way, way away from that. We estimated how much power was needed to do that with an aerodynamically loaded car—2,400 bhp. Then you would truly need a very talented driver to hold that car all the way down the straightaway. Can you imagine what a thrill that would be? I'm a horsepower freak."

Having done the initial development of the car in 1972 Donohue had a crash at Road Atlanta and missed four races; George Follmer, brought in to take his place, won the CanAm Championship. The 917/10 was clearly much faster than anything else by the end of the season. Why build another new car? "The 1972 car was a compromise, we ran out of time. It was a good car, but sensitive, critical to the axis between balance and performance. We wanted a car that was more level.

"We redesigned the basics, changed everything. We length-

Porsche engineer Helmut Flegl looks on as mechanics work on the 917/30. With engine specialist Valentin Schaefer he was in charge of the development of the CanAm car from the factory end

ened the wheelbase—primarily to get more fuel in the middle. Porsche were typically thorough. 'Mark Donohue wants to lengthen the wheelbase—how much?' Nobody is smart enough to know how much, so they built an adjustable chassis." News of this chassis —a three piece tubular frame with three different centre sections of different lengths and located by eight bolts—prompted the opposition to think that Penske's team would be using different wheelbase cars for different circuits. In fact they settled on the longest at 97 in., 6.5 in. more than the previous car.

With the long wheelbase came the long tailed body, 22 in. longer than the 917/10. "For years racing cars have had a terminal speed of between 212–214 mph. Indy cars went that fast in 1968 and they still do. The 917/10 did the same. Only two cars have gone quicker. The 917/30 reflects recognition of that problem," Donohue explains intriguingly.

"Log" inlet manifolds above each bank of cylinders are fed by turbochargers at the rear, conceal a clever valve system. Note twin distributors and transmission oil cooler; engine oil is cooled from front-mounted radiator

"We are testing in France at Paul Ricard, a circuit with a long straight. The weather was bad, and things were going wrong. Over a few drinks one night I said to Helmut Flegl (Porsche chassis engineer), 'All cars are doing 214 mph, which cars are quicker? Two —the 600 bhp long-tailed Le Mans 917 coupé and the 485 bhp Ford Mark IV. What's the difference between those cars and ours? Only one thing—their long tails. And who is more talented at making long-tailed cars than Porsche?

"Flegl wasn't enthusiastic—he said it was difficult to make them work properly. So we had a few more drinks and I persuaded him to give it a try. The next day they built one from an old tail with ally sheet and tubing. It was quite wrong to start with but it showed

promise—the maximum speed immediately jumped to 240 mph!

"The lap times weren't faster; we were giving away the extra speed by loss of balance. But at that point we had to make a decision—do we go long-tail or not? Porsche weren't keen, they said that there are not many fast tracks in America. But I said that it was the only thing that made any sense to me from an engineering standpoint. I'd live with it no matter what."

The tail was developed, styled and wind-tunnel tested to give an entirely new body shape. But Donohue didn't have a chance to demonstrate the 917/30's fantastic straight line speed during the season. The only opportunity should have been at the final race at Riverside, but the organizers decided to use the shorter, twistier, infield circuit instead of the 3.27 mile full track with its long straight. "I'm so *disappointed*," said Mark.

Other novelties

There is more to the 917/30 story than this. The car has, for example, no differential, despite its 19 in. wide tyres. For the last race of the season it had the rear anti-roll bar hydraulically adjustable from the cockpit. The team admit to a few failures—bearings at drive shafts, the carrier for the diff. that isn't—but none with the tubular frame which most designers would now regard as old fashioned. Like the coupés of a few years back it is gas pressurized so that any cracks can be detected by a simple gauge check—and it is made of aluminium. The 917/10 that Donohue crashed had a magnesium frame (He joked with enquiring journalists that it was "unobtanium") which saved 40 lb in weight but doubled the cost.

Now costs have become a primary reason for the 5·4-litre turbo 917/30 being banned. Donohue had little sympathy for the changes. "Five years ago we suggested a 7-litre stock block/5-litre racing engine formula and it was rejected. We got out of the CanAm as we couldn't be competitive. Now we have come to the fight with the sharpest knife and everyone is bitching at us." He doesn't like the sound of the move towards 5-litre and 3-litre engines for 1975. "All the thrill has gone for me at that point."

There is something appropriate about Mark Donohue, CanAm Champion, and some say a potential World Champion, retiring from racing when his "perfect race car" had reached the end of the line. □

SHADOWS IN ACTION

WATKINS GLEN

A "FIVE STAR" race meeting at Watkins Glen, New York State in July was the most ambitious SCCA programme ever staged, with events for sports cars, Formula 5000, Can-Am, Trans-Am and Super Vee. Crowds flock in to see the powerful Can-Am cars, domination this year having passed to the UOP Shadow team. George Follmer and Jackie Oliver (above) led the pack, Oliver completing a hat-trick of wins to lead the championship.

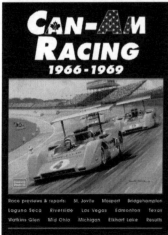

Made in the USA
Monee, IL
08 June 2021